*Lessons
in the
Correllian
Tradition*

. . . .

About the Author

Rev. Donald Lewis-Highcorrell (Illinois) is the CEO of Witch School International, the largest online school of Witchcraft and Wicca. He is also the long-seated First Priest and Chancellor of the Correllian Nativist Tradition and principal author of the tradition's degree materials. Rev. Lewis-Highcorrell co-founded the Pagan Interfaith Embassy, where he serves as a Pagan Interfaith Ambassador to the United States. He is currently the studio head of Magick TV and producer and host of *Living the Wiccan Life*.

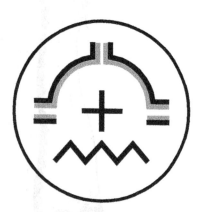

The Correllium, above, is the symbol of the Highcorrell family and the Correllian Tradition as a whole. The Correllium represents the oneness of being and is usually explained in this way: at the top, the Vault of Heaven is represented by (usually) a double line representing the elements of air and fire (light). At the center, a cross represents the element of earth and the four directions. At the bottom, a wave represents the element of water. The circle encompassing all is Spirit. The Correllium has its origin as a personal vision symbol and was later used in the manner of a familial crest.

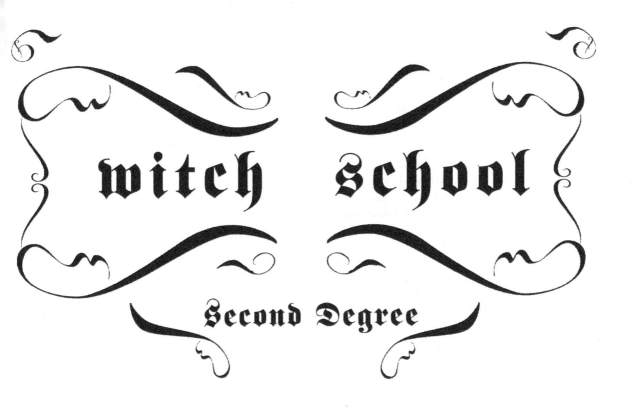

witch school

Second Degree

Rev. Donald
Lewis-Highcorrell

Lessons
in the
Correllian
Tradition

Llewellyn Publications
Woodbury, Minnesota

Third Printing, 2012
SECOND EDITION
(first edition ©2003, 2007 Witchschool.com)

Book design by Rebecca Zins
Cover design by Kevin R. Brown
Interior priest and priestess
illustrations from Dover Publications;
other interior artwork by
Llewellyn Art Department

Library of Congress
Cataloging-in-Publication Data
Lewis-Highcorrell, Donald.
  Witch school second degree : lessons in the
Correllian tradition / Donald Lewis-Highcorrell.
      p. cm.—(The witch school series; 2)
    ISBN 978-0-7387-1302-1
    1. Wicca—Textbooks. I. Title.
    BP605.W53L49 2008
    299'.94—dc22
                          2007051080

Llewellyn Publications
A Division of Llewellyn Worldwide, Ltd.
2143 Wooddale Drive,
Dept. 978-0-7387-1302-1
Woodbury, MN 55125-2989
www.llewellyn.com

Printed in the United States of America

• • • •

Other Books by
Rev. Donald Lewis-Highcorrell

Witch School First Degree

Witch School Third Degree

Witch School Ritual, Theory & Practice

Contents

Greetings, and welcome to Correllian Wicca's lessons for the Second Degree of clergy.

The Correllian Tradition follows the three-degree system of TRADITIONAL WITCHCRAFT. Today, many Wiccan traditions have moved to a two-degree system, eliminating the Third Degree. We, however, favor the traditional system, believing that each of the three degrees has an importance of its own.

The symbol of the First Degree is the downward-facing triangle, which symbolizes the Goddess. This triangle portrays Spirit (Goddess) descending into Matter (God) through the medium of the journey of the soul. This represents the First Degree as a phase in which the initiate is suffused with the spirit of the Goddess and immersed in spiritual study and practice.

A First Degree priest/ess is expected to be familiar with the details of the Wiccan faith and have a thorough grounding in Wiccan philosophy and traditions. The First Degree priest/ess should be able to

Introduction

First Degree symbol

Second Degree symbol

Third Degree symbol

answer most questions about Wicca on a practical (as opposed to theosophical) level. At First Degree, a priest/ess should be able to take any role in ritual with reasonable confidence, short of ritual leader.

The symbol of the Second Degree of clergy is the pentagram, the five-pointed star facing upwards, which represents the union of Spirit with the four elements. This also represents the union of Goddess and God—the Goddess being Spirit and the God being the lord of the material world, which is defined by the four elements. In this context, the pentagram represents taking the spiritual knowledge learned in the First Degree and applying it on a practical level, thus uniting Spirit and Matter through action. This is the role of the Second Degree.

Clergy of the Second Degree should be able to take any role in ritual and answer most questions about Wicca, whether practical or philosophical. Second Degree clergy should be able to manipulate energy in ritual and other settings with reasonable competence. The Second Degree priest/ess should be familiar with most Wiccan rituals and techniques and be able to undertake them without direct guidance.

The symbol of the Third Degree of clergy is the pentagram surmounted by the upward-facing triangle. This represents the soul's return to Source (Goddess) after achieving a perfect union of Spirit and

Matter. In this context, it symbolizes the ability of a Third Degree high priest/ess to momentarily unite with Deity through trance in order to access divine energy or guidance.

A high priest/ess of the Third Degree should be able to achieve this union with Deity through the rite of DRAWING DOWN THE MOON or its equivalent. This allows High Clergy to bring through divine messages, and it is this skill that gives the Third Degree the ability to facilitate initiation. Initiation is a difficult and easily misunderstood technique that is not used lightly—nor is it infallible.

When initiation is performed through self-initiation, or by a First or Second Degree priest/ess under the imperium of a Third Degree, it still uses the channel established by the Third Degree to facilitate it.

As this brief description points out, the role of the Second Degree clergy is one of practical application of the spiritual arts. The Correllian lessons for Second Degree have been crafted with the intention of providing a broad knowledge of practical metaphysical skills, as well as the theories behind them. Many of the basic ideas will be familiar to you from the First Degree lessons, but here you will find much more information about how to actually implement them in practice.

• • • •

The Lessons

Like the lessons for First Degree, the Second Degree coursework in this book includes the following:

The Lesson

The main body of each lesson will be devoted to a single subject, examined in as much detail as space permits. Many of these lessons are noticeably longer than the First Degree lessons, as the Second Degree material is somewhat more complex, and we have attempted to provide as thorough a grounding as possible. Many of these subjects could easily fill a book in themselves. Obviously, these lessons provide only an introduction and a good basic understanding of these different topics, and we strongly encourage you to follow them with further research on your own. Some of the subjects we will deal with in the Second Degree lessons include traditional arts such as tarot and astrology, as well as deeper mysteries such as death and the spirit world.

Exercises

Each lesson will also include a section of exercises to help you continue to expand your psychic development. These exercises are meant to follow and complement the exercises given with the First Degree lessons. (Note that Lesson XII has no exercise; this is intentional.)

Spell

Each lesson will include a spell to help you expand upon your knowledge of spellcraft and the practical application of the magical arts.

Glossary

Every lesson will include a glossary to explain words that may be unfamiliar to some of our students; glossary terms are set in SMALL CAPS. Some of our references are obscure and may give more information than you at first think you need, but it is necessary for clergy to be well informed and to have a wide acquaintance with the terms and concepts that they work with; therefore, if we use a term that is not explained in the lesson proper, we always try to include it in the glossary. Though some of these may seem excessive or redundant, we think you will benefit from knowing this information.

. . . .

Content

The Second Degree lessons have been created with the intention of giving the Second Degree student as wide a range of knowledge as possible. This is necessary for the Second Degree priest/ess to function effectively and credibly.

The First Degree constitutes the lowest degree of initiated priesthood, but First Degree clergy are understood to still be in the process of learning their role as clergy. Second Degree clergy, once initiated, are expected to know and be confident of their role, as it is the Second Degree that often handles much of the running of a temple or shrine. First Degree clergy are expected to still have many questions; Second Degree clergy are expected to be able to answer all but the most difficult of them. Consequently, it behooves the priesthood of the Second Degree to be as well informed as possible.

Also, many Second Degree clergy will choose a particular area in which to specialize their vocation. This specialization is not required, but it is strongly recommended. The Second Degree cleric may choose one or several specialties to focus on, and these may change with time. Thus one might specialize in ritual work, psychic work, healing, teaching, or any of many possibilities. These specialties may be pursued through private study. In some cases, orders exist within the Correllian Tradition that one may join to further the study of one's specialty.

In keeping with this, the Second Degree lessons are both longer and more in-depth than the First Degree lessons. They are intended to give you a well-rounded magical education, building upon your foundation as a First Degree, as well as to familiarize you with many of the options for specialization that are open to you.

The subject matter of the twelve Second Degree lessons includes the following:

0: Introduction (you are here)

I: Tarot

II: Physiognomy

III: Astrology

IV: Magical Alphabets

V: Numerology

VI: Death, Spirits, and Spirit Guides

VII: Sex Magic

VIII: Magical Calendars

IX: Advanced Chakra and Energy Working

X: Ley Lines

XI: The Ba Gua

XII: Group Dynamics

In addition to completing these lessons, the Second Degree student must complete a Second Degree project that has been agreed upon with their mentor and make a final defense of their project. If it is your intention to pursue Second Degree initiation, you may acquire a mentor at www.witchschool.com or www.correllian.com.

We hope that you enjoy the Second Degree lessons and that they may be of benefit to you in your journey. As with the First Degree lessons, we remind you that we can only provide you with information—how much or how little benefit you derive from it depends wholly upon the extent to which you implement that information in your life. Knowledge is like a muscle: the more you use it, the more it grows.

Blessed be,

Rev. Donald Lewis-Highcorrell

FIRST PRIEST AND CHANCELLOR,
CORRELLIAN NATIVIST TRADITION

• • • •
Glossary

Drawing Down the Moon—Drawing Down the Moon is a rite in which a priestess embodies the Spirit of the Goddess through trance in order to bring through divine energy or messages. This term was coined in reference to the Moon Goddess, but it can also be used broadly to describe bringing through an oracle from any aspect of Deity or even the beloved ancestors. Sometimes, it is simply referred to as an oracle. In Correllian Wicca, the ability to bring through such an oracle is the defining aspect of the Third Degree high priest/ess.

Traditional Witchcraft—*Traditional Witchcraft* is a term that has come into vogue to describe the practice of Witchcraft before Gerald Gardner. Traditional Witchcraft is made up of familial traditions which come from a variety of cultural backgrounds. Some of these familial traditions, like Correllian, consider their practices to be religious in nature, with an element of magic. Other familial traditions view their practice as being purely magical in nature, with little or no religious component. This difference in viewpoint comes from the fact that the different traditions within Traditional Witchcraft come from a variety of cultural and historical origins. There has been considerable tension between the Traditional and Gardnerian branches of Wicca, and some people consider them to be separate movements today; the Correllian Tradition rejects this view, however.

Lesson

I

The Tarot

Few things are associated with Witchcraft as strongly as tarot cards.

For hundreds of years, tarot's colorful and highly symbolic cards have been used for fortunetelling, psychism, and magic.

How many magical images are as familiar in mainstream culture as that of the Gypsy reader extending her palm so that it may be CROSSED WITH SILVER prior to a card reading?

Over the centuries, the cards have collected many legends and superstitions. For the uninitiated, the cards have often become a focus of fear and misunderstanding, much like any other magical art. They have sometimes been outlawed and their practitioners persecuted. Indeed, the tarot's first appearance in history is in an edict forbidding its use. Yet the cards have also remained fashionable at every level of society, no matter how strongly opposed by repressive laws.

Some believe that the tarot contains within it all of the secrets of the universe—

that, correctly interpreted, the tarot is a scripture, visual rather than written, which preserves ancient teachings of metaphysics handed down from the Platonic, Hermetic, and Pythagorean teachers of the classical world. This is a view with which the Correllian Tradition is substantially in agreement.

. . . .

History

The tarot cards are often thought of as mysterious and elusive, and so they are—especially in their origins. No one really knows when tarot cards were invented, or by whom, though people have advanced many theories over the centuries.

Certain aspects of the tarot's history, however, are clear.

The tarot seems to have made its first appearance in Europe in the AD 1300s (900s Pisces). No one is entirely certain how it got there, and there have been a number of theories advanced over the centuries. Some hold that the cards were brought to Europe from Egypt by returning crusaders, such as the KNIGHTS TEMPLAR. Others hold that the cards were invented in the aristocratic courts of Italy. Still others hold that the cards were carried to Europe by the wandering ROMANY tribes, with whom the tarot has always been closely associated.

The earliest mention of the tarot comes from an edict of the city of Bern, Germany, issued in AD 1367 (967 Pisces). The edict bans the use of the cards, but it is directed against gambling, not divination. The same is true of an edict banning tarot issued in Florence, Italy, in AD 1376 (976 Pisces).

At this time, the cards were called by the name Nahipi (or Naippe, or Naibbe), and they may have consisted only of the playing cards we know today as the MINOR ARCANA. The earliest description of a tarot deck, written by Frater Johannes von Rheinfelden in AD 1377 (977 Pisces), describes only the four suits of the Minor Arcana. Similarly, the oldest surviving card deck, the so-called "Hunting Deck" (because it is illustrated with a hunting theme) of Stuttgart, dating from AD 1420 (1020 Pisces), consists only of Minor Arcana cards.

The MAJOR ARCANA cards make their first verifiable appearance in the early AD 1400s (1000s Pisces), with the Visconti-Sforza cards providing the oldest surviving examples—also AD 1420 (1020 Pisces).

There is a belief that the Major Arcana and Minor Arcana originally constituted two separate decks. Anyone might own the Minor Arcana, which were disseminated as playing cards and used for gaming and gambling, thence the origin of modern playing cards. Only diviners owned the Major Arcana, which they kept as a distinct deck and added to their client's existing Minor Arcana deck when they did a reading. In this way, the ordinary person who owned a Minor Arcana deck could only be accused of gambling, while the diviner alone risked the accusation of Witchcraft should their Major Arcana be found. When it became safer to own tarot cards, full decks comprising both sets of Arcana were produced.

The early Major Arcana—which were called *Trionfi* or Triumphs (thence Trumps), were very different from the modern. There does not appear to have been an agreed-upon system of Major Arcana cards at first. Instead, symbols were drawn from many sources. Early decks include among their Major Arcana such images as the planets, the zodiacal signs, the seven virtues, the muses, figures from Pagan mythology, etc. Some of the modern Major Arcana cards appeared from the beginning, such as the Fool. Others did not make their initial appearance until much later. In particular, the Devil and the Tower cards were added to the Major Arcana during the era of the REFORMATION/BURNING TIMES.

The early Major Arcana also did not follow a set number of cards, unlike the Minor Arcana, which have been stable since the beginning at 52–56 cards. The Major Arcana varied considerably in number when it first appeared. Some RENAIS-SANCE tarots may have had as many as 100 cards. Only over time did the Major Arcana assume the twenty-two card form prevalent today.

. . . .

Origins

As has been said, there are many theories regarding the origin of tarot cards and how they came to Europe. Each competing theory has both pros and cons associated with it, and there is, as so often happens in metaphysical history, no conclusive evidence for any of them. I favor the theory that the cards were brought to Europe by the Romany, if only because this is what I was taught by the beloved REGENT LA VEDA.

Playing cards seem to have first been used in China. The first cards were often made from wood or ivory; only later were cards made from heavy paper.

From China, the idea of cards spread to India, where they were a popular pastime. It was in India that the Romany first would have acquired the cards.

Like the tarot, the origins of the Romany people have inspired many theories and legends over the centuries. European Christians, who had no clue of the Romany's origins, often treated them as sub-human, categorizing them with Christianity's scapegoats, Witches and Jews.

The Romany themselves often had no clue of their true origins. They did not identify themselves with a nation of origin but knew only that they had always traveled from place to place.

Today, through the miracles of anthropology and linguistics, we know that the Romany come originally from India, where their close cousins still live. They appear to be closely related to a number of Indian groups, including the Dom and the Luri.

According to the SHAH NAMEH, the Persian Shah Behram Gour imported a large number of Luri from the Hindu ruler Shankar, intending to use them as entertainers. Displeased with the Luri's nomadic lifestyle and inability to adapt to settled habitation, Behram Gour expelled them from Persia.

They are recorded as having been present in the BYZANTINE empire as early as AD 855 (455 Pisces). From there, they seem to have moved into and through the Muslim world (perhaps as a consequence of the long, slow Muslim conquest of Byzantium). At length they traveled up through Egypt, then crossed the Mediterranean to enter Europe in the AD 1300s (900s Pisces).

Because they came up through Egypt, Europeans thought the Romany originated there and called them 'Gypcians, which later shortened to "Gypsies."

The supposed Egyptian origin of the Romany is the real reason for the long-standing belief that the tarot came from Egypt, and indeed the tarot's form may owe something to Egypt because of the Romany's travels there.

. . . .

A Visual Scripture

The tarot has long been said to contain the secrets of the universe—a view with which, as you shall shortly see, we agree.

The BOOK RELIGIONS (Judaism, Christianity, Islam, and Satanism) regard the written word as the highest achievement of human thought and the only suitable medium for the transmission of religious (or any other) teaching. They personify the creative force as "The Word" (Logos) and regard written scriptures as infallible. It often seems that they feel the very act of writing a thing down makes it so, and that written material is incontrovertible by the very fact of its being written. The book religions are so reliant on the written word as the only acceptable transmitter of information that most of them have actually banned visual depictions of people or things.

The Pagan religions, on the other hand, have usually preferred visual to written forms as a means of transmitting religious ideas. All over the world, Pagans have used artwork as the principal method of conveying their beliefs, relying on words primarily as an auxiliary method—and even then the words are often used to convey "visual" images.

The book religions prefer the written word because it is (theoretically, at least) straightforward and unambiguous, allowing for literal interpretation. The written word creates an unchanging standard with a single meaning that does not easily vary. The book religions reject images because they are ambiguous, have multiple levels of meaning, and can be interpreted in different ways that are prone to change and adapt over time—the precise reasons that Pagans prefer visual images.

Moreover, though pictures may be understood by the mind, they primarily speak directly to the inner consciousness. When we read a written passage, we understand it only when we have finished all the words. When we see a painting or sculpture, we form our first understanding the second we see it—an understanding informed by our inborn emotional and psychological reaction, as well as by our cultivated understanding of symbols and images.

The idea of a visual "scripture" such as the tarot is quintessentially Pagan. You need only look at the walls of most historical Pagan temples, covered in murals or sculpture, to see how images have been used to convey allegorical myths in emotionally and psychologically touching ways. The lion's head of Sekhmet is meant to convey the Goddess's qualities of strength and courage, not genetic anomaly. The many arms of Shiva, each holding a different implement or assuming a significant posture, are meant to convey the deity's many attributes. The very surrealism of the image helps make clear that the reference is to spiritual qualities, not physical features.

According to Barbara Walker, in her book *The Women's Encyclopedia of Myths and Secrets*, the Romany considered the tarot to be their people's "Veda"—that is, their sacred "scripture" (*Veda* literally means "wisdom"). Readers of the tarot were called *Vedavica*. The tarot was considered relevant not only for divining the future of everyday situations, but also to convey timeless and cosmic teachings about Deity.

· · · ·

Other Influences

The cosmic wisdom of the tarot was believed to reside in the Major Arcana. As we have said, the Trionfi, or Major Arcana, did not conform to the modern order when they first appeared but developed over time. Many different systems of thought claim credit for the form the Major Arcana finally took.

One of the principal influences on the development of the Major Arcana was Hermeticism. Based on the writings attributed to Hermes Trismegistus, Hermeticism was based on ancient Egyptian teachings as filtered through HELLENISTIC thought. Hermeticism puts a strong emphasis on the relationship between Deity, the soul, and the consciousness, focusing strongly on the idea of oneness with Deity as the cure for all difficulties.

Another major influence on the cards was alchemy. Alchemy also developed out of late classical thought, coming from very ancient antecedents. Most people very much misunderstand the nature of alchemy, being familiar only with the overly literal interpretation of it, created in large part by its opponents. Though some alchemists did shade into an early form of chemistry, at its best, alchemy was first and foremost a subtle and highly developed philosophical system closely related to modern Wicca.

Alchemy focused strongly upon the idea of the relation between, and resolution of, the cosmic polarities, which they personified as king and queen. The king's death and resurrection was a major theme of alchemy, being a metaphor for the development of the soul. Alchemy was very concerned with the development and evolution of the soul, described in extremely allegorical terms. The famous image of

the alchemist laboring to turn lead into gold is, in reality, a reference to the idea of developing from physical consciousness (lead) to divine consciousness (gold).

Both Hermeticism and alchemy were extremely popular in the Renaissance, when the Major Arcana were taking shape, and they each contributed greatly to the cards. Indeed, the principal message of the Major Arcana is one that any Hermeticist or alchemist would recognize as easily as any Wiccan. Spiritual development brings one closer to Deity; being closer to Deity puts us in control of our lives and leads us ultimately to conscious union with Deity and the full access of divine power from within ourselves.

Another major influence on the Major Arcana is said to be the Hebrew CABALA. The idea that the Cabala might be the basis of the tarot was put forward in the nineteenth century AD (fourteenth century Pisces) by the CEREMONIAL movement and is encapsulated in the famous WAITE-SMITH tarot deck.

Cabala is a system of understanding the divine through numerology. Its most famous aspect is the well-known TREE OF LIFE, which arranges the numbers in a symbolic layout said to reveal the secrets of the universe. Cabalists have been known to claim that the great Pagan philosopher and numerologist Pythagoras was a student of pre-existing Hebrew Cabala and adapted its teachings for Pagan use; however, it is much more likely that Pythagorean numerology influenced Cabalistic numerology than vice versa.

The idea that the tarot was based on Cabala became dominant when author EDEN GRAY chose the Waite-Smith deck as the basis for her groundbreaking books on the tarot. Gray was the first author to write on the subject of tarot for a mass audience. Previous works on tarot had been written in an intellectual, somewhat impenetrable style, and printed only in small runs. Gray's books were written in simple, easily understandable language that made tarot easily accessible to all and sparked the tarot renaissance of the 1960s (1560s Pisces).

However, while numerology has undoubtedly become important to tarot, it is important to bear in mind that the earliest existing Cabalistic Tree of Life chart dates only to the AD 1100s (700s Pisces) and is not fully developed into its modern form. Therefore, while many people may associate the Cabala with tarot, it is clearly not part of the cards' origin.

The most fundamental influence upon the tarot, however, must surely be the beliefs of the people most closely associated with it: Gypsies and Witches. The beliefs of the Romany have their origin in popular Hinduism, often overlaid with a thin veneer of Christian HAGIOGRAPHY (thus the goddess Kali Ma becomes the "Christian" Black Madonna or the black St. Sarah), while the Witches came from many sources, including the tribal religions of old Europe and the cosmopolitan philosophies of Greece and Rome, also often mixed up with Christian hagiography (thus the goddess Anu, a Celtic reflex of Kali Ma, became the "Christian" St. Anne). Both religions have a strong emphasis on development through reincarnation and the IMMANENCE of Deity.

However, in discussing the cosmic meaning of the tarot, it is not so much with its origins that we are concerned, but with what it means to us today, in the light of contemporary thought.

It must always be remembered that as we are living, growing beings, so too our knowledge lives and grows, adapting to new understandings and changing circumstances. Therefore, we must always ask ourselves not "What did this mean to our ancestors?" but rather "What does this tell me now?"

• • • •

La Veda De Vita

Let us speak, then, of the meaning of the tarot in its present form and for the contemporary Wiccan audience.

The Major Arcana—the Trumps, or *Trionfi*—are the part of the tarot which is

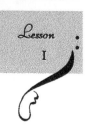

said to speak to cosmic issues, and so we shall start there.

In most contemporary tarot decks, the Major Arcana consist of twenty-two cards. As we have said, this was not always so, nor is it always so today, but it is the most common form, and so it is the form we shall deal with.

The Major Arcana, or Trumps, are considered the fifth suit of the tarot, but they are markedly different from the other four suits. It is said that this is because the Major Arcana deal with spiritual things, while the other four suits, or Minor Arcana, deal with everyday situations.

Supposedly in the days when tarot reading was forbidden by the Catholic Church, card readers would carry a deck of cards consisting only of the Major Arcana. When asked to read, they would join this deck of Major Arcana cards to their client's deck of ordinary playing cards. This was to ensure the client's safety, since if the client were caught with playing cards the punishment was much lighter than if they were caught with "fortunetelling" cards. Though its veracity is doubtful, this story is often given as the reason why the Major Arcana are not found in playing cards.

It is often said that all of the secrets of the universe are to be found in the Major Arcana. While that may be stretching it a little, it is nonetheless true that the Major Arcana do contain a coherent spiritual statement. Whether that statement was in the cards originally, as legend would have it, or was superimposed upon them later is debatable, but it is certainly to be found in today's tarot decks.

There are many interpretations of the Major Arcana's spiritual meaning, differing mainly according to the religious persuasion of the interpreter. But the basic meaning remains the same, no matter who interprets it: that life is a spiritual journey of the soul, whose origin and destination are the same—God, or Spirit, if you will.

It is an ancient belief that all matter is composed of five elements. The four physical elements are air, fire, water, and earth. These four elements are believed to be present in varying amounts in all things and creatures, though it must be understood that we are not referring to the physical substances named, but rather to their qualities. Roughly stated, those qualities are these: air—awareness and thought, fire—action and manifestation, water—reaction and emotion, and earth—integration and structure. The fifth element is spirit, which gives life to all things and without which nothing would exist.

This concept runs throughout the tarot and is key to understanding its structure. Consequently, in considering the meanings of the twenty-two Major Arcana cards, I have divided the cards into five groups of four—one group for each element. The remaining two cards, the Fool and the Universe, as will be seen, are naturally outside this system.

In each of these five quartets, the first three cards refer to conditions, the fourth card to the natural result of those conditions. Thus, if you consider the quartet of spirit, you will see that the Star, the Moon, and the Sun, separately or together, lead naturally to Judgement.

These twenty-two cards are:

0) The Fool—Deity before creation

Air

1) The Magus—Creation/the God

2) The High Priestess—Spirit/ the Goddess

3) The Empress—the ensouled universe

4) The Emperor—time and structure of perception

Fire

5) The HIEROPHANT— communication between Spirit and human

6) The Lovers—choice and lessons

7) The Chariot—Material advancement and success

8) Strength—spiritual advancement and success

Water

9) The Hermit—the seeker

10) The Wheel of Fortune—what Fate gives the seeker

11) Justice—what fate the seeker makes

12) The Hanged Man—the process of learning and growing

Earth

13) Death and Rebirth—the eternal cycle which facilitates growth

14) Temperance—acquisition and integration of knowledge

15) The Devil—material illusion, the veil

16) The Tower—piercing material illusion

Spirit

17) The Star—piercing illusion through vision and inner work

18) The Moon—piercing illusion through religion and ritual

19) The Sun—piercing illusion through material experiences

20) Judgement—the enlightened person who has overcome illusion

21) The Universe—union with Deity after enlightenment

VARIATIONS IN ELEMENTAL SUITS

Element	Tarot	English	German	Swiss
Air	Swords	Spades	Leaves	Shields
Fire	Wands	Clubs	Acorns	Acorns
Water	Cups	Hearts	Hearts	Roses
Earth	Pentacles	Diamonds	Bells	Shells

Here it will be seen that the Major Arcana of the tarot tell the story of existence, from before the first creation, through the journey of the soul, to the ultimate reunion of the soul with Deity. Thus it might be said to be true that the tarot does indeed contain the fabled secrets of the universe.

. . . .

The Minor Arcana

The Minor Arcana are divided into four suits corresponding to the four elements of the physical world: air, fire, water, and earth—thought, action, reaction, and integration. These four suits are retained in modern playing cards.

Different peoples have seen these elemental suits in different ways over the centuries. Some of the variations are included in the table at the top of this page.

One difference you will often see, however, is that in most tarot decks, the order of the elements is given differently—air, water, fire, and earth—and the attributions vary. Most commonly, for example, tarologists will class wands as the suit of air and swords as the suit of fire. This is because of the strong influence of European Ceremonialism, which uses this same attribution. Here I have chosen to use the common Wiccan system.

Each of the four suits of the Minor Arcana has ten pip cards and four court cards. In playing cards, the fourth court card, the Page (or Princess, in some versions), has been eliminated.

Each of these cards has a meaning, and these are usually believed to have a numerological origin.

As the Major Arcana are held to refer to cosmic, spiritual issues, so the Minor Arcana are generally held to refer to mundane, personal issues.

The Minor Arcana cards are as follows:

Ace

Ruled by the sun, the ace represents the cardinal qualities of the element of the suit. The Ace of Swords represents the powers of air/mind: thought, intelligence, judgment; usually it indicates a specific decision to be made. The Ace of Wands represents the power of fire/action: energy, enthusiasm, passion for the situation. The Ace of Cups indicates the powers of water/ emotion and is usually taken as happiness and good fortune. The Ace of Pentacles represents the powers of earth/integration: prosperity and stability, often perceived directly as money or financial growth.

Two

Ruled by the Moon, the two represents the element of the suit in dealings with others in private ways. Thus the Two of Swords represents alliances toward mutual aims. The Two of Wands represents new opportunities for growth and expansion through personal connections. The Two of Cups represents an important relationship, usually romantic in nature. The Two of Pentacles represents learning from experiences with others and being very busy.

Three

Ruled by Jupiter, the three represents the element of the suit in dealings with others in public ways. Thus the Three of Swords represents endings, separations, or major changes in important relationships. The Three of Wands represents help from a friend, mentor, or advisor. The Three of Cups represents shared happiness and cel-

ebration with others. The Three of Pentacles represents the employment of skills or abilities to the benefit of others.

Four

Ruled by Saturn, the four represents the element of the suit in a state of stability, with lack of movement. Thus the Four of Swords represents a rest or time-out period. The Four of Wands represents the achievement of a goal. The Four of Cups represents a good situation but still the desire for more. The Four of Pentacles represents miserliness, holding back from others, and reticence to become involved or take action.

Five

Ruled by Mercury, the five represents the element of the suit in a state of transformation and movement, but also a consequent fear of the unknown and unseen future into which one is moving. Thus the Five of Swords represents a feeling of being oppressed or held back by others. The Five of Wands represents inner or outer conflict. The Five of Cups represents disappointment or sorrow. The Five of Pentacles represents loss or fear of loss.

Six

Ruled by Venus, the six represents the element of the suit assisted by a gift of fate. Thus the Six of Swords represents travel,

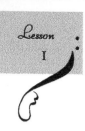

movement, and starting over. The Six of Wands represents victory, success, and popularity. The Six of Cups represents people or patterns from one's past. The Six of Pentacles represents receiving help from another, assistance, or a gift.

Seven

Ruled by Uranus, the seven represents the element of the suit crossed by obstacles that, if overcome, bring great benefit. Thus the Seven of Swords represents an uphill battle that may yet be won, but only through great effort. The Seven of Wands represents hard work that leads to victory. The Seven of Cups represents illusions and misunderstandings that contain the seeds of self-knowledge. The Seven of Pentacles represents many choices not yet decided upon, which can lead to great success once chosen and focused upon.

Eight

Ruled by Mars, the eight represents the element of the suit in extreme circumstances—good, bad, or indifferent. Thus the Eight of Swords represents feeling held back, unable to maneuver. The Eight of Wands represents speed, sudden happenings, and unexpected developments. The Eight of Cups represents exaggerated fears and obsessions. The Eight of Pentacles represents mastering one's craft and honing personal skills.

Nine

Ruled by Neptune, the nine represents the element of the suit in its greatest skill. Thus the Nine of Swords represents confronting and overcoming one's fears. The Nine of Wands represents patience, perseverance, and long-term plans. The Nine of Cups represents the ability to manifest what one desires from one's Higher Self. The Nine of Pentacles represents personal power and the ability to make one's own decisions and live life as one wishes.

Ten

Ruled by Pluto, the ten represents the element of the suit in its ultimate fulfillment. Thus the Ten of Swords represents leaving the old behind to make way for the new. The Ten of Wands represents a situation on the verge but not yet ready for change. The Ten of Cups represents personal happiness and fulfillment. The Ten of Pentacles represents having a strong and rewarding base in home, family, or a personal mission.

Princess

The princess (sometimes rendered "page") represents the powers of the element of the suit in a state of stasis or immobility (earth), the potential for change and growth not yet in motion. Thus the Princess of Swords represents diplomacy and circumspection. The Princess of Wands represents a person or situation on the verge of action. The Princess of Cups represents moodiness and overwhelming emotions. The Princess of Pentacles represents holding back from what one knows one should do.

Knight

The knight represents the powers of the element of the suit expressed through thought and intention (air). Thus the Knight of Swords represents a need for healthy self-interest. The Knight of Wands represents uncontrolled expansion and a need for greater focus. The Knight of Cups represents speaking, writing, the arts, and all other means of communication. The Knight of Pentacles represents slow but steady growth.

Queen

The queen represents the powers of the element of the suit experienced as an internal reaction (water) to one's understanding. Thus the Queen of Swords represents inner reflection and the ability to learn from past experience. The Queen of Wands represents satisfaction and being in an emotionally positive situation. The Queen of Cups represents happiness and joy. The Queen of Pentacles represents security, stability, and prosperity, enough for oneself and more to share with others.

King

The king represents the powers of the element of the suit as expressed in action (fire). Thus the King of Swords represents good judgment and the ability to make sound decisions. The King of Wands represents mental focus and successful practical action. The King of Cups represents the ability to experience one's emotions without being overwhelmed by them. The King of Pentacles represents prosperity and financial success.

. . . .

Beliefs About Tarot Cards

There are many beliefs about tarot cards and how to use them, as is to be expected for anything that has been around so long.

Some of these beliefs are good and useful, at least if used sensibly. Others, however, can be very limiting—these are SUPERSTITIONS and should be eschewed.

More than an age ago, the great Pagan philosopher PLUTARCH defined *superstition* as being beliefs based on the fear of Spirit, as opposed to religion, which is based on the love of Spirit. The wise know that there is never a need to fear Spirit, for Spirit, in all of her manifestations, is good. Superstitions limit and confine; spirituality should never confine you, save only to the sacred Rede, "Harm none."

Which of these beliefs about tarot cards are helpful spiritual tools, and which are superstitions? This you must answer for yourself. What works well for one may be unnecessary or limiting to another, and what is unnecessary or limiting to one may be another's helpful psychic key, assisting their shift of consciousness. The question is, what works for *you*? Any of these beliefs could be helpful, but none of them should ever be regarded as necessary.

What are these beliefs? Some of them include the following:

Some people believe that you should never buy a tarot deck for yourself but only receive one as a gift. I would venture to suggest that this belief arises from the idea of letting "the right deck for you" seek you out, like a found stone or object. Of course, this belief is only practical if you know people who use tarot cards.

Some people believe that this only refers to a person's first tarot deck, while others hold that it is true for any tarot deck.

Another belief that some hold is that you should never use a tarot deck that has previously belonged to another person. The idea here is that the deck will have bonded with its first owner and will not work well for any other.

However, some people believe that one's first tarot deck should be a deck that has been previously owned, preferably by one's teacher.

Personally, I have used both new and previously owned tarot decks, both purchased and given, with equal success.

As for the vibrations of previous owners, these are easily enough cleared. Anytime you acquire a new tarot deck, however you acquire it, you should cleanse and bless it as you might cleanse and bless any ritual object. This should clear any preexisting vibrations.

Another belief about tarot cards is that you should ATTUNE to a new deck, so that it bonds to you and you to it. The most common way for this to be done is to sleep with the deck for three nights in succession. Usually these are the three nights of the full Moon, when the ambient energy is strongest. The deck is placed either under the pillow or under the bed itself. Some people prefer to place the deck upon their altar.

Some people, having attuned to their deck, don't want anyone else to touch it, sometimes even the people they are reading for. They feel that other people's energy will disturb their bond with the cards. And, of course, if you choose to believe that, it will become true: "energy is shaped by thought and emotion, usually unconsciously," remember?

Personally, I let everyone handle my cards and have never had any trouble of this kind. On the contrary, I pride myself on having friendly cards. Though cards are meant to respond to energy, I do not feel that they pick up energy that casually. Many readers I know, both professional and recreational, feel the same. But who you let handle your cards is a personal choice, and when it comes to your cards you should do what feels right to you.

For this same reason—the idea that cards will casually pick up unwanted energy and give skewed readings as a result— many people make it a habit to wrap their cards in silk and keep them in a special box. Some people believe that silk has a special ability to shield unwanted energy, and this idea was particularly popular at the turn of the last century. As for the boxes, these are often lovely works of art in their own right, especially the wooden boxes import- ed from India for this purpose, which are often elaborately carved and inlaid.

Storing your cards in silk and fine wooden boxes is a nice thing to do. It makes for great atmosphere and thus can serve as a psychic key, helping you to align with your Higher Self and come into the right state of mind for reading. However, it is not necessary. I have read with cards straight from the box or carried in baggies and done just as well.

Some people also like to place a special stone or stones, usually quartz crystal, with their cards when they are not in use. The crystal is meant to amplify the cards' ener- gy, thus aiding the reader's native psychic

ability as well as the cards' ability to attune to the questioner. Other stones that might be placed with the cards include lapis lazu- li, amethyst, and Moonstone, all intended to increase the reader's ability to use the cards psychically. Of course, any stone can be used in this way if one desires to imbue the cards with its particular energy. Herbs can be used in the same way.

In the days, back a few years, when I was a well-known reader on the psychic fair circuit, my tarot cards were usually kept in a wooden box along with quartz crystal, a hunk of amethyst with a pewter wizard figure mounted on it (a gift from one of our Correllian high priestesses), and whole cloves (a favorite herb of mine). The inside of the box had been swabbed with essential oils chosen to promote psychic ability. The cards themselves were a Morgan-Greer deck, the gift of my altar-sister Bitterwind, who was later ACCLAIMED First Elder of the Correllian Tradition. I still use the same cards for most readings, even after a quarter of a century, although I have come to have a substantial collection.

One other common belief about tarot cards must be mentioned here. That is the idea that each tarot deck has its own spirit and personality.

Now this is an idea with which we agree generally, for what existing thing does not have a spirit? And just as you can visual- ize the spirit of a stone to attune to it, or

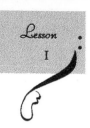

receive advice or assistance from it, so too can you communicate with the spirit of your tarot cards.

Obviously, such a practice can be helpful, but often it is not. Unlike a stone, which has existed long before it came to you and thus has a well-developed nature of its own, a tarot deck will take on much of its character through use, and much of that character will be shaped by you. The obvious consequence of this is that you should shape the cards as you want them.

I have known a number of people who had tarot decks that were extremely temperamental, finicky about who they would read for, and when or even if they could be read at all. All this is very dramatic, but if you ask me, it's also a pain in the neck. But these people loved it. They would supplicate their cards, cater to them, and treat them as prima donnas. Of course, that's just how these people liked their cards to be—it was their "atmosphere," their "key." They have programmed their cards to be this way (perhaps unconsciously) and reinforced it through their own behavior. Nice if you like things like that, I suppose. I prefer a simpler, friendlier world.

Personally, I do not accept those sorts of complications in my life (at least not from a deck of cards), and consequently I am never presented with them. I expect my cards to be user-friendly and trouble-free, and they are. I acknowledge that they have

a spirit, but I limit my interactions with it to blessing, cleansing, and asking questions of the cards. My advice? Treat your cards as colleagues and expect them to act professionally, and they will oblige.

. . . .

How to Read the Tarot

Enough with the history, enough with the beliefs. You have a tarot deck. How do you use it?

Well, you can pretty much distill all of the above into one simple sentence: "They have little pictures on them, and you read them by the way they come up in a reading."

Before you begin a tarot reading, you might want to light a candle to act as a battery, providing extra energy for the reading. You might also imagine four pillars of white light, one in each corner of the room, for the same reason (to act as batteries). Extra energy is always good for a reading. (If you use the pillars or other energy constructs, remember to take them down when you're finished, and *always* clear and release when you're done.)

To do a reading, begin by shuffling the cards. It doesn't matter how you shuffle them, though people often develop a favorite method, as long as the cards get good and mixed up, and their order gets switched all around.

As you're shuffling, concentrate on cleansing the cards of all previous IMPRES-SIONS. You might visualize the cards being flushed with cleansing yellow-white light. You might also want to think, or even say, something like "I cleanse you, I cleanse you, I cleanse you." This is an example of interacting with the card's spirit, which we discussed above.

Once you've cleansed your cards, you are ready to ask your question. The question can be as simple as the all-purpose "What do I need to know at this time?" which will produce an answer relating to present or upcoming circumstances. Or the question can be much more specific.

You can ask pretty much anything of the cards, if you phrase it right. Cards can be used to give yes or no answers, or to describe conditions in current or future circumstances or the unfolding of situations. However, they cannot be easily used to pick one of several options in a single question. When several options or subjects are being considered, these should be listed separately. An example of this is the question "How will my family be?" The answer to this question will be hopelessly confused unless you break down the question to deal with each separate family member, whose fortunes may be quite different.

Once you have your question, get it clear in your mind and concentrate on it. Anything that helps you to focus on the question is good. You might want to repeat the question over and over in your mind, or imagine it in visual terms or anything that will assist your focus, for it is through focus that you communicate the question to the cards, and thence to Spirit.

Now shuffle the cards again, while continuing to focus on your question. Keep shuffling until the cards are good and mixed up. When it feels "right," stop. Practice will make it easier to determine how long the cards need to be shuffled. If you are reading for another person, they should shuffle the cards this time, concentrating on their question, then give you back the cards when they are done.

It is traditional to cut the deck at this point. I normally hold either my left hand or both hands over the deck and open a channel to the divine energy to bless the cards. I visualize them being flooded with blue-white light. As I do this, I charge them (usually silently) to "show me not the hopes and fears of this person, but show me only truth."

Now, using your left hand (which represents the Goddess and spirituality), cut the cards into three stacks. Then reassemble them in a different order.

Now, to obtain your answer, you must draw some cards. There are some things to be aware of, however, before you do.

Many people believe that it is unlucky to read for yourself. This is nonsense.

Reading for yourself can be problematic, however. It is very difficult to have objectivity when dealing with questions that directly affect you or your loved ones. This is particularly true when you are just learning. Though the cards may give a perfectly accurate answer, you may not be able to read them properly because of your own hopes and fears.

Also, though the cards are the tool through which your answer is divined, the answer comes from Spirit, who may or may not want you to have the information you are asking for at the time you are asking. If this is the case, it will often be obvious: the answers obtained will be so obtuse as to be meaningless.

Consequently, when reading for yourself, you should remember this and take the results with a grain of salt—that is, use common sense in applying them. Indeed, this is good advice for all readings. Regard a reading as giving good advice that can be helpful, but do not take a reading as "GOSPEL" or you may be in for the Five of Cups.

How many cards should you draw?

The number of cards that you draw, and the pattern in which you lay them down, is called a SPREAD. There are many, many spreads that are in common use. Some of these are very simple, and others are hopelessly complicated. There are whole books on tarot whose main virtue is in presenting different spreads that the reader may use. Some readers pride themselves on always having the right spread for the right question. Personally, I confine myself to the spreads which follow.

. . . .

Spreads

One-Card Spread

The simplest of all spreads is the one-card spread. There are several ways to do it; it need be no more complicated than cutting the deck in any place that feels "right" and reading the card that comes up. Or, if you prefer, one card may be drawn from the deck and laid upon the table.

This one card will not give you much information, but sometimes it's all you need. It is not an especially good technique for a beginning student but can be quite serviceable to a seasoned reader who has a good understanding of the cards.

The card can be read according to its normal meaning. This will give you basic information as to the situation you are asking about. Many people make it a point to draw a single tarot card in this manner each morning, asking what will be the basic energy of the upcoming day. This is an excellent practice and can be very helpful in getting acquainted with the cards.

A variation of this is to ask a yes or no question. The card is then read yes or no according to whether it is upright or upside down, respectively.

If the single card does not give you enough information, you might want to draw two more and see if that helps.

Three-Card Spread

I learned this spread under the name "Las Vegas Quickie Reading" and have found it to be very useful. As you might imagine from the name, the spread requires three cards. These may be obtained by cutting the deck into three stacks or by selecting three cards at random. The three cards are then interpreted together. Sometimes they represent a sequential situation, each one leading to the next, but more often they should be interpreted as blending their meanings to refer to a single situation.

For example, the Knight of Wands, the Eight of Pentacles, and the Six of Pentacles (below, shown left to right) might be taken to indicate a need for greater focus and application of knowledge the QUERENT already possesses, which will attract needed help or assistance.

This is another spread which some people like to do for themselves each morning to divine the character of the upcoming day.

A variation on this spread, which will provide more detailed information, is to repeat it three or four times for a single question, thus yielding nine to twelve cards. Depending upon what they yield, these cards might be taken as all referring to a single situation or as successive events in a chain resulting from the initial situation.

Celtic Cross Spread

The Celtic Cross is certainly the most popular of tarot spreads currently in use. The term *Celtic Cross* refers to the equal-armed cross that we enact in our magic circle

Universal Tarot (Lo Scarabeo, ©Roberto De Angelis, 2000)

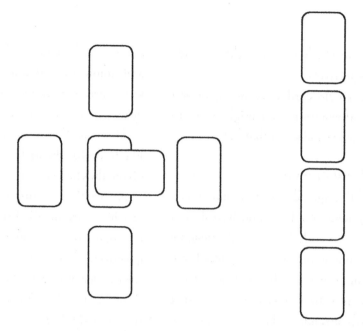

Celtic Cross spread

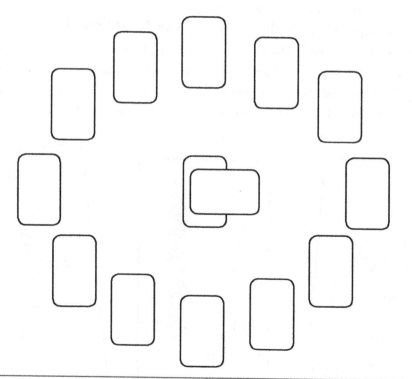

Zodiac spread

every time we invoke the four quarters. This is the solar cross, which represents the four directions and the four elements, or physical existence. The solar cross and the pentagram are sometimes taken to represent God and Goddess, respectively.

To perform a Celtic Cross spread, draw the needed cards one at a time at random. The first card goes in the center. This card represents the basic energy of the querent's situation as regards the question. The second card is laid across the first. This card represents any obstacles to the querent's objectives in the question.

Now, place one card above—to the north, so to speak. This card represents the past, things which have led the querent to their current situation regarding the issue in question.

Now, place a card to the right, as if to the east. This card represents the immediate future, what is about to happen regarding the situation.

Next, place a card below, as if to the south. This card represents the querent's desire regarding the question. This desire may or may not be fully conscious. Sometimes the desire will come up as failure, in which case the querent has seriously crossed mental wires regarding what they truly want.

Now, lay a card to the left, as if to the west. This represents the best that can be hoped for from the situation. This is by no means what must come but is the best that can come, the highest potential.

Now, to the right side, lay out four cards vertically. These represent as follows:

1. Where the querent is now regarding the question; the querent's current conditions.

2. What will be around the querent as this situation unfolds; what conditions will influence the querent.

3. What emotions the querent will primarily feel in reaction to this situation.

4. And finally, the most likely outcome of the question.

It sometimes follows that the most likely outcome may appear better than the best possible outcome. What this means is that the situation is likely to succeed, but it may not be the best course for the querent.

In addition, three more cards may be drawn to add extra information of a general nature.

It should be noted that there are a number of variations on the Celtic Cross spread in which the cards have slightly different meanings. You can discover this through your own research, and decide what works best for you.

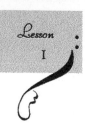

Zodiac Spread

The zodiac spread is meant to show the general conditions for the year ahead. It requires fourteen cards, one for each month from the time of the reading and two for the general energy of the year. The first card is placed at the center, and it represents the prevailing energy the querent will encounter in the year ahead. The second card "crosses" the first and should be laid upon, across, or beside it. The second card represents the principle lesson or lessons that will be placed before the querent by Spirit during this time. These lessons may appear to be blockages or obstacles to overcome, but they are sent by Spirit to stimulate needed growth.

Now, lay out the remaining twelve cards in a circle around the first two. Each card represents one month and shows the principal circumstances or events of that month. If clarification is needed, additional cards may be selected at random and added alongside the card to add more information.

Yes/No Spread

For a yes/no spread, you need either three or five cards. Obtain them either by cutting the deck into the appropriate number of stacks and taking the first card off the top or by drawing them at random. The answer is obtained by analyzing the number of cards which are upright versus the number which are upside down. If more are upright, the answer is yes. If more are upside down, the answer is no. In addition, the specific cards can be read to give information about the conditions surrounding the situation.

. . . .

These are the basic spreads I recommend. There are literally hundreds of others—far more than I choose to use, let alone relate here. There is a tarot spread for every temperament and every occasion. You may find that you want to learn more spreads, and if so, a little independent tarot research will yield a number of books containing any number of spreads. Personally, I find simplest is best.

Once you have completed your reading, you should clear the cards again, as you did to start with, and also clear and release excess energy from yourself. This is especially important if you are reading for someone else but should be done even if you are reading for yourself.

A final comment on reading technique. Readings can be remarkably accurate, but they are not always. The wise take the results of a psychic reading with a grain of salt and use common sense in applying them. A psychic reading, whether by tarot or any other means, constitutes a kind of advice, which like other advice should be considered on its merits. Any number of variables can interfere with a reading's accuracy, so you should judge the information a reading gives in light of common sense and whether circumstances seem to support it as the situation goes forward. This is only practical.

• • • •

To Charge or Not to Charge?

There is a great deal of controversy among Wiccans over whether or not one should charge for psychic and magical services. Many Wiccans feel that psychism/magic is a gift from God/dess and must be shared freely, as it was freely given. Members of some Wiccan traditions get quite dogmatic about not charging for the employment of spiritual abilities and are deeply offended when others do charge.

We in the Correllian Tradition take the position that psychism and magic are not gifts that one is born with so much as skills that one develops. Granted, one may be born with these skills fully developed, but this is only because the skills have already been built in previous lifetimes. The flowering of psychic abilities is the reward of effort, often a great deal of effort, and we feel that one is entitled to the fair reward of that effort—that is to say, reasonable payment.

When I was in training in the '70s, I was taught that psychic work was an important part of the priestly calling. I was taught that a Wiccan priest/ess was not only expected to master psychic skills, but use them to help people, especially the members of their own temple. This was only one part of the great responsibility that came with the priesthood.

But, my teachers maintained, the compensation for this was that these same skills could be used to earn or augment one's living. God/dess does not place these skills into your hands so that you can hide them away from the world, but rather so that they can be used to do good. Those who do not accept compensation for psychic work usually do not do very much of it. They read for friends and people they know, when the occasion arises. But a paid psychic is likely to read for many more people, thus building a much higher degree of skill, as well as using their skills to benefit a much wider audience.

This does not mean that all Correllian clergy are expected to be professional psychics—far from it. We know that different people will excel in different areas and thus take different specialties as time passes. Though we do expect all Correllian clergy to be familiar with psychic techniques, have a good understanding of them, and be capable of employing them if they choose to, we know that only a few will make it their specialty. But those who do develop their psychic skills as their primary specialty, in our opinion, should be entitled to the just reward of their labors and should be able to employ their skills as a recognized aspect of the priesthood.

Of course, this endorsement of paid psychic work is hardly surprising, considering that the Correllian Tradition was founded by a woman who worked for years as a professional psychic reader and spiritual healer, Orpheis Caroline Highcorrell. Not only did Orpheis Caroline charge for her psychic readings, especially during her years with the circus, but also for her healings, herbal remedies, and charms. In this she was the very image of the traditional Witch.

From centuries of written and pictorial records, we all know that practitioners of the psychic and magical arts traditionally charged for their services. Usually they asked for a modest fee, enough to make it possible for them to continue practicing. After all, you can't be of help to anyone if you can't afford to live yourself.

It is our official position that the ban on charging for psychic work observed by certain Wiccan traditions is a reaction to the antispiritualist laws of the last century's teens and '20s. These laws were written in response to the exposure of fraud on the part of a few SPIRITUALIST mediums, though most spiritualists were entirely honest. The exposure of the dishonest few was, and continues to be, taken advantage of by conservative Christian forces whose goal was not the prevention of fraud but the elimination of competing beliefs. To avoid any appearance of dishonesty, not to mention possible arrest, many spiritualists and Witches adopted the view that one should never charge for spiritual work.

The Correllian Tradition considers the employment of the psychic arts to be an integral and essential element of our faith. Use of psychic skills is not an adjunct to, or a byproduct of, the Wiccan religion, but is a fully integrated aspect of it. We regard that it is the absolute moral right of our priesthood to employ the psychic and magical arts and to be justly compensated for them, just as the priesthood of other religions expect just compensation for the enactment of the spiritual rites of their faiths. Nonetheless, this is a moral position, and by it we do not mean to encourage you to violate your local laws if they prohibit charging for psychic work, only to state our formal opposition to such laws.

• • • •

Exercises

The series of exercises included with the Second Degree lessons are separate from but similar to the exercises that accompanied the First Degree lessons. Parts of these exercises will seem very familiar to you, while other parts will be very different.

As we said in the First Degree lessons, you can gain a great deal of knowledge by reading the text of each lesson, but the true value of the lessons comes from putting that knowledge into practice. The exercises section of each lesson lays out a course of practice to build your psychic muscles and thus increase your magical skills.

Just as with the First Degree exercises, you should set aside a time each day to perform the exercises, preferably the same time each day. Of course this is not always workable, but you should try to be as regular as possible.

When doing the exercises, you should be as comfortable and relaxed as possible. Do whatever you wish to put yourself in the right frame of mind. You may wish to burn incense, anoint yourself with oil, or play a restful meditation tape. Make sure you are in a comfortable position. You should wear loose, easy-fitting clothes or no clothes at all.

To help you with your exercises, you should set up several "batteries." Physically you can do this by lighting candles—the flame will help to raise energy for your exercises. You should always light at least one candle if possible, but you may light as many as you wish. You can also use stones as batteries. Simply select an appropriate stone and charge it for this purpose. If you recall from the First Degree lessons, stones like quartz crystal, amethyst, and lapis lazuli are among those that make excellent aids to psychic work.

You can also create energy constructs to serve as batteries to help you in your exercises. A good way to do this is to create four pillars of white light at the corners of the room you are working in or simply in a vortex around you.

Once you are set up, as always you should begin by clearing and releasing all excess energy.

Exercise 1

This exercise deals with the transformative power of sound.

Sound has long been used to affect the vibrational rate of energy. Vibration, as you'll recall, is the rate at which energy moves, thus affecting its position in the seven planes of existence.

The priestesses of ancient Egypt used the sacred SISTRA (s. sistrum), a kind of rattle, to purify energy, thus creating sacred space and dispersing negative energy. Native Americans are famous for using drumming in the same way: to disperse negative energy, as well as to induce altered states of consciousness for shamanic work. Chanting, too, has a long history of use by disparate peoples for the purpose of affecting energy, the most famous contemporary example being the Buddhist monks of Tibet.

Historically, many have attempted to quantify the qualities of sound—the exact energetic effect of a given note or pitch, the particular "sound" to be associated with a given plane or zodiacal sign or planet. We will not go into this here except to say that the Hindus have such a system, according to which the sound Ohm (or Aum) is said to be the sound of creation.

Begin the exercise by becoming aware of your solar plexus chakra, in the area of your navel or just above.

Just behind your navel, in the center of your body, imagine a ball of clear, white light. Imagine it like a sun shining out from the center of your being. Have this image visualized as clearly as possible, then take a deep breath. As you expel it, vocalize the sacred syllable Ohm.

As you vocalize the syllable, imagine the ball of light expanding within you. See it grow to fill your abdomen, your torso, your whole body. See it expand and grow beyond you as you continue to vocalize the sacred syllable Ohm.

Continue to simultaneously vocalize and expand the ball of light until it is at least six feet in diameter, then stop the sound. Visualize a flash of white light, and let the ball collapse back into you.

Although I have said six feet, you should allow your ball of light to expand as far as you can easily expand it. As you gain facility with the exercise, you will be able to expand the ball farther and farther. Try to extend the exercise as far and as long as possible.

Similarly, you may need to take additional breaths during the exercise in order to be able to maintain your Ohm when you first begin it, but as you practice, you will find it easier and easier to maintain the sound. Try to keep the sound as even and steady as possible.

This exercise will help to raise your vibrational frequency, open your throat chakra, and also be good for your lung capacity.

Once you have finished the exercise, you should then go ahead and open your chakras, as you learned to do while training for First Degree. Create a ball of colored light in each of the seven major chakras. When you have all seven balls of colored light, go back and change each ball to white light. When you have all seven balls of white light, then go back and turn each ball into purple light.

You should now again clear and release all excess energy, as you know to do after all psychic and magical workings.

Continue this exercise until it is easy for you; then you will be ready to try some variations.

Variation A: If you are like most of us, you will have been making your sound from your throat. Once you have practiced the exercise enough to become comfortable with it, you should try moving the sound around. Instead of your throat, try making the sound from your diaphragm, the bottom of your rib cage.

If you have never done this before, you may find it rather difficult, but keep trying and soon you'll get it. As you vocalize, imagine the sound moving farther down your windpipe, toward the diaphragm. Focus on the diaphragm, and "push" the sound down to it. It may take a few tries.

If necessary, you can practice vocalizing the sound separately, to gain greater control over where it is being generated.

Once you've got it, do the exercise as usual, except for generating the Ohm sound from the diaphragm. Keep trying to expand the ball of light farther before collapsing it. Repeat the exercise this way, vocalizing from the diaphragm, until it is easy for you to do.

Follow by opening the chakras first as colored balls of light, then white, then purple. Clear and release, as always.

Variation B: When you are able to make your Ohm sound from the diaphragm without difficulty, you are ready for more variations.

Try moving the sound upwards, back up to your throat, then up the back of your throat and into the nasal cavity. It may

take a few tries to be able to generate the Ohm sound from the nasal cavity, but be persistent. You will find it a very distinctive feeling. Again, you can practice the vocalization separately from the visualization to gain facility with it, if need be.

Once you can generate the sound from the nasal cavity, perform the exercise as usual, expanding the ball of light as far as possible.

Follow by opening the chakras first as colored balls of light, then white, then purple. Clear and release, as always.

. . . .

Spell for Lesson I
Creating Artificial Vortices, Part 1

If you recall from First Degree, Lesson III, a vortex is an energy center. A vortex differs from a chakra only in that chakras are the internal energy centers of our body, while vortices are external energy centers of the world around us. Vortices can be natural, as energy centers of the earth (the context in which they are most often thought of), or vortices can be created. The magic circle and other energy constructs serve as synthetic vortices, amplifying our natural energies.

In this lesson's spell, we are going to talk about how to create synthetic vortices through the use of crystals. These synthetic

vortices can be used to help charge an object or to amplify the energy of a candle burning or a ritual.

Normally these techniques are reserved for rare occasions when we really want to focus a lot of energy into what we are doing, but some people use them more often. How much, or even if you use any of these techniques, is purely a matter of taste. Some people find them very useful, others find them cumbersome; everyone is different.

Our first technique is designed to create a simple vortex whose purpose is to amplify energy. You will need a number of crystal points. These can be natural quartz crystal points, or they can be other crystalline stones (such as citrine or amethyst) that have been cut to a crystal-point shape. The crystal points should be pointed at one end only; you would not use double terminals for this.

How many crystals you use depends on your purposes. Select the appropriate number from the number chart included on the next page.

Next, you will want to charge the crystals. You should be very familiar with this practice already from the First Degree lessons, but let's review it here.

Take the crystal in your hands; do each one separately. Imagine the crystal surrounded by a ball of yellow-white light that fills the stone. Concentrate on cleans-

ing the stone of all negative or unfocused energy. Then create a ball of blue-white light around the stone, filling it with light. Now bless the stone and charge it to your purpose. Tell the stone what you want it to do, and concentrate strongly upon this. You may find it helpful to call forth the stone's spirit and address it that way. You should remember this technique from First Degree, Lesson XII.

Once you have charged your stones, you are ready to create your vortex. The vortex can be set up around any object or person. You could even do a whole magic circle, if you wished, placing one crystal at each quarter. Most commonly, though, this sort of vortex is used to help charge a ritual item or amulet, or is set up around a candle to amplify a candle burning.

Place the item to be amplified on the altar. Set up your crystals in a circle around it, with their points all facing deosil, as if they were chasing one another. Now draw down divine energy to fill the vortex and start it moving. Imagine the divine energy coming down as a thick column of blue-white light. See it enter the crystals and begin to flow deosil through the crystal circle. Imagine the column of light as a pipeline filling the crystals with a limitless amount of energy, which enters them and flows deosil through them. You have now created your vortex and may proceed to charge the actual item at the center, or do your candle burning or other working.

The vortex will remain until you take it down. To do this, you should first remove the charged item, lest you dissipate the charge you have worked to create. Then thank the stones and the divine energy for their help. Visualize the same column of divine energy, still in place. Now pull down a yellow-white light through this column. Let that light fill the vortex and swirl through it. Then let the image dissipate and the energy with it. Take a moment to cleanse and release all excess energy from yourself and the altar as well (the whole area).

Take each crystal and run it under cold running water to further cleanse the excess energy from it.

NUMBER CHART

3: Luck, prosperity, success

4: Stability, strength, endurance

5: Communication, speed, increase

6: Peace, harmony, tranquility

7: Spirituality, insight, understanding

• • • •

Glossary

acclaimed—In the Corellian Tradition, we speak of our officers as being acclaimed—that is to say, recognized—rather than chosen. This is in keeping with the idea that we have come into the world with specific purposes and specific tasks. It is our responsibility to recognize and act on these. When we acclaim an officer, we are recognizing that their soul came into life with this among its purposes—thus we are not really choosing them so much as acknowledging their role in the divine plan. This is partly due to our belief that the Tradition is a multigenerational project whose actual blueprint is in the spirit realm. When an officer is acclaimed, it is because we believe that they are already fulfilling the purposes of the office to the extent available to them. Thus, when an elder is acclaimed, it is because we are recognizing that that person is already functioning as an elder. To determine this, we rely upon the judgment of our conscious mind, divination, and the advice of the beloved ancestors.

attune—To attune to something is to tune into it—to seek out its particular qualities and align with them. This forms a bond through which energy may be shared. In magic, attunement refers to processes by which we enter a state of sympathy with another person or thing. A common example is attuning to a particular place or to a magical tool or item. In this way, we build a relationship that allows us to draw upon the qualities of that place or item to enhance our working or our knowledge. One can also attune to people and things that are far away. We do this by feeling for their energy in the universe and aligning with it, creating a remote bond. In this way, people who are physically far away can share a ritual or other experience by joining their energy at the same time.

book religions—The book religions are those religions whose principal basis is the supposed bargain between Jehovah/Allah and Abraham, which set one people above all others. Of course, the book religions cannot agree on which people currently hold that position, as each one thinks it's them alone. The beloved Caroline Highcorrell, founder of the Correllian Nativist Tradition, held that there were only two religions in the world: the Native, or Pagan, religions that grew out of custom and experience of the divine and that are growing and evolving, and the book religions, which were set out in scriptures that could not be changed or deviated from. These religions are Judaism, Christianity, Islam, and Satanism, plus a variety of smaller offshoots. Each has its own version of The Book (Torah, Bible, Koran, etc.), but all share the same basic beliefs—resurrection as opposed to reincarnation, divine judgment, heaven and hell,

a devil or spirit of evil incarnate, the superiority of the male sex, rejection of sexuality in general, and the importance of obedience over enquiry, literality over symbolism, and "faith over works." Most of these views are diametrically opposed to Pagan views, which tend to believe in reincarnation through many lifetimes and karmic balance rather than judgment, reject ideas of "evil" as such, honor the female sex and embrace sexuality as a healthy part of life, consider allegorical symbolism among our greatest achievements, welcome enquiry, and regard literalism as silly. Of course, these are blanket statements, and there are many variations within each of these types of religion, including groups which overlap.

Byzantine—The term *Byzantine* refers to the Eastern Roman Empire, which had its capital at Constantinople, a city that had originally been called Byzantium and is today called Istanbul. The term *Byzantine* was applied by Western Europeans who refused to acknowledge the Byzantines as Roman. In 1530 Aries (AD 330), the Roman Emperor Constantine, a Christian usually credited with the crime of suppressing Pagan religion (though some of that blame should be shared with his successors), established the Greek city of Byzantium as his capital, forsaking Rome because he could not control its powerful aristocracy or suppress its strong Pagan traditions. When the empire later permanently split in half, Rome became capital of the Western Empire, and Byzantium—renamed Constantinople—was capital of the Eastern Empire. The Western Empire promptly disintegrated. The Eastern Empire continued for a thousand years more, though on an increasingly rickety basis, finally being conquered by the Turks in 1053 Pisces (AD 1453). The Byzantine empire was governed by an immense and complicated bureaucracy and characterized by vicious and bloody struggles for power—hence the word *Byzantine* is sometimes used as an adjective to describe anything which is extremely intricate or overly political.

Cabala—The Cabala is an important school of Jewish mysticism, which has been adopted by certain metaphysical Christians and even by some Pagans. Cabala is based on numerological significances and is strongly influenced by Pythagorean ideas. Much of Cabala is centered around the image of the Tree of Life, whose ten spheres, or sephiroth, are considered to delineate existence. These are very similar to the seven planes of Pagan thought. Caba-

listic scholars believe that the Cabala is essential to the understanding of the Hebrew scriptures, which they feel cannot be taken at face value but must be interpreted symbolically. Because of this enlightened view, Cabalistic thought is much more appealing to Pagans than the other variations of book religion. Though they obviously differ on many points, Cabalistic and Pagan ideas also have much common ground.

Ceremonial—The Ceremonial Tradition, or Ceremonial magic, shares many elements with Wicca, which has been strongly influenced by it. Like Wicca, Ceremonialism has a number of branches that differ from each other, sometimes considerably. Ceremonialism draws heavily from the ideas of the Judeo-Christian Tradition, notably Cabala, but like Wicca is also strongly influenced by Hermeticism and alchemy. Many Ceremonials consider themselves to be Judeo-Christian, while others would consider themselves to be Pagan or Christo-Pagan. In Ceremonialism, the adept works with a variety of external spirits, notably angels and demons, with the intention of gaining assistance from or control over these entities. Many Ceremonials also work diligently on personal spiritual growth. Ceremonialism shares many features with the Wiccan religion—the magic circle, emphasis on the elements, the four sacred tools, etc.—mainly because Wiccans have adapted these things from Ceremonialism. Ceremonialism differs from Wicca chiefly in emphasizing external matters—Ceremonials place great importance on the externals of ritual—the use of exact words, exact astrological timing, etc., as well as an emphasis on external powers. The most noted exponent of Ceremonialism in the modern era was Aliester Crowley. Other famous Ceremonials include Samuel L. MacGregor Mathers, A. E. Waite, and Israel Regardie. The leading Ceremonial organizations have been the Order of the Golden Dawn and the *Ordo Templi Orientis*.

crossed with silver—Everyone has heard the phrase "Cross my palm with silver," but how many people know what it means? Most people assume it only refers to payment; indeed, as a request for payment, it has become somewhat synonymous with greed. In fact, however, it refers to a very specific ritual. It was the custom of former times that when one went to a reader, if one had training in magical or psychic matters, one would enact this little rite before the reading began. One would take the silver coin with which the reading was

to be paid for and make the sign of the equal-armed cross—the Pagan Cross of the Four Quarters—above the outstretched hand of the reader. In this way, the reader knew that s/he was dealing with a fellow adept and would know to take this into consideration in the reading. It also served to identify magical people in the age when public identification was not always safe.

gospel—The term *gospel* comes from the Anglo-Saxon *God spell*, meaning "divine words." The term is usually used by Christians to refer to portions of their religious scripture, which they consider to have been channeled to them from their God Jehovah. These Christians consider their scriptures to be infallible and unquestionable. In wider usage, the word *gospel* is used to refer to anything that is viewed as infallible or beyond question. To "take something as gospel" is to give up one's own free will and judgment and assume that there could be no possibility that the thing in question might be either wrong or misinterpreted. However, since we are given the conscious mind to question and form judgments so that we might better understand, there is nothing that should ever be taken "as gospel."

Gray, Eden—A noted actress, author, and radio personality, Eden Gray ranks among the foremost authors on the subject of tarot. More than any other author, her works have made tarot accessible to the average reader and were instrumental in the tarot renaissance of the 1560s Pisces (AD 1960s). Eden Gray wrote only three books on tarot—*Guide to the Tarot, Mastering the Tarot,* and *The Tarot Revealed*—but these were and are the standard works for beginning tarot students to read. For many years, Eden Gray owned a metaphysical bookstore and publishing house in New York, through which she published a number of books on metaphysical themes. She said that she decided to write about tarot when customers at her store began asking for books on the cards (which were first imported into the United States in large numbers by Stuart Kaplan in the '60s) and she was unable to find any. The books she did eventually find on tarot were written in obscure and pedantic language, which she felt made them unsatisfactory. Consequently, when she wrote her own books on the subject, she was at pains to make them easily readable for most people. The result was that the books were immensely and immediately popular. Ms. Gray said that she stopped writing books on the tarot after she was asked to write a tarot cookbook combining tarot information with recipes;

at that point, she figured enough was enough. Although she was instrumental in sparking the tarot renaissance, which has led to the proliferation of thousands of different tarot decks, Ms. Gray was a purist who preferred the more traditional decks. Shortly before her death at the age of ninety-eight, Ms. Gray appeared as guest of honor at the first World Tarot Congress held in Chicago, sponsored by the International Tarot Society and its president, Janet Berres, where she was honored for her lifetime of achievement.

Gypsy—*Gypsy* is a term that is commonly used to describe the Romany people. The term comes from 'Gypcian, meaning "Egyptian," since in former times many Europeans thought that the Romany were originally from ancient Egypt. This is because the first big migration of the Romany into Europe came by way of Egypt in the late 900s or early 1000s of the Piscean era (late AD 1300s or early 1400s). Records indicate the presence of wandering bands of Gypsies in Europe as early as the 700s Pisces (AD 1100s), but many scholars suggest that the term was first used to describe *any* wanderers, and that these earlier "Gypsies" were not Romany. The matter is open to debate, however.

hagiography—Hagiography is the study of saints. A saint is a particularly holy person through whom Deity is seen to manifest strongly. Usually this is demonstrated through great wisdom, good works, and/or very high-level magic. In life such people are teachers, and after death they often manifest as spirit guides, helping anyone who calls on them. The word *saint* is usually associated with Christianity and the book religions, but in fact the concept is found in all religions. Most Pagan religions have saints, but they are usually known by different terms, which vary according to the religion in question. In Hinduism particularly, great spiritual teachers, both living and in spirit, are considered *sadhus*, or saints: examples being Mahatma Gandhi or Sai Baba. In Buddhism, a saint is called a boddhisattva—one who has attained spiritual enlightenment but acts as a guide to help those who have not, an example being Avalokitesvara/Kuan Yin or Ksitigarbha/Ti Tsang. In Taoism, a saint is an Immortal (*Hsien*), examples being T'ieh-Kuai Li or Lan Ts'ai-Ho. In Greco-Roman Paganism, saints were often termed demi-gods, examples being Herakles or Orpheus. In Wicca, saints are usually referred to either as Beloved Ancestors or Mighty Ones, though the exact usage of these terms varies with tradition.

Hellenistic—The term *Hellenistic* refers to the international culture based on Greek ("Hellenic") philosophy and education that came to dominate first the Mediterranean and then the Near East as well around the middle of the Arian Age (1200 BC–AD 400). The term particularly refers to the Greek-ruled kingdoms founded after the death of Alexander the Great in 877 Aries (323 BC). These kingdoms included Ptolemaic Egypt, Seleucid Syria, Pergamum, Pontus, and Bactria, among others. These kingdoms were strongly influenced by the Greek culture of their ruling dynasties, but they were enriched by their native cultures and by cultural sharing that went on between them all. Hellenistic Egypt, ruled by the Ptolemies, was particularly noted as a center of metaphysical study, and many schools of metaphysics and magic flourished there. Thousands of magical papyri survive from this period, which show us the practices of the day. The cosmopolitan attitudes of Hellenistic Egypt strongly influenced Hermetics, alchemy, and Ceremonial magic.

Hierophant—From the Greek *Hierophantes*, the term *Hierophant* refers to a cleric who initiates. In particular, it was the title of the presiding cleric in the Eleusinian Mysteries in ancient Greece.

Dedicated to the goddess Demeter and her daughter Kore/Persephone, the mysteries of Eleusis had to do with death and rebirth, though the ceremonies were kept so secret that we cannot really say what occurred in them. We do know a great deal about the worship and mythology of these goddesses, and we know a lot about the outer ceremonies that surrounded the Eleusinian initiation, but as to the inner ceremonies, we can only guess—people took their oaths of secrecy much more seriously in those days. In the tarot deck, the term *Hierophant* is used because it is through the inner transformation triggered by initiation that the doors to higher spiritual knowledge are opened.

immanence—Immanence is the idea that Deity is within all things, rather than being an outside force. This is the ultimate meaning of the ancient phrase "As above, so below." Deity is the spark that gives us life through our soul, and Deity is the true inner nature of all things that exist—but our divine inner nature is obscured by successive layers of incarnation. By penetrating these various levels of incarnation and healing the blockages associated with them, we can return to our true divine nature. Most Pagan religions believe in the immanence of Deity, though their beliefs about it, of course, vary.

impressions—The universe is composed of energy. Energy reacts to thought and emotion (and also to physical stimuli: action). Because of this, every thought, emotion, and action leaves behind an impression in the ambient energy. Sometimes these impressions are slight; sometimes they are strong. We all respond to these impressions, but we are not usually aware of the fact. Psychic readers, however, react to these impressions consciously, picking up on them and interpreting them: "reading" them, if you would. Most of these impressions are incidental, meaningless static: "negative" energy. While we can choose to focus on which impressions we wish to concentrate on, it is easier to do this if we cleanse unwanted impressions. This is why it is always a good idea to cleanse a psychic tool, such as a tarot deck, between uses.

Knights Templar—The Knights Templar were originally founded as the Order of the Poor Knights of the Temple of Solomon. Organized and led by the aristocratic Hugue de Payns, the Knights of the Temple were a chivalric association of laymen sworn to poverty and a monastic life. In its early days, the order was under the jurisdiction of King Baldwin of Jerusalem, and its principal duty was to protect Christian pilgrims traveling in the Near East, primarily between the port city of Jaffa and the Judeo-Christian holy city of Jerusalem. The Knights of the Temple became an official order of the Catholic Church at the Council of Troyes in 728 Pisces (AD 1128), through the influence of the powerful Abbot Bernard of Clairvaux, a friend and patron of de Payns. As an order of the church, the Knights Templar played a leading military role in the Crusades and in the government of the territories conquered by the Crusades. They also became immensely rich, and within just a few years of their founding were already filling what would become their most vital role: as the principal bankers of Europe and the Near East. The Templars remained powerful and respected throughout the entire period of the Crusades, with extensive land holdings in both Europe and the Near East. It was only when Europe's Near Eastern territories were lost in the 890s Pisces (AD 1290s) that the Templars began to have problems. The European kingdoms loved the Templars as crusading knights in the Near East, but when they fell back to Europe after losing their Eastern possessions, it was another matter—the Templars' vast wealth and ecclesiastical privileges led to much jealousy. Within only a few years, the powerful and acquisitive King

Philip the Fair of France moved against the Templars, tricking the Templar leadership into coming to France and then arresting every last Templar in the kingdom, more or less simultaneously, on the morning of Friday, October 13, 907 Pisces (AD 1307). Though a number of Templars escaped, and Templars in other parts of Europe did not all fare so badly, the Templar leadership and the French Templar knights were subjected to horrendous tortures and in most cases were executed. What makes this relevant to the Wiccan and metaphysical audience are the charges under which the Templars were arrested: the Knights Templar were charged with being a secret Pagan society disguised as a Christian religious-military order, who worshiped a deity called Baphomet (Bathos Métis—"Initiated in Wisdom") and practiced ritual homosexuality. Ever since the Templars' arrest, theory after theory has been proposed to explain why the charges either were or were not true, and the Templars have been portrayed as everything from Christian saints to Pagan saints to merely tawdry Satanists. One of the more interesting theories suggests that the surviving Templars went underground and reformed to become the Masons. This theory is put forth in the intriguing book *Born in Blood* by John J. Robinson.

Major Arcana—The Major Arcana are a series of allegorical images added to playing cards to create tarot. Today the Major Arcana are commonly—but not always—twenty-two in number. In earlier times, the number appears to have varied considerably. The Major Arcana appear to have been developed in Renaissance Italy and drew their themes from a variety of sources, including alchemy, Hermeticism, and classical and medieval Paganism. Some of the cards now in the Major Arcana were there from the beginning, such as the Fool and the Wheel of Fortune. Others did not appear until much later, notably the Tower and the Devil cards. Others, such as the Papess, have changed considerably, though the transformation of the Papess into the High Priestess is not as big a change as it appears; medieval Pagans often referred to the Goddess or her priestesses using terms like *Abbess* or *Papess.*

Minor Arcana—The Minor Arcana are the four suits of the tarot, which correspond to the four suits of playing cards. These are commonly rendered as Swords/Spades, Wands/Clubs, Cups/Hearts, and Pentacles/Diamonds. The suits of the Minor Arcana differ from those of playing cards by having four court cards rather than three. For most of tarot's history, the artwork in the Minor Arcana was handled much like that in playing cards, with the requisite number of each item per card—two cups, three cups, and so on. However, the famous Rider-Waite-Smith tarot deck introduced the idea of illustrating each Minor Arcana card, and that has since become the standard practice for contemporary decks. In tarot, the Minor Arcana are generally said to refer to the more mundane aspects of life, while the Major Arcana refer to more spiritual aspects, or events of greater importance. It is believed that playing cards predate tarot, so the Minor Arcana are actually the older part of the deck.

Plutarch—Plutarch was born in the city of Chaeronea around 1246 Aries (AD 46). He was educated at Athens, then the intellectual center of Greco-Roman civilization, and traveled widely throughout Egypt and Italy. He lectured in Rome and served as a priest at the Temple of Delphi (the principal oracle of the Greek world), but he eventually returned to settle in Chaeronea. Plutarch wrote many books on a variety of subjects but is best known for *Parallel Lives*, a book of biographies paralleling the lives of famous Greeks and Romans. Plutarch also wrote a number of works on religion and philosophy, including volumes on the nature of oracles and the worship of Isis and Osiris. For the modern Pagan, Plutarch's most important work is *De Superstitione*, in which he discusses the differences between superstitions and true religious feeling. Plutarch died around 1320 Aries (AD 120).

querent—The querent in a reading is the person asking the question—that is, making the query. If you are reading for yourself, you are the querent. If you are reading for another, they are the querent.

Reformation/Burning Times—The Reformation, called the Burning Times by many Wiccans, is the period in European history that follows the Renaissance and precedes the Enlightenment. The Reformation/Burning Times are generally considered to belong to the 1100s and 1200s Pisces (AD 1500s and 1600s). The Reformation was a period of intense religious strife, persecution, and bloodshed. The open and enquiring spirit of the Renaissance brought about many new ideas about society and religion, including Christian religion, and these new ideas brought deep conflicts. Spurred along by the invention of the printing press, which made the Christian Bible available to the common people for the first time, splinter

movements within the Catholic Church began to demand reforms to bring the church in line with the Bible, and some even wanted to eliminate the Catholic Church altogether. These movements came to be called Protestants. The Protestants were extremely zealous and considered violence an acceptable tool of their agenda—as indeed the Catholics traditionally had as well. The result was a cataclysmic conflict, fought both in the form of civil war and religious persecution. Though this conflict was largely between Catholics and Protestants, both sides also turned their attention toward non-Christian or pseudo-Christian movements as well. Some feel that they did this to divert attention from the behavior of their own churches. The Inquisition and similar organizations throughout Europe carried out massive persecutions focused on the extermination of Witchcraft, which was deliberately confounded with Satanism, as well as dissident Christians and metaphysical practitioners of all kinds. The Christians became obsessed with demonology and ideas of Satanism—especially the idea of demonic possession, which was used to explain a variety of mental illnesses. Though some so-called scholars are currently suggesting that these persecutions barely caused a ripple in the fabric of society, contemporary opinion and all previous memory held the Reformation/Burning Times to be an awful and violent period. Eventually the bloodshed became too much and a backlash set in against Christianity, giving rise to the Age of Enlightenment, in which all these things were pooh-poohed.

Regent LaVeda—The Regent LaVeda was the former head of the Correllian Tradition and the person who saved the tradition from extinction in the 1570s Pisces (AD 1970s). Lady LaVeda was the daughter of beloved Mable Highcorrell and the granddaughter of beloved Orpheis Caroline Highcorrell, who founded the tradition. After the death of the First Priestess Mable in '66 and the First Priest William Highcorrell in '68, Lady LaVeda found herself the last living Correllian priestess. For a time she abandoned the faith, feeling unable to pass on the tradition because of its rigid matrilineal rules, for her only daughter had died. These strict matrilineal rules excluded two other pseudo-Correllian lineages; the Louisine lineage and the Carline lineage, which were considered separate entities because their progenerators were male (sons of Orpheis Caroline). Then in the early '70s, Lady LaVeda and her cousin Gloria joined together to change the elder

rules, allowing for mixed descent. The beloved Gloria, and the Louisine lineage of which she was head, re-entered the tradition and were trained to carry it on. So far as is known, the Carline lineage subsequently died out with the last of its elderly members. In '79, it was decided that Lady Gloria's eldest daughter, Krystel, should take up the role of First Priestess, while Lady LaVeda's son Don would become First Priest, thus ending the regency and reinstating the traditional Correllian leadership. Krystel and Don decided to abandon the element of descent altogether and open the tradition to the public. Because she was the heir of Lady Mable but never actually took on the title of First Priestess, Lady LaVeda is always referred to as the Regent LaVeda. In Correllian usage, the term *regent* is used to describe the heir to a leadership office until that person has actually succeeded to the office (at least one year of mourning must pass). Lady LaVeda wrote under the pseudonym Lady Elizabeth Greenwood. The beloved LaVeda passed into spirit on 13 September 1589 Pisces (AD 1989).

Renaissance—The Renaissance is the period in European history that follows the Middle Ages and precedes the Reformation. The word *renaissance* means "rebirth," and this period was

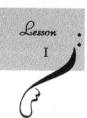

marked by a rekindling of interest in the skills and learning of Pagan antiquity and a flowering of philosophy and the arts. The period was characterized by free-thinking social change and philosophical questioning. From these qualities, modern science was born. The same qualities gave rise to a huge revival in metaphysics. Alchemy, Hermetics, and Ceremonial magic were extremely popular. So was Witchcraft, and some Italian Streghe consider this to have been the formative period for Italian Witchcraft. The Renaissance is particularly associated with the arts. Many great artists thrived at this time, and there was a rapid advancement in artistic techniques; among the most famous Renaissance artists are Michelangelo, da Vinci, Rafael, and Botticelli. The Renaissance is considered to have begun first in the Italian city of Firenza (Florence) in the 900s Pisces (AD 1300s), then spread through Italy and thence through the rest of Europe. The term is particularly associated with the 1000s Pisces (AD 1400s). After the openness and advancements of the Renaissance, a backlash followed that plunged Europe into the religious Dark Age of the Reformation.

Romany—*Romany* is the proper name for the people commonly known as Gypsies.

The Romany appear to have originated in India, but their nomadic lifestyle has spread them throughout the Near East and Europe and thence to the Americas. The Romany are split into tribes, including the Kalderash, Gitanos, and Manush (also called Sinti). The Romany tend to practice "double faith," adopting the dominant religion of the area they are in while still maintaining many of the animistic beliefs of their ancestors. Thus in the Near East they are usually Muslim, while in Europe and the Americas they profess Christianity, without having sacrificed their ancestral culture. The Romany tend to have a particular devotion to the Black Goddess, often in the form of Black Madonnas or their own patron saint SanSara, said to be the dark-skinned maid of the Three Marys. Traditionally a Romany tribe is headed by a Council of Elders (Elder=*Kako*), above which is a diarchy very similar to our Correllian diarchy: a tribal chief or king, the *Vataf* or *Voivode*, whose power is political and executive, and a matriarch or queen, the *Phuri Dai*, whose power is primarily spiritual. Historically the Romany have often been closely associated with Christian Europe's other outcasts, Jews and Witches.

Shah Nameh—The *Shah Nameh* is an epic poem telling the mythological history of the kings of ancient Persia. The *Shah Nameh* contains 60,000 rhyming couplets and is said to have taken thirty-five years to complete, finally being finished in 610 Pisces (AD 1010) when its author was seventy years old. The author was Abu al-Qasim Firdawsi (540–620 Pisces/940–AD 1020), who built upon an earlier poem by the poet Daqiqi. The work tells of the legendary kings of early Persia through to historical times and the death of King Yazdegerd III in 251 Pisces (AD 651) during the Muslim invasion of Persia.

sistra—A sistrum (pl. sistra) is a kind of ceremonial rattle that was used in ancient Egypt to purify sacred space. It was believed that the sound of the sistrum dissipated negative energy; this is because the frequency of its sound vibrations raised the vibrational frequency of the surrounding area. Sistra are still used today, especially by Temples with an Egyptian bent. They are very popular among the devotees of Isis and other Egyptian deities. Egyptian sistra have a very distinctive appearance, looking rather like the sacred ankh. They have a handle, often in the shape of a *T*, above which is a narrow hoop set with rows of metal cymbals that jingle when the sistrum is shaken. The sistrum is considered particularly sacred to the goddess Hat-Hor and often bears her image where the handle connects to the hoop.

spiritualist—A spiritualist is one who works with spirits, usually to bring through messages from them. These may be the spirits of the dead, of elemental or astral entities, or even forms of Deity. This skill is sometimes called mediumship or channeling. It may be performed in either a light or a deep trance, the spiritualist retaining consciousness in the former and being unconscious in the latter. Spiritualism is an intrinsic part of almost all religions; for example, the book religions, which mostly repudiate the psychic arts, still claim that their books were "divinely inspired"—that is, channeled. Often, however, the term *spiritualist* is used to refer more specifically to the spiritualist movement and its adherents. The spiritualist movement arose as a coherent entity during the 1400s Pisces (AD 1800s) in part as a result of publicity surrounding the Fox sisters, who are generally considered its founders. Though certainly not the first people to practice communication with spirits, the Fox sisters added a note of showbiz and commercialism, which led to many problems down the line. The fact that many mediums accepted money for their efforts attracted charlatans and frauds. The movement grew rapidly in popularity, even as it became mired in scandals. By the 1520s Pisces (AD 1920s), many laws were being passed against spiritualists, despite their rights to freedom of religion—laws which have since been used against Wiccans and others who practice psychic and magical traditions. Many spiritualists responded to these laws by becoming pointedly noncommercial, frowning upon any exchange of monies. Many of the people involved in Wicca at the turn of the last century also had ties to the spiritualist movement, one result of which is the deep split between those who believe in charging for teaching and other services and those who reject all financial compensation as inappropriate. The spiritualist movement, notably the Spiritualist Church, remains active and is still very much in existence today.

spreads—Spreads are different ways of laying out (or "spreading") tarot or other divinational cards. There are many different spreads that accommodate different tastes and purposes. The most popular spread is probably the Celtic Cross, in which six cards are laid out in the form of the equal-armed Celtic Cross, representing the four quarters (two in the center and four around). An additional four cards are laid to one side. Though there are many different popular spreads, there is no "correct" spread: each reader must decide for themselves what works best for them.

superstitions—Superstitions are spiritual practices that bind rather than strengthen an individual. True religion and spirituality enrich the individual and set them free; spiritual practices should be tools to help one realize one's highest potential. The great Pagan philosopher Plutarch summed it up nicely in his book *De Superstitione,* in a manner that may be paraphrased as follows: "*Superstition* refers to practices which are followed out of fear of Deity; *religion* refers to practices which are followed out of love for Deity." Terms such as "God-fearing" and "fear of God" represent the ultimate in superstitious motivations. A truly religious person never does things out of fear of Deity, but rather acts always from love for Deity.

Tree of Life—The Tree of Life is the central symbol of Cabalistic thought. The tree symbolically depicts the relationship of the ten Cabalistic spheres, or sephiroth (s. sephira), which are used to delineate the qualities of existence. The tree is arranged as a central trunk with branches to each side, forming three vertical lines, or pillars, on which the Sephiroth are arranged. The ten Sephiroth are Malkuth (Kingdom), Yesod (Foundation), Hod (Splendor), Netzach (Victory), Tiphareth (Beauty), Geburah (Power or Firmness), Chesed (Mercy), Binah (Understanding), Chokma (Wisdom), and Kether (Crown). It is believed that the Cabala is an outgrowth of Pythagorean thought, and that the Sephiroth are based upon Pythagorean numerology, which used numbers to symbolize the states of existence and the nature of the universe. The idea of a Tree of Life—a tree used to symbolize the universe—long predates Cabala as such. It is an ancient and widespread symbol, found in ancient Sumeria and Egypt as well as in Europe and the Far East. Most often it is represented as an apple tree, but in Asia it is commonly a peach tree, and the Germanic world tree Yggdrasil was an ash. Certain ancient representations of the Sumerian Tree of Life somewhat resemble the later Cabalistic tree, but have eight spheres, rather than ten, and may possibly have had a similar significance. However, the particular arrangement of the Cabalistic Tree of Life is unique to it alone.

Waite-Smith—One of the most famous of all tarot decks, the Waite-Smith, also called the Rider, Rider-Waite, or Rider-Waite-Smith tarot, was created around 1510 Pisces (AD 1910) in conjunction with the book *A Pictorial Key to the Tarot*, and it takes its name(s) from the those responsible for its creation: publisher William Rider & Son, author A. E. Waite, and long-neglected artist Pamela Colman Smith. The deck, which was beautifully illustrated by Smith, broke with precedent in making the number cards of the Minor Arcana as beautiful as the court cards and Major Arcana. Previously a card such as the Four of Cups just had a picture of four cups on it. In the Waite-Smith, each number card was turned into an illustration that helped to convey its meaning and that formed a story to help remember the meanings. Thus, the Four of Cups in the Waite-Smith deck shows not four cups but a person who possesses three perfectly good cups being tempted by a phantom cup held by a disembodied hand. It was partly this innovation that made the Waite-Smith so popular and led to its becoming the dominant tarot deck and the model for most subsequent ones.

Lesson

II

Physiognomy

A physiognomist named Zopyrus once visited the great Greek philosopher SOCRATES. The sage consented to be read, and Zopyrus commenced to study his features. At length Zopyrus pronounced Socrates' features to reveal him as slow-witted, sensual, and dull—which may not sound like much of an advertisement for physiognomy.

But Socrates' reply was to congratulate Zopyrus and tell him that he was absolutely correct—this had been exactly Socrates' character before he transformed it through the study of philosophy.

This is a famous anecdote, sometimes interpreted to demonstrate the salutatory effects of the study of philosophy, and sometimes interpreted to demonstrate Socrates' wit, but definitely demonstrating the importance and acceptance of physiognomy in the ancient world.

Physiognomy is the art of reading the human body, just as we might read tarot cards or an astrological chart. The purpose

of physiognomy is to divine personality characteristics of the individual, aspects of their potential future, and their present psychological/emotional state.

Physiognomy is older than most other forms of divination, as we had our bodies long before we had tarot cards or crystal balls. It is a natural human trait to analyze and categorize whatever is at hand and to use the data so gained as a gauge for what to expect from the future. Divination has always been with us. It is only to be expected that one of the earliest forms of divination should have been the mystical interpretation of the features of our own bodies.

Physiognomy was much more important in the ancient world than it is today. Physiognomists, such as Zopyrus described above, were not unusual at that time. One reason for this is that people wore fewer clothes in the Greco-Roman era and before than they did during the Christian—dominated centuries that followed. It was much easier to observe the body and thus divine from it. Only quite recently has the body come back out from under multiple layers of voluminous clothes to be readily observable again.

Physiognomy is the living proof of Trismegistus's maxim "As above, so below," for through physiognomy we observe the DIVINE PLAN spelled out in the very features of our bodies. Every part of the body

can be so divined, and many schools of physiognomy have developed that focus on only a single area of the body, such as the palms, the ears, or the bumps of the head, and derive an equal amount of relevant information from each of these limited areas.

The most famous of these forms of physiognomy that study only a limited area of the body is PALMISTRY, which we shall deal with later in this lesson.

Other schools of physiognomy utilize the whole body; mole reading, for example. A drawback to whole-body physiognomy is that it requires the subject to be nude or lightly clad. However, this need be no impediment to the massage therapist, acupuncturist, or other healer whose patients are fully or partly disrobed. Moreover, people today often wear clothing that reveals enough of the body that it may be read without anything having to be removed at all.

• • • •

What Possible Good Can Physiognomy Do Me?

Physiognomy can tell you a lot about yourself or another person. It reveals basic character traits and potentials, and it can therefore help you to deal with a person by telling you what to expect from them.

Physiognomy can also be of help to the healer: if you can factor in the physiognomical meaning of an injury or an energetic blockage, you can use this knowledge to help in healing it: for example, a twisted ankle shows a person who is having difficulty remaining flexible in relation to their life path, and who may feel that circumstances regarding their life path are currently overwhelming them. Addressing this issue may tend to speed healing.

Moreover, you will be surprised how much you see the influence of physiognomy in modern culture, once you know what to look for. Physiognomical assumptions, such as the meaning of a firm or a receding chin, the desirability of a large or a small nose, or what constitutes an "honest" face, are still prominent in people's consciousness, even if they often have no idea where these assumptions come from. These assumptions influence not only the advertising and entertainment professions, where you might expect them, but also exert an influence on such unexpected things as corporate hiring practices, jury decisions, and other places where appearance plays a prominent, if often unconscious, role.

This is not to say that physiognomy *should* be used in all of these ways: people should not be judged based on appearance, and we are certainly not suggesting that they should. Rather, physiognomy should be used like other forms of divinatory reading, including its subset, palmistry. Moreover, results should always be taken in accord with common sense.

There follow several forms of physiognomy. You will notice that they don't absolutely agree in every detail. This is because they have been developed in different times and places, influenced by differing cultural assumptions. I have not, for the most part, tried to reconcile them when they differ, but rather leave it for the student to consider the differences where they occur and decide for themselves which meaning makes most sense to them.

Each person who uses any form of divination brings to it their own individuality; in using physiognomy—as with any other form of divination—you may find that certain things may take on a significance to you that is different from anything you would find in a book or in another person's practice. This is normal and desirable, for divination is a language through which we allow Spirit to speak to us, and it is only right that we should give Spirit flexibility in her communication. Always remember that all forms of divination were developed by people who allowed Spirit to speak freely to them, not handed down from heaven engraved on tablets of stone.

• • • •

Reading the Body

Hair
Independence, originality, self-direction. Hair that is very thick indicates a vital and

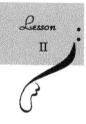

Lesson
II

original mind. Hair's connection to free-dom and self-governance is one reason why some people are afraid of long, loose hair.

Forehead

Intelligence. The forehead is said to indi-cate the individual's intelligence; width of the forehead indicates the individual's breadth of thought and adaptability of ideas; and height of the forehead indicates the individual's depth of thought—their ability to develop an idea and to get more out of it.

Ears

Understanding. Ears are said to indicate the ability to learn from outside sources and to understand what one has learned. Large ears indicate a person who is strong-ly influenced by external sources. Small ears indicate a person who tends to keep their own counsel. Long earlobes indicate wisdom and understanding, though not necessarily about all things.

Eyes

The soul, inner self. Eyes are said to be the "mirror of the soul," and they indicate both the state of the inner self and also the extent to which the individual expresses it. Large, wide eyes indicate a person who is very open about themselves and who puts up few emotional defenses. Deep-set eyes indicate an individual who tends not to show their inner self so quickly, and who reveals their inner feelings only to those they trust. Similarly, wide-set eyes are said to indicate an emotionally open nature, while close-set eyes indicate one who puts up many emotional protections to shield the inner self.

Nose

Ego, outer self. The nose is said to repre-sent the ego and the outer persona. The size of the nose indicates whether a per-son measures the world in terms of their own needs and ideas or the needs and ideas of others. The larger the nose, the firmer the ego. The smaller the nose, the more accommodating the individual is likely to be toward other people. That is not to say that a larger nose indicates in any way a lack of interest in or concern for others, rather the relative firmness or flexibility in their reactions to others.

Mouth

Sensuality, emotional openness. The mouth tends to indicate the pleasure one derives from sensation and from interac-tion with others. The fuller the lips, the more one enjoys sensation and physical pleasure (as, for example, the taste of food, the various textures of things, the sight of beauty, and so on). The width of the mouth tends to indicate emotional openness: a wide mouth with thin lips might indicate a person who enjoys interacting with people and is open in expression, but whose nature is mental rather than sensual. A small mouth with thick lips would suggest a person who tends to keep their emotions to themselves, but who derives much enjoyment from the senses.

Jaw

Determination, ambition, and resolve. A square jaw indicates a person who can be very focused and single-minded. If it's too square, the person may not know when to quit and will continue trying to force goals through long after they have ceased to be relevant. A more narrow jaw indicates a person who will vary their approach and is more likely to work around than confront impediments. A too-narrow jaw indicates irresolution and inability to persevere.

Chin

Willpower. The chin indicates self-confidence and self-image. A prominent chin indicates self-assurance and confidence in getting one's points across. A receding chin indicates one who tends to be reticent and who may have issues of inferiority.

Neck

Self-control, self-image: how much one puts up a public façade. Most people are concerned with how other people perceive them, whether they admit it or not. This concern often shows in the neck area. The relative thickness of the neck indicates the extent to which the person attempts to control their image. A thin neck indicates a relatively open expression with little emotional façade. A thick neck, or one with many lines or markings, indicates that the person exercises conscious control in how they present themselves to others, and tends not to show their thoughts and feelings to everyone.

Shoulders

Issues of responsibility, duties, and obligations. The relative width of the shoulders, not the muscle but the frame, indicates one's capacity to bear up under responsibility. Broad shoulders indicate the ability to take on and fulfill more responsibility. Narrow shoulders indicate a person who is more likely to be of help to others in positions of authority. Broad but sloping shoulders indicate one who will incline toward intellectual responsibilities more than material ones.

Upper Back

Emotional responsibilities. The upper back indicates one's relationship with emotional responsibilities toward others and the struggle that can arise between duties one has assumed toward others versus one's duty to oneself. Trouble with the

upper back tends to indicate that the individual has damaged themselves through their duties to others, either by being overwhelmed by them, being unable to fulfill them, or sometimes through anxiety regarding these duties. Most often, such trouble in the upper back indicates that the person has either gone well beyond their real responsibilities or has assumed responsibility for duties that should never have been theirs in the first place.

Lower Back

The lower back indicates one's relationship with financial and material obligations. If a person is having troubles with their lower back, they are likely to be either weighed down by bills and/or disturbed by financial losses or the fear of potential losses, or they may have been extending themselves too far in providing financial or material help to others, so that they have done damage to themselves through overgenerosity.

Arms

Skills and abilities, talents, career. The upper part of the arm has to do with duties and responsibilities involved with career—what the career demands from the person. The forearm deals with personal expression and enjoyment through career—what the career offers the person. The upper arm will almost always be the larger, but their relative size and strength speak to

the balance of responsibility and pleasure in regard to career. Whichever is firmer or more muscular represents where the person places their emphasis.

Underarms

How much of the inner self one expresses in daily life. The more deep-set or otherwise obscured the underarm, the more the person masks their private feelings. This is also shown by the relative hairiness of the underarm; shaving the underarm indicates a desire to wear one's feelings very openly, at least when it is done as a personal choice rather than in response to cultural dictates.

Elbows

Flexibility in dealing with others. If the elbow is stiff, the person does not like to cater to other people. If the elbow is callused, the person may have been hurt through accommodating others.

Wrists

Ability to master multiple skills or talents—multitasking ability. A delicate wrist indicates greater focus in activity, while a thicker wrist indicates more varied skills. Difficulty connected with the wrist suggests that the person may be spreading themselves too thin for their own good. A stiff wrist suggests that the person may resent the need to take on divergent tasks.

Hands

Self-expression, creative ability. The overall shape of the hand shows the manner in which the individual expresses their creativity in life. A conical hand, wider at the wrist than at the base of the fingers, shows the creative energy expressed in mental and intellectual ways. A spatulate hand, wider at the base of the fingers than at the wrist, shows an original, inventive creativity. A pointed hand, wide and rounded at the wrist and narrower at the base of the fingers, is emotional and artistic in expression. A square-shaped hand shows practical expression of creativity. You will find more information on hand shape in this lesson's palmistry section.

Fingers

Indicate the degree to which the self is expressed through career or vocation. Each finger has a meaning relative to career, and which is longest and how they are formed show how the career can express the self. The index finger indicates a career that carries authority and prestige. The middle finger indicates a career that deals with spirituality and introspection, or with duty. The ring finger indicates a career dealing with creativity, and the little finger indicates a career in business or communication. You will find more information on the fingers and how to read them in this lesson's palmistry section.

Breast/Pectorals

Indicates the ability to nurture and protect people, things, or oneself. Problems with the breast area indicate a person who has issues with their dependants, especially with people using them or taking too much of their energy on a protracted basis, or other situations which cause resentment or anger.

Nipple

Indicates the ability to derive pleasure from interactions with others. Large, dark, or unusually prominent nipples indicate a person who greatly enjoys contact with others and needs this in their life. In some cases, they may tend to measure themselves by how others see them. Small or inverted nipples indicate a very self-contained person, with less need for interpersonal interaction.

Diaphragm

Confidence in dealing with others. If the area of the diaphragm is wide and flat, it indicates a person who is very sure of their abilities in dealing with other people. If the diaphragm seems squeezed between the chest and upper belly, then confidence is lacking.

Upper Belly

Determination, perseverance, "guts." If the upper region of the belly should happen to be prominent, it indicates a person who is very focused in pursuit of their goals. This person is very determined and likely to be stubborn. Once they have set their path, few things can deter them. Similarly, if the upper stomach has a sunken appearance, the person is likely to vacillate and defer their own goals because of the needs of others or because of circumstances. If this region is unusually hairy (proportionate to gender), it indicates a person who can be very focused and determined, but who may appear vacillating or accommodating on the surface.

Lower Belly

Ability to break down and understand complex ideas and situations. This is the area around and just under the navel. If it is prominent, it indicates one who can comprehend difficult concepts and see below the surface of things to grasp their causes. (This has nothing to do with whether or not the subject is heavyset; this area can protrude on even very slender people. Likewise, this region may not be prominent even with a very large belly.)

Navel

Introspection and self-understanding. This can be judged by how deep-set the bel-lybutton is. (Again, this is not based upon slenderness versus stoutness, as even very thin people can have comparatively deep-set bellybuttons, while the heavyset can sometimes have very prominent navels.)

Hips

Indicates desire for comfort, material things, and the need for support. The larger the hips, the more the person desires external support of various sorts. Slender hips indicate a person not too concerned with material things.

Buttocks

Inner emotions, inner needs. The smaller the buttocks, the more self-contained the individual. The larger the buttocks (not necessarily in terms of fat, nor including the size of the hips), the more the person needs other people to validate their inner selves. Hairiness or pronounced cellulite indicate a tendency to mask one's inner emotions.

Thighs

Ambition, willingness, and ability to get ahead. The thighs indicate not only a person's ambition, but also the nature of the person's ambitions. The degree of fleshiness in the thigh tends to suggest whether and to what extent the person's ambitions are directed toward internally or externally motivated goals. This can be either in terms of whether the goals are set by the person or set up for them by others, or in terms of whether the goals are directed toward internal or external results: spiritual versus career goals, for example. The thicker the thigh, the more likely the person's goals are internal to themselves. This can be difficult to read, however, since an internal goal is sometimes expressed in a very external manner, and vice versa. The relative firmness of the thigh indicates the degree of the person's resolve: both how strongly they focus on achieving their goals and also how able they are to alter them if need be.

Knees

Ability to adapt to situations, changes, and the unexpected. The knees indicate one's ability to "roll with the punches"—how a person reacts to sudden challenges, difficulties, or the need to make unexpected changes. This is especially true in reference to dealing with authority figures or institutions. Stiff knees indicate a person who does not easily bend to circumstances or to the will of others. Weak knees indicate a person who bends too easily, thus losing their sense of self and giving away their own power.

Calves

Ability to enjoy the fruits of one's life path. A thick calf—be it fleshy or muscular—suggests a person who takes much pleasure in achievement, whether of a personal or a career-oriented nature. A thin calf indicates a person who takes a less emotional and more mental approach to their achievements.

Ankles

Flexibility in one's life path. Security, confidence, satisfaction. Strong, thick ankles suggest a person who can adapt to and withstand most of the challenges that life throws them—not to say that they will be unaffected by them. Delicate ankles indicate a less adaptive nature, with clear beliefs and goals that are altered only with difficulty. Fat ankles indicate a person who takes change with difficulty and has created emotional protections within themselves to shield them from the pain they associate with change/loss. A person who twists their ankle unusually often, or who has more serious ankle problems, is having difficulty adjusting to the changes required by their life path or is resisting a need to change the life path itself.

Feet

Life path: the direction or quality of life. Feet indicate the life path and the conditions surrounding it. While the heel indicates the core beliefs and desires on which the life path is built, the foot as a whole indicates the current conditions of the life

path—whether the individual is satisfied with their life, and what they are getting out of it. Callused and battered feet tend to suggest a person who is not enjoying the way they are living, or perhaps who is facing one challenge after another. Foot pain indicates a person for whom major issues of life path are giving difficulty; perhaps the life path is too narrow or involves great challenges or difficulties, or very often the life path has come to involve giving away their power to others.

Heel

Foundation of life path. The relative firmness and prominence of the heel, together with whether it is smooth or callused, indicate how strong the base is upon which the person has built their life. While the foot itself speaks more to how the person is living at the moment, the heel speaks to their inner ideals and direction in life as they experience it at their core—whether their direction in life is based on strong convictions and focused desires, or shifts and vacillates; whether they are happy with their goals in life, or not; whether their core beliefs have been challenged or battered by life's experiences. For many people, the inner foundations of their life path are suborned by crossed wires, contradictory beliefs they may not even know are there. This might be expected to show up in a weakness of the heel. However, it should

be kept in mind that spiritual people are always in a process of addressing such issues, consciously or otherwise, as they come into greater and greater self-awareness; this too will show up on the heel, but should not be interpreted as an affliction, rather as a challenge.

Toes

Degree to which the inner self is expressed in the life path. Long, thin toes suggest a person who expresses their inner self a great deal through the life path; that is, the outer direction of their life expresses strongly their inner being. Shorter toes often express a person whose inner self is distinctly separate from their worldly expression.

Soles

The sole of the foot indicates the inner resources with which the individual supports their life path: beliefs, emotions, and inner strengths with which to deal with the experiences encountered in life. A fleshy sole suggests a person who has many such inner resources. A bony sole suggests one who must look outside of themselves for strength in times of difficulty. A heavily callused sole suggests one who keeps their inner self very private, and who does not permit others to see them dealing with inner issues.

Physiognomy deals not only with the appearance and condition of these body parts, it can also be used to interpret the spiritual sources of a pain or illness by its location. This does not mean that a given pain or illness should be treated on the basis of its spiritual source, but rather that the spiritual source of the pain should be treated along with the physical manifestation.

You will also notice that it is not only the body itself that these definitions are relevant to, but also clothing. For example, a person's choice of hats often reveals their mental attitudes. Their choice in shoes speaks to the nature of their life path. Tight neckwear often reveals a person's concern with self-control and willpower.

. . . .

Mole Reading

A quaint old form of physiognomy not much met with anymore is mole reading.

Mole reading was especially popular in those eras when "patching," the use of artificial moles to accentuate beauty, was fashionable.

This is only a brief overview of mole reading. If one really wished to get into it, the exact placement of each mole, and its color and shape, have meanings. We will not go that far into it because of the relative obscurity of this art today.

Though the presence of a mole is said to show a given character trait or potential, the absence of a mole does not necessarily mean that trait is absent, only that it is not accented in this particular way.

A mole on the right side of the forehead is said to indicate one who will achieve a high status in life and who will receive much honor and respect.

A mole on the left side of the forehead is said to show a person who has a strong mind and a great depth of understanding.

In the center of the forehead, a mole is said to indicate emotional detachment and lack of empathy, unless it is a raised mole, in which it indicates great good luck and psychic ability.

If on or just above the eyebrow, a mole indicates a person who will be happy in love and most likely have a strong and stable marriage.

A red mole above the left eye indicates strong psychic ability.

A mole on the nose indicates a person who will travel widely.

A mole on or about the lip indicates popularity, persuasiveness, and the ability to get one's own way.

A mole on the chin shows a person who will achieve wealth and prosperity.

A mole on the lower jaw indicates a person who may tend to suffer from depression or frustration in their goals.

A mole on the front of the throat indicates a person with good luck.

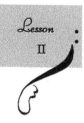

On the back of the neck, a mole was traditionally said to show death by the gallows. A more modern interpretation might be rebelliousness and a tendency to buck authority.

A mole on the left breast indicates a person with many admirers who help and assist them.

A mole on the right breast indicates a person who helps and assists others, sometimes too much; likewise a mole on the left knee.

Many moles between the elbow and the wrist indicate problems and frustrations in mid-life, which give way to a happy and prosperous old age.

A mole on either hand is said to indicate a person who will have many children or students.

A mole on the stomach shows strength and perseverance.

A mole on either thigh indicates that the person will have to work hard to get ahead in life.

A mole on the right foot shows good luck and success.

A mole on the left foot indicates that the person will have to work hard to achieve their goals.

. . . .

Now that we have techniques that examine the body as a whole, let us look at some techniques which focus on some of its individual parts; we will start with the face.

. . . .

Face Reading

The art of reading the facial features is very ancient and well developed. There are several schools of face reading, including European, Indian, and Chinese. There are also sub-branches within these.

The method of face reading we will present here owes much to both European and Chinese models, but might best be described as "contemporary."

Shape of the Face

The first consideration in reading the face is its shape. The shape of the face shows the overall nature of the personality, much as the SUN SIGN does in astrology.

There are seven basic facial shapes countenanced by traditional physiognomy, and these correspond to the seven planets of astrology and thus to the seven chakras and the seven archetypes of Deity. These facial types include:

The Saturnine Face

Ruled by Saturn, the saturnine face is pear—shaped, the jaw being wider than the forehead. This facial type indicates a reserved, cautious, and introverted nature, given to deep thoughts and soul searching. The saturnine face is not particularly social but has great self-control, concentration, and focus.

The Jovial Face

Ruled by Jupiter, the jovial face is rectangular, its length exceeding its height. The jovial face indicates good character—one who is honest, forthright, and optimistic—with a great deal of energy and ability to focus. It is considered a very fortunate facial type, indicating a propensity to success.

The Martial Face

Ruled by Mars, the martial face is square, being roughly as wide as it is long, with a squarish jaw and forehead. The martial face indicates a dynamic, confident, and assertive individual, who may also tend to be impatient and temperamental.

The Venusian Face

Ruled by Venus, the venusian face is oval, rounded but being narrower at the bottom than at the top. It is the so-called "ideal" facial proportion often used by artists, especially in portrayals of women. The venusian face indicates a warm, affectionate nature, outgoing and compassionate, with a love for romance.

The Mercurial Face

Ruled by Mercury, the mercurial face resembles a downward-facing triangle, being wide at the forehead and pointed at the chin. The mercurial face indicates a disposition that is mentally bright, is quick

but restless, tends to be talkative, and likes new challenges.

The Lunar Face

Ruled by the Moon, the lunar face is round and tends to a low, wide forehead and short nose. The lunar face indicates deep emotions and strong imagination. It is compassionate but can be stubborn, and tends less to act than to react to situations.

The Solar Face

Ruled by the Sun, the solar face is the rarest facial type, resembling an upward-pointing triangle, wide at the jaw but markedly narrower at the brow. The solar face indicates an ambitious and fiery individual with great drive and strong desires. The solar face tends to be deeply passionate but impatient and temperamental.

. . . .

It is within the context of the facial shape that all other features are studied, their meanings taken into account together with the basic shape to explain the personality.

Divisions of the Face

Regardless of the shape of the face, each face has three divisions. The first division is from the hairline to the eyebrows; the second division is from the eyebrows to the tip of the nose; and the third division is from the tip of the nose to the chin.

These divisions are interpreted in two ways: according to personality and according to chronology. These two means of interpretation are not mutually exclusive, but both may be used as separate systems in the same reading.

To interpret the three divisions according to personality, think of them in this manner: the first division indicates the mind and mentality; the second division indicates flexibility and adaptability; and the third division indicates vitality and physical energy. If any of the three divisions is more pronounced or possesses stronger features than the others, then this area of the personality will be strongest.

To interpret the three divisions chronologically, consider them thusly: the first division represents youth and young adulthood; the second division represents the prime of life and middle age; and the third division represents old age. The relative strength or weakness of the features in each area of the face suggests the quality of life in the years indicated.

Ideally each of the three divisions should be about equal in length, creating a balanced appearance. This indicates a well-integrated individual.

· · · ·
Individual Features

Forehead
The forehead is generally considered to denote the intelligence of the individual.

Height: The height of the forehead indicates mental acuity and speed. A high forehead thinks fast and is quick to adopt new ideas. A low forehead thinks in a more cautious and deliberate fashion, though it may be just as intelligent. (Baldness, by the way, does not constitute a high forehead.)

Width: The width or narrowness of the forehead indicates breadth of knowledge and openness to new ideas and unfamiliar concepts. A broad forehead indicates a tolerant and adaptable mind, while a narrow forehead indicates fixed opinions and definite ideas.

Shape: The forehead may be divided horizontally into three parts. The first part, just above the eyebrows, indicates the powers of observation. The second part, at the center of the forehead, represents the powers of memory. The third part, just under the hairline, indicates the powers of imagination. The prominence of each zone and presence of any bulges, lines, etc., indicate the prominence and character of the indicated quality in the subject's mental makeup.

Angle: The angle at which the forehead slopes is also significant. If the forehead is more or less straight up and down, it indicates that the subject approaches matters in an intellectual fashion, thinking them through. If the forehead slopes back, it indicates that the subject takes a more emotional approach to situations, tending to feel them through rather than think them through. How much either is the case depends on the angle.

Hairline: Different kinds of hairline are also to be considered in evaluating the forehead. A straight hairline indicates practicality and common sense. A rounded hairline indicates imagination, openness, and individuality. If the subject has a widow's peak, a downward point at the center of the hairline resembling the traditional mourning cap of European widows, ambition and drive are indicated. If the hairline is jagged, a rebellious nature and need for freedom are strong, as, again, is ambition. And if the hairline is M shaped, the individual is likely to be artistic, emotionally sensitive, and fond of attention.

Forehead Lines

The art of reading forehead lines is called metaposcopy. This art was most fully developed by GEROLAMO CARDANO, who wrote a number of books about it in the 1100s Pisces (AD 1500s).

In metaposcopy, the lines of the forehead are categorized according to where they appear on the forehead and what planetary ruler is associated with that area. The forehead is divided into seven zones, each with its own planetary ruler. These are, starting at the brow and working up toward the hairline, the Moon, Mercury, Venus, the Sun, Mars, Jupiter, and Saturn.

The strength and nature of each planetary influence is determined by whether there is a line in the given planetary zone and the nature of the line—deep or shallow, straight or wavy, continuous or broken, marked by moles or not, etc.

It is generally considered best to have just a few lines, and for those to be straight and clear. For a better idea of how to read these lines in respect to clarity, see the section on palmistry (page 64), and apply the same techniques used to read the lines in the hand.

Eyebrows

Eyebrows are an extremely mobile part of the face and are generally regarded as representing the subject's temperament.

They also have the distinction of being one of the most frequently altered parts of the face, especially for women. This has the effect of hiding the temperament, as if behind a mask.

Eyebrows that have been shaped or painted can be difficult to correctly read, but this in itself tells you something about the subject: that they are trying to keep their emotions hidden.

Natural eyebrows have a wide variety of shapes and thicknesses.

Eyebrows that are longer than the eye itself indicate intelligence and good judgment.

Eyebrows that are shorter than the eye tend to indicate emotional reserve and reticence.

Full, bushy eyebrows tend to indicate ambition and determination, but eyebrows that are too bushy can indicate a lack of conscience and a willingness to succeed at all costs.

Very thin brows, on the other hand, indicate low energy and lack of resolution.

High-set brows show an impetuous, confident temperament.

Low brows indicate a cautious and hesitant nature, perhaps calculating.

Straight brows indicate practicality and perseverance, ability to concentrate and focus, and a tendency to dislike changes.

Arched brows indicate strong will, independence, and passion.

Eyebrows that slope upward, toward the outside of the face, indicate confidence and a strong ego, sometimes too strong.

Eyebrows that slope downward, toward the edge of the face, indicate a lack of confidence and resulting reserve and reticence.

A monobrow—eyebrows that meet in the middle—tends to indicate dissociation of the mental and emotional processes, how much so depending on how thick the brow.

Eyes

The eyes are said to be the "mirror of the soul," and certainly they are the most prominent feature on the face. Eyes tend to indicate how we interact with others.

Large eyes indicate a bold and adventurous person, confident and creative, who enjoys working with others.

Small eyes show a cautious and reserved person who enjoys challenges but works best alone.

Eyes that slope upward at the outside edges indicate pride, ambition, and a tendency to put the self first.

Eyes that slope downward at the outside edges indicate a good-natured and generous person who tends to put others first.

Eyes that protrude—so that the eye white is visible both above and below—tend to be nervous, excitable, restless, and full of energy. The more the eye protrudes, the more this is the case.

Eyes with a high iris—with the eye white visible below the iris—indicate people in a state of spiritual unrest and emotional disturbance.

Eyes with a low iris—so that the eye white is visible above the iris—indicate a person who can be cruel or destructive without apparent reason.

The presence of a blotch in the eye white is a sign of poor financial sense, which portends possible financial loss.

The spacing of the eyes is important as well. Ideally, eyes should be set about as far apart from one another as each eye is long. This indicates an individual with a well—balanced outlook.

Eyes that are set too close indicate a narrowness of personal scope and inability to see all of one's options. This can manifest as selfishness or even dishonesty in some cases, if the narrowness of vision leaves the subject feeling that they have no other options.

Eyes that are set too wide indicate an honest but gullible mindset, easily taken advantage of. Eyes set extremely wide apart may indicate mental slowness.

Nose

The nose is generally considered to represent the ego.

In observing the nose, both the length and the width should be considered together, as each affects the other.

A long nose represents pride, reserve, and aloofness.

A short nose indicates a free and independent mind and a sensuous nature.

A broad nose indicates stability, patience, and ability to concentrate and focus.

A narrow nose indicates lack of direction and difficulty in following through on things.

An arched nose represents confidence, energy, and firmness.

A hawk nose indicates success in business and ability to make money.

A pointed nose indicates curiosity and an agile, restless mind.

A too-flat nose indicates a lack of ambition or confidence.

A snub nose, which is concave with an upturned end, indicates happiness and optimism, but also a lack of focus and a tendency to squander resources.

The so-called "celestial" nose, which is concave but not upturned, indicates an optimistic but passive nature.

If a nose has a pronounced bump at the end, it indicates ambition and a strong ego.

If a nose has a pronounced bump on the bridge, it indicates a concern for the less fortunate.

Cheeks

The cheeks, or more precisely the cheek-bones, indicate desire for power and control over others.

Low cheekbones show a person who is not especially interested in controlling anyone or acquiring power.

High but flat cheekbones indicate that one will have influence over situations but no actual power.

High, bony cheekbones indicate the tendency to acquire but misuse power.

High, well-formed cheekbones indicate power gained and used fairly.

Philtrum

The philtrum is the groove that runs from your nose to your upper lip.

The philtrum should be clear and well marked. This indicates fertility and good fortune in life.

If the philtrum is shallow, the subject is likely to dissipate their energies or their substance unless they are careful not to.

If the philtrum is wider at the base than at the top, it indicates that the subject will have a stable home and the opportunity to have several children.

If the philtrum is wider at the top than at the base, there may be difficulties in the home or the career.

If the philtrum is widest at the midpoint, the subject must work to avoid stagnation. If it bends to either side, the subject must work to avoid losing direction.

Mouth

The mouth represents the subject's emotional nature, especially in regard to expression of emotion.

A large mouth indicates a generous and outgoing individual, spontaneous and open, often very popular. Their energy is expansive and optimistic but may tend to be over-expansive, self-indulgent, and lacking in focus.

A small mouth indicates a person who is cautious and reserved with others, but who can be very focused and precise.

The ideal is a medium-sized mouth, which gives a warm and caring personality, honest and open, but still able to focus.

The lips refer more specifically to romance.

The upper lip indicates the ability to love. The lower lip indicates the need for love. Ideally they are about the same size and well formed. But the size, shape, and other characteristics of each lip reflect the quality it represents. If one lip is notably larger than the other, then the qualities of giving and receiving love are out of balance.

Thin lips indicate emotional reserve and a lack of communication. If they are twisted or do not meet properly, they may also indicate a tendency to cruelty.

Thick lips indicate a sensuous nature and outgoing personality.

If the outer edge of the upper lip is convex, as it usually is, it indicates open communications in relationships.

If the outer edge of the upper lip is concave, it indicates extreme emotional reserve and difficulty in communicating on emotional subjects.

Chin

The chin is considered to represent willpower and one's ability to focus and persevere.

A broad chin indicates good character and strong will.

A chin both broad and round indicates a warm and generous personality.

A chin that is broad but square indicates honesty, trustworthiness, and willingness to work hard for one's goals.

A chin that juts forward indicates a very strong will and an exceptional sex drive.

A narrow or pointed chin indicates a lack of energy or ambition.

A receding chin indicates lack of confidence and indecision.

A cleft chin indicates a strong desire to be loved.

Jaw

The jaw must be considered in light of the shape of the chin, which is a major component of it. Generally a jaw is either broad or narrow.

A broad jaw indicates energy, vitality, and willpower; ambition and ability to focus on goals; and a strong sex drive.

A narrow jaw indicates a lack of energy and an inability to focus or concentrate.

Ears

Like the eyebrow, the ear is a frequent subject of intentional modification. Many cultures, especially in Asia and the Americas, have distended the earlobes, sometimes down to the shoulders. Large ear spools would then be worn in the extended holes in the lobes. This was often an indication of high rank. Members of the "modern primitive" movement sometimes do this today.

Most people you will encounter, however, leave their earlobes as they are, except perhaps for one or more sedate piercings, which will not interfere with interpretation.

How close the ear lies to the head indicates how socially outgoing the subject is. Ideally the ear is neither flat to the head nor protruding; this indicates a normal sociability and ability to communicate.

Ears that lie too close to the head indicate a person who is reserved and introspective.

Ears that markedly protrude indicate one who is outgoing, but may be scattered or disruptive.

Ears that are set high on the head indicate intelligence.

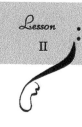

Ears that are set low on the head indicate a lack of confidence in one's intelligence.

Ears that are too small tend to indicate a person too receptive to others, easily influenced and lacking the will to say no.

Ears that are too big tend to indicate overconfidence, lack of self-control, impulsiveness, and perhaps immaturity.

Large earlobes indicate wisdom and spiritual understanding. Large lobes also indicate a potential for very long life.

. . . .

Palmistry

Next, let us look at the hands.

The best-known and most popular form of physiognomy is undoubtedly palmistry: the study of the shape and lines of the hand.

Everyone is familiar with the stereotyped image of the Gypsy-like palm reader bending over her client's hand to decipher the future from its lines. The scene has been repeated in countless paintings, novels, movies, and TV shows. It is a cultural icon.

Perhaps the most famous prediction ever made through palmistry concerns the young Contessa de Montijo. The Contessa and her mother were walking near the sea one day in their native Spain, when they spied a Gypsy fortuneteller. Though noble, they were impoverished and uncertain about the future. So they hired a reading for the young Contessa, whose name

was Eugenia. In a scene as stereotyped as any, the palmist looked at the young girl's hand, then looked up amazed; she predicted that little Eugenia would grow up to wear a crown and live for a hundred years! "Yeah, right," Eugenia's mother must have thought.

As it was, little Eugenia grew up to make an improbable marriage to the future French Emperor Napoleon III and reign at his side as Empress Eugenie, the most glamorous woman in Europe. She lived to be ninety-seven.

What's In a Hand?

Everyone knows that to do palmistry, you look at the hand. But what exactly do you look for?

There are six major components: 1) the shape of the hand; 2) the horizontal lines; 3) the vertical lines; 4) special markings; 5) the mounds; and 6) the fingers.

But first, you have to pick which hand.

The left hand is said to show the person's potential; what *can* be. The right hand shows the person's present (and most likely future); what *is*. Though opinions vary, we feel that it does not make a difference to this polarity if the subject is right or left handed.

Ideally you should look at both hands, so that you can speak both to what is currently the case as well as to what potential is present for other possibilities.

Many skills or opportunities that you may see in the left hand are not present in the right, but they can be manifested there if the person works on it. Many restrictions or difficulties present in the right hand are not present in the left, because they can be overcome through effort.

The lines in the palms are constantly changing: often minutely, sometimes dramatically. You are likely to see small changes in your palms every few months. Consequently you should go back and look periodically to see if new potentials have emerged that were not present before.

Shape

There are four basic hand shapes: conical, spatulate, pointed, and square. These correspond to the four elements: the conical being air, the spatulate fire, the pointed water, and the square earth. In addition, there is also a mixed hand, which combines elements from the other types.

The Conical Hand: Ruled by air, the conical hand is broader at the base of the palm than at the top of the palm, tends to be fleshy, and has longish fingers. The conical hand indicates someone who is intellectually creative, with a strong imagination and an analytical mind. The person with a conical hand is often more interested in understanding than in doing.

The Spatulate Hand: Ruled by fire, the spatulate hand, so called because of its resemblance to a spatula, is narrower at the base of the palm that at the top of the palm. The fingers tend to be broad, with squared, or spatulate, tips and knotty knuckles. The spatulate hand indicates practical creativity, originality, and inventiveness. A person who has a spatulate hand tends to put creativity into practice.

The Pointed Hand: Ruled by water, the pointed hand has a wide but rounded base that tapers up to slender, pointed fingers. The pointed hand indicates a person who is emotionally and often psychically receptive, who loves beauty and the arts, and who desires to be surrounded by peace and harmony.

The Square Hand: Ruled by earth, the square hand is as broad as it is long, with a squarish base and square—tipped fingers. It indicates a practical mind, common sense, perseverance, and hard work.

The Mixed Hand: The mixed hand displays a mixture of the elements of the other types of hands, but not merely a mixture of finger types, for all hands have a mixture of finger types. The mixed hand shows a mixture of elements in the construction of the lower part of the hand itself. This is said to indicate adaptability and flexibility.

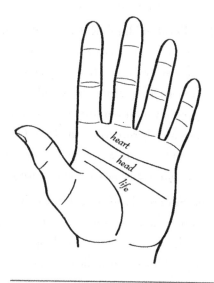

The major horizontal lines of the hand: the heart, head, and life lines

Horizontal Lines

The lines in the palm are both the best known and probably the most important part of a palm reading. Almost everyone knows which is their life line, but the palm's other lines are less well-known. Still, it is from the lines—their character and markings—that a palmist will derive most of their information.

There are three horizontal lines on the palm that speak to the inner nature of the person. These are the heart line, head line, and life line. Technically speaking, the life line isn't exactly horizontal but more diagonal, as it curves down around the thumb. This indicates that the life line deals with external aspects of the person as well.

Heart Line: "Heart over head" is a famous saying among palmists, both as a formula to help the novice remember which line is which, and also as serious advice, for if the heart isn't happy, the head can never make up for it. The heart line is the highest of the palm's horizontal lines, rising from the inside edge of the hand near the index finger and crossing the palm. The heart line speaks to the individual's emotional nature and its expressions, especially but not exclusively in a romantic sense. The deeper and clearer the heart line is, the warmer and more loving the person. If the heart line is faint or broken, it indicates emotional reserve or unwillingness to deal with strong emotions. If the heart line begins at the inside edge of the hand, it shows a person who tends to idealize their mate, or the opposite sex in general, placing them on too high a pedestal. If the heart line starts under the index finger, it shows a warm and stable nature. If the heart line starts between the index and middle fingers, the person may tend to fall in love too quickly or without considering the consequences; they wear their heart on their sleeve. If the heart line starts under the middle finger, the person may tend to put themselves first and have a selfish attitude toward love situations. If the heart line is doubled—that is, there appear to be two of them running close together—it shows that the person is sheltered and protected by a romantic partner. If the heart line is long and curved, it indicates emotional stability and enduring affections. If the heart line is short but deep, it also indicates emotional stability, but if it is short and faint, it shows a lack of interest in romantic and emotional matters. If the heart line runs close to and parallel with the head line, it shows a person with strong emo-

tional control. Sometimes the heart line may appear to be missing from the palm; in this case, it is considered that the heart and head lines are conjoined. This shows a person has extreme emotional self-control, to the point of denying their emotions.

Head Line: The head line is the second horizontal line on the palm, falling between the heart line above and the life line below. The head line shows mental strength and problem-solving ability. If the head line and the heart line are joined at the start, then diverge, it shows a person who is cautious and dislikes taking unnecessary risks. If the head line and heart line are not conjoined at the start, it shows a person who is adventurous and welcomes challenges. If the head line is long and straight, it shows a logical mind and a direct manner. If the head line is faint or wavy, it shows a person who has difficulty in concentration and focus. If the head line is doubled—that is, there appear to be two of them running in close parallel—it shows great mental ability. A short head line shows a person who is a doer, not a thinker. If the head line curves upward as it crosses to the outer side of the hand, it shows a person with a retentive memory

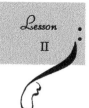

and a tendency toward acquisition of things as well as knowledge. If the head line slopes downward as it crosses the palm, it shows an inventive and creative mind.

Life Line: By far the most famous of the palm's lines, and popularly considered the most ominous, the life line is the third of the hand's horizontal lines. The life line begins between the thumb and the index finger and slopes down around the thumb, sometimes but not always all the way down to the wrist. The ominous reputation of the life line comes from the conception that its length indicates the length of the subject's life; this is not so. Though the potential length of life can be divined from the life line, the soul's choices can and do alter this. The length of the life line has as much to do with the person's vitality and range of experience as with their longevity. If the life line is long and strongly marked, it shows strength and vitality and can indicate longevity. If it is long and faint, it indicates a life with many changes and lowered vitality, perhaps poor health. A short but strongly marked life line shows great ambition and drive, especially in a square hand. If the life line curves around the base of the thumb, it shows that the person will remain active till the end of their life. If the degree of the life line's swoop around the thumb is wide, it indicates much strength and vitality, as well as a strong sex drive. If the angle of the life line's swoop around the thumb is narrow, it shows a cautious and emotionally reserved nature. If the life line swoops all the way across to the opposite side of the base of the palm, it shows a person with a broad and flexible nature who is likely to travel widely.

Special markings on the life line indicate events or phases in the life of the individual (special markings being discussed on page 70). For example, an island might indicate a period of illness or other confinement.

Where these markings occur indicates the age at which the event can be expected to occur. To read ages from the life line, divide it into equal thirds: the first third being youth, the second third being adulthood, and the final third indicating old age.

Vertical Lines

There are three vertical lines on the palm as well, which speak to the person's experiences in the outer world. These are the fate line, the fame line, and the money line.

Fate Line: The fate line runs from the wrist up toward the middle finger. How strongly this line is marked on the hand indicates how much a role fate plays in the person's life. If it is too strongly marked, the person's life may seem beyond their control, wholly mapped out by their karma. If it is weak while other lines are strong, the person's life is entirely built on their own efforts. Special markings on this line indicate times in life when the person is greatly affected by their karma, for good or ill. If the fate line begins not in the middle base of the palm but from the outside base, opposite the thumb, it indicates a person who will be before the public in some way. If the fate line arises from the life line at the beginning of the latter, it shows a self-made person who builds their own success. If the fate line arises from well up the life line, it indicates a person who will derive much help from their family or ancestors. If the fate line begins independently but then joins with the life line for a while, it indicates

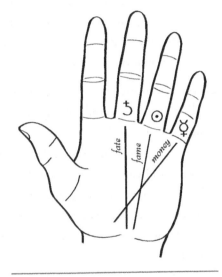

The major vertical lines of the hand: fate, fame, and money lines

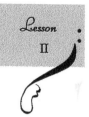

that the person will sacrifice their own interests for their family at the point indicated. If a secondary line arises from the outside base of the hand and rises to join with the fate line, it shows that a romantic interest will greatly affect the person's fate.

Fame Line: The fame line begins at the base of the palm and runs up to the ring finger. As its name suggests, it indicates fame and public recognition. Not everyone has one. If this line is clear and strong, it indicates both recognition and satisfaction. If the fame line goes directly to the ring finger, it indicates success through creativity or self-expression, as in the arts. If the fame line arises not at the base of the palm but from the head line, it indicates greater renown in the middle and later years. If it arises from the heart line, recognition will come in old age.

Money Line: The money line arises from the area at the base of the thumb and rises across the hand to the little finger. If this line is strong and straight, it shows financial success. If it is light or wavy, it indicates financial or health problems. If the money line joins the life line, the point on the life line where it does so is often held to show a potential

age of death (that is, a point when the soul will have a juncture at which it may choose to either live on or die), even if the life line itself is much longer.

Special Markings

There are a number of special markings that may appear either on the hand itself or on one of the lines discussed above. Each has its own special meaning. How these meanings affect the person is evaluated by where the marking occurs on the hand. These special markings are as follows:

Stars: The presence of a star (resembling an asterisk) indicates good luck and success in the area it appears in (for example, appearing on the heart line, it indicates success in love). This is true everywhere except the life line, where it indicates a crisis at the point in life indicated by the star's position on the line.

Triangles: A triangle also betokens good fortune, wherever it appears.

Crosses: A cross indicates challenges or oppositions the person must overcome.

Crosshatchings: A crosshatching (many little lines crossing each other like a grid) indicates that the person will encounter difficulties or opposition in the part of life indicated by the place in the hand where it appears, and will need grit and perseverance to overcome it.

Squares: Squares indicate protection or assistance from others, in the area where they appear.

Islands: An island (which is a circle or oblong appearing on a line) indicates that the person will experience restriction or confinement due to circumstances or ill health.

Circles (rare): A circle is like a free—standing island and also indicates restriction or confinement in the area of life indicated by its location.

Chaining: If a line is chained (that is, it has a "knitted" appearance rather than being a solid line), it indicates nervousness, worry, or unease in the area indicated by that line.

Forks or Frays: If the end of a line is forked or frayed, it indicates that the energies of that line may be dispersed or frittered away.

Breaks: A break in a line indicates that the person will experience a change in direction or a radical rearrangement of feelings or ideas, according to where the break occurs.

In addition to these general markings, which may appear anywhere on the hand,

there are several special markings that appear in specific places. These are:

Mystic Cross: The mystic cross is a cross in the area between the heart and the head lines. The mystic cross indicates one who is skilled in magic or metaphysics.

Battle Cross: The battle cross is a cross that is found in the triangle formed by the life, head, and money lines. This indicates a person who sacrifices much for their cause and is looked to by others as a champion or martyr. It often indicates suffering or death in the line of duty.

Magic M: The magic *M* is a rare marking formed by the arrangement of the heart, head, life, and fate lines when they fall in such a way as to clearly mark the letter *M* in the palm of the hand. This is the mark of the Mother Goddess; it is a sign of good fortune, luck, and success. If the fame line happens to run close to the fate line, as if to reinforce its stroke in the *M*, the good fortune is doubled.

Pentagram: A very rare marking formed by the confluence of the head line, life line, fate line, and money line that clearly marks the sign of a pentagram in the palm of the hand. This is a sign of great spiritual power

and advancement, and it indicates one who is highly adept. The Pythagoreans used to mark the pentagram on their palm as a sign to recognize one another by; thus the presence of the pentagram marking may indicate a soul who was one of this ancient and highly advanced mystical school in lives gone by and still bears the mark to this day.

Ring of Solon: The Ring of Solon (called by Judeo-Christians the Ring of Solomon) is a line that encircles the base of the index finger, rather like a drooping ring. The Ring of Solon indicates a person with great spiritual ability, which may or may not be conscious.

Ring of Saturn: The Ring of Saturn is a line that encircles the middle finger, again rather like a drooping ring. The Ring of Saturn is rare and indicates restrictions (self-imposed or otherwise) or depression.

Girdle of Venus: The Girdle of Venus is a line that encircles both the middle and the ring fingers. It indicates sex appeal and sexual drive. If broken, the Girdle of Venus indicates a sexual athlete.

The Mounds

The term *mound* refers to the fleshy pads on the palm of the hand. Five of these are the base of the fingers and thumb. Two more are located in the center and outside base of the palm. Each has a planetary ruler, and is evaluated in light of its qualities.

The Mound of Jupiter: The Mound of Jupiter is the fleshy pad at the base of the index finger. It indicates one's position in life and the respect and regard one achieves. If well developed and firm, it indicates a good status, comfort, and an optimistic outlook. If this mound is positioned more toward the middle finger, it indicates status based on steadiness and ability to concentrate and focus. If it is broad and soft, it may indicate self-indulgence and a tendency to squander one's substance. If the Mound of Jupiter is marked with a triangle, it indicates good luck and protection. A star indicates happiness in home and marriage, and respect from others. Lots of little lines indicate ambition and drive. A crosshatch of lines indicates overconfidence and a tendency to overreach. A cross suggests that one's goals may be unattainable in their present form, and a square suggests that one will face opposition but not succumb to it.

The Mound of Saturn: The Mound of Saturn is the fleshy pad at the base of the middle finger. Most people do not have a Mound of Saturn, nor is it good if one does. The region where the Mound of Saturn would be is usually flat or even concave like a valley between the Mound of Jupiter and the Mound of the Sun. If the Mound of Saturn is present as such, it indicates, at best, that one is very self-contained and introspective, not caring much for the company of other humans. If the Mound of Saturn is firm and well developed, the subject may be a full-blown misanthropist who holds out little hope for the human race. If the Mound of Saturn is large but soft, the person is likely to be given to depression or obsession. If the heart line begins where the Mound of Saturn would be, rather than from the Mound of Jupiter, it indicates a tendency to be selfish in love. If the region of the Mound of Saturn is marked with a star, the individual is strongly marked by karma, for good or ill. If there is a cross in the region of the Mound of Saturn, the person is in danger from accidents, even an accidental death, a fate they should be careful to avoid. A triangle here indicates magical skill. A circle indicates confinement, either self-imposed through isolationism or

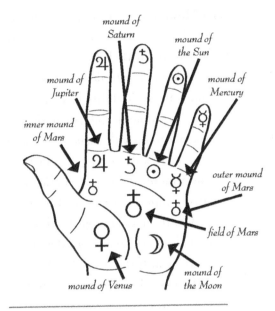

The mounds of the hand: Jupiter, Saturn, Sun, Mercury, Venus, Moon, and Mars

perhaps in a prison or other restrictive environment. If the Mound of Jupiter drifts into the region of the Mound of Saturn, it indicates steadiness and practicality. If the Mound of the Sun drifts toward the Mound of Saturn, it indicates the practical application of creative abilities.

The Mound of the Sun: The Mound of Sun, also called the Mound of Apollo, is the fleshy pad at the base of the ring finger. It represents creativity, self-expression, and the arts. If well developed and firm, it indicates talent and creative ability. If the Mound of the Sun drifts into the region of the Mound of Saturn, it indicates the practical application of creative skills. If the Mound of the Sun drifts toward the Mound of Mercury, it indicates involvement in the business side of the creative arts. If the Mound of the Sun is underdeveloped, it suggests more ability to appreciate the arts than to create it oneself. If there is no solar mound, it suggests a very practical person with little use for imagination and creativity. When the Mound of the Sun is marked with a star, it indicates that the person will achieve recognition and perhaps fame through their creative work. A triangle indicates that the person will

receive the admiration and respect of others for their creative work. A crosshatching of lines suggests that the individual must work hard for whatever recognition they achieve, while a cross suggests that they may be unable to achieve much recognition at all and should pursue creativity for its own sake, if at all.

The Mound of Mercury: The Mound of Mercury is the fleshy pad at the base of the little finger. The Mound of Mercury has to do with the mind and with one's ability to communicate, to promote, and to sell; thus, it also has to do with business and with money. If well-developed and firm, the Mound of Mercury indicates a strong mind and practical business ability. If underdeveloped, it suggests that the individual is scattered and unfocused. If the Mound of Mercury drifts toward the Mound of the Sun, it indicates involvement in a creative business. If the Mound of Mercury is marked by a star, it indicates success in business or financial acumen. A square indicates one who has a keen decision-making ability. A circle shows one that tends to vacillate or be indecisive. A cross here suggests a self-serving nature and perhaps dishonesty.

The Mound of Venus: The Mound of Venus is the fleshy region at the base of the thumb. It is connected to love—both sexual love and sensuality, and spiritual love and compassion. If it is firm and well-developed, the Mound of Venus shows a capacity for both sexual and spiritual love. If it is overfleshed, it suggests a strongly sensual nature and perhaps a sexual athlete. If underfleshed, it shows a person who suffers for or through love, though they may seek out situations that cause them suffering. If the Mound of Venus is marked with stars or triangles, it shows happiness and success in love. A square suggests protection in romantic situations. Crosses or crosshatchings suggest that the person will be unhappy or frustrated romantically.

The Mound of the Moon: The Mound of the Moon is the fleshy region at the outside base of the palm, opposite the thumb. The Mound of the Moon has to do with imagination and creativity. If the Mound of the Moon is well-developed and firm, it indicates a person with a good imagination and original ideas. If the head line comes down onto the Mound of the Moon, it indicates an adventurous and inventive individual who may blaze new trails. However, if the head line comes too far onto the Mound of the Moon, it suggests that the imagination may be too strong, and that the person may have trouble distinguishing between reality and fantasy. A star on the Mound of the Moon represents one who makes new discoveries or creates new ways of doing things. Lots of little horizontal lines on the Mound of the Moon indicate an adventurous person who may make many journeys to faraway places during their lifetime. A cross on the Mound of the Moon suggests a person who may have trouble focusing in the real world.

The Mounds and Field of Mars: The Field of Mars is the flattish area in the center of the hand. If the Field of Mars is flat, it indicates an open and outgoing person. If the Field of Mars is hollow—that is to say, it appears sunken in the hand—then the individual is likely to be very private, even secretive, and likely to be cautious or calculating. The Mounds of Mars are located to either side of the Field of Mars, at the outside middle of the hand, or opposite, in the space between the thumb and forefinger. The inner Mound of Mars represents ambition and drive. The outer Mound of

Mars represents self-discipline. If the inner Mound of Mars is well-developed, it shows desire for success and ability to focus on one's goals. If it is overdeveloped, the individual may be too assertive in pursuit of those goals and tend to steamroll others. If the inner Mound of Mars is underdeveloped, the person may lack confidence and tend to be steamrolled by others. If the outer Mound of Mars is well—developed, it indicates self-control and discipline. If it is too firm, the person may tend to be too hard on themselves. If it is soft and fleshy, the person may lack self-discipline. A star in any of the Martian areas indicates success through one's own efforts, a self-made person. Crosses or crosshatchings on the Martian areas suggest that the individual has many opponents or enemies, of whom they may or may not have knowledge. A square suggests the same thing, but says that these enemies will not be able to damage the person. A circle warns that the person must be careful not to leave themselves open to attack.

The Fingers

A number of things can be told from the fingers. Each finger has a planetary ruler, to which its specific qualities correspond.

The Index Finger: The index finger is ruled by Jupiter. Its special qualities relate to position, prosperity, and authority.

The Middle Finger: The middle finger is ruled by Saturn. Its special qualities relate to duty, to one's life's work, and to karma. The middle finger is also related to psychic and spiritual matters, and to introspection.

The Ring Finger: The ring finger is ruled by the Sun. Its special qualities relate to creativity, self-fulfillment, the arts, and fame.

The Little Finger: The little finger is ruled by Mercury. Its special qualities relate to the mind, business, communication, and money.

In addition, each finger is divided into three sections, separated by the knuckles, which show how the individual relates to the qualities of the particular finger in question.

The bottom section of each finger, nearest the palm, represents intuition and instinct—one's native talent for the things the given finger represents. The center section represents practicality and common sense, and how these are (or are not) applied to those things that the finger represents. The top section represents the intellect; how much one consciously knows, or consciously applies oneself, to the things represented by the finger; whether or not one is learned in these areas.

The extent to which each of these is the case is determined by the characteristics of that section of the finger. Is the section plump or skinny, is the flesh firm or soft, is it longer or shorter than the other sections?

The shape of the fingertips speaks to how the qualities of the finger are expressed in the world. Often the fingertips will match the shape of the hand; thus, a square hand will be likely to possess square fingertips. In that case, the energy of the square shape is dominant throughout the personality. More often, however, different fingers will have differently shaped tips, which speak only to the qualities of the finger itself.

Conical Fingertips: Indicate strong imagination.

Spatulate Fingertips: Indicate inventiveness and originality.

Pointed Fingertips: Indicate artistic sense and love of harmony.

Square Fingertips: Indicate practicality and common sense.

It is also important whether or not the fingers drift. What this means is that when the fingers are extended in a relaxed manner, they will all either stand equally apart or some will drift toward others. When fingers drift in this way, it shows the relative strength of their qualities, as respects the other fingers.

Thus, if the index finger drifts toward the middle finger, it shows that one's life's work will win respect and position.

If the ring finger drifts toward the middle finger, it shows that one's creativity will be of help to others and that one's destiny is met through self-expression.

If the little finger drifts toward the ring finger, it shows that success will come through creativity and self-promotion.

If the little finger stands well apart from all the others, it shows that the mind is strong and independent, and issues of learning and teaching are likely to be important.

The Thumb

The thumb is built differently from the other fingers, and thus it is interpreted differently as well. The thumb is ruled by Venus, and it represents the will.

A very long thumb represents a strong mind and ability to concentrate. A very short thumb represents a person for whom physicality means more than mind.

The thumb, too, is divided into parts. The top joint of the thumb represents ego and willpower. The lower joint of the thumb represents logic and reason. Ideally, they should be about equal in length.

If the top part of the thumb is much longer than the bottom, it represents stubbornness and egotism.

If the top part of the thumb is much shorter than the bottom, it shows a weak will.

The thumb is also evaluated according to its flexibility. How far back the top part of the thumb can bend indicates how flexible the person is in dealing with others. If the top part of the thumb bends well back, the person is very adaptable and can easily adjust to circumstances. If it bends too far back, however, (near a ninety-degree angle), they may be a pushover. If the top of the thumb does not bend back far, the person is set in their ways of doing things and does not like disruptions.

How far the thumb can be spread out from the hand indicates the person's generosity. If it spreads far out, it shows a person who is generous and giving. If it only spreads out a little way, they are more likely to be concerned with what they have for themselves.

· · · ·

Exercises

Exercise 2

It may come as no surprise to you that Exercise 2 begins the same way as Exercise 1. Begin by doing the Ohm exercise, vocalizing the sacred syllable "Ohm" while simultaneously expanding a ball of white light around you, then open each chakra, visualizing balls of colored light in each chakra, beginning with the root chakra and working your way up, as you learned to do in the First Degree lessons. Now go back through the chakras and replace each colored ball of light with a ball of pure white light. Finally, replace each ball of pure white light with a ball of violet light. This is where Exercise 1 left off.

Now, go back through each chakra and change the color of the balls of light again. This time, fill each ball of light with glittering silver energy, silver energy sparkling and swirling with thousands of tiny silver stars, kind of like glitter or a more vibrant version of the static you sometimes see on a television channel that is off the air. You will remember being introduced to this kind of energy in First Degree, Exercise 20.

Go through all seven chakras and open balls of this silver stellar light.

Now focus on your crown chakra and the ball of silver stellar light you have created there. Imagine that ball of light beginning to grow. Visualize the silver stellar light spreading from the crown chakra to fill your whole body. Let the silver stellar light move through every part of you, filling you completely. Now, visualize the silver stellar light moving out from your body to fill your aura as well. See the silver stellar light expand around you, forming a ball. See the ball grow larger and larger until it is approximately six feet (two meters) in diameter. You can let the ball grow farther than that if it is comfortable to do so, but for most people this will be a good size.

Stay within the ball of silver stellar light as long as you like; let it suffuse you and move through you. The energy is strengthening your aura and raising your energetic vibration. Don't overdo it, however; as soon as you feel tired or strained, you are ready to close.

Let the image of the large ball of silver stellar light filling your aura fade away. Now go back and close each chakra. Then ground and release as usual.

Exercise 3

When you have come to the point that you can do Exercise 2 easily, you are ready for Exercise 3. It begins the same way: the Ohm exercise, opening the chakras with balls of colored light, changing the balls of colored light to balls of white light, changing the balls of white light to balls of purple light, changing the balls of purple light to balls of silver stellar light, and then filling your aura with silver stellar light.

After letting the silver stellar light move through your aura for a bit, turn your attention back to your chakras. Starting from the root chakra, go back through the chakras and change each ball of silver stellar light into a ball of golden stellar light—a swirling, glittering light filled with tiny golden stars. Fill each chakra with golden stellar light, until you have done all seven.

Now, let the ball of golden stellar light in your crown chakra expand to fill your body, just as you did with the silver stellar light in Exercise 2. Let the golden stellar light fill your body, then expand to fill your aura, so that you are within a great ball of golden stellar light. Remain this way as long as you are comfortable, and then close it down. Let the image of the golden stellar light filling your aura fade, then close each chakra down and finally clear and release all excess energy.

Exercise 4

When you are able to do Exercise 3 easily, you are ready to add Exercise 4 to your routine. When you finish Exercise 3 and are within a great ball of golden stellar light filling your aura, turn your attention again to the chakras. Beginning with the root chakra, change each ball of golden stellar light to a ball of amber light.

What is meant by amber light is best described as resembling lava. It is mottled darkly on the outside, with bits of vibrant reddish-gold energy showing through, not unlike the embers of a fire that has died down.

As in Exercises 2 and 3, fill each chakra with amber light, then let the crown chakra expand to fill your whole aura with amber light. Again, stay within the amber energy as long as you feel comfortable, then let the image of the energy in the aura fade, close the chakras, and clear and release as always.

. . . .

Spell for Lesson II
Creating Artificial Vortices, Part 2

The previous spell was creating an artificial energy vortex with a deosil circle of crystals. In this spell, we will examine other methods of creating artificial vortices with crystals.

Method 1

Our first technique is a method of charging an item for use. This essentially makes the item—for example, an amulet or a ritual candle—into a battery that stores extra energy for release at the appropriate time.

To do this, first cleanse the item to be charged of all excess or unwanted energies, a technique you should know well. Then place the item on your altar or in a place specially set aside for this purpose.

Select an appropriate number of crystals; refer back to the number chart on page 29, if you wish. These would most commonly be clear quartz crystals, but any other stone or crystal shaped into a point like a clear quartz can also be used, provided the stone's properties are appropriate to the working.

Cleanse and charge each crystal separately. Hold the crystal in your hands, and imagine it surrounded by a ball of yellow-white light. Concentrate on cleansing the stone of all negative or unfocused energy. Then create a ball of blue-white light around the stone, filling it with light. Now bless the stone and charge it to your purpose. Tell the stone what you want it to do, and concentrate strongly on this. You may wish to call forth the stone's spirit and address it directly.

Place the crystals around the item in a circle, but with their points facing inwards, toward the item.

Call on divine energy to fill the vortex. Imagine divine energy rushing from all around you, focused by the crystals into the object being charged. As the divine energy fills the vortex, imagine the item beginning to fill with light, shining brightly, like a sun upon your altar.

Now address the item being charged, and direct it to absorb and hold the energy until called upon to release it. Direct the item to absorb only as much energy as it can hold, lest it be overcharged and damaged.

The vortex you have created will remain until you take it down. You can leave it for a few minutes or a few days. During this time, it will continue to charge the item at a steady pace until the item is full or until you take the vortex down.

To do this, you should first remove the charged item, lest you dissipate the charge you have worked to create. Then thank the stones and the divine energy for their help. Visualize the vortex of energy still in place. Now pull down through the vortex a wave of yellow-white light, and let that light fill the vortex and swirl through it. Then let the image dissipate and the energy with it. Take a moment to cleanse and release all excess energy from yourself and the altar as well (the whole area).

Take each crystal and hold it under cold running water to further cleanse the excess energy from it.

Method 2

Our second technique is opposite from the first. This technique is intended to assist in the gradual dispersion of energy from a charged object—for example, the energy from a candle-burning spell. As the energy disperses, the spell takes effect. By dispersing gradually, a steady flow of energy is maintained.

For this technique, surround your object, which has already been charged for the purpose, with three, five, or seven crystal points, also cleansed and charged for the purpose, as described earlier. These crystals may be either natural or artificially ground points. They would most commonly be clear quartz, but they could also be other crystals, such as amethyst, chosen for qualities that augment the working. The points of the crystals should point outward, away from the object. In this way, they will conduct the energy outward into the world.

Unlike Method 1, which is a spell in itself, this technique is intended to assist another spell whose energy you wish to disperse over a period of time. Therefore, once you have assembled the crystals around the object, do the spell, then call upon divine energy. Imagine divine energy coming down upon the central object, then radiating out through the crystals, thus forming the vortex. Charge the vortex to carry the energy of the spell out into the world for a specific amount of time, and visualize this happening.

When the specific amount of time you have indicated has expired, you must dismantle the vortex. Thank the stones and divine energy for their help. Visualize the

vortex of energy still in place and pull down through the vortex a wave of yellow-white light, filling the vortex and disseminating through the crystals. Then let the image dissipate and the energy with it. Take a moment to cleanse and release all excess energy from yourself and the altar as well (the whole area).

This technique can also be used to bless an area—a temple, for example, or a room, or a place of business—whose energies need to be carried out into the world. To do this, you would place the crystal points around the area to be blessed. As above, you would create the vortex after the working. It might be a specific ritual, such as an earth-healing ritual, or if there is not a specific ritual but the ordinary activities of the place are to be carried outward, do a basic space blessing, then create the vortex.

The vortex should be set up for a specific period of time; usually a modest period of a few days or weeks is best. If you wish to set up a more permanent vortex—at a temple, for example—you should still create it for a specific time period, and when that period has expired, cleanse the crystals and again set up the vortex from scratch.

· · · ·

Glossary

Cardano, Gerolamo—Also rendered in Latin as Hieronymus Cardanus, Gerolamo Cardano was born on September 23 in 1101 Pisces (AD 1501) in the Italian town of Pavia, near Milan. Cardano was considered one of the greatest physicians of his age, and he wrote eighty-three books on medicine. He was also acknowledged as a great mathematician, his most noted mathematical work being the *Ars Magna*. In addition, he wrote many other books on many other subjects, including astrology, astronomy, dream interpretation, theology, and physics. Cardano also perfected the art of metaposcopy, or the physiognomic reading of the lines on the forehead. Cardano assigned horizontal regions of the forehead to astrological rulers and interpreted the lines using palmistic techniques. He wrote a total of thirteen books on metaposcopy. Cardano died in 1176 Pisces (AD 1576).

divine plan—The term *divine plan* refers to the idea that nothing happens accidentally or randomly, but that everything is united as part of a single, divine whole, all of whose parts have meaning. The divine plan is an intrinsic part of Deity that is contained within everything that exists, since everything that exists is ultimately a manifestation of Deity. The divine plan can be accessed through the monadic level of the being, which though separate from Deity retains all of the essential nature of Deity at the core of the individual soul. The idea that the totality of the divine plan is present in all things, and can be seen through them, is the ultimate meaning of the ancient maxim of Hermes Trismegistus: "As above, so below."

palmistry—Palmistry is the most famous form of physiognomy, and it consists of divining the character and potential future of a person from the palm, fingers, and other features of the hand. Palmistry is very ancient, having been widely practiced in the ancient world. A famous mosaic from Pompeii, itself believed to be copied from a much earlier Greek work, is thought by many to show a palmist and her client. Palmistry works on the premise of planetary correspondences—that is, that certain parts of the hand correspond to certain planets and may be read in light of the planetary qualities—according to the idea of "As above, so below." The shape of the hand and fingers, lines and markings on the palm and elsewhere— all have meaning in palmistry and go toward the complete reading. The best-known palmist of modern times was probably Count Louis Hammond, who read under the name Chiero during the Edwardian era and the jazz age.

Socrates—Socrates was a great Athenian philosopher, born in 732 Aries (469 BC). Socrates was the teacher of Plato and thus had a huge effect on later Greek philosophy. Socrates' own teaching was primarily concerned with issues of virtue and right behavior. Socrates taught that the highest virtue was to "know yourself," and that no one knowingly does wrong but rather always does the best thing they know to do. Socrates taught with a method termed *socratic dialogue* or *dialectic*: teaching through question and discussion, a technique which forced the student to evaluate the matter for themselves. Socrates is said to have created the teleological argument for the existence of Deity, which states that anything which exists to fulfill a useful purpose must be the work of an intelligence which designed it to fulfill that purpose. Socrates was an opponent of the powerful Sophist movement, and his activities against them led to his being accused of impiety and corrupting the morals of the young. Some say that these charges arose partly because two of Socrates' intimates, Alcibiades and Critias, had recently betrayed Athens. Socrates denied having done anything wrong, but he refused to offer arguments to support his point of view and was convicted and sentenced to commit suicide by drinking hemlock,

an herbal poison. Socrates' trial and death occurred in 801 Aries (399 BC). Socrates left no writings of his own, our knowledge of his teachings being derived from the works of his student Plato and the memoirs of the historian Xenophon, plus a few comments in the works of Plato's student Aristotle.

Sun sign—In astrology, the Sun sign is the zodiacal sign the Sun was in at the time of one's birth. Though many other elements go into an astrological chart, the Sun sign is the most prominent, as it most expresses the nature of the individual.

Lesson
~ III ~

Astrology

The purpose of this lesson is not to be an exhaustive study of astrology. An exhaustive study of astrology would more than fill a book in itself and require months or years to learn and understand. Astrology is a complicated art that has been developed and embellished over the course of millennia, and it is still developing in the present day.

The purpose here is to acquaint you with the basic principles of astrology. This lesson will give you an understanding of astrological terms and practices, so that you can read an astrological chart and understand astrological archetypes, which are sometimes important in magic as well as allegory. With this knowledge as a base, you can pursue a study of more advanced astrological material on your own, should you choose to.

History

Astrology is known to have been developed in ancient Mesopotamia. Exactly when it began is unknown, but astrological records date from the 700s BC (600s Aries), showing it as a highly developed art at that time. The oldest existing NATAL HORO-SCOPE (birth chart) was cast on April 30, 409 BC (791 Aries), for the son of Shuma-usur.

The flat plains and clear skies of Meso-potamia made it easy to observe the stars and read portents from them.

The earliest form of astrology to devel-op was ASTROGANCY, the study of the visual appearance of stars, their relative brightness and position on the horizon being the primary factors. From astrogan-cy, the planets and zodiacal constellations were identified and beliefs grew up around them, their respective qualities and char-acter, their good and bad positions, etc.

In time, the Mesopotamians developed astrogancy further, ultimately creating astrology. Astrology was more complex than astrogancy, relying on the relation-ships between planets rather than their physical appearance.

The Mesopotamians identified the plan-ets with their principal deities: Shamash the Sun, Ishtar the planet Venus, and Marduk the planet Mars. This practice would continue as the practice of astrol-ogy spread from Mesopotamia to the Near East, Egypt, Greece, and Rome, and thence through Europe to us. This is an important part of the origin of the idea of the seven divine archetypes. Thus, as you read below, you will see each of the seven traditional planets identified with one of the seven divine archetypes.

In the early years of its existence, astrol-ogy was used exclusively for divination about governments, royal houses, and civil situations, such as the success or failure of harvests, building projects, or wars.

In the third century BC (900s Aries), the Babylonian priest Berosus brought astrology to Greece, establishing an astro-logical school on the Greek island of Cos. Berosus and his students introduced the idea of personal astrology, applying astro-logical arts to ordinary people and their lives for the first time.

Astrology became extremely popular in Greco-Roman culture, despite periodic attempts to suppress it. The Roman emper-or Tiberius expelled all astrologers from the city of Rome in AD 19 (1219 Aries), yet one of history's best-known astrolo-gers is Tiberius's own personal astrologer, Thrasyllus.

In the millennia of its existence, astrol-ogy has been applied to every sphere of life, developing many side specialties along the way. In Medieval and Renaissance Europe, both medical and judicial astrology enjoyed great popularity and legal support.

Medical astrology used the position of the planets to select auspicious times for medical procedures, and the PLANETARY CORRESPONDENCES to treat physical maladies through the use of sympathetic stones and herbs chosen for their planetary attributions.

Judicial astrology sought to forecast the future by studying the past; the historical events connected with past planetary alignments were believed to repeat when those alignments reappeared. It was on this idea that the celebrated prophet Michele de Nostre Dame, called NOSTRADAMUS, among many other things a judicial astrologer, based his famous predictions.

· · · ·

Astrological Theory

The principle behind astrology is that by studying the position of the planets, their relationships to each other (called ASPECTS), and their position in the ZODIAC (the band of constellations used to divide the sky into zones of study), one can interpret the inner nature of people and situations, and predict the future course of events.

This does not mean that the planets cause the character or shape the events, but rather that they reflect it in their position by virtue of Trismegistus's maxim,

"As above, so below." All things that exist reflect the divine plan, which can be divined through them. Thus, the system of astrology reflects by virtue of its minute detail the minute details of life on earth.

We would augment this with the Correllian argument that astrology is not really the study of the stars as such, but rather the cycles of time, those cycles being identified with the movement of the planets rather than caused by them. Thus the accuracy of astrology is not based on cause and effect, but on reflection of the inborn cycles that guide all things.

· · · ·

The Planets

The most basic component of astrology, and the first to develop historically, is the study of the planets.

In astrology, we use the seven planets visible with the naked eye, called the Ptolemaic planets after the great astrologer PTOLEMY. These planets are the basis of astrology, as it was from the observation and interpretation of their visible presence in the sky that astrology was invented.

Modern astrology also makes use of the three outer planets visible only by telescope: Uranus, Neptune, and Pluto, as well as a number of asteroids, such as Chiron. Though these additional heavenly bodies have come to be an integral part of contemporary astrology, it is generally agreed that opinion about them is still taking shape, and the seven Ptolemaic planets remain primary to astrological interpretation.

The planets are the active element in astrology; their position is ever-changing, in some cases quite rapidly. When an astrological chart is cast, whether for a person, thing, or event, it is the position of the planets that is being read.

Everything that exists is said to be influenced by all seven planets—that is, they show information about it.

Each planet has its own character, corresponding to the seven divine archetypes. This character never changes but is influenced by the perceived position of the planet. The zodiacal sign (see below) a planet is in influences its meaning; planet Mercury rules the mind and thought. Planet Mercury in the sign of Taurus represents a strong, conservative mental state, slow to learn but with strong powers of concentration and retention.

The Sun

The Sun corresponds to the divine archetype of the Lover.

In astrology, the Sun represents the conscious self.

The Sun rules all the hoped-for virtues of the self: courage, integrity, honesty, loyalty, and generosity. The Sun governs the rules of ordinary conduct: honor, hospitality, adherence to contracts. The Sun has

to do with one's position in the world, and as such is connected to institutions and governments. The Sun is connected to the physical body and issues of health; as such, it is important in questions of medicine or surgery.

In negative terms, the Sun is prideful, self-centered, and egotistic. The negative Sun is concerned only for itself and can pursue its interests to the exclusion of all else. The negative Sun can be rigid, hidebound, and overly legalistic.

Symbology: The hieroglyph for the Sun is the Sphere of the Conscious Self: ☉ The "navel" usually added to the center represents the Divine Spark within, which is surrounded by the field of conscious perception.

Correspondences: The Sun rules the sign of Leo. His metal is gold.

The Moon

The Moon corresponds to the divine archetype of the Mother.

In astrology, the Moon represents the Higher Self, psychism, intuition, dreams, and the subconscious. The Moon represents the emotional, reactive, internal self.

The Moon is the patron of religion and spirituality; she rules visions, clairvoyance, and relationship to Spirit. In the advanced person, this is a beneficial, nurturing relationship that informs and spiritualizes the life. To the unadvanced, it is confusing, unclear, and appears to be a source of misery and frustration, thence the Moon's negative reputation among Christian astrologers.

In negative terms, the Moon is too emotional, overly psychic, and so strongly influenced by her surroundings and the feelings of others that she cannot know her own mind. The negative Moon is associated with fear, subconscious inhibitions, and lack of clarity. This is, of course, a matter of perception; these different qualities are all signs telling us that we need to look inside, to take counsel of the Higher Self, which the Moon represents. When fear and disfocus lead us to spiritual introspection (and thus the rectification of situations), they are good friends to us.

> Symbology: The symbol of the Moon is the Crescent of the Higher Self: ☽ We interact with our Higher Self through the subconscious when the veil of our conscious mind is thick, and through meditation and psychism when the veil is thin. The Higher Self nourishes, sustains, and guides us when we have a strong relationship with it. When that relationship is weak, our "subconscious" appears to trip us up, when it truly seeks to inform us.

> Correspondences: The Moon rules the sign of Cancer. Her metal is silver.

Mercury

Mercury corresponds to the divine archetype of the Sorcerer.

In astrology, Mercury represents intelligence, thought, and ingenuity. Mercury rules communication of all sorts, teaching, and expression of ideas. Mercury is facile, versatile, and easily adaptable. Mercury rules education, invention, and innovation.

Mercury also rules money and commerce. It is the patron of merchants and businesspeople, as well as journalism and the media. Mercury is strongly connected to movement and is associated with speed and quickness.

Mercury is also connected with the idea of will and the ability to influence matter through concentrated thought. As such, Mercury is a patron of metaphysics. In this sense, Mercury might be thought of as ruling the active powers of magic, while Saturn (see below) might be associated with the more internal virtues of psychism.

In negative terms, Mercury is shallow, fickle, and inconstant, and can be cunning but self-serving, even dishonest.

> Symbology: The hieroglyph for Mercury is also a sign for the Horned God; it shows the Crescent of the Soul above the Sphere of the Conscious Self, above the Cross of Matter. That is to say, it represents the

correct alignment of the self—the soul expressed and expanded by the self (mind) and focused into physical action: ☿

Correspondences: Mercury rules the signs of Gemini and Virgo. His metals are quicksilver (Mercury) and aluminum.

Venus

Venus corresponds to the divine archetype of the Maiden.

In astrology, Venus represents both romantic and sensual love, creativity, artistry, and self-expression. Venus rules beauty and pleasure, arts and crafts, and all of the sweet things of life. She is particularly associated with sexuality, but, like the Maiden, her most essential quality is strength of self.

In negative terms, Venus is associated with selfishness, greed, and indulgence. Negative Venus thinks of herself first and others second, if at all. Overindulgence of all sorts, but especially sexual, is associated with negative Venus, as well as a conspicuous lack of concern over consequences.

Symbology: The hieroglyph for Venus is the Sphere of the Conscious Self over the Cross of Matter; that is to say, the conscious self expressing itself in the physical, with little reference to the Higher Self: ♀

Correspondences: Venus rules the signs of Taurus and Libra. Her metal is copper.

Mars

Mars corresponds to the divine archetype of the Hero.

In astrology, Mars represents courage, action, and forward movement. It is associated with self-confidence, pursuit of goals, and expansion of limits. Mars is decisive, forward-looking, and sure of itself. Mars is a doer, not a thinker, and its movements are quick and sure.

In negative terms, Mars rules aggression, discord, and anger. Mars is associated with quarrels, arrogance, and violence. Mars is the planet of war and disruptions; it is associated with accidents and natural disasters. Negative Mars is associated with recklessness, carelessness, and hasty actions.

Symbology: The hieroglyph for Mars is the Cross of Matter (usually rendered as a point, but still the same symbol) over the Sphere of the Conscious Mind; that is to say, action paramount over the self, with no reference to the Higher Self: ♂ Positive Mars uses that action to express the self. Negative Mars uses that action in spite of—and perhaps against the better judgment of—the self.

Lesson III

90

Correspondences: Mars rules the signs of Aries and Scorpio. His metal is iron.

Jupiter

Jupiter corresponds to the divine archetype of the King.

In astrology, Jupiter represents optimism, generosity, and expansion. Jupiter is associated with satisfaction, humor, and self-confidence; it is connected to good luck, progress, and success. Jupiter is a happy planet and very beneficent. Jupiter is also strongly connected to the idea of justice, as is the King archetype itself.

Jupiter rules the legal profession, the structure of governments and organizations, as well as accumulated wealth.

In its negative aspect, Jupiter is connected to all sorts of overdoing: overconfidence, overexpansion, overindulgence. Though Jupiter rules wealth, in its negative aspect it also causes it to be frittered away. Negative Jupiter is so confident as to miss or ignore problems, disregard threats, or take foolhardy actions. Negative Jupiter is also connected to procrastination.

Symbology: The hieroglyph for Jupiter is the Crescent of the Soul above the Cross of Matter; that is to say, the Higher Self informing the physical life, or physical action in harmony with inner guidance: ♃

Correspondences: Jupiter rules the signs of Sagittarius and Pisces. His metal is tin.

Saturn

Saturn corresponds to the divine archetype of the Crone.

In astrology, Saturn represents introspection, learning, and knowledge. Saturn governs practicality, common sense, and understanding. Saturn rules magic and metaphysics, and controls the gateway to the Higher Self. Saturn is associated with death and the decay that precedes regeneration.

In the negative aspect, Saturn rules depression, negative thinking, and emotional disconnection. Negative Saturn is perceived as limiting, blocking, or preventing movement or progress.

Most astrologers consider the influence of Saturn to be negative and inhibiting, the cause of difficulties, problems, and grief. But this is a matter of perception; like the Crone Goddess, Saturn shows us the flaws in our systems, the cracks in our foundations. She warns us of potential problems. If we do not listen to her warning and look within for solutions, disaster often overtakes us, and we falsely blame the Crone and feel she has brought disaster on us. When we do listen and take the necessary corrective action, however, the Crone has

been our benefactor. Thus the presence of Saturn warns of, rather than causes, problems, and in the hands of the adept is a powerful key for self-improvement.

Symbology: The hieroglyph for Saturn shows the Cross of Matter above the Crescent of the Soul; that is to say, a focus on structure and form, based on inner guidance: $\hbar$ In positive terms, that structure comes from and carries forward the fruits of inner guidance. In negative terms, that structure obscures or denies inner guidance.

Correspondences: Saturn rules the signs of Capricorn and Aquarius. Her metals are lead and pewter.

. . . .

The Outer Planets and Asteroids

The outer planets have only been discovered in recent times and are still in some cases (notably Pluto) a subject of debate today. These planets are outside of the sphere of traditional astrology, but have become increasingly integral to the practice of modern astrology.

Similarly many modern astrologers include the position of a number of asteroids in their charts, which are outside the sphere of traditional astrology.

Some astrologers choose to ignore the outer planets (especially Pluto) and/or the asteroids, because they are still in the process of becoming fully understood and fully integrated into the astrological system.

Whether to use the outer planets and asteroids is, of course, a matter of personal taste, but changes in the astrological system are nothing new. Any system so long in use has undergone many changes and will no doubt experience many more.

The outer planets are usually considered to represent "higher octaves" of the inner planets—that is to say, they are a more intense, more spiritual aspect of the same energies. All of the outer planets have to do with issues of intuition, spirituality, and psychic and magical energies expressed in differing ways.

Uranus

Uranus is generally considered to represent a higher octave of Mercury, or in other words, a more intense version of the Mercurial energy. As such, it manifests all of the intellectual powers of Mercury, but in a much more frenetic form.

In astrology, Uranus represents inspiration, originality, and the unexpected. New ideas, new ways of doing things, and deeper understandings are governed by Uranus. Sudden flashes of insight, the breaking of old patterns, sudden developments and new beginnings are connected to Uranus. Uranus is also connected to ideas of spiritual enlightenment and "cosmic consciousness."

Uranus is also sometimes considered the planet of destiny—its position indicating the workings of fate, those things we receive unexpectedly from Spirit due to the machinations of karma and the divine plan.

In the negative aspect, Uranus is considered flighty, erratic, and unpredictable. Its energy can be rebellious, moody, and unstable. If extremely ill-aspected, it is believed to be connected to accidents, natural disasters, and violence.

Uranus was discovered in 1381 Pisces (AD 1781) by British astronomer William Herschel.

Symbology: The hieroglyph for Uranus shows two Crescents of the Soul joined by the Cross of Matter, surmounting the Sphere of the Conscious Mind: ♅ The two crescents form a Janus-face looking forward and backward, inward and outward, at once. This represents self-knowledge and inner insights. That the two crescents are joined by the cross and surmounting the sphere indicates the integration of these qualities into the physical and their expression through the conscious mind and intellectual understanding. An alternate symbol for Uranus is a single crescent pointing upward, above the cross and above the sphere.

Neptune

Neptune is generally considered to represent a higher octave of Venus. As such, it represents all of the emotional qualities of Venus but in a deeper and more encompassing way.

The emotionality of Neptune is such that it overwhelms the ego. This can be positive in the sense of selflessness and devotion to purposes outside of oneself. Or it can be negative in the sense of wallowing in emotion and an inability to find direction.

Neptune is connected to intuition, psychism, and mysticism. It is a planet of spirituality and magic. Neptune is compassionate, emotionally sensitive, and deeply feeling. It is a planet of strong imagination and creative ability. Neptune likes to be of service to others and is capable of great self-sacrifice.

In a negative aspect, however, Neptune is overly emotional, lacks physical drive and direction, and is prone to view itself as a victim or passive observer rather than a participant in its own circumstances. Neptune tends toward drifting, addiction, and confusion. Neptune is also easily subject to deception (especially self-deception).

Though its discovery was predicted a generation before it happened, based upon the discovery of Uranus, Neptune was not in fact discovered until 1446 Pisces (AD 1846).

Symbology: The hieroglyph for Neptune shows the Crescent of the Soul with points upward, above and usually impaled upon the Cross of Matter: ♆ The crescent in this position represents psychic abilities and the reception of spiritual messages and energies from outside the mundane self. These are then channeled into the physical life, represented by the cross. The fact that the crescent is impaled upon the cross shows that the reception of these energies is often unconscious or beyond conscious control, and confusion may arise between spiritual and physical input.

Pluto

Pluto is generally considered to represent a higher octave of Mars. As such, it shares Mars' explosive, sometimes violent energy, manifested in an even stronger fashion.

Pluto is primarily associated with change and transformation, cleansing and regeneration, the clearing away of old structures to make way for the new, and looking below the surface to grasp the inner workings of situations before fine-tuning them accordingly.

Pluto is connected with the pursuit of self-knowledge and inner development, and with trying to find one's place in the world and in the universe. Pluto is connected with magic and psychism, development and use of spiritual energies. Pluto is also strongly connected to sexuality and sexual magic.

In a negative sense, Pluto is connected to obsession and overindulgence, being governed by one's passions and uncontrollable emotions. Extreme actions and reactions and sudden changes characterize Pluto in its negative aspect.

Pluto is the most recent of the planets discovered, though there has been some debate as to whether or not it should be properly considered a planet. Pluto was discovered in 1530 Pisces (AD 1930) by astronomer Percy Lovell.

Symbology: The scientific symbol for Pluto is a monogram of the letters "P" and "L," initials of the planet's discoverer: ♇ This monogram is not to be confused with the planet's astrological symbol, however, which is quite different: ♀

The hieroglyph for Pluto is similar to that of Uranus, showing the crescent of the soul with points upward, above the cross of matter. However, in Pluto, the crescent is not impaled by the cross, showing a clear understanding of what is spiritual and what is physical, and the two are surmounted by the sphere of the Conscious Mind. This represents the conscious reception and integration of psychic and spiritual energies intentionally focused into the physical, the work of the Witch.

. . . .

Along with the outer planets, there are several asteroids that many contemporary astrologers also make use of. Opinion about the asteroids, even whether or not to use them, varies widely—but a growing number of astrologers have adopted their use, and so it behooves the student to be familiar with them. The asteroids most commonly used are:

Chiron

The asteroid Chiron is named for the wise CENTAUR who schooled the mighty ACHILLES, as well as a number of other HEROES in Greek mythology. In keeping with Greek custom, Chiron taught his students not only academic subjects like reading and writing, but also philosophy and how to solve life's problems. The asteroid Chiron is believed to act in the same way, showing us what needs to be fixed in our lives and teaching us how to fix it. The position of Chiron in a chart is said to show where we are tripping ourselves up, often unconsciously. Aspects to

Chiron help give direction as to how to fix the situation.

> **Symbology:** The symbology used for the asteroids is entirely unrelated to that used for the traditional planets. These symbols, which are quite modern, are much cruder and more self-evident in meaning than the older signs. The symbol for Chiron is a stylized key: ⚷

Ceres

Ceres is named for the Mother Goddess in her form as goddess of grain. The asteroid Ceres deals with issues of self-esteem and self-worth. Ceres shows how one deals with nurturing and sustaining oneself and others. It is said the Ceres placement in the signs shows how one nurtures others, while her placement in the houses shows where one requires nurturing for oneself.

> **Symbology:** The symbol for Ceres is a stylized sickle, resembling an inverted Saturn, looking rather like a question mark with a cross through the shaft: ⚳

Pallas

Pallas, or PALLAS ATHENA, is named for the virgin warrior goddess of Greek mythology, who ruled all arts and crafts as well. Thus, Pallas deals with practical

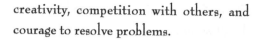

creativity, competition with others, and courage to resolve problems.

Symbology: The symbol for Pallas is similar to the symbol for Venus, except it is a square above a cross rather than a circle above a cross: ♀

Vesta

VESTA is named for the Greco-Roman goddess of fire and inspiration. The asteroid Vesta deals with issues of focus and commitment: family, work, idealistic causes, etc. The position of Vesta in the chart shows one's capacity for loyalty, perseverance, and putting the interests of others above one's own.

Symbology: The symbol for Vesta is a stylized hearth or altar with a central flame burning: ⚶

Juno

Juno is named for the Queen of the Gods in Greco-Roman mythology. Though the Greek HERA was portrayed as having a rocky relationship with her consort ZEUS, each one plagued by jealousy and possessiveness, the Roman Juno and her consort Jupiter were perceived as living in perfect concord, a model couple. The asteroid Juno deals with both of these extremes, representing how one deals with relationships and sharing in general. Issues of trust

and compatibility, as well as insecurity and jealousy, are revealed by the good or bad placement of Juno in the chart.

Symbology: The symbol for Juno resembles the symbol for Venus, except that instead of a sphere surmounting a cross, it is a star surmounting a cross: ⚵

. . . .

Positions and Aspects

The significance of the planets in astrology comes not only from their innate qualities but also from their positions in the astrological chart. The position marks the planet's perceived location in space relative to the zodiacal constellations and the other planets. Of course, this is not the planet's literal position, but rather how it appears from Earth.

The position of the planet in the zodiac indicates the relative strength of the planet's qualities and in what manner they can be expected to manifest in a given person or situation.

Planetary position also indicates the relationships of the planets to each other. These relationships are described as *aspects*. An aspect between two planets affects the meaning of each, describing a specific effect. There are a number of aspects that can occur between planets, including the four major aspects that follow:

Conjunction

Planets are said to be in conjunction when they are so close to one another as to be considered "conjoined," or occupying the same space. This is usually considered to be between 0 and 10°. The conjunction blends the qualities of the two planets involved in a way that can be either positive or negative, depending upon which planets they are.

Opposition

Planets are regarded as being in opposition when they are placed at a 180° angle, or exactly opposite. The opposition is considered to be a difficult aspect, in which the qualities of the two planets strain against each other, often bringing the worst qualities to the fore. The presence of an opposition in a chart indicates a need to learn a more positive way to interact with the planetary qualities in question.

Trine

Planets are said to be in trine when they are at a 120° angle to each other. The trine is considered to be a positive aspect that brings out the best in both planets.

Square

Planets are said to square one another when their positions are at a 90° angle. The square is considered to be a difficult aspect that indicates tension between the qualities of the two planets.

. . . .

The Zodiac

The zodiac is a series of twelve stellar constellations, which are represented as forming a band around the Earth, through which the planets move. Of course, this is a purely symbolic description, based on how space looks from Earth. In reality, the stars forming any given constellation are millions of miles apart and have no actual relationship to one another, save how they look from here; they serve as a handy marker.

The word *zodiac* is Greek and means "animal signs." There are twelve zodiacal signs, which originally corresponded to the twelve months of the year. Each of the twelve signs is represented by an animal or human symbol. The same signs have been used since Babylonian times, with only minor changes.

Each sign is associated with a planet, which is said to be its "ruler." Each sign also has an attribution to one of the four elements. In addition, the signs are said to fall into one of three further categories, called modes: cardinal, fixed, and mutable. These three modes are said to define the state of the sign's relationship to its element.

The Elements

The elements used in astrology are exactly the same four elements you have already learned about. The elements are used in a different order in astrology, perhaps because of astrology's place of origin in Mesopotamia. As you may recall from the First Degree lessons, the order of elements in regards to the directions and the quarters of the magic circle is believed to have originated in the topography of a given area.

Below is a description of the elements and modes in terms of their relevance to the zodiacal signs.

Fire

Fire has to do with movement, action, and ambition. The three fire signs—Aries, Leo, and Sagittarius—are quick and passionate.

Earth

Earth has to do with stability and integration. The three earth signs—Taurus, Virgo, and Capricorn—are focused and practical in material matters.

Air

Air has to do with thought and communication. The three air signs—Gemini, Libra, and Aquarius—are all concerned with ideas and understanding.

Water

Water has to do with emotion and feeling. The three water signs—Cancer, Scorpio, and Pisces—are all deeply emotive and concerned with interpersonal relationships.

• • • •

The Modes

Cardinal

The cardinal signs are those that most directly express the qualities of their element. They are associated with action and with bringing their elemental qualities into practical form. The cardinal signs exemplify both the positive and negative aspects of their respective elements. Aries, Cancer, Libra, and Capricorn are said to be cardinal signs.

Fixed

The fixed signs express stability and structure. They exemplify determination and persistence. In a negative sense, the fixed signs can be stubborn or inflexible. Taurus, Leo, Scorpio, and Aquarius are said to be fixed signs.

Mutable

The mutable signs express change and movement. They exemplify flexibility and adaptability. In a negative sense, the mutable signs can be unreliable and inconstant.

Gemini, Virgo, Sagittarius, and Pisces are said to be mutable signs.

• • • •
The Signs

Aries

Aries is fiery and ambitious, with a bright, quick mind. Energetic and fast-moving, Aries is full of enthusiasm. Aries is excellent at beginning and developing projects, but is not always good with follow-through.

When negative, Aries can be overambitious but scattered, with a tendency to drop projects in the middle.

Aries is ruled by the planet Mars and assigned to the element of fire. Aries is considered to be the cardinal fire sign, which is to say that it is very passionate and enthusiastic.

Symbology: The symbol of Aries is the ram: ♈

Taurus

Taurus is conservative and stable, strong—willed, and determined. Taurus is capable of great concentration and perseverance. Taurus is very security oriented and enjoys the comforts of life.

When negative, Taurus can be stubborn, self-centered, and rigid.

Taurus is ruled by the planet Venus and assigned to the element of earth. Taurus is considered to be the fixed earth sign, which is to say that it is very practical, materialistic, and stable.

Symbology: The symbol of Taurus is the bull, or sometimes the cow: ♉

Gemini

Gemini is extremely clever and versatile, with great ability in communication. Gemini has a quick, subtle mind and great perceptivity. Gemini is capable of moving in several directions at once, and can usually juggle them all well.

When negative, Gemini can be superficial and fickle, with a tendency to be spread too thin.

Gemini is ruled by the planet Mercury and assigned to the element of air. Gemini is considered to be the mutable air sign, which is to say that it is very mental and very fluid and adaptive.

Symbology: The symbol of Gemini is the twins. These are the polar opposites, which while appearing to be diametrically opposed are, in fact, different forms of the same essence: ♊

Cancer

Cancer is sensitive and deeply emotional. Cancer is strongly attached to home and family, and picks up easily on the moods of others. Cancer is nurturing and highly intuitive.

When negative, Cancer can be thin-skinned, brooding, and lacking in confidence.

Cancer is ruled by the Moon. Cancer is assigned to the element of water and is considered to be the cardinal water sign, which is to say that it is very emotional and reactive in nature.

> **Symbology:** The symbol of Cancer is the crab: ♋ Cancer is also sometimes represented by the scarab beetle.

Leo

Leo is proud, dramatic, and full of energy. Leo is honest and honorable, and tends to be very generous and nurturing. Leo has a very strong sense of self and enjoys being the center of attention.

When negative, Leo can be self-centered, arrogant, and short-sighted.

Leo is ruled by the Sun and assigned to the element of fire. Leo is considered to be the fixed fire sign, which is to say that it is passionate, dynamic, and stable.

> **Symbology:** The symbol of Leo is the lion: ♌

Virgo

Virgo is precise, orderly, and perfectionistic. Virgo cultivates skill and artistry in every pursuit, and is always looking to self-improvement.

When negative, Virgo can be overly critical or self-defeating.

Virgo is ruled by the planet Mercury and assigned to the element of earth. Virgo is considered to be the mutable earth sign, which is to say that it is practical but adaptive.

> **Symbology:** The symbol of Virgo is a woman. Who this woman is and what she represents varies, according to the religion and personal ideas of the speaker. She is usually considered to represent the Maiden Goddess, as is suggested by the name (*Virgo*—"Virgin"). However, some suggest that she is actually meant to be the Mother Goddess, since the sign coincides with the harvest: ♍

Libra

Libra is constantly seeking balance, peace, and tranquility, though not always finding them. Libra is creative, expressive, and enjoys beauty. Libra is sensitive and strongly emotive.

When negative, Libra can be vacillating, indecisive, and prone to mood swings.

Libra is ruled by the planet Venus and assigned to the element of air. Libra is considered to be the cardinal air sign, which is to say that it is essentially mental and analytical.

Symbology: The symbol of Libra is the scales (sometimes shown as a person holding scales): ♎

Scorpio

Scorpio is deeply emotional and capable of great focus and concentration. Scorpio excels at long-term projects and is capable of tremendous and sustained effort. Scorpio is highly psychic and can be very spiritual.

When negative, Scorpio can be brooding, petty, and vengeful.

Scorpio is ruled by the planet Mars and/or Pluto. Scorpio is assigned to the element of water and is considered to be the fixed water sign, which is to say that it is emotional but that it holds on strongly to things.

> **Symbology:** The symbol of Scorpio is the scorpion: ♏ Occasionally a lobster will be used to symbolize the sign instead of a scorpion, especially in older works.

Sagittarius

Sagittarius is optimistic, expansive, and has a high capacity for adventure. Sagittarius is devoted to learning and having new experiences. Sagittarius is highly social and also makes an excellent teacher.

When negative, Sagittarius can be unfocused, short-sighted, and self-indulgent.

Sagittarius is ruled by the planet Jupiter and assigned to the element of fire. Sagittarius is considered to be the mutable fire sign, which is to say that it is active and passionate but adaptive.

> **Symbology:** The symbol of Sagittarius is the archer: ♐ Commonly, the archer is shown as a centaur, half human and half horse.

Capricorn

Capricorn is ambitious, practical, and pragmatic. Capricorn is highly goal-oriented and is capable of sustained, focused effort. Capricorn has tremendous skill in organizing and structuring.

When negative, Capricorn can be cold, calculating, and overly materialistic.

Capricorn is ruled by the planet Saturn and assigned with the element of earth. Capricorn is considered to be the cardinal earth sign, which is to say that it is very solid and material.

> **Symbology:** The symbol of Capricorn is the goat (originally this was the sea-goat, a creature having the head and foreparts of a goat and the tail of a fish; sometimes this symbol is still used): ♑

Aquarius

Aquarius is brilliant, inspired, and often sees things in new ways. Original and unconventional, Aquarius is capable of deep insights. Aquarius is deeply concerned with issues of justice and balance.

When negative, Aquarius can be misanthropic, self-absorbed, and quirky.

Aquarius is ruled by the planet Saturn and/or Uranus. Aquarius is assigned to the element of air and considered to be the fixed air sign, which is to say that it is mental and inspirational but steady and holds on to things.

Symbology: The symbol of Aquarius is the water bearer:—

Pisces

Pisces is creative, emotive, and humanitarian. Pisces is generous and sympathetic. Pisces is often highly psychic, in an empathic way.

When negative, Pisces can be unfocused, indecisive, and has an overly active imagination.

Pisces is ruled by the planet Jupiter and/or Neptune. Pisces is assigned to the element of water and considered to be the mutable water sign, which is to say that it is both emotional and changeable.

Symbology: The symbol of Pisces is the fish: ♓

Houses

In addition to the twelve zodiacal signs, there are also twelve houses, or divisions of the chart, whose position is determined by the Ascendant sign. The Ascendant is the sign that was exactly above the horizon at the moment the chart depicts (the moment of birth in a natal chart). Exactly opposite the Ascendant is the Descendant. Between them is the Midheaven, coinciding with the tenth house.

The houses explain where in a person's life the various planets and signs will have their effect, what parts of life they will influence most strongly.

Every two hours during the day the Ascendant sign changes, thus changing all of the house information. It is through the houses that you can see the differences between people born at different times on the same day. If you do not know the time of birth, you cannot calculate the position of the Ascendant, and thus you cannot place the houses correctly.

The Ascendant is very important in a chart, as it speaks to the person's outlook on the world.

First House

(Ascendant) Personality, appearance, and outlook. How one views the world and is viewed.

Second House

Inner goals and values. Possessions, money, wealth. One's financial status.

Third House

Surroundings, friends and neighbors, ability to communicate and make oneself understood. Memory and cognitive ability, native skills and talents. Childhood and early education.

Fourth House

(Nadir) Home and inner self. Property. The less-influential parent. The later years of life.

Fifth House

Self-expression, creativity, romance. Amusements and pastimes. Books, artworks, and other expressive creations. Children. Also hidden karma and misuse of power.

Sixth House

Profession, work, service to or from others. Creature comforts, employees, and dependants of all sorts.

Seventh House

(Descendant) Relationships, partnerships, and romances. Ability to work and play well with others. Also adversaries.

Eighth House

Magic, psychism, sexuality. Addictions. Transformation and regeneration. Inheritances, one's mate's wealth, death and the end of life.

Ninth House

Higher education, religion and spirituality, travel, and international activities.

Tenth House

(Midheaven) Fame, reputation, professional standing. The dominant parent. Employers. How the world perceives you.

Eleventh House

Wishes, goals, and ambitions. Friends and social contacts.

Twelfth House

Subconscious issues. Inner transformation. The issues that hold you back, which must be addressed for transformation to occur. Principal life lessons. Charity to or from others.

. . . .

How to Read a Chart

An astrological chart, or HOROSCOPE, is a map showing the exact position of the planets at any given moment. Traditionally, a chart was created using laborious mathematical formulae, which were used to determine the placement of the planets and the aspects between them. Happily, we now have computers to do all that for us, so today charts are fairly easy to cast, at least if you have the right software.

The chart is read using all of the various elements we have discussed above. The planets are the primary concern; the sign they are placed in affects the expression of their qualities; the house they are placed in tells what part of life their influence will be strongest in. The aspects formed between the planets show how their dynamic forces interact.

Thus, the planet Mercury by itself represents the mind and communication. Placed in Taurus, Mercury represents a strong, if conservative, mind, a superior memory, and perhaps also a tendency to stubbornness. Placed in the sixth house, Mercury in Taurus will manifest through career or vocation, which will be strengthened by or even dependent upon strength of mind, intellect, and steadfastness of purpose. Now an aspect: let us say our Mercury in Taurus in the sixth house is also conjunct Venus. The aesthetic and artistic qualities of Venus will unite with the mental qualities of Mercury, both being strengthened by Taurus and expressed in life through the vocation.

It is in this way that the chart is read.

The most common use of an astrological chart is the NATAL CHART. The natal chart shows the position of the planets at the moment of a person's birth. Astrologers use natal charts to divine details of the person's personality traits, talents, strengths, and weaknesses.

Though the natal is the most common form of chart, there are other ways in which charts are used as well. An example is the COMPARATIVE CHART.

A comparative chart uses the natal charts of two (or more) people to divine the nature of their potential interaction; will they help or hinder each other, get on well or badly, etc. To do this, the two natal charts are compared and examined for similarities and differences. The planetary positions are examined to see what aspects the planets in chart A form to those in chart B, to reveal the dynamic interactions between the two people.

Another common chart is the TRANSIT CHART. To do a transit chart, you compare the person's natal chart with the chart for a given day or the charts for a period of time. This will show the transits of the planets; that is, the position of the planets now, as compared with where they were at the subject's birth. This will show what the subject can expect from the period of time in question. The aspects formed between the natal and transiting planets can be very revealing.

Another kind of chart, no longer much used, is the HORARY CHART. Horary astrology, once widely used for judicial purposes, is the art of studying history from an astrological perspective and applying the knowledge gained to contemporary or future events. In horary astrology, the planetary conditions around an event are compared to events that are known to have happened historically when the same planetary aspects were in play.

In judicial astrology, the astrological chart of the time when a crime occurred, or of the accused in a criminal case, is compared to its historical precedents to gain greater insight. For the purpose of divining the future through horary means, one takes the chart of a major event, say the GREAT FIRE OF CHICAGO for example, and looks for points in the future when the same astrological conditions recur, on the premise that a similar event can be expected to happen then.

. . . .

Now, having read all of this, you should be able to read an astrological chart pretty well, though you have a lot of study ahead if you really want to learn astrology, for this has been only a brief overview. Astrology is an ancient art, and consequently it is highly developed. But a basic understanding of astrology and its principles is essential to a Wiccan priest/ess, as so many things refer back to it through correspondence and allegorical interpretation. This lesson should give you that basic understanding.

Exercise 5

Exercise 5 begins where Exercise 4 left off. Start with the Ohm exercise. Then open the chakras with balls of colored light, changing the balls of colored light to balls of white light, changing the balls of white light to balls of purple light, changing the balls of purple light to balls of silver stellar light, and then filling your aura with silver stellar light. Next, change the balls of silver stellar light to balls of golden stellar light, then fill your aura with golden stellar light. Finally, change the balls of golden stellar light to balls of amber light, and fill your aura with the amber light.

At this point, become aware of your solar plexus chakra. From the solar plexus chakra, send out a beam of red or multicolored light. Visualize this beam of light clearly; extend it from your solar plexus chakra across the room to the far wall.

Use this beam of light just as you did the beams of light from your third eye and palm chakras in the exercises accompanying the First Degree lessons. That is, draw shapes with it on the wall, write words, and practice your skill with controlling the beam.

Then, after a few minutes' practice, close down your chakras as usual, clear, and release.

If this exercise should cause you discomfort, then immediately after doing it, before you close your chakras, flood the solar plexus chakra with yellow light. Like any exercise, these psychic exercises may occasionally strain unused or little-used psychic muscles. Flushing the chakra with yellow light will eliminate any such discomfort. Such psychic muscle strain only happens the first time or two an undeveloped muscle is put to work, and it quickly ceases.

Exercise 6

When you feel proficient in manipulating the beam of light from the solar plexus chakra, you are ready to move on.

Go through all the steps above, until you fill your aura with amber energy. Then, instead of going to your solar plexus chakra, go to your root chakra, low in your pelvis. From the root chakra, extend a beam of red or multicolored energy across the room to the opposite wall, and draw or write with it in just the same way you have been doing with your solar plexus chakra.

After a few minutes, move on to the second chakra; do the same thing here.

Continue through all the chakras. You may not be able to do this all at once the first few times. It is okay to work up to it; perhaps add a chakra per day until you can do them all.

When you can make and use light beams from all seven major chakras, you are proficient with this exercise.

These exercises will greatly strengthen your chakras in preparation for much more serious chakra working, which we will begin to discuss in Lesson IV.

. . . .

Spell for Lesson III
Creating a Guardian

In this spell, we are going to introduce you to the concept of thoughtforms. A thoughtform is an energy construct created for a specific purpose, such as to be a guardian, but it has the form and reactions of an astral being.

The thoughtform takes its shape and behavior from the specification of its creator, then carries on independently, according to programming. It is not unlike a psychic robot or a psychic computer program: you create it, tell it what to do, then it does it on its own. Like any good robot or computer program, however, it does need proper maintenance.

Thoughtforms need not be difficult to create and use, but certain important rules apply. You must act with a pure heart when you create a thoughtform, as your purity of motive will color the thoughtform's own behaviors. You must be clear on what you want; you must treat your thoughtform with respect; you must not create a thoughtform and then just forget about it.

A thoughtform is also sometimes referred to as a GOLEM.

There are differing views on exactly how a thoughtform is made. Some say that it is created from the ambient energy around you and given existence only by your act of magic, dissipating back into the ambient energy when you are done. Others hold that you are creating it out of your own energy, separating off a soul from your own soul, which—when its time as a thoughtform is finished—will go on to other existences, as any other soul would. Still others hold that it is actually an existing spirit willing to fill the job, not a new creation at all.

Our view is that a thoughtform is created from ambient energy but given form by you, thus being, in a sense, a part of you, since it is imprinted with your energy pattern. The thoughtform may or may not become a soul in its own right, depending upon how strongly it is shaped and how long it is used, but it is definitely alive, since all energy is alive, whatever its form.

Thoughtforms can be created for a number of purposes—for example, a fetch to retrieve desired or lost items. But by far the most common use of a thoughtform is as a guardian, either for a person or for a building or area. There are many fine examples of sculptures of temple and house

guardians from ages past that served as keys to the thoughtforms they represent.

For the purposes of this spell, a guardian would normally be created if a person felt they were in danger. It is not altogether unlike an artificial spirit guide. The guardian would then be retained until the danger had passed, when it would be deconsecrated and allowed to move on. This should not be done lightly.

A guardian could also be created to guard a building or a family for a longer period of time, or indefinitely.

To create your guardian, you will first need a statue or picture whose image you wish to create your guardian in. If you prefer to create a guardian purely from your imagination, then you should have a token that represents it. The guardian should appear formidable and serious. Buddhist temple guardians, for example, are often extremely fierce-looking warriors with terrifying countenances. However, a guardian need not be frightening, merely strong.

You will need:

- The image or token of your guardian
- As many candles as you wish, the more the better
- An offering of some sort: milk with a bit of whisky in it, cornmeal, or incense

This is best done in a circle, as the circle will enhance the energy. Cast the circle as usual, and when you come to the body of the ritual, charge the image/token in this way:

From below the image, imagine a column of white light arising from the earth. Pull it up into the image, and form a ball of white light around it. Imagine the earth energy filled with strength, courage, and protective love. Now, from above the image, imagine a column of white light coming down from the heavens. Let this light enter the image, mixing with the earth energy. Imagine this energy as filled with intelligence and vigor. Let the two energies mix and come into perfect balance. Now invoke your guardian into being. Say something like:

> *"Behold, from this energy*
> *of Mother Earth and Father Sky,*
> *I fashion a guardian—a protector*
> *and champion. I call you into being,*
> *O guardian; I call you forth.*
> *I imbue you with energy and*
> *will, and I give you form. May*
> *you take this form, may you*
> *animate this form, may it be*
> *my key to you, O guardian."*

Imagine the guardian in the form of the image (or, if you are using a token, in the form you desire). See the guardian begin to grow, expanding from the size of the image to life size, then to larger than life size. Imagine it taking on the appearance and movement of a living being.

Make your offering now. Say something like:

> *"Greetings, O guardian. Accept*
> *this nourishment from me in token*
> *of the bond between us. As you*
> *give service to me, so do I also*
> *give service to you. As you protect*
> *me and mine, so likewise I honor*
> *you and nourish you. Accept this*
> *offering, I pray, and take of it what*
> *you desire; when you have finished,*
> *I will dispose of what remains."*

Place the offering before the image. Imagine the offering glowing with light, very brightly. Imagine the guardian taking the offering and consuming it. It should be noted that the nourishment is not the offering. Spiritual beings have no use for physical food but rather the act of respect in offering it and the energy included with it.

Now charge your guardian. Say something like this, depending on what exactly you need:

> *"O guardian, I charge you to*
> *protect me and mine from all*
> *harm, shield us from negativity,*

stand with us and aid us against any dangers, and keep us safe and strong. Protect us in our home and away from home. Be alert to all dangers, and avert them! And when we no longer have need of you, and no longer make offerings to you, return to the Goddess and let her guide you forward! We thank you, O guardian, and offer you our love and our respect. May the blessing be upon you, beloved guardian!"

Now close the circle as usual. Then set the image of the guardian in a place of honor, either on your altar or on an altar of its own. If it is to protect your home, place it near the front door.

Make frequent offerings to the guardian in the same way as above. The offering should be respectful and accompanied by thanks for the guardian's service; once a week is normally good. This nourishes the guardian, partly in the sense of keeping it focused. Do not forget, or your guardian will dissipate and be of no good to you.

When you no longer need the guardian, you should do a ritual of thanksgiving, honoring it for its service and formally releasing it to the Goddess. If you are creating a guardian who is meant to serve indefinitely, you would alter your charge accordingly, instructing it to go dissipate and return to the Goddess when it is no longer needed and thanking it for its service in advance.

. . . .

Glossary

Achilles—Greatest of the Greek warriors during the Trojan War, Achilles' story is presented in the *Iliad* and other ancient sources, and while there may have been a real Achilles, his story is heavily overlaid with myth. Achilles was said to be the son of the sea goddess Thetis and the mortal Peleus, king of Phthia. The marriage of Thetis and Peleus was the mythical starting point for the Trojan War, for it was here that the goddess Eris (Discordia) threw the famous golden apple marked "Kallisti" ("To the fairest"). This caused the goddesses Hera, Athena, and Aphrodite to vie with each other as to which of them most deserved the apple. Accepting the Trojan prince Paris as judge, the three goddesses endeavored to bribe him, Aphrodite offering to make the most beautiful woman in the world—Helen, hereditary queen of Sparta—fall in love with him. Paris duly judged Aphrodite the fairest and began his affair with Queen Helen, which sparked the war. When Achilles was born, his mother, Thetis, dipped him in the river Styx, making him invulnerable to physical injury everywhere except his heel, which she held him by. Thetis tried to keep Achilles out of the Trojan War by hiding him at the royal court in Skiros disguised as a girl—but this ploy was unsuccessful and resulted in the birth of Achilles' own son, Neoptolemus. At Troy, Achilles became the Greeks' greatest warrior, fighting with his *eronemos* Patrocles at the head of a band of myrmidon soldiers. Achilles defeated Troy's greatest defender, Prince Hector, in revenge after Hector slew Patrocles. Achilles was killed near the end of the Trojan War, when Prince Paris shot an arrow that accidentally hit Achilles in the heel, his one vulnerable spot. This is the origin of the phrase "Achilles' heel."

aspects—In astrology, the position of one planet as regards another is termed an *aspect*. There are a number of aspects, including conjunction (very close together), opposition (opposite from one another), and square (at right angles to each other), as well as many others. The aspects between planets are very important in astrology, and much information is divined from them.

astrogancy—Astrogancy is divination based upon celestial events: observation of comets, coronas, and so on. It is believed that the practice of astrogancy gave rise to astrology when ancient astrogancers realized that certain heavenly phenomena repeated on a regular schedule and began to study their sequence.

centaur—In Greek mythology, centaurs are creatures that were half human and half horse, who lived on the plains of Thessaly. Centaurs are usually portrayed as combining the best characteristics of both humankind and horsekind—but occasionally they are shown as combining the worst of each. The two most famous centaurs in Greek mythology are Nessus and Chiron. Nessus attempted to seduce Deianeira, the wife of Hercules, and was killed by the irate husband. Before he died, however, Nessus was able to persuade Deianeira that if she saved a vial of his blood, she could use it restore Hercules' love, should it ever wander. In time, Hercules did begin to turn from Deianeira, and so she took the vial of Nessus's blood and applied it to a tunic that Hercules owned. When Hercules put on the tunic impregnated with Nessus's blood, far from falling back in love with Deianeira, he was poisoned and burned by the blood of the centaur, dying in terrible pain and agony. The other famous centaur, Chiron, was a wise sage who tutored many Greek heroes, including Jason, Hercules, Peleus, Achilles, and Aeneas. Chiron was also among the teachers of the great healer Asclepius, who became the god of healing.

Ceres—Ceres is the Roman name for the goddess Demeter, goddess of the earth and fields. The name *Demeter* means "The Mother," and Demeter is above all a Mother Goddess. Demeter's primary myth is the story of how her daughter Persephone was taken by Hades, god of the dead, to be his wife. Demeter mourned her daughter's loss, and the earth fell into the first winter. In time, Demeter's persistence led to an entente: Persephone would live six months of the year with her mother and the world would be in summer, and six months with her husband, Hades, when the earth would be in winter. Some versions say Persephone was to spend four months on Olympus (spring), four months with her mother (harvest), and four months with her husband (winter), which reflects the older three-season Greek year. The preeminent site of Demeter's worship was Eleusis, near Athens, where each year the Eleusinian Mysteries celebrated the story of Demeter, Persephone, and Hades, and proclaimed the immortal nature of the soul. The Eleusinian Mysteries were considered the greatest of the Greek Mysteries. In some places, such as Arcadia, Demeter was portrayed with a horse's head, linking her to the more northerly Earth Mothers like Danu, Rhiannon, and Macha.

comparative chart—In astrology, a comparative chart is the combined chart of two persons (usually) in order to divine their compatibility and the nature of the interactions that might be expected between them. Comparative charts are commonly done for romantic or business partners, but they can also be done for parents and children, friends, or anyone who might desire it. A comparative chart can also be done for countries and institutions.

golem—An entity artificially created to fulfill a specific purpose. In the original sense of the word, derived from Jewish legend, the golem was an image made of clay, brought to life by magic. In contemporary Correllian parlance, a golem is an astral entity usually created to serve as a guardian or spirit helper.

Great Fire of Chicago—A tragedy comparable to the Great Fire of London or the Tokyo Earthquake, the Great Chicago Fire began on 8 October 1471 Pisces (AD 1871) and raged out of control for more than twenty-four hours, destroying much of the city. Contemporary investigators found that the fire started at a barn belonging to one Patrick O'Leary, but they could not identify the cause—although the famous legend attributes it to a stubborn cow and an overturned lantern. The fire left 300 dead and 90,000 homeless.

Hera—Hera is a Greek Mother Goddess with aspects of both Maiden and Crone. Hera, Queen of the Gods, was the sister and wife of Zeus. Hera, whose name means "the Lady," was a patron of women and children, of the home and family. She was the particular guardian of marriage and childbirth. In her Crone aspect, Hera becomes jealous and persecuting—yet, in common with all Crones, her apparent persecution must be thought of in terms of hard lessons that cause the recipient to grow and rise to their highest potential. Although her worship was universal in the Greek world, the primary seat of Hera's worship was at Argos, in the Peloponnesus. Her festival, known as the Heraia, was held here and was considered the women's answer to the Olympic games. Hera is considered cognate with the Roman Juno.

heroes—In the metaphysical sense, a hero is a man or woman who goes on a spiritual quest, often in the form of a physical adventure. Greek mythology is full of such heroes, their exciting, semi-historical quests forming a large part of Greek mythology. Almost always, Greek heroes date from Mycenean times, before the advent of Classical Greece. This may be because the stories of heroes are a legacy of the earlier culture (much as Germanic Europeans relished the adventures of the Celtic King Arthur), or it may be because the Classical Greeks could not conceive of such heroes in their own day. Some notable Greek heroes include Hercules, Odysseus, Jason, Theseus, and Atalanta, to name a few.

horary chart—Horary astrology is based on the idea that conditions repeat, and that if a given set of astrological aspects led to one thing in the past, it will lead to something similar in the future.

horoscope—A horoscope is an astrological chart showing the position of the planets and the relationships between them at any given time. There are many different kinds of horoscope, but the most common is the natal chart, which shows the position of the planets at the time of a person's birth. The term *horoscope* is Greek and means roughly "to see the hour."

natal chart—The natal chart is the most common chart used in astrology. The natal, or birth, chart is drawn up to show the position of the planets and the aspects between them at the time of a person's birth. From this, character traits and potential future events are divined. The natal chart is the basis of most other astrological operations. Natal charts can also be done for countries, institutions, businesses, or anything that may be said to have an official "birth."

natal horoscope—The natal horoscope is the most common form of horoscope and is necessary for any astrological evaluation. A natal horoscope is a horoscope cast to show where the planets were positioned at the time of a person's birth. The natal horoscope shows personality traits, strengths and weaknesses, and potentials for the future.

Nostradamus—The famous French prophet Michele de Nostre Dame, better known as Nostradamus, was born in Provence in 1103 Pisces (AD 1503). The prophet was born into a wealthy Catholic family of Jewish ancestry. He grew up to be an astrologer and medical doctor—an expected combination in that era. After losing his young wife and children to the plague in 1134 Pisces (AD 1534), Nostradamus made the plague his specialty and had unusual success in its treatment. For many years, he worked as an itinerant doctor, traveling wherever he was needed. In

1147 Pisces (AD 1547), Nostradamus married his second wife, Anne Ponsart (or Anne Pons Gemelle), and settled in Salon. Beginning in 1150 Pisces (AD 1550) Nostradamus published an annual almanac, which included his predictions for the coming year. This proved to be very popular, and in 1155 Pisces (AD 1555), he published the first part of his famous *Prophecies*. The success of the *Prophecies* brought Nostradamus to the attention of the French royal house, and in 1156 Pisces (AD 1556), he was summoned to Paris to meet King Henri II and Queen Marie de Medicis. The Queen asked Nostradamus to make predictions for the royal house and the royal children. After this, Nostradamus received royal patronage from the House of Valois. When King Henri II died in 1159 Pisces (AD 1559) in circumstances which seemed to confirm Nostradamus's prediction with uncanny accuracy, the prophet's reputation was set. The Dowager Queen Marie de Medicis appointed him Physician in Ordinary in 1164 Pisces (AD 1564), a high honor. Nostradamus died in 1166 Pisces (AD 1566), and the definitive edition of his *Prophecies* was published posthumously in 1158 Pisces (AD 1568) by his widow and his student, Chavigny. Nostradamus's prophecies are decidedly obscure but have been

Lesson
III

held to predict a wide range of events, including the English civil war and French Revolution, Napoleon, and Hitler. Indeed, in WWII, both the British and German propaganda departments had special subsections dedicated to interpreting (and, if need be, manufacturing) Nostradamus prophecies of their eventual victory.

Pallas Athena—Athena is a Greek Maiden Goddess. Athena is the goddess of the mind and of intelligence, and mistress of all arts, crafts, and sciences. Athena was also a warrior goddess who served as a protector and a patron of heroes; she is nearly always shown in armor. Athena was the tutelary goddess of Athens, but her worship was found all through the Greek world. Athena was the daughter of Metis by Zeus, but Zeus, fearing that Metis's offspring would be greater than he, swallowed Metis whole; later, Athena sprang fully grown and fully armed from Zeus's head. Athena is cognate to the Roman Minerva and is considered to be closely related to the Hindu goddess Durga as well. The warrior aspect of the goddess is less pronounced in Minerva but more pronounced in Durga. Pallas is either an earlier or variant name for Athena or a Mycenean-era goddess assimilated to Athena: later Greek myth describes Pallas as the daughter of the Titan Triton and a childhood friend of Athena's whom she accidentally killed and whose name she took in remorse.

planetary correspondences—Planetary correspondence, also termed planetary rulership, is an important idea in metaphysics. Simply stated, the idea is this: because the microcosm can be understood through the macrocosm—As above, so below—everything that exists can be studied through other aspects of existence with which it has correspondence. The seven Ptolemaic planets, which also correspond to the seven divine archetypes, are a frequently used tool for interpreting in this manner. Thus, any given thing can be said to have one or more planetary correspondences or planetary rulers. For example, anything romantic is commonly said to be ruled by Venus. The outer planets—Uranus, Neptune, and Pluto—can also be used in this manner; for example, Uranus is usually said to be ruler of technological issues.

Ptolemy—Claudius Ptolemy is author of the astrological treatise *Tetrabiblos*, written in the second century AD (1300s Aries). The *Tetrabiblos* was a compendium of all astrological knowledge of the time and served as the major reference on the subject for centuries. For this reason, traditional astrology is sometimes termed *Ptolemaic astrology*.

transit chart—In astrology, a transit chart compares the position of the planets at the time of birth with their position at a given moment later in life. The relationships thus revealed between the natal chart and the later positions of the planets are used to divine the influences around the person and how these might influence present or future events.

Vesta—Vesta is the Roman equivalent of Hestia, Greek goddess of fire, especially the hearth fire. Vesta was considered the guardian of the Roman state, and her priestesses, the celebrated vestal virgins, were of extreme importance among the Roman clergy. The vestal virgins—originally the daughters of kings, later of aristocratic families—were sworn to serve the goddess for thirty years each, during which time they must remain celibate; at the end of the thirty years, they could leave the order and marry if they chose, or remain in the Goddess's service. The principal duty of the vestal virgins was to maintain the sacred flame, which was never allowed to go out. If it did go out, it was a very ill omen, and the vestal responsible was considered guilty of a terrible crime. The chief vestal was something of a female equivalent of the Pontifex Maximus, the chief priest of

Rome, and chief vestals wielded tremendous influence. The chief vestal Vibidia attempted to intercede on behalf of the condemned Empress Messalina during the reign of Claudius, and though she was unsuccessful in this, the eminent Vibidia was one of the few people powerful enough to be able to make an attempt. Another prominent vestal was Aquilia Severa, who briefly became the wife of Emperor Elagabalus as part of the emperor's attempt to emphasize the unity of all religious thought; high—minded reasons notwithstanding, the Roman public was outraged, and Aquilia was ceremoniously re-virginified by order of the Roman Senate.

Zeus—Greek King of the Gods, Zeus was thought of as the son of Cronos (Time) and Rhea (Earth). According to the most common myth of Zeus's birth, Cronos feared that his children would overthrow him, so he swallowed each child whole as it was born. When Zeus was born, Cronos's wife, Rhea, grieving for her earlier children and not willing to lose another, fed Cronos a stone wrapped in baby's swaddling and hid the real baby at Mt. Ida in Crete. Here Zeus was suckled by the goat goddess Amalthea (identified by the Greeks with Capricorn). Grown up, Zeus returned to overthrow his father Cronos, just

as predicted, and liberated his siblings
whom Cronos had swallowed. A war
between Zeus and the gods and Cronos
and the Titans followed, which became
the subject of quite a few pieces of
Greek art. Ultimately Zeus prevailed,
and Cronos was killed. The freed siblings of Zeus were Demeter, Hera, Hestia, Hades, and Poseidon. Zeus is considered cognate to the Roman Jupiter.

zodiac—The zodiac is a system of constellations used since ancient times
to structure the practice of astrology.
Developed in the ancient Near East,
astrology uses the theoretical position
of stars and planets to address issues
of internal character and future events.
Though tied to the position of heavenly
bodies, it could be argued that astrology
really has more to do with the mathematical calculation of repeating cycles
of time and their individual character,
using the stars and planets as markers.

Lesson
IV

Magical Alphabets

The term *magical alphabets* conjures up images of ancient, dusty tomes written in arcane scripts decipherable only by adepts—and, indeed, in this lesson we will be commenting upon a number of arcane scripts of this sort, including our own Correllian alphabet. But in reality, the idea of a magical alphabet need be neither so difficult nor so mysterious.

All alphabets have magical dimensions and applications that have been with us since the beginning of alphabets, when even the idea of communicating by written word was considered magical. The modern Latin alphabet, which we use in English and other languages of Western European descent, is full of magical significance and lends itself to many magical practices unknown to most people. Among these are gematria and isopsephos, which are spoken of at length below. In our examination of magical alphabets, we will deal with our own Latin alphabet first.

Before we speak of the metaphysical aspects of alphabets, however, let us first examine the origins of the alphabet itself.

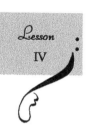

. . . .
History of the Alphabet

An alphabet is a system of symbols, each of which stands for a single sound. Alphabets are one of several methods of writing, which humanity has employed over the course of many ages. Similar to the alphabet is the syllabary, a system whereby symbols are used to stand for the syllables, of which the words of a language are constructed. The most famous example of a syllabary is the Cherokee syllabary created by GEORGE GUEST, better known as "Sequoia." The third form of writing is pictographic, a system in which symbols are used to represent objects, actions, or ideas. Mesopotamian cuneiform, Egyptian hieroglyphics, and traditional Chinese writing are all examples of pictographic writing.

The earliest forms of writing were pictographic. The Sumerians and the Egyptians developed their respective systems, cuneiform and hieroglyphics, about the same time, around 1300 Gemini (3100 BC). It is usually thought that cuneiform was invented first, and hieroglyphics was inspired by it; however, this is debatable and may be due to the biblical bias of early archeologists. At any rate, whether it was

cuneiform or hieroglyphics that came first, neither preceded the other by much. And while one may have inspired the other, they have no shared components beyond the basic idea.

Long after they had ceased to be the ordinary method of writing in their areas, cuneiform and hieroglyphics continued to be used for religious and magical purposes, which might be considered the first example of a magical "alphabet."

The first example of an alphabet proper makes its appearance during the 1200s Taurus (1600s BC), in the trading city of Ugarit. The Ugaritic alphabet has thirty letters, which were incised into clay like cuneiform but otherwise bear little resemblance to it. The Ugaritic alphabet even had a standardized form, an ABC if you will, whose order was basically the same as the later Phoenician alphabet. The Ugaritic alphabet was used for several hundred years but seems to have ceased being used when the city was destroyed by the Sea Peoples around year 0 Aries (1200 BC).

In subsequent years, a new alphabet was developed, perhaps based upon the Ugaritic. This new alphabet was the Phoenician. The Phoenician alphabet had the same basic order of letters as the Ugaritic but used very different signs to express them. The Phoenicians were a Semitic people who lived in the area now known as Syria, Palestine, and Jordan. They were noted for trading and seafaring.

The first evidence of the Phoenician alphabet comes from the city of Byblos, a Phoenician city that had a long connection with Egypt. The people of Byblos had developed a syllabary of eighty letters, apparently based somewhat on Egyptian hieroglyphs, but by at least 200 Aries (1000 BC), they had abandoned their syllabary in favor of the Phoenician alphabet. This Phoenician alphabet is the ancestor of most of the alphabets used today.

The Phoenician alphabet had twenty-two letters, all of which were consonants. Vowels were not developed until later. The Phoenician alphabet was written from right to left, following the path of the moon, whose cycle progresses from right to left. Its descendants in the Middle East, Hebrew and Arabic writing, are still written this way.

Within a few hundred years, the Phoenicians were being challenged for control of the Mediterranean waterways by the Greeks. Both the Phoenicians and the Greeks based much of their economy on trade. They competed for the same markets and the same trade routes. By 450 Aries (750 BC), the Greeks had adopted the Phoenician alphabet and began adapting it to the needs of their language.

Around 600 Aries (600 BC), the Greeks changed the direction in which the alphabet was written, writing from left to right instead of right to left. In doing so,

they also changed the direction in which many of the individual letters faced. In addition, the Greeks created symbols for vowel sounds, as well as for consonants that existed in their language but not in Phoenician. Thus, the basic form of the alphabet we use today was established.

The Greek alphabet, in its turn, was adopted and altered by many other peoples. The Etruscans of Italy used it as a base for their alphabet, as did the Romans. Farther north, the Germanic peoples adapted the Greek and Roman alphabets into a runic alphabet, which we will speak about later. In Egypt, a Coptic alphabet was developed that displaced hieroglyphics for everyday purposes. The Celtic peoples developed an alphabet, called Ogham or Bethluisnion, which though totally different from the Greek or Latin alphabets was probably inspired by them.

In time, the Latin alphabet would replace all of the alphabets of Western Europe, while the Arabic alphabet replaced the alphabets of the Middle East. The Greek alphabet continued to be used in Greece and the Eastern Mediterranean, and was developed into the Cyrillic alphabet, which spread through Eastern Europe. This, then, is the history of the Western alphabets, and how the Latin alphabet we use in English came to be.

. . . .

Gematria

One of the principle metaphysical applications of alphabets is gematria.

Gematria is the art of interpreting letters, words, and phrases in order to expand upon their meaning. Each letter has its own gematrical qualities, which will be outlined below. The qualities of the individual letters, as well as their number in the particular word, are taken to expand upon the word's significance and explain aspects of its inner nature.

For example, the word *letter* contains two letter *E*s and two letter *T*s, as well as an *L* and an *R*. The letter *L* represents artistic and personal expression. Because it is the first letter of the word, its qualities are predominant. The letter *R* represents new beginnings, overcoming obstacles, and inner growth. Because there are two *E*s in the word, the *E* vibration in the word is especially strong. The letter *E* represents communication. Similarly, the two *T*s strengthen the *T* influences in the word. The letter *T* represents diplomacy and cooperation. Thus the word *letter* may be said to DENOTE a symbol used to represent a sound (in this instance), also having the further CONNOTATION of aiding communication and personal expression, fostering cooperation and the overcoming of obstacles. For a further discussion of the meaning of each letter, consult the chart below.

Other practices that may be said to come under the heading of gematria are expanding upon the meaning of a word by finding other words within it, or by arranging its component letters to form other words (which is technically called *temurah*).

Thus, for example, the word *letter* will be seen to contain the word *let* (meaning to allow another to do or to use something), the word *tee* (having the connotation of a base or a beginning), the word *reel* (meaning to pull in), and the word *leer* (meaning a gaze, intense to the point of salaciousness). This could be taken to say, of letters, that they enable others, engender beginnings, bring things (or, rather, bring their meanings) to one, and also that they facilitate intensity and focus, sometimes taken to extreme.

Of course, people already familiar with gematria will know that its primary use is numerological—the interpretation of words through the numerical values attributed to the letters in a word, and the sums thereof. We will discuss numerology at length in Lesson V, where we will examine how words may be interpreted by number.

Gematria is closely related to Cabala. Both gematria and Cabala are metaphysical systems developed primarily by Jewish mystics, who elaborated upon the ideas of the great Greek teacher Pythagoras, which strongly influenced Judaism during the Hellenistic and Roman periods. The principal Greek form of word interpretation is called *isopsephos*.

Isopsephos is also highly numerological. In isopsephos, we consider the numerological value of words not only on the basis of the meaning of the number value, but also by comparing words whose numerological value is the same, to find correspondences between words and thus expand upon their meaning (this will be discussed further in Lesson V). However, by extension, the comparison of letter values between words might also be considered a kind of isopsephos. Thus we might look for correspondences between words based upon their containing the same letters or the same groups of letters, and thus having similar qualities.

In this way, the word *letter* and the word *better* will be seen to have similar isopsephic properties, based upon possession of similar letters and groups of letters, though not a full correspondence because the initial letters differ. Here the word *letter* may be said to have connotations of creativity, personal expression, communication, strong cooperation, new beginnings, and overcoming obstacles. The word *better* may be said to have connotations of nurturing, passivity, communication, strong cooperation, new beginnings, and overcoming obstacles, the letter *B* representing focus on the needs of others.

Here follow a list of the meanings of individual letters in the Latin alphabet, which you may use as a guide to interpreting words and names by letter value.

A: The qualities of the letter *A* are ambition, leadership, initiative, self-knowledge, strength of character, integrity, and self-control.

The negative qualities of *A* are a tendency to be egotistical and self-important.

B: The qualities of the letter *B* include concern for others, nurturing, charity, receptivity, reticence, fixed ideas, and a preference for reaction over action.

The negative qualities of *B* are secrecy and deception.

C: The qualities of the letter *C* focus on communication, self-expression, creativity, and self-absorption.

The negative qualities of *C* include shallowness and the dissipation of energies.

D: The qualities of the letter *D* are conservative, self-limiting, concerned with safety and security, loyal, hardworking, and dependable. *D*s tend to create unnecessary limitations for themselves, especially if there is more than one *D* in a name or word. *D*s usually benefit from stretching their boundaries.

The negative qualities of *D* are stubbornness, unwillingness to move or change, and a tendency toward depression.

E: The qualities of the letter *E* focus on words and communication, personal expression, freedom, and expansion. A double *E* in a word gives a quality of extreme expansionism and progressive ideas.

The negative qualities of *E* are extravagance, impracticality, ungroundedness, and a tendency to overthink things.

F: The qualities of the letter *F* deal with duty, responsibility, and caretaking. *F* is orderly, supportive, and organized. *F* also deals with issues of structure and practicality.

The negative qualities of *F* are overwork and a tendency to self-righteousness.

G: The qualities of the letter *G* include desire for understanding, examination and interpretation, precision and perfectionism, inner seeking and self-improvement. *G* is idealistic, meditative, and questioning.

The negative qualities of *G* include being overly critical, hard to please, and intolerant of imperfection.

H: The qualities of the letter *H* include inner and outer growth, desire for self-expansion and accomplishment, intellectual and spiritual curiosity, and personal self-control.

The negative qualities of *H* are being overly demanding, possessive, and having a tendency to be judgmental.

I: The qualities of the letter *I* are focus, concentration, self-direction, ability to achieve and accomplish, and connection to the Higher Self. When *I* is at the beginning of a name or word, it indicates focus upon a goal in process. When *I* is found at the end of a word, it indicates the achievement of a goal.

The negative qualities of *I* are a tendency to be self-centered and to expect too much from others.

J: The qualities of the letter *J* focus on intelligence, practicality, knowledge, memory, and the ability to use all of these traits in a constructive manner. *J* can envision and create what it desires, with little need for assistance.

The negative qualities of *J* include self-centeredness and dishonesty.

K: The qualities of the letter *K* focus upon mastery of self, inner balance, and issues of internal and external control.

The negative qualities of *K* are over-focus, nervous strain, and impatience with interference or delay.

L: The qualities of the letter *L* are creativity, self-expression, artistry, empathy, intuition, optimism, warmth, impartiality, and a tendency to do things with extreme passion and drive.

The negative qualities of *L* include indecisiveness, playing both sides against the middle, and impatience with distraction.

M: The qualities of the letter *M* include the ability to guide and teach others, practicality, protectiveness, nurturing of people or projects, and willingness to focus upon the needs of others. *M* is said to be the letter of the Mother Goddess, its shape representing her nurturing breasts. It is the thirteenth letter of all Indo-European alphabets, and the word for *mother* in most languages begins with *M*.

The negative qualities of *M* include overprotectiveness and inability to see differing points of view.

N: The qualities of the letter *N* have to do with cleansing and purification, personal and spiritual growth, releasing the old to make way for the new, spiritual initiation and spiritual

teaching, and balance of inner and outer self.

The negative qualities of *N* include strong emotions and sensuality, which may tend to be overwhelming.

O: The qualities of the letter *O* focus upon responsibility and practicality, stability, family, security, material success, and money. *O* is acquisitive and protective.

The negative qualities of *O* include jealousy, possessiveness, and resentment of others.

P: The qualities of the letter *P* focus upon persuasiveness, ability to use communication to get one's way, concentration, mental strength, magical ability, curiosity, and desire for growth and expansion.

The negative qualities of *P* include stubbornness and a tendency to force one's will upon others.

Q: The qualities of the letter *Q* include balance, centeredness, psychic ability, connection to Spirit, and integration of masculine and feminine elements.

The negative qualities of *Q* are difficulty in taking action, overcoming inertia, and a tendency to need a push from others to get moving.

R: The qualities of the letter *R* include rebirth and new beginnings, spiritual

growth and overcoming obstacles, and release of the old to make way for new growth.

The negative qualities of R include frustration and overemotionality, which result if one fights against necessary release.

S: The qualities of the letter S focus on individuality, self-reliance, self-direction, self-expression, creativity, sensitivity, psychic receptivity, and the ability to see below surfaces. The letter S also deals with sudden changes and also sudden inspirations.

The negative qualities of S are overconfidence and disinterest in others.

T: The qualities of the letter T focus on cooperation, concern for others, altruism, and the desire for and ability to make peace.

The negative qualities of T include oversensitivity and inability to deal with distractions.

U: The qualities of the letter U include emotional sensitivity, inspiration, creativity, and high ideals. U tends to hide the inner feelings behind a façade, which may vary with the audience.

The negative qualities of U include being double-faced, indecisive, overly hesitant, and easily annoyed.

V: The qualities of the letter V center on the idea of making connections between things: people, ideas, resources. V is practical, cooperative, and good at getting things done.

The negative qualities of V are emotional insecurity and a tendency to overreach.

W: The qualities of the letter W include emotionality, sensuality, intensity, and a strong need for freedom from all restriction. W in a name or a word also indicates flashes of inspiration and enlightenment.

The negative qualities of W are indulgence and dissipation.

X: The qualities of the letter X are those of high idealism, charity, and desire to improve the world.

The negative qualities of X are egocentrism and such an attachment to one's ideals as to have difficulty seeing other points of view.

Y: The qualities of the letter Y focus on the idea of separation between the spiritual and the material, which is, of course, an illusion. Y indicates the need to integrate the spiritual and the material together, to bring spirituality into daily life and greater "earthiness" into spirituality. Y shows a need for meditation and for working with the Higher Self, but also the need not to rarify the spiritual experience.

The negative qualities of *Y* include the illusion of separation between spirit and matter, difficulty in balancing these, and a tendency to be overly inward-focusing.

Z: The qualities of the letter *Z* include the ability to understand motivations, to see below the surface of things, to gather and systematize knowledge. To uncover secrets and discover the inner nature of things.

The negative qualities of *Z* include a tendency to be too focused, too determined, so that other aspects of life suffer.

• • • •

Other Alphabets

There are, of course, many other alphabets in the world beside the Latin alphabet. Many of these are used as magical alphabets. These include ancient alphabets once in common use, such as the runes, and ancient pictographic systems, such as Egyptian hieroglyphics, which have been adapted to alphabetic use. Alphabets such as the Enochian and Theban alphabets were created specifically to be magical alphabets and have never been used for any other purpose.

"But," you might say, "of what possible use are magical alphabets in the modern world?"

Well, it is certainly true that the primary use of magical alphabets in past times is both unnecessary and even a bit silly today—that is, as a cipher to keep information secret. In the past, adepts used magical alphabets to hide their knowledge from the uninitiated, which, in most instances, would be considered counterproductive today. Magical alphabets were also used to hide information, and especially identities, from the forces of unfriendly powers, such as the INQUISITION, a situation which no longer exists today.

Other uses of magical alphabets remain relevant, however, such as in the writing of spells and sacred documents, and the decoration of robes and altar furnishings. Through uses like these, magical alphabets can create a magical atmosphere, serving as a key to help induce a shift of consciousness, which you learned about way back in Lesson I, First Degree. The use of magical alphabets as decoration on robes and magical tools not only helps to put one into a magical mindset, but it can also help one to connect to knowledge gained in past lives, where the alphabets in question were used. An example of this would be using items decorated with hieroglyphics when trying to connect to knowledge from Egyptian lifetimes. If you are drawn to a particular

	A	Aped, the eagle
	A	Ah, the forearm; pl Awi
	B	Beh, the leg
	C	Kehen, the cup
	D	Det, the hand
	E	Eyahit, the plant
	F	Fennu, the slug
	G	Ga, the vessel
	H	Hebsit, cloth
	I	Eyaht, the plants
	J	Jaht, the serpent
	K	Kehen, the cup
	L	Ru, the lion
	M	M'sha, the owl
	N	Nui, the waters
	O	Oahr, the rope
	P	Pat, the seat/mat
	Q	Qaa, the hill
	R	Re, the mouth
	S	Sebseba, the fillet
	T	Ta, the loaf
	Th	Thit, the tying cord
	U	Uahr, the newborn chick
	W	Uahr, the newborn chick
	Y	Eyaht, the plants
	Z	Zhat, the door-bolt

The basic phonetic symbols used in hieroglyphics.

magical alphabet for no apparent reason, you have probably used it in past lifetimes.

Another virtue some find in the use of magical alphabets is in spellwork. When a written component of a spell is written in a magical alphabet rather than in the Latin alphabet, it forces the spellworker to concentrate more upon what they are writing, since it must be "translated" from the Latin alphabet used in everyday life to the less-familiar magical alphabet. Some people find that this increases their mental concentration and thus adds more energy to the spell.

Hieroglyphics

Although hieroglyphics are not actually an alphabet but rather a pictographic system, they have since, early on, had alphabetic functions. That is to say, certain signs came to stand for certain sounds and were used alphabetically.

The hieroglyphic system included several categories of signs. There were signs with alphabetic meanings, which were used to spell words phonetically just as we do with an alphabet—for example, an owl stood for the sound "M." There were also signs with syllabic meanings, which stood for single syllables, which might be words themselves as well as part of other words. For example, a goose stood for the syllable "sa," which was also the word *son*. And, of course, there were symbols that stood for

whole words, which is how the system originated. For example, a lute-like instrument stood for the word *nefer*, meaning "good, pleasant, or beautiful." All three types of signs were used together. In addition, many words included a determinative sign at the end, which helped determine what a word meant, since many words were spelled alike or very similarly. Thus, the word *sat*, meaning "daughter," might be spelled out with a goose (the syllable "sa"), a loaf (the letter *T*), and the image of a woman, to indicate that a woman was being referred to instead of any synonym of "sat."

The development of writing belongs, as you might expect, to the Age of Gemini (4400–2800 BC). The Mesopotamians were using clay symbols to represent objects for tallying and recordkeeping as early as 1200 Virgo (8000 BC). These symbols were small clay tokens with distinctive shapes that represented goods and were used to indicate the quantity of a given item. These were particularly used in commerce, where the tokens were sealed inside clay packages to indicate how much of an item was being bought or sold. A drawing was made on top of the package to indicate how many tokens it contained. These packages served as a kind of contract and as a record of the transaction. In time, the package was dispensed with, and only the picture was used. Eventually, people began to use pictures to represent many other

Lesson
IV

things as well. This kind of pictographic or ideogrammatic writing was in use by 1100 Gemini (3300 BC) in both Mesopotamia and Egypt, and from that time on, it developed separately in both cultures.

Hieroglyphics make their first appearance around 1100 Gemini (3300 BC). Unlike Mesopotamia, there was no history of symbols being used before this for records or anything else—that we know of, at least. This is one reason why hieroglyphics are generally thought to have been inspired by Mesopotamian cuneiform. However, hieroglyphics were clearly not just copied from cuneiform, as the two systems do not share sign meanings, nor do they much resemble each other even in their most basic form. For this reason, most people think that the Egyptians became familiar with the cuneiform system, presumably through trade, and then independently created their own system. A few people think that while cuneiform was already developed as a record-keeping system, it was the Egyptians who first used symbols for writing ideas, and that the Mesopotamians then adopted the idea from them.

Egyptian hieroglyphics were certainly the first magical alphabet. By 1500 Gemini (2900 BC), the Egyptians developed the hieratic system of writing. This might be best described as cursive hieroglyphics.

While the hieroglyphic system was developed for carving, hieratic was developed specifically for writing on papyrus, a kind of paper made from the fibers of the abundant papyrus plant. Soon hieratic was used for ordinary writing, and hieroglyphics was reserved for formal subjects.

By the time Egypt came to be ruled by foreign dynasties late in its history, its culture began to decline and become classicizing and rigid. Hieroglyphics became the preserve of the priesthood and were no longer understood by ordinary people. At this point, hieroglyphics had become a purely magical alphabet. The last hieroglyphic inscription was made in 1594 Aries (AD 394), in a time of increasing anti-Pagan persecution by the now-Christian Roman emperors. After this, the meaning of the hieroglyphic symbols was forgotten.

Hieroglyphics were not deciphered again for over a thousand years. In 1399 Pisces (AD 1799), the famous Rosetta stone was discovered during Napoleon's campaign in Egypt. The Rosetta stone includes copies of the same proclamation praising Pharaoh Ptolemy V in Greek, demotic Egyptian, and hieroglyphics. Scholars at once knew that the Rosetta stone was the key to deciphering hieroglyphics, but it would take many years for this to happen. The French linguist Jean-François Chompollion worked from 1408 till 1422 Pisces (AD 1808 till 1822) to decipher the

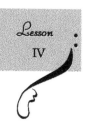

inscription, working only through copies, without ever seeing the stone itself.

The table on page 126 contains the basic phonetic symbols used in hieroglyphics, which can be used as you would use an alphabet. There are a few that we have not included, but these are the most common ones. There is neither time nor space for us to include either syllabic symbols, of which there are very many, or those symbols that stand for words, of which there are also very many. If you wish to learn these things, you will need to do further research.

Divination with Hieroglyphics

Hieroglyphics were certainly never used for divination in ancient Egypt, but they are sometimes used for divination today. A number of Egyptian-based divination systems are available, which no ancient Egyptian would ever recognize. However, as we aren't ancient Egyptians, we need not be limited to what they knew or did.

The following system is a fairly easy form of hieroglyphic divination. Each of the phonetic hieroglyphs is assigned a meaning. These meanings can be used gematrically to augment the interpretation of hieroglyphic words or purely for divination. The symbols can be drawn on cards or incised on plaster or wood lots, then drawn at random or laid out in patterns like tarot spreads. Or they could be

arranged in a circle and read with the aid of a pendulum held over the center. There are many potential variations.

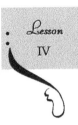

The names given for the symbols are based upon modern assumptions; we have no idea what, if anything, the ancient Egyptians called individual hieroglyphs. The names have been rendered phonetically to aid in pronunciation. It should be noted, incidentally, that no one knows how the ancient Egyptian language was pronounced; all attempts to reconstruct it are educated guesses, and by no means do they all agree.

Aped—The Eagle: Aped indicates the need to have emotional distance in a situation, to step back from it and not get caught up. Aped indicates that the emotions of the moment may be blinding one, and that it is necessary to look at one's situation as from a distance.

Ah—The Forearm (pl. Awi): Ah indicates receiving something positive: a gift of fate, the help of another, things falling into place unexpectedly and through no effort of one's own.

Beh—The Leg: Beh indicates travel, movement, and influences from other locations.

Kehen—The Cup: Kehen indicates pleasure, enjoyment, good friends, and positive situations. Happiness.

Det—The Hand: Det indicates personal skill and ability, being able to do whatever one wants in the situation and making the situation into whatever one wants it to be.

Eyahit—The Plant: Eyahit indicates growth, expansion, and being very busy with many projects. Creativity and self-expression.

Fennu—The Slug: Fennu indicates slow movement and the need for patience. Let the situation develop at its own pace, which is likely to be slow. Things need to fall into place before they can move forward.

Ga—The Vessel: Ga indicates change, transformation, and development from one thing to another: Ga will be seen to be a cooking vessel, with a stylized flame at its base. Just as cooking in a stew pot changes diverse ingredients into a coherent dish, so Ga represents the development of a situation from chaos to order.

Hebsit—Cloth: Hebsit indicates cleansing, releasing, letting go of the old to make way for the new. The need not to hold on to what one has outgrown.

Eyaht—The Plants: Eyaht indicates being overextended, having too much to do, too many obligations, having taken on too much: the need to cut back, to simplify one's life.

Jaht—The Serpent: Jaht indicates power and authority, whether of a person or an institution. Jaht indicates the need to take a humble role in the situation and work within a system controlled by others.

Ru—The Lion: Ru indicates bravery, courage, self-confidence; the strength to face every situation and stand up to every challenge. (The Egyptian language had no "L" and only adapted this symbol to serve for "L" in late times to translate foreign words.)

M'sha—The Owl: M'Sha indicates wisdom, insight, knowledge: having an overview of a situation and seeing it clearly.

Nui—The Waters: Nui indicates that Deity is guiding one, and that one should relax and go with it, even if the destination is not yet clear. Divine providence.

Oahr—The Rope: Oahr indicates unseen problems, obstacles, or challenges. One must be careful and should take a second look at the situation to try to see what was missed at first glance.

Pat—The Seat (Mat): Pat indicates the help and support of others: friends, family, associates. Good advice or aid from others will help the querent.

Qaa—The Hill: Qaa indicates challenges and difficulties: what is desired may be possible but will take much effort to attain. An uphill battle.

Re—The Mouth: Re indicates communication, meetings, and working out details with others.

Sebseba—The Fillet: Sebseba indicates success, positive attention, and admiration of others: the reward of effort. Honor, recognition.

Ta—The Loaf: Ta indicates taking care of others, fulfilling duties or requirements in a situation, attending to necessary details, and making sure that what needs to be done gets done. Doing one's part to make the situation successful.

Thit—The Tying Cord: Thit indicates wealth and prosperity: having the things one desires.

Uahr—The Newborn Chick: Uahr indicates new beginnings, new directions, new doors opening. Opportunity and potential.

Zhat—The Door-bolt: Zhat indicates safety and protection. Nothing in the situation will harm the individual or damage them in any way, so they should have no fear.

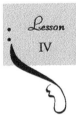

• • • •
Runes

The term *rune* can be used to describe any magical marking or form of writing, and you will encounter the word used thusly, especially in older works. However, the term *runes* is most often used today to refer to the ancient Germanic alphabet. This alphabet, which is also sometimes called Futhark after its initial letters, or the Futhark runes, was developed in northern Europe sometime around 1200 Aries (AD Year 1) using the Latin and Greek alphabets as models. It is generally thought that the runic alphabet was developed in Denmark, where the oldest-known inscriptions are found. The runic alphabet was used throughout Scandinavia and Germania over a period of many hundreds of years. Viking adventurers carried the alphabet far and wide in their travels.

There are many variations on the runic alphabet, as is to be expected in an alphabet so long in use. The form we are using here are the Germanic runes. The runes are very rectilinear in form, because they were developed to be carved, rather than written. And indeed, many runic inscriptions carved in stone have survived; there are 3,000 in Sweden alone. Other inscriptions carved in more perishable materials such as wood or ivory are more rare. Often, the runes appear to have been painted with red paint after being carved, presumably to magically empower them, for one of the chief uses of runes was for magic.

The original runes were divided into three *Aettir*, or groups of eight, whose meanings were considered to be related. The first of the Aettir belonged to Freya, the second to Hagal, and the third to Tyr.

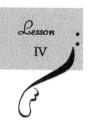

In latter centuries, the runes underwent a number of reorganizations and transformations. Beginning about 200 Pisces (AD 600), two strikingly different traditions took shape. The Germanic tribes of England and western Europe began to expand the runic alphabet to better fit the needs of their language, which would eventually become English. Meanwhile, the Germanic peoples of Scandinavia were doing the opposite, reducing both the number and the shape of their runes. However, the Scandinavians so simplified the runes that they became inadequate for writing their language and so had to then create new runes to replace the runes they had discarded. The most extreme of these unwieldy "simplifications" are the so-called "staveless runes," which removed the vertical elements (staves) of many of the runes, leaving them extremely difficult to read.

It is interesting to note that those who worked with runes were known as *Vitka* or *Witka*, a term which may be related to the word *Witch*, and which forms all or part of the name of several Wiccan traditions.

Divination with Runes

In recent years, divination with runes has become extremely popular. Though runes were certainly used in magic by the ancient Germanic peoples, it is a subject of debate whether or not the runes were used for divination. Most people feel that the use of runes for divination is a modern practice, but that certainly does not make it in any way illegitimate.

Most people who use runes for divination have a set of runestones, actual stones, or lots made from wood or plaster upon which the individual symbols of the runic alphabet have been painted or carved. The querent may be asked to randomly draw these stones from a bag or basket to get the answer to their question. The rune reader may simply ask for a runestone or number of runestones, which are then read according to their meaning, or the runestones may be laid out in patterns similar to tarot spreads. Indeed, runes are now available as cards, which are read much as one reads tarot cards. This is by far the most common method of reading runes today.

Another way that runestones may be read is to have the querent ask their question and meditate over the runestones for a few moments. The reader then throws the runestones onto a special diagram, using all the runes at once and interpreting by where and how they fall. In one version of this style, the diagram resembles a bull's— eye, and how close to or far from the center the runestones land indicates various aspects of the answer, notably timing. In addition, whether the runestones are face-up or face-down adds to the answer: some reading only face-up runestones, others reading face-up as positive applications of the runestone's meaning and face-down as negative applications of the runestone's meaning.

A third method of reading runes is by casting long, narrow sticks. The patterns formed by the sticks when they fall will be read according to which runes they resemble.

As has been remarked, there are many versions of the runic alphabet; here is a commonly encountered version of Germonic Futhark:

Ⅴ (F): Called Fehu, meaning "cattle," this rune represents money, prosperity, and success.

Ⅾ (U): Called Uruz, referring to the "aurochs," an ancient kind of wild cattle, this rune means strength of will, determination, and perseverance.

Ⅾ (Th): Called Thurisaz, meaning "giant," this rune indicates a time of waiting before progress can occur. A time to reexamine and reassess one's situations and to gather the tools one needs for the time coming when things will move forward.

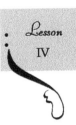

Ⅰ (A): Called Ansuz, meaning "god," a title of Odin, this rune represents wisdom, insight, and self-mastery; having within yourself the knowledge you need to get what you want from the situation.

Ⅰ (R): Called Raidu, meaning "chariot," this rune indicates communication, messages, getting to the truth of situations, and constructive interaction with others.

Ⅰ (K): Called Kenaz, meaning "inflammation," this rune means disappointment or dissatisfaction with a situation, a need to heal or fix something.

Ⅹ (G): Called Gebo, meaning "gift," this rune represents receiving or achieving something you have wanted, having your desire, a goal accomplished.

Ⅾ (W): Called Wunjo, or "joy," this rune represents happiness, pleasure, and having many blessings.

Ⅰ (H): Called Hagalaz, meaning "hail," this rune represents situations beyond one's control, setbacks, delays, and the need for clearer understanding before proceeding.

Ⅰ (N): Called Nauthiz, meaning "need," this rune indicates the need not to be overwhelmed by one's emotions and fears, but rather to step back and more coolly assess the situation—

which may not be nearly as bad as it first seems.

ᛁ **(I):** Called Isaz, meaning "ice," this rune represents lack of movement, situations at a standstill, and inability to move forward at this time.

ᛃ **(J):** Called Jara, meaning "year," this rune represents prosperity and good fortune.

ᛇ **(E):** Called Eiwaz, meaning "yew tree," this rune represents the end of a problem, a positive change in situation, and overcoming adversity.

ᛈ **(P):** Called Pertha, meaning "fruit tree," this rune represents positive effects from fate, chance happenings, and unexpected benefit or gain.

ᛉ **(Z):** Called Algiz, meaning the "European elk" (which is also the American moose), this rune shows success through effort, the overcoming of obstacles, the achievement of one's goals despite difficulty or opposition. It indicates that effort will be required but success can be had.

ᛋ **(S):** Called Sowelu, meaning "sun," this rune represents change, reversal of circumstances, change of plans; current conditions will pass away and be replaced by very different, perhaps unexpected ones.

ᛏ **(T):** Called Tiwaz, the god of war who gives his name to Tuesday, this rune means victory, success in one's situations, overcoming of opposition, and achievement of one's desires.

ᛒ **(B):** Called Berkana, meaning "birch tree" (a symbol of the Goddess), this rune represents healing, regeneration, and new beginnings.

ᛖ **(E):** Called Ehwaz, meaning "horse," this rune means travel and movement.

ᛗ **(M):** Called Manaz, meaning "human," this rune indicates another person influencing the situation, giving advice or support, or perhaps offering opportunities.

ᛚ **(L):** Called Laguz, meaning "lake," this rune represents intuition, the ability to see below the surface of things, psychic guidance, and looking within. Some authorities, notably Dr. James Peterson, consider the original meaning of this rune to have been not Laguz/lake but Lakz, meaning "leek," giving the rune a greater protective quality.

(Ng): Called Inwaz, a title of the god Freyr, this rune means peace, prosperity, and support from those around one; being in a good situation.

ᛞ **(D):** Called Dagaz, meaning "day," this rune indicates sudden realization or inspiration, new ideas or new opportunities.

⚷ **(O):** Called Othala, meaning "ancestral home," this rune means that you should rely on your own skills, tools, and qualities in dealing with the situation at hand, rather than looking for help from outside.

In modern use, rune readers often include as part of their runes a blank rune. If drawn, the blank rune means that the situation is in the hands of Fate, and the querent should not try to rush a conclusion or force their will upon it but allow the situation to develop and unfold at its own pace.

. . . .

Ogham

Ogham (pronounced O-uhm or Oh-yam) is believed to have been invented by the Irish Celts around 1500 Aries (AD 300), though some place its development closer to 1200 Aries (AD 1). Markings similar to Ogham have been found on standing stones in northern Spain and Portugal dating to 700 Aries (500 BC), but their relationship to Ogham is unclear.

Ogham is a comparatively simple alphabet, composed of vertical and diagonal lines drawn above and below a central baseline. It is thought that the Celts adopted the concept of an alphabet from the Romans, but the form of the Ogham alphabet is entirely original.

It is generally thought that Ogham was developed from a system of hand signs, and that the letters indicate how many fingers should be pointing up or down, and on which or both hands, to represent a certain sound. In this sense, Ogham is absolutely unique and superbly fitted for silent communication. It is possible that the druids may have used Ogham as a sign language long before developing the written form.

Ogham was obviously meant to be carved; it is not especially well suited to being written. The baseline is necessary to understand the letters, and often in inscriptions the baseline is formed by the edge of the stone or wood being carved on, with the upper lines on one side of the edge and the lower lines on the other.

In Celtic mythology, Ogham was invented by the hero god Ogmios, who was also known as Maponos, Mabon, and Aengus Og. This is the ithyphallic young god that the Romans identified with Hercules. The name *Ogham* probably derives from Ogmios.

At first, knowledge of Ogham was restricted to the druids, the priestly caste of the Celts, who used it for religious purposes. Over time, however, Ogham came to be used by ordinary people as well, for more mundane purposes. To keep their own writings secret, the druids then created secret codes to use with Ogham.

Possibly because of druidic secret codes, possibly because of ordinary regional variations, there are several forms of the Ogham alphabet. Some make use of dots as well as lines. Others include extra letters formed by crossed lines. We have included the simplest, and we think purest, form.

Ogham is also sometimes called *Bethluisnion*, after the first, second, and fifth letters of the alphabet: Beth, Luis, and Nuin. The term *Bethluisnion* was coined during the Pagan revival of the late 1400s Pisces (AD 1800s).

Another name for Ogham is the "tree alphabet" because each of the letters is named for a tree or plant. Many people who have little or no knowledge of its historical origins have come to know Ogham as the tree alphabet.

Ogham was a latecomer to the history of the Celts, and its use was limited to the British Isles. Nonetheless, it can be very useful as a magical alphabet, especially when silence is desired.

Divination with Ogham

Although it does not appear that Ogham was used for divinatory purposes in ancient times, it has certainly been adapted to divinatory use in modern times. This is usually done with cards bearing the individual Ogham letters.

Each letter is named for a tree, upon whose qualities the divinatory qualities of the letter are based. The letters are:

B, Beth, "Birch": Beth represents the Mother Goddess, spirituality, purification.

L, Luis, "Rowan": Luis represents protection, safety, stability.

F, Fearn, "Alder": Fearn represents movement, flexibility, going with the flow.

S, Saille, "Willow": Saille represents balance, harmony, natural cycles in situations.

N, Nuin, "Ash": Nuin represents rebirth, new beginnings, new directions.

H, Huath, "Hawthorn": Huath represents the Maiden Goddess, sexuality, fertility, growth.

D, Duire, "Oak": Duire represents the Lover God who dies and is reborn; also initiation, growth, expansion.

T, Tinne, "Holly": Tinne represents courage, leadership, responsibility.

C, Coll, "Hazel": Coll represents the psychic arts, ability to see below the surface of things, insight and inspiration.

Q, Quert, "Apple": Quert represents rebirth, reincarnation, new forms, new situations, changes.

M, Muin, "Bramble": Muin represents learning, knowledge, understanding.

G, Gort, "Ivy": Gort represents difficulty, obstruction, lack of what is needed.

Ng, Ngetal, "Reed": Ngetal represents memory, knowledge, inheritance from the past.

St, Straif, "Blackthorn": Straif represents karmic justice, challenges, obstructions.

R, Ruis, "Elder": Ruis represents the Crone Goddess, magic, the spirit world.

A, Ailm, "Elm": Ailm represents overcoming obstacles, insight, healing of situations.

O, On, "Gorse": On represents fertility, growth, expansion.

U, Ur, "Heather": Ur represents luck, new opportunities, new beginnings.

E, Eadha, "Aspen": Eadha represents stubbornness, rigidity, difficulty in accepting change and the need to do so.

I, Ioh, "Yew": Ioh represents situations about to change, potential, release of old forms. It is said that Ioh represents the final day of the old year, or the intercalary days between years.

• • • •

The Correllian Alphabet

The Correllian alphabet was designed in the mid 1570s Pisces (AD 1970s) at the request of the beloved Regent LaVeda. It was intended to serve both as a code—for the writing of secret records—and for decorative purposes. Of course, it can also be used for writing sacred and magical documents, serving to help focus the writer's attention and energies.

The Correllian alphabet will be seen to be extremely rectilinear and heavily square. It will be remembered that four is the number of physical manifestation, and thus the square is the shape of manifestation as well as practicality, and practicality is one of the cornerstones of Correllian ideology.

The Correllian alphabet is meant to be written in vertical rows, as shown here, rather than horizontal rows. The alphabet can be written horizontally as well; however, over the twenty-five-odd years of its use, the methods for using it horizontally have varied. The current recommendation for using the alphabet horizontally is to turn the letters on their sides, so that in effect you have a vertical row that has just been turned sideways. The reason that vertical columns were chosen when the alphabet was designed was to facilitate its use in the Correllian state robes—which at that time featured a central CLAVIS, or vertical stripe. However, the alphabet is only rarely used on the state robes today.

The alphabet features forty letters, which include a variety of vowels and diphthongs that are represented differently than in English. This is to be born in mind when translating to or from this alphabet—words are spelled more or less phonetically with the Correllian alphabet. However, there have never been any hard-and-fast rules, and certain inscriptions you may see in older Correllian regalia or artwork sometimes simply use the common English spelling of words.

To make the alphabet more legible, word dividers are used between each word so that the letters do not run together. Usually the word divider resembles the English letter *I*, but again there has been variation over the years, and occasionally you may see older Correllian inscriptions where the words are divided by simple dots.

To help illustrate the use of the Correllian alphabet, let us here present a few familiar names rendered in their Correllian form:

	R		R
	e		e
	v		v
	D		e
	o		d
	n		
			H
	L		u
	e		b
	w		b
	i		er
	s		d

or more calligraphically to the right:

Divination with the Correllian Alphabet

Like the other magical alphabets discussed above, the Correllian alphabet can also be used for divination. Each letter has a meaning: the meanings can be used for gematria, or for divinatory reading.

There are a number of ways to divine with the Correllian alphabet. The most obvious is to inscribe the forty letters on forty slips of paper or on lots of wood, plaster, or stone (à la runes). You would then ask your question and draw at random for your answer, interpreting the answer according to the meaning of the letter drawn. You could, of course, also draw without a specific question, simply to see what the universe has to tell you.

Another method is to draw three or more lots and read them all together, averaging their meanings into a single answer.

If by chance the letters should also spell a word, this would also be part of your answer. For example, if the letters you drew spelled "d-o-g," you might interpret the answer as having to do with your understanding of the word "dog"—for example, issues of loyalty or dependence.

A different method is to arrange the letters in a circle, and use a pendulum. Ask your question, and whatever letter the pendulum swings to is your answer.

Of course, as with tarot or the Chinese I CHING, these methods of divination require practice with interpretation, since most of the basic meanings can assume a number of variations, depending upon the question or circumstances.

X ("f") **Crossroad:** Decisions, choices, changes, need to move forward.

X| ("v") **A Person at the Crossroad:** Ability to make one's own decisions.

X|| ("b") **Many People at the Crossroad:** Chaos, confusion, uncertainty.

∏ ("p") **Fence:** Claiming your due, getting what you want, justice, reward of effort.

— ("k") **Path:** Swift movements, sudden developments.

⌐ ("t") **Single Bed:** Independence, standing on your own two feet, having all you need to do whatever needs to be done.

⊒ ("x") **Double Bed:** Love, support, fellowship.

╪ ("g") **Telephone Pole:** Messages, receiving communications, information.

╪ ("j") **Spine, Skeleton:** Transformation, release of old for new; may register as loss or disappointment, but brings new possibilities as well.

⊢ ("y" as in yellow) City Gate: Conscious control of one's environment, choosing one's companions and/or surroundings, setting life to order.

⊩ ("d") City Wall: Protection, security, stability. Can also indicate reticence and a tendency to hold back.

⊫ ("h") Side Streets: Knowing what to do, having a plan, having an overview of the situation, making needed connections.

⌐ ("er") East Wall: Think the situation through. Meditate. New ideas and inspiration.

∟ ("uh") West Wall: Help others, give of yourself. Love, charity, kindness, a helping hand.

⌐ ("oo" as in smooth) North Wall: Keep what is yours. Consolidate, integrate.

⌐ ("oo" as in took) South Wall: Do what you know you should do, take action, do not hold back; you have the necessary knowledge, put it into practice.

⊓ ("aw") One Leading Another: Eloquence, skillful communication, teaching.

⊓‖ ("ah" as in father, but also used as the final "a" in names like "Anna" or "Livia") One Leading Many: Persuasion, salesmanship, force of will.

⊐ ("ow") Bedroom: Inner self, inner emotions, privacy, protection.

⊔ (short "a" as in apple) House: Stability, home, family, security, comfort, happiness.

⊟ (long "a" as in ale) Two-Story House: Wealth, prosperity, good fortune.

⊟ ("eh" as in element) Palace: Power, authority, influence, dominance over situation.

⋂ ("o") The God: Action, achievement, remaking situation as you want it; taking action. (On an existential level, this represents the ongoing process of creation, God/dess's descent into matter.)

< ("ee" as in eagle) River: Relax, trust, go with the flow. Spirit will provide. (On an existential level, this represents the ever-flowing energy of the universe/Spirit—the Tao, if you would.)

⊲ ("ih" as in Illinois) One in the River: Looking within. Spiritual guidance, inner growth. Dependence on Spirit. (On an existential level, this represents the soul's journey from matter back to Spirit through incarnation.)

○ ("i" as in eye) Goddess: Love, compassion, understanding. Approach the situation from within. (On an existential level, this represents Spirit, the origin and ultimate nature of the soul.)

⋀ **("r") Man Leading Woman:** Worldly concerns, ambition, focus on the material. (On an existential level, this represents matter dominating Spirit.)

⋀ **("oi" as in oil) Woman Leading Man:** Spiritual and emotional concerns. Harmony, equality, peace. (On an existential level, this represents Spirit dominating matter.)

∪ **("m") The Valley:** Easy tasks, little effort needed for success, good luck. Being in harmony with Spirit. (The valley also carries the connotation of the sacred yoni, and thus is another reference to Goddess/Spirit.)

∩ **("n") The Mountain:** Obstacles, blockages, challenges. Need to stop fighting the situation and go with the flow. (The mountain also carries the connotation of the sacred lingam, and thus is a reference to the God/Matter.)

∩| **("ng" as in king) One Before the Mountain:** Overcoming obstacles, meeting challenges, effort brings success.

⊐ **("s" as in sack) The Seat:** Education, knowledge, learning. (A seat is literally a chair or place to sit, but in this

sense also connotes a rank or office, as a "seated high priest/ess" who is a member of the Witan council or the "county seat" of a landed squire.)

ⵝ **("z" as in zoo) The Throne:** Responsibility, duty, teaching.

▯| **("sh" as in shift) One Before the Gate:** Change, new beginnings, unexpected developments, facing the unknown.

▯|| **(soft "th" as in them) Many Before the Gate:** Changes around one.

|▯ **(hard "th" as in three) One Inside the Gate:** Fear of change. Stubbornness. Rigidity.

||▯ **("ch" as in chess) Many Inside the Gate:** Social censure. Fear of others' disapproval. Others' opinions influence one too much.

△ **("l") The Cone of Power:** Magic, manifestation, ability to work one's will in the situation.

▢ **("w" as in was) The Gate:** Openings, opportunities, potential.

⊢ **("ll, ly" as in caballero) The Kitchen Chair:** Rest, respite, recovery, rejuvenation.

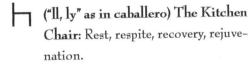

Other Magical Alphabets

There are a variety of other mystical alphabets with which you should also be acquainted. Most of these do not have such highly developed uses as the alphabets given above but are still frequently met with in metaphysical use. Several such alphabets follow.

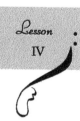

Theban: Witches' Runes

Theban runes are supposed to have been created or at least favored by Pope HONO-RIUS II, who was famous in his day as a sorcerer. For this reason they are also called the Honorian alphabet. The Theban runes are one of the few magical alphabets in common use among Ceremonial magicians that are not based on the Hebrew alphabet. It is for this reason that they are the preferred alphabet of English Traditional and Gardnerian Witches, who call them the Witches' runes. Common knowledge will tell you that the term *rune* is incorrectly applied here, but in fact the term *rune* has been used historically to refer to almost any magical alphabet or symbol, rather as the term "hieroglyphic" is used to refer to Mayan and other picto-graphic forms of writing.

Enochian

The term "Enochian" refers to a system of magic originating with DR. JOHN DEE.

Like many ancient sorcerers, Dee used a separate clairvoyant, in this case Edward Kelly, and together they channeled a great deal of information, which they identified as angelic. A Christian mystic, Dee became quite frightened when the angels informed him that Jesus was not God and that Christianity was not the One True Religion. Enochian magic takes its name from Enoch, a character in the Judeo-Christian Bible who was said to be a great sorcerer and an immortal who never died. Enochian magic is not to be confused with the equally fascinating BOOK OF ENOCH.

It should be noted that the Enochian script can be used as an alphabet as well as a syllabary, that is, each letter can be taken to stand for a full syllable rather than a single sound. Thus, if "D-O-N" is spelled out in Enochian letters, it may be read by alphabet as "Don" or by syllabary as "Dee-Oh-Ehn." Thus it will be seen that as a syllabary Enochian is unusually well-suited to use as a cipher, and indeed it is suggested that Dr. Dee used it in just that way during espionage assignments he undertook for his employer, Queen Elizabeth I.

Malachim

Another magical alphabet popular with Ceremonials.

As was mentioned earlier, most of the alphabets used by the Ceremonials were

	Theban	*Enochian*	*Malachim*	*Passing the River*	*Daggers*
A					
B					
C					
D					
E					
F					
G					
H					
I					
J					
K					
L					
M					
N					
O					
P					
Q					
R					
S					
T					
U					
V					
W					
X					
Y					
Z					

based upon the Hebrew alphabet. They therefore require a certain amount of adaptation to be used for English. This sometimes gives rise to considerable variation in the forms of the alphabet that may be encountered. In the table on page 143, for example, is an alternate form of the Malachim alphabet adapted for English use, given by RAYMOND BUCKLAND in his famous magnum opus "Big Blue," or *Buckland's Complete Book of Witchcraft*.

Passing the River

Again, an alphabet primarily used by Ceremonials, here adapted for use with English.

Daggers

This is an interesting and, in my opinion, pretty much unusable alphabet that comes from Crowley's *Equinox*. Again, it is primarily used by Ceremonials.

. . . .

This concludes our look at magical alphabets and how they are used. Whether and to what extent you use magical alphabets in your own practice is up to you. Many people are drawn to them for either past-life or aesthetic considerations. They can certainly add to mood and can be beautifully used to enhance ritual objects in ways that are both decorative and meaningful. But the reasons that gave impetus to the devel-

opment of numerous arcane alphabets and made them so popular among Ceremonials have little application to us today: secrecy and the desire for exclusiveness.

Whereas our grandparents (to a greater or lesser extent) had to hide their Pagan beliefs and metaphysical practices, we do not. We today live proudly in a New Age of tolerance and respect in which we are no longer content to be second-class citizens but rather equals; as such, secrecy does not become us.

And while there are still some temples that shroud themselves in mystery and work hard to exclude people from their meetings and membership, we (the Correllian Tradition and most other contemporary traditions) believe that spiritual knowledge should be for the benefit of all people, not just a chosen few. Not everyone will want to become a priest/ess, of course, nor should they, as it is not a path for everyone. But everyone can benefit from the knowledge contained in our religion: the nature of Spirit/Goddess and our relationship to her, the nature of the soul and of the Higher Self, what magic is and is not, etc. Thus, exclusivity of the Ceremonial type also does not become us.

What does become us is that we use our knowledge to the good of all and to the fulfillment of our soul's higher purposes. Magical alphabets can aid us in this through the many ways outlined above, which basically come down to strengthening our personal connection to our Higher Self and to God/dess. When this connection is strong we improve the world even when we're not trying, simply by expressing our highest and best self in life, not to mention all those things we consciously do as a priesthood. This, in the end, is what it's all about.

. . . .

Exercises

At this point, your daily routine should go like this: begin with the Ohm exercise, then open the chakras with balls of colored light, changing the balls of colored light to balls of white light, changing the balls of white light to balls of purple light, changing the balls of purple light to balls of silver stellar light, and then filling your aura with silver stellar light. Next, change the balls of silver stellar light to balls of golden stellar light, then fill your aura with golden stellar light. Finally, change the balls of golden stellar light to balls of amber light, and fill your aura with the amber light. Now, from each chakra project a beam of light across the room to the opposing wall, and exercise it by using it to "draw" pictures on the wall or "write" on the wall, etc.

When you can do this comfortably, you are ready for Exercise 7.

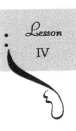
Exercise 7

Go through the whole sequence above until you come to the part where you send out beams of light from the chakras. Begin from the solar plexus and send out a beam of light as you have been doing, but instead of sending it all the way to the wall, send it to the middle of the room and let the end of the beam of light form into a person, so that it is as if you are two people joined by a beam of light from solar plexus to solar plexus. This "person" is your solar plexus chakra externalized.

Try not to control the image the chakra-person takes, but let it look any way it chooses: let it take the form it needs. For some of you this will be easy, perhaps even automatic; this means that you have done this before in other lifetimes, and are not so much learning as remembering it now. For others it will be harder. You may have to give your chakra-person their form, imagining the person in a way that conveys the qualities of the chakra. For example, the solar plexus chakra might resemble a solar deity or be dressed in yellow or be a being of golden light—however you can best work with it.

Once the image of the chakra-person has taken form and you can see it clearly, you can let the beam of light fade.

Dealing with a personified chakra is a lot like working with a spirit guide. They

145

can be surprisingly autonomous. Talk to the chakra-person, interact with it. It can answer you and give you information on the state of the chakra as well as information and advice on the various qualities and skills the chakra deals with and how best to employ or develop them. In essence, you are now personifying a part of yourself in order to better work with it in the same way that you learned to personify the Higher Self of a stone or crystal or anything else in First Degree, Lesson XII. Your chakra can now give you feedback in verbal rather than merely energetic form.

You can work with your personified chakra toward cleansing, healing, or further developing the chakra. There are also more advanced techniques, which we will discuss in future lessons.

When you are done working with your solar plexus chakra-person, allow it to come back inside you, and then close down, just as you ordinarily close your chakra. A personified chakra is still just your chakra; do not leave them open, as it will be a great drain on your energy.

Continue doing the full routine and then evoking the solar plexus chakra until it is easy for you. You are then ready to move on to Exercise 8.

Exercise 8

I doubt that you will be surprised that Exercise 8 goes on to evoke the remaining chakras. Do your whole routine, until you have evoked your solar plexus chakra-person. Then, beginning with the root chakra, evoke the remaining chakras in the same way, beginning by sending forth a beam of light, which fades when the image of the chakra-person is clearly formed.

You may not be able to do all of them at once and should not expect to. You may want to add one new chakra-person to the routine at a time, a few days apart, taking time to gain facility with each.

When you have successfully evoked all seven major chakras, do your palm chakras as well.

Remember to bring the personified chakras back inside yourself and shut them back down when you are done.

The chakra people may have any appearance, gender, race, etc. Some of them may not make sense to you now, but do not second-guess them. For example, the chakra-person of my left palm usually appears as a little person dressed as a columbine, or female clown. I have learned that when spirits appear as little people that they usually deal expressly with healing—at least, that's how they usually appear to me. And in fact my left hand is my primary healing hand, even though I tend to be mostly right-handed. Clowns are associated with Spirit and magic. Her appearance makes sense to me now, but when I first learned this exercise I didn't know these things, and I could only wonder why she appeared in this guise, but I didn't second-guess or censor the image, and you should not either.

When you can go through the whole routine, then personify all of the seven major chakras plus the two palm chakras, you will have mastered this exercise. At that point, you will be ready for Exercise 9, which will follow in the next lesson.

• • • •

Spell for Lesson IV
Magical Automatons

In our last spell, we created a golem, a magical thoughtform created for a specific purpose. In this spell, we will be creating a magical automaton. The golem is a spiritual creation intended to have an effect in the physical world. An automaton is a physical creation intended to have an effect in the spiritual world.

The purpose of an automaton is to extend and multiply the energy put into a prayer or a spell. The automaton is activated by means of physical motion, which releases the energy of the prayer/spell without further mental focus from the person who created it.

An excellent example of an automaton is the use of prayer ties. Prayer ties have been used on both sides of the Atlantic since ancient times. Basically, a length of cloth or ribbon is blessed and tied to a

tree limb to represent the person's prayer. The wind blowing through the trees then continually activates the prayer by rustling the hanging ends of the ribbon or cloth tie. The prayer tie is left on the tree until it is destroyed by the elements. The yellow ribbons often tied around trees for the sake of absent loved ones—especially prisoners, hostages, or soldiers—is the same basic idea.

A single prayer tie may be made and attached to a tree by one person, or a great number may be made and attached by many people as part of or after a ritual. At Irish sacred wells in ages past, and also still today, prayer ties would be tied to adjoining trees by pilgrims to the site, building up over time to a mass of ribbons. This can be a beautiful sight to behold and is probably one of the earliest forms of decorating trees.

Native American prayer ties often include an offering, whether at the base of the tree or in the prayer tie itself. A common example is a bit of tobacco tied in a small square of cloth and attached to the tree by the prayer tie.

Another famous example of an automaton is the prayer wheel used by Buddhists. A prayer wheel has a cylinder that spins around a handle when the prayer wheel is turned. Inside the cylinder is a prayer written out on paper and wrapped into a scroll. Sometimes the prayer is written upon the

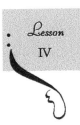

cylinder itself. The idea is that as the cylinder turns it activates the power of the prayer, just as the wind activates the prayer in a prayer tie.

In the ancient world, the priesthood of Hecate utilized a similar device, a prayer ball with sacred figures inscribed upon it at the end of a length of string or chain. The prayer ball would be spun at the end of the string, activating the energies represented by the markings.

To make an automaton, you must first assemble the needed pieces. The easiest kind of automaton to make is a prayer tie. If you are making a prayer tie, you will need a length of ribbon; any kind of ribbon will do. We would recommend also a square of cloth and an offering of some sort, along with some string.

You must also select a tree to which you will tie your completed prayer tie. You should ask the tree's permission; determine its answer through clairvoyance, through an omen, or through divination.

Use the string to tie up your offering in the square of cloth. Now take both the offering and the ribbon in your hands, or if you are doing this as part of a group, place them in the center of the circle. Focus energy into the items. Imagine them filling with energy and glowing with power. Concentrate on what you wish to have happen. Pray to God/dess for aid. Then tie the prayer tie together with the offering to the limb of the tree you have selected for the purpose.

A prayer wheel or other automaton would be blessed in the same way. The active ingredient—the prayer that will be put into the prayer wheel, for example, or the ball on the end of the prayer ball string—is blessed, then the automaton is assembled. Then whenever motion is introduced, the prayer/spell will be activated.

Of course, the perceptive student will recognize that elements of many spells could be considered automatons, and this is certainly so. It is a common-enough technique but one that bears being pointed out. Now that you know the basic idea, you can apply it in any way that seems good to you.

. . . .

Glossary

Book of Enoch—In Judeo-Christian mythology, Enoch was an early patriarch especially favored by God who was assumed bodily into heaven without experiencing physical death. The Book of Enoch was at one time a popular part of Judeo-Christian scripture, and is quoted in the New Testament as such. In the time of the Jewish philosopher Jesus, the Book of Enoch was very important, but later Christians suppressed the book, and no copies of it survived in Europe—leading to great curiosity as to what it had contained. In 1373 Pisces (AD 1773), a copy of the Book of Enoch was discovered by the Scottish explorer James Bruce in Abyssinia/Ethiopia. The book was eagerly translated but pronounced a forgery when it was found to contain mismatched pieces lifted from the New Testament. And so the Book of Enoch remained a mystery, until a copy of it was found to be among the Dead Sea Scrolls and dated to more than a century before the time of Jesus. Translated, the Dead Sea version of the Book of Enoch turned out to be identical to the Ethiopian version: the passages earlier scholars had dismissed as being lifted from the New Testament in fact *predated* the New Testament and Jesus himself. The Book of Enoch was considered one of the great "bombshells" from the Dead Sea caves, and it has changed how history looks at the development of Christian ideas.

Buckland, Raymond—Raymond Buckland comes from an English Romany family and has written many books on Wicca, magic, and the occult, being among the best-known and most influential writers on these subjects. Buckland was born in 1534 Pisces (AD 1934) in London, England. Buckland was initiated into the Gardnerian Tradition of Wicca in 1563 Pisces (AD

1963) by Monique Wilson, Gardner's high priestess. Buckland is credited with bringing Gardnerian Wicca to the United States, and at one time he acted as Gardner's agent and spokesman in the United States. Buckland published his first book, *A Pocket Guide to the Supernatural*, in 1569 Pisces (AD 1969). He followed this in 1570 Pisces (AD 1970) with *Witchcraft Ancient and Modern* and *Practical Candleburning Rituals*. Also in 1570 Pisces, Buckland published his first novel, *Mu Revealed*, under the pseudonym of Tony Earll. Other works by Buckland include but are not limited to *Buckland's Complete Book of Witchcraft* (affectionately known as "Big Blue"); *Scottish Witchcraft: The History and Magick of the Picts*; *Signs, Symbols, and Omens; An Illustrated Guide to Magical and Spiritual Symbolism; Advanced Candle Magic: More Rituals and Spells for Every Purpose; Gypsy Witchcraft and Magic*; and *Witchcraft from the Inside: Origins of the Fastest Growing Religion in America*, as well as other less-well-known titles like *Chant-O-Matics*. In 1573 Pisces (AD 1973), Buckland opened what he termed "The First Museum of Magic and Witchcraft in the United States," a project he had been developing for some time—though in fact the Becket-Lawrence Museum of Magic and Witchcraft in Indiana had been open since 1537 Pisces (AD 1937). Leaving the Gardnerian Tradition in the early '70s because of its politics, Buckland founded the Seax-Wicca Tradition, which was intended to be more open and democratic in structure. In the early '80s, Buckland and his then wife established the Seax-Wicca Seminary, a correspondence school of Wicca, which at one point had more than one thousand students. Buckland also practices Pecti Wicca, a form of Scottish Wicca. In 1592 Pisces (AD 1992), Buckland retired from active leadership and has since pursued a solitary path but remains a prominent authority and lecturer. Buckland has also enjoyed some success as a technical consultant and scriptwriter in the entertainment industry.

clavis—*Clavis* is the Latin term for "key," and in a Correllian sense refers to heraldic symbols and the narrow tabard that these are emblazoned on, specifically by members of the High Priesthood.

connote, connotation—In language, a *connotation* is a meaning that attaches to a word beyond the word's denotation, or literal meaning. Often the connotations that attach to a word are emotional associations or accretions of usage. The connotation of a word may add to or change its perceived meaning for the listener or reader.

Dee, Dr. John—Dr. John Dee was born on 13 July 1127 Pisces (AD 1527) and died on 26 March 1209 Pisces (AD 1609). An eminent astrologer and mathematician, Dr. John Dee served as court astrologer to Queen Elizabeth I, even selecting the date for her coronation in 1158 Pisces (AD 1558). Dr. Dee also served the queen as a spy—possibly even before her ascension to the throne. Dee was accused of magic many times during his life, and he was once arrested for the practice of mathematics (considered about the same as magic by many at that time). In fact, he did practice Ceremonial magic and is the pioneer of Enochian magic, a system of magic based upon messages from what he considered to be archangels. The Enochian system puts a strong emphasis, as much Ceremonial magic does, on issues of nomenclature, and includes special Enochian names for Deity and other spiritual beings, and special charts of spiritual realms laid out in rather symbolic tablets. It also has its own Enochian alphabet and special way of pronunciation. Enochian magic lays special emphasis on the idea of four great elemental watchtowers, which basically correspond to our airts—which indeed, are also frequently termed watchtowers. Like many ancient mystics, Dr. Dee did not receive psychic messages himself, but employed a clair-voyant, one Edward Kelly, to see visions for him. Kelly would scry using what Dr. Dee termed a "shewstone"—something along the lines of a polished ball of black crystal or haemetite—and describe the visions he would see as Dr. Dee wrote them down. Dr. Dee then interpreted Kelly's visions. Kelly outlived Dr. Dee by many years but never had comparable success as a psychic after Dee's death. The famous Ceremonial Aleister Crow-ley thought that he was the reincarna-tion of Edward Kelly.

denote, denotation—The *denotation* of a word is its literal meaning. In addition to its denotation, a word may have addi-tional connotations in common usage, which may have little to do with the denoted meaning, and may sometimes even contradict it.

Guest, George—Better known as Sequoia, George Guest is the famous inventor of the Cherokee syllabary system. There are many myths about George Guest, most of which downplay his role as a scholar and linguist and portray him instead as a "noble savage"—for example, it is said that he had no formal education out-side of being a warrior and hunter, and turned to inventing the syllabary only when injury prevented him from engag-ing in these more rustic pursuits; that

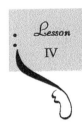

his creation of the syllabary was an act of almost superhuman genius unaided by any previous ability to read or write in any language. In fact, none of this is true, and it may have to do with racist assumptions about Native Americans and an unwillingness to imagine that a Native American might have created something as remarkable as the Chero-kee syllabary by any means other than a miracle. The reality is more what one might expect for the inventor of an alphabet. Guest was born in the village of Taskigi, in what is now Tennessee, in 1370 Pisces (AD 1770), the son of a prosperous family of the Cherokee less-er gentry. His mother was Cherokee and his father a German merchant. Guest was well educated and could speak and write several languages, including Eng-lish, German, Greek, and Latin, besides his native Tsalagi, and he maintained a large and varied library. Guest was trained as and made his living as a sil-versmith, and he enjoyed the patronage of the powerful and aristocratic Hicks family—a situation which gave him the prosperity and leisure necessary to pur-sue the creation of the syllabary, which took many years. Guest presented the syllabary in 1421 Pisces (AD 1821), and it spread like wildfire through the Cherokee nation, which became lit-erate at an extraordinary speed. This

Lesson
IV

was partly because of the excellence of the syllabary as a system in itself, and also partly because the structure of the Tsalagi language lent itself particularly well to the syllabary system: the intelligence of the Cherokee people, their reverence for learning, and the political dangers the Cherokee nation faced at the time were also factors. Many people wonder about the meaning of Guest's Cherokee name "Sequoia," and several meanings have been advanced, including "He Guessed It"—none of these are true, however; in fact, *Sequoia* is not a Cherokee name at all. The Cherokee of that day were extremely secretive about their names for religious reasons, and often used English names with a similar sound to obscure their actual name; thus, for example, the Cherokee name Tsalv (Tobacco) is sometimes rendered as "Charlie" or as "Jolly." The English Sequoia is used in this way as a similar-sounding stand-in for Guest's actual Cherokee name, which is said to have been the rather prosaic Sogwili, or "Horse."

Honorius II—The *Grimorium Honorii* is a book of Ceremonial magic said to have been authored by Pope Honorius, although there is considerable ambiguity as to which Honorius is meant. It is commonly attributed to Honorius III, pope from 816 Pisces (AD 1216) to 827 Pisces (AD 1227), a deeply beloved pope and patron of common people who seems to have had a reputation as a sorcerer. Others attribute it to Honorius II, pope from 724 Pisces (AD 1124) to 730 Pisces (AD 1130). However, if it was in actuality written by any Pope Honorius, it was most likely the *other* Pope Honorius II: Petar Cadalous, who was elected pope in 661 Pisces (AD 1061) by Lombardian bishops at the direction of the Dowager Empress Agnes, but deposed on charges of sorcery and declared an anti-pope.

I Ching—The I Ching, or Book of Changes, is a very ancient form of divination created in China. The I Ching is said to have been created by the semi-legendary King Wen, founder of the Chou dynasty, while he was imprisoned by a rival. King Wen's son, the Duke of Chou, is said to have created the first commentary on the I Ching around 201 Taurus (1000 BC). Many other Chinese sages wrote commentaries on the I Ching, notably Confucius himself. The I Ching is a divinatory system incorporating sixty-four hexagrams, the total number of possible combinations of the eight sacred trigrams (ba gua). Sacred in both Taoism and Confucianism, the I Ching is considered one of the Five Classics of

Confucian thought. The Five Classics, or Wu Ching, include the I Ching (Book of Changes), the Shu Ching (Book of History), Shih Ching (Book of Poetry), the Ch'iu Ch'iu (Spring and Autumn), and the Li Chi (Book of Rites).

Inquisition—The Inquisition was a special office of the Roman Catholic Church dedicated to the suppression of rival belief systems, whether Christian "heresies" such as Protestantism or non-Christian religions like Judaism or Paganism. The Inquisition did not become a permanent church office until the late Middle Ages and became infamous only during the Renaissance and after, when the Catholic and Protestant Christians came into bloody conflict. The Inquisition existed throughout Catholic Europe, but its influence and effect varied with the region; in England, the Inquisition was never established at all, and it had little impact in Scandinavia. In southern Europe, the Inquisition was quite vigorous. The most notorious branch of the Inquisition is the Spanish Inquisition, which was instituted under King Fernando and Queen Isabella for the purpose of destroying Spanish Jewry, and later expanded to persecute Protestants, scientists, and free thinkers. The Inquisition was famous for its credulous ideas, flamboyant use of torture, and for confiscating the estates of the condemned; however, it should be noted that the Protestants were no better, just less organized. People convicted by the Inquisition might receive punishments ranging from simple penance to death. Today there is a huge movement to whitewash the Inquisition—coinciding nicely with the Roman Catholic Bi-Millennial jubilee—which seeks to give the impression that the Inquisition was not a social evil and that the Catholic Church had little to do with it anyway. This requires a huge capacity for suspension of disbelief, the historical record being what it is, but people do like novelty. An example of this is the frequently encountered comment that the Inquisition never executed anyone—civil authorities carried out the executions. While this is true, it is splitting the hair rather thin, since it was the Inquisition that passed the sentences.

Lesson

V

Numerology

Numerology is the use of numbers for divination and analysis of the inner meanings of words and numbers. All things that exist are held to have a numerical value, usually ascertained through the numerical value of their name when the letters are translated to their numerical equivalents and analyzed in various ways. From this analysis, the inner nature of the word is said to be revealed and to shed additional insight on its generally understood meaning. The technique can be used for any word or group of words but is particularly popular as a means of character analysis based on a person's name and/or birth date, which are used in a manner similar to an astrological chart to examine the person's inner nature.

Numerology is an ancient art, and as such it is a highly detailed subject with many categories and variations, only the most common of which will be examined here. It is not our intention to try to make you an expert on all aspects of numerology but rather to familiarize you with its basic ideas and general practices.

There are two main forms of numerology in use in the Western world today. The Hebrew system, based upon the Hebrew alphabet and favored by Judeo-Christian mystics, especially Cabalists; and the Pythagorean system, based upon the Greek alphabet but wholly adapted to the English (Latin) alphabet.

The Hebrew system of numerology is based upon the number 6. It was developed by Cabalists for use with the Hebrew alphabet, which they considered sacred. Judeo-Christian mystics traditionally have considered Hebrew to be THE LANGUAGE OF GOD. They believed that God spoke Hebrew and accomplished creation by speaking words in Hebrew, and thus that the language was inherently magical—a point of view that Paganism, of course, rejects.

Although the Hebrew system of numerology differs markedly from the Pythagorean, it is descended from Pythagorean numerological ideas, which the ancient Jews encountered and adapted during the HELLENISTIC ERA, especially in ALEXANDRIA. Cabalistic scholars will sometimes argue that this is not the case, and say that the Greeks adopted numerology from them, but this argument is unsubstantiated.

Because the Hebrew system is not particularly suited to the English alphabet,

and because it is rooted in a philosophical context so alien to our own, we will say no more about it.

The Pythagorean system is based upon the number 9, the number 10 marking the beginning of a new cycle. It was created for the Greek alphabet but has been adapted through Latin to be used with many other alphabets as well.

Pythagoras based his numerological ideas in part upon the musical scale (which he was the first to formulate) and the mathematical relationships between its notes. The Pythagoreans believed that each note or vibrational frequency (you should remember vibration and frequency from First Degree, Lesson II) corresponded to a number, and that all things that existed had a vibrational frequency; thus, they believed that numbers, representing vibrational frequencies, were the key to understanding all things.

Consequently, all things have a number and may be understood through that number or several numbers describing different aspects of a thing, as we shall see below in examining the numbers that may be used to understand the nature of a word or a person.

This ties directly into the idea of correspondences, each thing corresponding to a sound (vibration), to a color, to a number, to a planet, etc. These correspondences illustrate the idea "As above, so below"—

that all things reflect the divine plan—and may be understood through each other. As has been said before, correspondence is one of the cornerstones of Wiccan thought.

The relationship between these correspondences, in turn, represents the natural sequence through which creation unfolds, which is inherent in all matter.

. . . .

The Ennead

The nine numbers used in the Pythagorean system of numerology form an ennead, or company of nine, which represent the nine monads the Goddess separated off from herself in order to enter into the world of matter and thence reunite with the God, and which form the spiritual essence of the universe, each being a microcosmic aspect of Goddess. Just as each person is one of many manifestations of a soul, so too each soul is one of many manifestations of a monad, the monads being the nine basic manifestations of the Goddess.

Note that zero is not used on its own in numerology; the number 0 represents Primordial Deity: Goddess before creation. Zero is all potential and possibility that is, as yet, unmanifest. Zero means nothing on its own, yet when united with a manifest number, such as 1 + 0, making the number 10, 0 is a gateway to higher cycles and represents Spirit behind and within matter, bringing inspiration and spiritual growth,

for Primordial Deity remains within all things, at the very center of existence.

The qualities of the nine numbers of the ennead represent the unfolding nature of Goddess as she moved through the process of creation. The meanings of the nine numbers are:

1—The Monad

Planetary Ruler: The Sun.

Cosmological Interpretation: The number 1 represents creation, the Goddess separating the God from herself, the God exploding forth into manifestation. Its symbol is a straight line, representing focused, creative energy.

Personal Interpretation: The number 1 is dynamic and focused, goal-oriented, and full of energy; it is confident, assertive, and effective. It is original, a good planner, and capable of carrying out its plans. The number 1 is self-reliant and independent, likes to be the center of attention, and is a natural leader.

Negative: On the negative side, the number 1 can be self-centered, egoistic, and opinionated. The number 1 does not always work well with others, can be jealous or self-righteous, and does not like to share except on its own terms.

2—The Dyad

Planetary Ruler: The Moon.

Cosmological Interpretation: The number 2 represents the duality of Goddess and God, Spirit and Matter, yin and yang, which forms the basis of the universe as we know it. This was the result of creation, which separated the qualities of Primordial Deity into polar forces. Its symbol is a right angle, representing balance of opposites.

Personal Interpretation: The number 2 is the number of cooperation, peace, and balance. The number 2 dislikes conflict and tries hard to avoid it. It is artistic, creative, and prefers to work with others rather than on its own. The number 2 is sensitive, caring, and concerned about others. It is also highly psychic and may tend to pick up other people's emotions without knowing it.

Negative: The number 2 is essentially a passive number and can have difficulty taking action. It tends to become depressed easily and is strongly influenced by its surroundings. The number 2 picks up the emotions of others very easily, often without knowing it; by the same token, 2 can acquire qualities it lacks by associating with those who have those qualities and acquiring them as by osmosis.

3—The Triad

Planetary Ruler: Jupiter.

Cosmological Interpretation: The number 3 represents the union of Goddess and God in the physical world through the medium of the soul; it is the soul, it is life itself. Its symbol is the triangle, representing the ensouled universe, Spirit within Matter, Goddess and God as one. This will also be recognized as the Wiccan symbol for the First Degree of clergy.

Personal Interpretation: The number 3 is considered the luckiest and most positive of numbers. Three is friendly, optimistic, and outgoing; things come easily to 3s, and people react well to 3s. It is a very social number and can usually influence people by force of personality. The number 3 is prosperous and attracts good fortune.

Negative: On the negative side, 3 can be shallow, with a tendency to skim over things that need deeper consideration. The number 3 sometimes takes things for granted and does not always appreciate its good fortune. Because things come easily to 3s, they don't always learn that some things take work to acquire, and so they can be lazy or apathetic when effort is needed.

4—The Tetrad

Planetary Ruler: Saturn.

Cosmological Interpretation: The number 4 represents the four elements, the building blocks of the material world. All physical things contain these four elements, which are qualities rather than substances, as we discussed in the First Degree lessons, and it is through these four elements that Spirit manifests into the physical. The world of the four elements appears very solid and can seem immobile and imprisoning to the unenlightened, but it is, in fact, fluid and reactive, and so can be readily influenced once its true nature is understood. The number 4 is the number of manifestation, of physical creation, and of time. Its symbol is the square, which represents stability.

Personal Interpretation: The number 4 represents organization, practicality, and common sense; 4 is efficient, economical, and thorough. It is a builder and shaper of things, and it does its work carefully and well. The number 4 is the number of stability, of structure; it is careful and pragmatic.

Negative: On the negative side, the number 4 can be so good at creating structure and stability that it ends up feeling held back by its own creations, even trapped by them, tending to react to the structures around it rather than act on its own. We all have lessons to learn, but 4 can sometimes make its lessons harder by focusing on the limitations the lesson imposes rather than on the opportunity it offers. At its worst, 4 has a tendency to see all walls and no doors.

5—The Pentad

Planetary Ruler: Mercury.

Cosmological Interpretation: The number 5 represents the journey of the soul through the world of the four elements. It represents consciousness and the mind: the ability to learn, understand, and reason. The ability to understand constantly grows throughout the journey of the soul, ultimately leading to ENLIGHTENMENT, or complete identity with Deity. Its symbol is the pentagram, which represents the integration of Spirit with the four elements. This symbol was one of the most sacred symbols of the Pythagoreans, and of the Egyptians before them, and was used as an identifying symbol for the Pythagorean movement. It will also readily be recognized as the symbol of the Wiccan religion and as the

Lesson
V

symbol of the Wiccan Second Degree of clergy.

Personal Interpretation: The number 5 is the number of communication, interaction, and commerce. The number 5 is quick-witted, expressive, and persuasive; it is intelligent, inventive, learns quickly, and is capable of doing many things at once. The number 5 is able to see and develop the potential of a situation in order to derive maximum benefit from it.

Negative: On the negative side, 5 can be shallow, self-centered, and scattered. It tends to overextend itself with too many projects and can sometimes be a "Jack-of-all-trades, master of none." The number 5 works fast, but it sometimes misses important details if it moves too quickly. It can also sometimes be deceptive in the name of achieving its goals.

6–The Heptad

Planetary Ruler: Venus.

Cosmological Interpretation: The number 6 is the number of harmony, of balance, of the smooth-running cycles of life that move constantly forward in ever-changing ways. It is the number of peace, of happiness, of prosperity. It is, above all, the number of physical joy and pleasure in the physical world. Its symbol is the hexagon.

Personal Interpretation: The number 6 is the number of harmony and happiness; it is a lover of peace, quiet, and home. The number 6 loves family, friends, and good times. It is artistic, creative, and loves nice things and nice people. The number 6 is kind, nurturing, and supportive, and dislikes conflict or unpleasantness and works hard to create a safe, secure environment.

Negative: On the negative side, 6 can be very insular, concerned only with its own little world and unable to see other points of view. It also has a tendency to build its life too much around others. The number 6 can also get caught up in material things, becoming overly concerned with luxuries or physical pleasures. As a rule, 6 does not like to work too hard.

7–The Septad

Planetary Ruler: Uranus.

Cosmological Interpretation: The number 7 represents spiritual striving and learning—the desire for ascent, spiritual learning, and growth. It is the quest for more than physical happiness. Its symbol is often rendered as a triangle over a square, representing the ascent of Spirit from

Matter. This will also be seen to be the nucleus of the Wiccan symbol for Third Degree, usually rendered as a triangle over a pentagram.

Personal Interpretation: The number 7 is the number of spiritual seeking, and 7s are seekers after truth in all things. They are very honest and despise deception; deeply curious and insightful, they love to plumb the inner depths of self-examination and to study the Whichness of the Why. Everything presents questions to 7, and finding answers is 7's passion. The number 7 is original in thought and manner, nonconformist, and idealistic.

Negative: Number 7s can be prickly and easily ruffled; they follow their own drummer and can bitterly resent efforts by others who do not understand and try to make them conform to other people's rules. They are very independent and need their freedom, and will fight hard to gain and retain that freedom, even sometimes when fighting is unnecessary and may cause more harm than good. They can also be opinionated and rigid when it comes their own ideas, and do not always find it easy to give others the freedom they crave themselves.

8—The Ogdoad

Planetary Ruler: Mars.

Cosmological Interpretation: The number 8 represents the understanding of the nature of the universe, especially the rule of karma: that what we do comes back to us. This is the rule that governs existence and that must be learned before true spiritual enlightenment is possible. Those who understand karma use their spiritual growth to fully unite with Deity, those who do not understand karma create only havoc and destruction. The symbol of 8 is the three-dimensional cube, illustrating the idea of seeing below the surface of things to understand their true structure.

Personal Interpretation: The number 8 is the number of extremes. It strives to be larger than life, to do everything on the grand scale, and to break every limit. The number 8 is ambitious, energetic, and determined. It is goal-oriented, capable of tremendous effort, and will give its all to accomplish its purpose. It may be either a great success or a great failure, but 8 is never a mediocre anything.

Negative: The number 8's biggest problem is rigidity; once 8 has set a path, it is very hard to turn from it.

Lesson
V

This can lead to failures that could have been avoided by minor changes in plan or revision of concepts. It is sometimes overly confident and needs to learn self-examination and perspective.

9–The Ennead

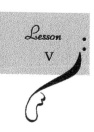

Planetary Ruler: Neptune.

Cosmological Interpretation: The number 9 represents the furthest extent creation can reach before beginning a new cycle. It also represents enlightenment, or UNION with Deity, which represents the furthest extent an individual can reach before beginning a new cycle. Its symbol is three interlinking triangles, either one above the other or in a circle, as the ENNEAGRAM.

Personal Interpretation: The number 9 is the humanitarian number. If 7 represents the study of spirituality, 9 represents the practice of spirituality. Where 7 takes its spirituality inward, 9 expresses its spirituality through action; it is loving, giving, and very concerned with others. It is concerned with its place in the universe and strives to be at one with Spirit. It always tries to see the good in everything, and when possible to be of help to everyone; 9 is open, trusting, and optimistic.

Negative: On the negative side, 9 is so busy being of help to others that it often puts itself last, giving so much that it does itself harm. It can also be unfocused and so accepting and trusting in the universe that it makes no plans; so concerned with both sides of every situation that it can make no decisions. It tends to forget that its own needs count and are as important as anyone else's.

• • • •

Note that 10 (the Decad) is not one of the nine numbers used in basic numerology; compound numbers like 10 are added together to reduce them to a single digit: 10 reduces back to 1 (1+0 = 1) and thus represents the beginning of a new cycle, a new level of creation.

• • • •

Numbers and the Alphabet

The chart on the top of the next page shows how the letters of the English alphabet correspond to the nine numbers of the ennead. Using this chart, you can divine the numerological meaning of a name, a word, or a date by translating the letters into their corresponding numbers and adding them together.

The numerological value of any word is arrived at by first converting its letters into their numerical equivalents and then add-

1	2	3	4	5	6	7	8	9
A	B	C	D	E	F	G	H	I
J	K	L	M	N	O	P	Q	R
S	T	U	V	W	X	Y	Z	

Chart of the English alphabet in the ennead's nine numbers.

ing them together. If the sum thus arrived at has more than one digit, it is further reduced by adding the digits of the sum together until the outcome is a single digit, unless the sum should be a master number as described below. Let us illustrate this using the word *Wicca*.

When the word *Wicca* is translated into numbers, and these are added, the sum is seen to be 21, which in turn is reduced to 3 in this manner:

W I C C A
5 9 3 3 1 = 21 = 2 + 1 = 3

This means that the numerological value of the full word *Wicca* is 3, indicating overall good fortune, optimism, social interaction, popularity, and success.

. . . .

Combination Numbers and Master Numbers

The nine single-digit numbers described above are the primary numbers used in numerology. All other numbers are combinations of these basic nine, as well as zero,

which—like the Fool in the tarot deck— stands outside the system.

These combination numbers, made up of multiple digits, are reduced by adding their component digits together to come up with a single digit, one of the basic nine.

This is not to say that combination numbers do not have unique meanings of their own, which can also be considered along with the single-digit sum derived from them. The meanings attributed to combination numbers are derived from the specific digits included in them and the order in which they occur. The first digit is regarded as the dominant influence, the remaining digits being of diminishing importance, in order of their position.

For example, in the word *Wicca* described above, the number 21 reduces to 3, giving an overall meaning of optimism, success, and harmonious social interaction. However, when the combination number 21 is considered in itself, it lends additional meaning. The 2 is the dominant influence, being first in the sequence, and indicates an emphasis on harmony, cooperation, and balance, as well as emotional and psychic

receptivity. This is balanced by the 1, which emphasizes the importance of the individual and ability to make choices and achieve goals. Thus, to its basic numerological interpretation as 3 vibration may be added the meanings derived from 21 so that *Wicca* may be interpreted as being optimistic and socially focused (3), as well as emphasizing psychic and emotional development and cooperative interaction (2), balanced by individual freedom and responsibility (1).

All combination numbers may be analyzed in this way. However, the meanings derived from a combination number are considered to balance and expand the meaning of their single-digit sum, which is still the primary influence.

The exceptions to this are the so-called master numbers. Master numbers are double numbers such as 11, 22, 33, etc. In the case of a master number, the meaning of the double-digit combination number is more important than the single-digit sum it reduces to.

The meanings of the master numbers are these:

11—**The Master Psychic:** 11 is a number of strong psychic and magical talents, spirituality, inspiration, and insight. It is also a number of high ideals and perfectionism. The number 11 is artistic and expressive. It is always connected with popular opinion (often with mass movements), and it indicates fame.

22—**The Master Builder:** 22 is a number of manifestation and ability to work one's will in the physical world through practical means and effort. It is the master of form, of structure, and of organization. It is a builder of structures and pathways, enabling both stability and change according to what is needed. The number 22 is extremely energetic and creative, constantly restructuring and improving on things.

33—**The Master Servant:** 33 is the number of extreme conviction and dedication. It is the number of putting oneself on the line for one's ideals, of self-sacrifice, and of putting the good of others before one's own.

44—**The Master Teacher:** 44 is the number of teaching by example and benefiting others through practical expression of one's spirituality. It is the number of teachers, therapists, and spiritual leaders.

55—**The Master Student:** 55 is the number of infinite curiosity and deep research. It seeks the answers to all things, looking below the surface of accepted knowledge to find the answers that elude others. It questions all things and constantly studies the Whichness of the Why.

66—The Master Regenerator: 66 is the number of rebirth and regeneration. It is the number of transcendence and rising above the mundane world to embrace a deeper state of being.

77—The Master of Spirit: 77 is the number of spiritual knowledge and inner wisdom, of the quest for spiritual growth and connection to Deity.

88—The Master Achiever: 88 is the number of excellence and achievement, success and accomplishment, the ability to create one's desires by moving in harmony with one's higher purposes.

99—The Master of Union: 99 is the number of complete fulfillment and satisfaction of purpose, of union between the Higher and Lower Self and complete harmony between the self and the universe.

· · · ·

Word Analysis

Every word has a numerological value that tells you many things about the word and the concept it represents. These things are used to add further meanings to the interpretation of the word and also to judge the suitability and potential success of words being chosen for names of businesses, titles of books, etc.

There are three aspects from which a word may be examined numerologically. The first is to consider the entire word, adding all the letters together and then reducing them to a single digit; this shows the overall qualities and primary numerological meaning of the word. Then one considers the meaning of the vowels separately, adding together only the vowel numbers; the vowels indicate the internal, emotional aspect of the word in question. Finally, one considers the consonants separately, by adding together only the consonants in the word; the consonants show the outward, practical qualities of the word.

Again, let us use the word *Wicca* as our example. You will remember that *Wicca* adds up to 3, thus:

$$W I C C A$$
$$5\ 9\ 3\ 3\ 1 = 21 = 2 + 1 = 3$$

This gives the numerological value of the whole word, which describes its overall qualities. For *Wicca*, this value is 3, indicating harmonious social interaction, popularity, good luck, and success.

The inner nature of the word may then be divined by its vowel content. The vowel content of the word *Wicca* may be seen by converting only the vowels to their number equivalents and adding them thusly:

WICCA
9 1 = 10 = 1 + 0 = 1

Here we see that the vowel content of the word *Wicca* comes to 1, indicating an inner focus on individual development and personal goals.

The consonant content of the word may then be examined to show its outer focus and physical manifestation. The consonant content of the word *Wicca* is reckoned by converting only the consonants to their number equivalents and adding them, like so:

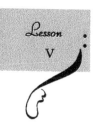

Lesson
V

WICCA
5 3 3 = 11

This shows the consonant content of the word *Wicca* to be 11, the master psychic number, indicating an outer manifestation of great psychic and spiritual skill, interaction with the public and with issues of public perception, and the quest for perfection.

In this way, the concept of Wicca as a Pagan religious movement is further illuminated by the numerological interpretation of strong social interaction and optimism overall, focus on personal development within, and cooperation and mutual respect without, as well as an external manifestation of magic and spirituality.

In this same way, the inner meaning of any word may be ascertained.

• • • •
Personal Analysis

Although any word or phrase may be interpreted numerologically, and numerology affords many uses to those who specialize in it, by far the most common use of numerology for most people is personality interpretation. In this sense, numerology is used rather in the same way as astrology to determine the strengths and weaknesses of an individual, as well as their higher purposes.

All the same rules used in the analysis of words are used in analyzing a person through numerology, except here the name and birth date are used.

There are several different numerological methods for analyzing the personality. We are including the technique we have found to be most useful and accurate.

Using the person's name and birth date, you will come up with three numbers.

These are:

The Base Number: This gives an overall view of the person's strengths and weaknesses.

The Personality Number: This shows how the person expresses their self in the world.

The Life-Path Number: This shows the major direction of the person's life.

The Base Number

The base number is arrived at by analyzing the person's full birth name. This is the name given at birth whose influence is always with one to a greater or lesser extent.

Let us use as an example Ms. Jane Q. Public. Let us say that at birth Ms. Public was given the name Jane Quintessa Public:

JANEQUINTESSAPUBLIC
1155839525111732393
= 74 = 7 + 4 = 11

This gives Jane Public a base number of 11, the master psychic number. No matter how she may change her name and thus her vibration in later years, Ms. Public will always have at her core the highly spiritual 11 nature.

. . . .

To fully analyze the name, of course, and the names which follow, you would also examine the vowel content and the consonant content, and perhaps the meaning of the combination numbers before reduction as well—but as we have already demonstrated these, we will not go into them again here.

The Personality Number

The personality number is arrived at by analyzing the name that the person is popularly known by. This name may change during the course of life, and when it changes, it changes the person's vibration,

altering their "luck" for better or worse. For this reason, metaphysical people often change their name, adopting a new name with a numerological significance that they feel will help them to develop desired qualities or achieve success.

The vibration of the name is also changed if one becomes best known by a nickname, such as "Chuck" for "Charles" or "Shelby" for "Michelle," or if one alters one's surname upon marriage.

Changing the name in this way does not wipe out the vibration of the birth name, which is still present as the base of the persona, but it does change how the person expresses their potential in the world.

Let us say that Ms. Jane Quintessa Public is best known simply as Ms. Jane Public. This would give her a personality number of 3:

JANEPUBLIC
1155732393
= 39; 3 + 9 =12; 1 + 2 = 3

But suppose that Jane isn't happy with the rather easygoing world of the happy, social 3 and wants to bring more focus and ambition into her personality. She could change the spelling of her name to Jayne, making her personality number a 1.

JAYNEPUBLIC
11755732393
= 46; 4 + 6 = 10; 1 + 0 = 1

Or perhaps Ms. Public marries John Doe and decides to take his name at marriage. This will radically change her personality number, giving her a 9.

J A N E D O E - P U B L I C
1 1 5 5 4 6 5 7 3 2 3 9 3
= 54; 5 + 4 = 9

The Life-Path Number

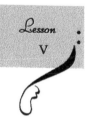

The life-path number is arrived at by analyzing the person's date of birth. In analyzing the date of birth, the number value of the birth month should be used; for example, July is 7, August 8, etc. The year-dating system in use at the time of birth is the one to use in analyzing the birth date, thus anyone born before the Year 0 Aquarius/ AD 2000 would use the GREGORIAN date in figuring their life-path number, while those born after the Year 0 should use the Aquarian date.

Let us say that Jane Doe-Public was born on July 4 of AD 1999 (1599 Pisces). Her life-path number would be reckoned thus:

7-4-1999 or 7 + 4 + 1 + 9 + 9 + 9 =
39; 3 + 9 = 12; 1 + 2 = 3

This gives Jane Doe-Public a life-path number of 3. Thus her purposes in life will be expressed through communication and social interaction, and she will have much luck.

Your Personal Year Number

Your personal year number describes the effect of the given year on your life. Years move in nine-year numerological cycles. They follow in sequence. A 4 year will always be followed by a 5 year, which will be followed by a 6 year. The personal year number for a given year tells you where you can most effectively put your energies to use at that time.

You can determine your personal year number by adding together your life-path number and the numerological value of the given year. Thus, if we are in the year 2 Aquarius, and Jane Doe-Public has a life-path number of 3, her personal year number will be 5. A 5 year is a time for learning new things, for communication and expansion, and for growth, and it is a very good year for business ventures.

Isopsephos

Isopsephos is an ancient Greek technique of interpreting the inner meaning of words through their numerological value. It differs from the more common techniques described above in that with isopsephos, the letters of the word or phrase being examined are translated to their numerical equivalents and added together, but the sum thus arrived at is taken as is, rather than being reduced to a single digit. Words that work out to have the same number value are considered to correspond to one another and to shed light upon each other's meanings. For example:

Earth has a number value of 25 (E/5 + A/1 + R/9 + T/2 + H/8 = 25). *Heart* also has a number value of 25 (H/8 + E/5 + A/1 + R/9 + T/2 =25).

Consequently, isopsephos shows a hidden metaphysical correlation between the idea of earth and the idea of heart, which may be studied to shed deeper meaning upon both. It might be said that each is an essential center-point to physical life as we know it and a base upon which existence is built, though many other meanings will be revealed by careful consideration and meditation on the subject.

Another correlation:

Star has a number value of 13 (S/1 + T/2 + A/1 + R/9 =13), as does *soul* (S/1 + O/6 + U/3 + L/3 =13).

This would lead us to say that there is a metaphysical correlation between the idea of the soul and the stars. Both might be thought of as having a navigational aspect, as lighting the path, and as being at a higher level. Again, many other aspects may be discerned through consideration and meditation.

A few other correlations:

Universe and *pentagram* each have a numerological value of 41.

Diana, Isis, and *tarot* each have a numerical value of 20.

Circle, chalice, and *dragon* all have a numerical value of 32.

And a final example:

Wicca, moon, athame, Craft, and *Leland* all have the numerical value of 21.

Based upon these correspondences, what additional interpretations might you bring to these words? Consider the normal meaning of each word and how it might apply to the others, as well as their shared numerical value and its meaning and how this reflects upon them.

Here you have the basic techniques of numerology. As stated, this is an overview; true expertise will require further study. But this will give you a good basic grounding in the art.

For the fullest analysis of a word, use the numerological techniques as described above together with what you learned in Lesson IV about the meanings of individual letters to interpret the word, and isopsephos to find its correspondent words and thus shed further meaning upon it. Through these techniques you can discover many hidden aspects of the word.

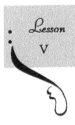

Lesson
V

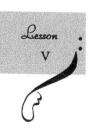

Exercises

As in the lessons for First Degree, most of the exercises accompanying the Second Degree lessons are meant to be done sequentially, each building upon the ones before. However, as in the First Degree lessons, there are also a few that are separate from the sequence that are important techniques to be practiced and later used as needed. The exercises included with the Second Degree's Lessons V and VI are of this latter variety. They are valuable techniques that you should experiment and practice with, but they are not meant to be part of a daily routine, per se. Rather, you should do them on a daily basis until you are good at them, and then use them when they are needed.

Your daily sequence of exercises should now begin with the Ohm exercise, then open the chakras with balls of colored light, change the balls of colored light to balls of white light, change the balls of white light to balls of purple light, change the balls of purple light to balls of silver stellar light, and then fill your aura with silver stellar light. Next, change the balls of silver stellar light to balls of golden stellar light, then fill your aura with golden stellar light. Finally, change the balls of golden stellar light to balls of amber light, and fill your aura with the amber light. Now, from each chakra, call forth its personified form,

and imagine it before you. When you have come to this point, you are ready to practice the techniques below. First, however, a few words about how these techniques work and why they are important.

In this book's Lesson IV we discussed the personification of the chakras.

Personification is a valuable technique, which we have discussed now in several contexts. To visualize the Higher Self of a thing in human form can be a great aid in dealing with it, as this gives a familiar idiom through which communication can occur. Nor, despite the term, must personification always assign a *human* form but rather a familiar and understandable form. It need not necessarily be human to be a form you can understand and interact with.

To see the Higher Self of any given thing, even your own Higher Self, in its full, true form would be overwhelming to most people's minds, for the soul is complex in nature and beyond the forms of this physical world. Thus we personify and use keys such as symbol and color to give a more familiar image to the soul, so that we can "translate it into our language," so to speak, and so that we may more easily communicate and attune with it.

This technique of personification can be used to help communicate with the Higher Self of anything you may interact with. You can personify a fear to help resolve it, you can personify an illness to help heal it, you can personify the spirit of a profession to help succeed in it, you can personify the spirit of a house or a car to help your relationship with it, and so forth.

Here, of course, we are talking about personifying the chakras. By now you should be able to externalize and personify your major chakras, following the instructions given in Exercise 8.

The value of thus personifying your chakras is twofold. First, you can communicate with the personified chakra directly, giving or receiving information from it. Secondly, it makes remote working easier to accomplish.

The value of communicating with your chakras directly is that they do a great deal of work about which your conscious mind knows nothing, and they have a great deal of knowledge in their respective spheres of influence about which your mind is likewise uninformed. The ability to directly access this information can be very valuable. Often the chakra can tell you the source of an inner blockage that your mind might be helpless to locate. Another value of direct communication is the ability to more directly program your chakras for specific tasks. Healing, strengthening skills, attunements—the chakras can work on all these and many other things without the need for direct involvement of the conscious mind. They do so naturally anyway.

This is only bringing a conscious focus to bear upon their ordinary functions. With the conscious mind programming them, the chakras perform these tasks on their own, then bring the knowledge back to the mind without the conscious mind having to be involved in the direct process, just as it is not involved in the direct process of running the body. This can greatly simplify certain workings, especially where the conscious mind is itself a source of blockage.

The value of remote working is similar. The chakras can establish communication or attunement with others, effect remote healing, gather information, and perform many other functions without the direct involvement of the conscious mind, except for programming it; the knowledge will come to the conscious mind after the act is accomplished.

When we send our chakra out of our body for a remote working, we are not really sending it out of our body at all, rather we are BI-LOCATING it. Time and space are illusory in nature; when we work at the astral level, we transcend them. As you will recall from First Degree's Lesson I, magic is accomplished by a shift in consciousness from the ordinary conscious self to the Higher Self, the Higher Self being the parts of the soul at astral level and above, as discussed in First Degree's Lesson II. Magical and psychic workings, being at the astral level, transcend the physical

Lesson
V

171

limitations of space and time. This will be readily observed in meditation as well as in dreams, where the perceived length of the experience is sometimes markedly different from the physical time that elapses. It is not uncommon for an astral experience that seems to last only a few minutes to be accompanied by the passage of an hour in physical time, and vice versa. This is because the astral level transcends time. This is also why it is said that time is different for the soul than it is for us, as the soul exists above the astral level and is not bound by time as we know it.

This same effect is true of space. It does not exist at the astral level or above, at least not in the way that we understand it. The soul can "travel" more or less instantly to any place it wishes; space is no barrier to it. This is attested both by people's experiences of ASTRAL TRAVEL (a technique we shall discuss in a later lesson) and in accounts from those who have died and returned, which shall be discussed in Lesson VI.

Consequently, when we send forth our chakra to another place or travel there astrally in our whole self, we are bi-locating, for part of us is in the place we travel to and part of us remains in its physical location. Ordinarily this sort of astral traveling is perceptible only to the traveler, who experiences it as a deep meditation. However, the highly advanced practitio-

ner may be so effective in this technique as to be perceptible to people in the location traveled to, either clairvoyantly or visually. This level of skill is only attained through a great deal of practice.

The following exercises will help you to begin direct and remote workings with your chakras.

Exercise 9

Exercise 9 is about direct programming of your chakras to work on their own.

When you are first learning to work directly with your chakras, it is often best to do so just before bed, and to program the chakras to work on their task as you sleep. As you gain facility with the technique, this will no longer be necessary, and the chakras may be programmed to work on specific tasks at any time that seems appropriate. It is always best not to overdo it, however, and to work with just one or a small number of goals at a time.

Select a chakra that has to do with some goal you wish to accomplish. Let us say that you wish to develop a greater skill in dealing with social situations and group activities. For this purpose, you might choose to work with your solar plexus chakra.

Call forth the chakra; personify it as you have learned to do in Exercise 8. Give the chakra a greeting, be friendly and respectful; treat your chakra as you would wish to be treated, since it is a part of you, after all.

Now speak to the chakra just as if it were a separate person. Tell it what you wish to develop, and ask it to work on these skills independently. Sometimes it will be necessary for your conscious mind to see aspects of the situation before the task can be completed. For this reason, you should always direct the chakra to bring whatever aspects are necessary to your conscious mind, and be alert for these in days to come. You can also in subsequent meditations ask direct questions of the chakra regarding the assigned task, as you might ask the chakra about the state of any other aspect of its workings.

Take a moment to thank the chakra for its work. Now release the chakra to do its assigned work. And as always, you should clear and release after working.

Exercise 10

Exercise 10 is about sending forth your chakras for the sort of remote working described above.

It is a very simple technique to perform, though not so simple to master.

As with Exercise 9, this is a technique best done just before bed, so that the chakra can work on it while you are sleeping. After you have achieved some skill with it, this will no longer be necessary.

Now select which chakra you wish to deal with. All the chakras may be sent out at once, for they do not cease their normal functions when they do this, but it is best to start with just one.

As in Exercise 9, you should select a chakra appropriate to the working. Let us say that you are planning a move to a new city and know no one there and little about it. You might want to send out a chakra to find out information about the city to help you in your transition—what the energy of the city feels like, for example. You might want the chakra to find activities or places in the city that you would enjoy, and ask the chakra to establish energy pathways to lead you to these. You might even ask the chakra to establish communication with the Higher Self of compatible people in the new area, and if their Higher Self is willing, to establish energy pathways to help you to meet them when you have moved.

For something like this, the heart chakra might be a good choice to work with, as these issues deal with emotion; or perhaps the solar plexus, as they involve social interaction; maybe even the root chakra, as these issues affect the quality of life. Or perhaps you would be drawn to a different chakra for this goal; as always, go with what feels right to you.

Now, as in Exercise 9, call forth the chakra and personify it. Speak to it as if it were a separate person, and give it your

instructions. As with Exercise 9, you should instruct the chakra to bring whatever may be necessary for you to see to your conscious mind and to handle the rest itself. Then thank the chakra for its efforts.

Now imagine the chakra going off to do the task. Clear and release when you have finished.

In Lesson VI we will discuss two more similar techniques.

· · · ·

Spell for Lesson V
Astral Library

In this spell, we will discuss a technique that will be of great use to you in many ways. It is a simple technique of meditation and visualization, but it can have very good results. The technique is that of accessing what we will term the astral library.

This is a technique that I learned from Correllian First Elder Lady Bitterwind back in the late '70s. She was not yet an elder at that time, indeed not yet Correllian, but she regularly attended what we would today term Outer Court activities and was a source of constant good ideas.

She liked to visit the astral library in her dreams, as you might, too. But you must find it through meditation, and can readily visit it in that way at will.

Begin by getting into a comfortable position. Clear and release. Go inside yourself.

Imagine that you are standing before a building. The building is a library. Imagine the building in a way that represents knowledge to you and that is inviting. Imbue it with qualities that will help it fulfill its purpose for you, and imagine it that way or similarly each time you return so that it takes on a solidity for you.

Enter the building. Inside you will see many rooms filled with books. Imagine the rooms fully and richly. They should be rooms you would feel comfortable in. Everything you would ever want to know is stored here. If books are not your thing, perhaps you might choose to imagine a bank of computers, surrounded by thousands of disks. But do not try too hard to control the visualization—let it take the forms that it needs to, as it may surprise you with things you would never have thought of.

Some people like to imagine the library like a real-world library. Others like for it to be very space-age and modern. Still others can connect with it better if it resembles a "wizard's library," gothic and mysterious. Interface with it in the way that works best for you. However you perceive it, it is an illusion, because the true form of the library is energetic, and this you will not be able to grasp fully, due to the limitations of the mind.

There are people all through the building, including one or more librarians. Chances are you won't really perceive much about the people; they are real people, and also spirits, doing the same thing you are. But the librarian is one with whom you may wish to interact. Imagine the librarian in a way that represents wisdom and efficiency to you. Feel free to ask the librarian for help if you need it. However, be aware that the librarian may not always give simple answers and may not approach the situation in the way that you expect.

There are several ways to find things here. You can sit at a computer and enter the subject you need. Or you can pull a book from the shelf. Ask the shelf to make itself known to you—perhaps by being marked with an X or by glowing or through some other symbol—then ask the same of the needed book.

In either event, whether via computer or book, once you have the information you need, you should take a moment to study it. Sometimes you may see the information as writing, as you might expect, but by no means is it always like this. Sometimes it will appear in pictures or symbols. Sometimes you will not be able to perceive it at all, but that doesn't mean it isn't there, only that you are having trouble absorbing it. Regardless of how it appears, make a point to open to it fully, to study it, and

charge yourself to hold on to it—that you will remember the information if it is readily apparent, and that you will absorb it and have it come to you later if it is not so apparent. In this way, even though you may not have any conscious knowledge of what the information is while you are in the library, the knowledge will enter you and rise up to your conscious mind later, like bubbles rising to the surface of water.

Once you have found your information, give thanks for it, leave the library, and return to yourself. Remember to clear and release after.

Lesson
V

This is an excellent technique to use whenever you need to know something and simply cannot find it, or need to remember something and cannot think of it. The results are not always immediate, but they are usually fairly quick.

Lady Bitterwind likes to visit the library in her dreams. You can do this by programming yourself just before you go to bed that you will visit the library while you sleep. Be clear in your intent on the information you are seeking. Of course, it is also possible to visit the astral library without a specific purpose, rather as you might go to a real-world library, just to see what pulls you. Even then, it will still steer you toward something you need to know.

Glossary

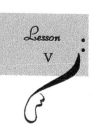

Alexandria—Termed the "capital *by* Egypt" rather than the "capital of Egypt" to indicate its technical status as a free Greek Polis, Alexandria was the largest and most glamorous city in the Hellenistic world. Founded by Ptolemy I Soter, Alexandria was a center of culture and learning unrivaled in its time. Among its greatest achievements were the Pharos light house, considered one of the Seven Wonders of the World, and the famous Library of Alexandria, actually a number of libraries centered on the Museion of Alexandria. Alexandria was considered separate from Egypt proper, which it ruled, and Alexandrian citizenship was almost as prized as (and considered a good recommendation toward) Roman citizenship. In Alexandria, Egyptian, Greek, and Jewish civilization co-existed side-by-side and intermingled, not without some strife; the result of this was an active and vigorous culture with a propensity for re-invigorating old ideas and creating new ones. Alexandria was especially noted for its highly developed ideas about magic, which have influenced magical theory and practice for centuries. Hermeticism and alchemy both trace their origins to Egypt through Alexandria: Hermeticism takes its name from Hermes Trismegistus, the Greek form of a title of the Egyptian god Thoth, while alchemy comes from *Al Chem*, meaning "black," as in *Kemet*, the Black Land, the native name of Egypt.

astral travel—Astral travel, or astral projection, is the term applied to traveling outside of the physical body while in a trance state. It is held that the part of the person that is able to do this is the astral body, a part of the consciousness associated with the astral plane. The astral body can assume any form but is generally perceived in the form of the physical body. Animal forms are sometimes preferred for astral travel, however—the astral body taking the form of a mouse, bird, wolf, or other animal for its out-of-body adventures. This is also called shape shifting, and is the origin of legends about werewolves and the like. Astral travel is a fairly advanced spiritual discipline, but it also can occur spontaneously without the person knowing that they are doing it, usually while sleeping or in moments of extreme crisis.

bi-locating—Bi-location is the art of being in two or more places at once. This is a kind of astral travel in which the person sends out their image to a secondary location from the body. Sometimes the image is experienced as solid and fully physical by people who see and interact with it; other times it may appear insubstantial, as if it were a ghost. Usually this is done intentionally and is a fairly high-level skill. Spontaneous bi-location, occurring without the conscious knowledge of the individual, most often occurs when sleeping.

enlightenment—Enlightenment is the state of having all seven levels of the being in alignment, so that the physical becomes a perfect vessel for Spirit and the entity experiences a state of conscious union with Deity. Enlightenment is sometimes spoken of as surrendering or extinguishing the conscious self or ego, but it is better to look at enlightenment as the expansion of the self to its full proportions; in this state, the conscious self becomes a conduit for Deity, increasing rather than losing its nature. Enlightenment is also sometimes described as *union* or *buddhahood*. Enlightenment is generally regarded as the ultimate destiny of the soul.

enneagram—An enneagram is a nine-pointed star sometimes drawn as a closed star made of three interlocking triangles, sometimes as an open-ended star with a more complex formation. The use of the enneagram as a spiritual and psychological tool was pioneered by Georg Gurdjief, a Christian mystic from Russian Georgia, and is based upon numerological theory. The open-ended enneagram symbol appears to have originated with Gurdjief, although some claim a more ancient origin for it, but complex theories involving the cosmological significance of the nine single digits date back to Pythagoras at least. The enneagram is used to represent and chart the relationships between these nine numbers. Use of the enneagram is very popular in psychology, although this is markedly different from its significance in Correllianism. In Correllian theology, the enneagram represents the nine monads, or ennead, each of which contains many souls, just as each soul contains many lives. The monads might be thought of as "oversouls" in the sense that the monad is to the soul what the soul is to the individual incarnation.

Gregorian—The Gregorian calendar was instituted in 1184 Pisces (AD 1584) at the order of Pope Gregory XIII in order to correct problems accreting with the Julian calendar, which had been in use since the time of Caius Julius Caesar. Over the course of centuries, the Julian calendar had fallen out of whack by ten days, offsetting the Christian religious calendar, to the annoyance of the papacy. On recommendations from a

panel headed by the Jesuit mathematician Christoph Clavius, Pope Gregory dropped ten days from the date and altered the system of leap years so that years ending in even hundreds were no longer counted as leap years unless divisible by 400. The new calendar was only gradually adopted outside of the Roman Catholic world, slowly displacing the Julian calendar.

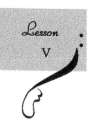

Hellenistic Era—The term *Hellenistic* refers to the international culture based upon Greek ("Hellenic") philosophy and education that came to dominate first the Mediterranean and then the Near East around the middle of the Arian Age (1200 BC–AD 400). The term particularly refers to the Greek-ruled kingdoms founded after the death of Alexander the Great in 877 Aries (323 BC). These kingdoms included Ptolemaic Egypt, Seleucid Syria, Pergamum, Pontus, and Bactria, among others. These kingdoms were strongly influenced by the Greek culture of their ruling dynasties, but they were enriched by their native cultures and by the cultural sharing that went on between them all. Hellenistic Egypt, ruled by the Ptolemies, was particularly noted as a center of metaphysical study, and many schools of metaphysics and magic flourished there. Thousands of magical papyri survive from this period, which show us the practices of the day. The cosmopolitan attitudes of Hellenistic Egypt strongly influenced Hermetics, alchemy, and Ceremonial magic.

language of God—Many cultures have had the idea that there is a specific "language of God," usually whatever language they themselves speak. They attribute metaphysical properties to the language and its parts, and regard that its words have an intrinsic magical power. Although several languages have been looked at in this way, one most commonly encounters the idea among Judeo-Christian mystics who regard the Hebrew language as the language of God. The Correllian Tradition would hold that human language, being by its very nature limited, cannot therefore be regarded as an appellation of Deity in this sense, Deity being by its nature unlimited in all ways. The Pythagoreans do, however, make an interesting argument for mathematics as the language of God, mathematics dealing as it does with universal concepts of number and pattern.

union—When we speak of union, we speak of being one with Deity. This is the state of enlightenment or buddhahood, in which all levels of the being are in sync and the physical self serves as a conscious vehicle for Deity. We taste a bit of this state when we draw down Deity to give an oracle or when we enter certain kinds of trance, but to be constantly in this state is to become a bridge between the worlds, eliminating the barrier between them so that the Lower Self and the Higher Self are at one and Deity is expressed through the being in a conscious manner.

Lesson
V

Lesson

VI

Death, Spirits, and Spirit Guides

"Don't worry for me, son. If Death comes to me, I will welcome him as a friend."

My mother spoke these words to me just before she went into the hospital for a lung biopsy. She had little reason to speak of death—a tiny spot on an x-ray—otherwise she was in perfect health. The words seemed meant to allay my disquiet; in fact, they told me she had chosen death.

My beloved mother met her friend Death three months later on September 13, AD 1989 (1589 Pisces). He had not kept her waiting long, yet he had given her all the time she needed to settle her affairs and speak what words her life had left unsaid. Soon after she died, a quiet rain began to fall, soft and gentle. "Rain is a blessing for the dead," my father said. It was an omen.

My mother met her death with quiet dignity and something of a conscious

181

premeditation. There was no fear, no hesitation. Indeed, it was an eager embrace, for she knew what lay beyond.

It was a fitting death. A Witch's death.

As far back as I can remember, Death was our friend. The rites and rituals of death were important in our family. Every spring brought pilgrimages to the cemeteries with carloads full of fragrant flowers: roses, irises, carnations, and always peonies, which my mother grew especially for the dead. At Yule there were always presents for the spirit of my dead sister, placed on her special altar with the snow-white miniature Yule tree, a practice discontinued when the family decided she had been reborn to us. The spirits were our friends, the beloved ancestors our guides. We spoke of them always, spoke to them often, and frequently they spoke back.

There was no need to fear death, no question of the soul's survival; surviving souls were all around us.

That does not mean that death occasioned no sadness, but fear was no component of that sadness.

. . . .

What Happens to You When You Die?

It is sometimes said, especially in the book religions, that we can only speculate or accept on faith what fate may follow death, for no one has ever returned to tell us what lies beyond.

This, however, is not true. Many people have returned from the OTHERSIDE, over the course of centuries and in modern times, and they are both coherent in their accounts of their experiences and in line with traditional Pagan teachings on the subject (thence the book religions' refusal to credit their experiences).

Those who have been on the Otherside and returned to tell about it fall basically into two categories: those whose experience of the Otherworld came to them accidentally and those whose experience of the Otherworld came to them intentionally.

Those who came to experience the Otherworld accidentally include those who have gone through the so-called near—death experience; that is to say, they have come near or experienced physical death yet been preserved from BRAIN DEATH and survived. Also, people who have been in comas or who have been grievously injured sometimes report near-death experiences.

The second group, those who have their Otherworld experiences intentionally, are people who walk between the worlds using visions and trance, arts that have been a major component of some traditions of Wicca, notably our own Correllian Tradition, in which they are considered Third Degree skills.

These two groups differ somewhat as to the details of crossing and initial reception, as is to be imagined; otherwise, they correlate quite nicely with each other, allowing for variations that are based in cultural perception.

. . . .

The First Group

So what do those who have died and returned have to say about it? Just what does happen to us when we die?

Those who know describe a distinct series of events.

First, the spirit leaves the body. How this is perceived depends, in part, on the manner of death. Many people describe the sensation of rushing through a dark tunnel and emerging into the light. It has been suggested that this is simply a natural reaction to oxygen deprivation to the brain, and perhaps this is so, for not everyone experiences this tunnel. Some simply find themselves outside of their bodies, with no particular perception of how they got there.

Having thus left the body, the spirit may cross directly to the Otherside or it may find itself lingering near its body. This depends partly on the frame of mind at the moment of death, as well as one's personal psychic experience or training; obviously it is easier for one who is psychically developed to make an easier transition to the Otherside, especially if one is proficient in astral travel or World Walking.

Those spirits who do linger near their own body often find themselves disoriented or confused. Commonly, they do not at first understand what has happened; they often don't realize that they are dead and in many cases do not recognize their body when they see it. Sometimes the spirit will remain near the body until this recognition comes. This is why the ancients sometimes buried a mirror with the deceased, and it is one of several reasons why they often used anthropoid coffins or effigies of the dead—to help the spirit recognize A) who it had been in life, and B) that it had, in fact, died.

Failure to recognize death can prevent the spirit from crossing over. The spirit may also be unable to cross to the Otherside if it is either afraid to do so (a particular problem for followers of the book religions) or if it is caught up in emotion over self-doubt (could have, would have, should have) or unfinished business. This is especially common in cases of unexpected or particularly traumatic deaths. Caught between the worlds, unable to participate in this world or cross fully into the other, these spirits are described by WORLD WALKERS as being enveloped by a grayish veil of negative energy, unable to perceive other spirits around them yet visible themselves to astral travelers as well as fully-crossed spirits. These spirits are stuck in place until they can either work out their

Lesson
VI

issues for themselves or until they allow themselves to be helped by their spirit guides or by a helpful world walker.

More commonly, however, the spirit crosses easily on its own. Either the spirit finds itself in the Otherside immediately or it lingers briefly near its body before perceiving the gateway to the Otherside. This gateway is usually described as a kind of doorway emitting a very bright white or bluish white light. This gate of light is the origin both of the now-hackneyed phrase "Go into the light" and of the term "Peret Em Heru" ("Coming Forth into Light"), the proper name of the famous Egyptian BOOK OF THE DEAD.

Sometimes the spirit will perceive this gateway as a river, characterized as Styx by the Greco-Romans and identified with the Jordan River by the book religions, but this is an older perception, not so commonly met with by modern people.

As the spirit passes through to the Otherside, it is usually greeted by other spirits—loved ones and spirit guides. Sometimes these spirits will appear to greet the new arrival even before it has crossed over and will help it through.

After being greeted by their loved ones and guides, the spirit is then brought before the Otherworld deity. How this deity is perceived by the spirit is very individual, for Deity always presents itself in the way that is most understandable to the indi-

vidual. Thus some perceive a God, others a Goddess, others simply an Essence. Christians who have returned from the Otherside often describe the Otherworld deity as Jesus, while Buddhists have spoken of AMIDA, and Wiccans the Goddess. Imperial Roman writings speak of Isis as welcoming arrivals on the Otherside.

Visually, the Otherworld deity is most often described as a Being of Light. This idea of Deity as a Being of Light is very ancient. It is spoken of in some classical myths, where a given deity (as Demeter in Eleusis or Zeus to Semele) is described as casting off its artificial human image to reveal its true nature as a Being of Light. It is also hinted at in the age-old identification of Deity with the heavenly bodies (sun, moon, and stars).

The deity greets the newcomer and is described as then proffering a sort of mirror. In this mirror, all of the events of the life just ending are replayed for the spirit. Those who have returned from the Otherside say that this is not just a passive viewing of the events of the life; it is accompanied by all of the emotion connected to the original living of those events. This allows the spirit to evaluate the life and the extent to which the life's intended purposes were achieved. This is the origin of the belief in divine judgment that has been so lamentably perverted by the book religions.

It is of extreme importance to emphasize that when Deity thus replays the events of the life just ended for the newly crossed-over spirit, Deity itself makes no judgment, according to those who have experienced it. Rather, the spirit itself evaluates the life according to its own understanding. This can be traumatic but often engenders considerable healing of old wounds.

The spirit then rejoins its loved ones and guides, who help it to settle in.

How the spirit perceives the Otherside seems to vary considerably. Always it is described as very pleasant and beautiful. Some people have described peaceful forests and rivers. Others speak of "cities of light" with "great libraries" that contain the AKASHIC wisdom of the universe. This is no doubt due in part to the varied ability of the conscious mind to understand what the spirit has experienced, among those who have died and returned. But it may also be due to variations in the level of development among the different spirits, for the spirit gains skill through its many lifetimes.

According to MABLE HIGHCORRELL, former head of the Correllian Tradition, there are many different places in the Otherworld, just as there are in this world. Though all go to the same Otherworld, where the spirits gravitate to within it is dependent upon both level of development and the amount of rest required to recover

from the life just ended. Perhaps the old joke is actually a pretty good description:

A Wiccan priestess dies and is greeted on the Otherside by her grandmother. After being settled in, the priestess is given the grand tour by the grandmother, who shows her many places and introduces her to many fellow spirits. They see druids cavorting in sacred groves, Norsefolk feasting and fighting in a banquet hall, Buddhists chanting in a pagoda, Native Americans dancing; everywhere the newcomer is made welcome and makes new friends. Then the priestess and her grandmother came to a large, dark stone building, within which they hear the sound of singing. "Shhh," says the grandmother, with her finger to her lips, "be very quiet." So the two tiptoe past, and when they have gone on a little way, the priestess asks about this curious building. "Oh," says the grandmother, "that's just the Christians. They think they're the only ones here."

Traditional Pagan theology teaches that the Otherworld is a kind of paradise, a place of feasting and celebration in an idyllic setting presided over by the Otherworld deity, who may be perceived as either Goddess or God. Those who have returned confirm rather than question this ancestral view. The world of the living is a place of challenges and transformation, typified by constant lessons and growth. But the Otherworld is a place of peace and joy, at least for those resting between lives.

Not all spirits rest, of course. More advanced spirits are often as busy between lives as during them; many act as SPIRIT GUIDES to the living. Spirit guides, what the book religions call GUARDIAN ANGELS, help the living in daily life and especially in matters of spiritual development. These are usually preexisting relationships built up over a number of lifetimes, probably originating in the Otherworld.

Often a spirit will be reborn many times into the same family or bloodline, for the purpose of achieving a multigenerational goal. This is also true for some organizations such as the LAMAS of Tibet or the Wiccan clergy. The purpose of such multigenerational projects is sometimes so that a given spirit or group of spirits can learn a particular lesson that cannot be achieved through one lifetime, or achieve a level of spiritual growth in a given system that requires more than one lifetime to accomplish, or it can be because a group of advanced spirits wishes to make a change in the world, for which it needs many generations of effort. Between lives, the spirits involved in these multigenerational projects will often act as spirit guides to the other members of the project, who may or may not have conscious knowledge of the multigenerational work they are involved in. This kind of spirit guide is called an ancestor, whether the bond to the living is one of blood or of common membership,

as in a clerical order. In the Correllian Tradition they are spoken of as "beloved" or sometimes with the more common phrase "of beloved memory."

The beloved ancestors are often spoken of as having been "DEIFIED"—that is, they are regarded in a manner very similar to a patron deity. The beloved ancestors are consulted for advice and help, and honored with ceremonies and symbolic offerings of food or gifts; these offerings represent the respect in which the beloved ones are held, for it is understood that they do not require any sort of sustenance. The beloved ancestors are also sometimes spoken of as the "Old Ones."

There are other jobs for spirit guides besides helping the living. Notably, guides help other spirits to cross over, just as world walkers do from this side. Spirit guides also help facilitate spiritual healing for the residents of both this world and the Otherworld.

. . . .

The Second Group

The second group we shall consider are those whose experience of the Otherworld comes through crossing over voluntarily. In this case, the crossing between the earthly world and the Otherworld comes not through death but through vision and trance.

This is not as rarified an experience as it may first sound; indeed, I dare say that anyone who has made a serious study of Pagan religion must have encountered, if not necessarily taken part in, this practice.

Among the most famous practitioners of this art are the followers of shamanic religions. The shamanic religions include, but need not be considered limited to, Siberian, East Asian, Native American, and Inuit tribal religions. Voluntarily crossing between the worlds is a major component of shamanic religion.

The shamans induce trance in a number of ways, including meditation, music, and dance. Some use mind-altering substances as well, such as the famous Peyote mushroom or hashish, but this is by no means the dominant practice.

Using trance, shamans travel between worlds to communicate with deities, spirit guides, and higher aspects of their own or others' souls. Among the spirit guides that shamans deal with are the ancestors, the spirits of those who are in the Otherworld. Shamans cross into the Otherworld to speak with the ancestors, to be taught by them, and to undergo initiatory experiences.

Shamanic descriptions of the Otherworld vary, according to the shaman's cultural perceptions and their purposes for dealing with the Otherworld. Usually the Otherworld is perceived as looking much like this world but having a dreamlike quality. The laws we perceive as physics do not apply there, nor does time exist there as we understand it. For this reason, the shaman may experience a time distortion between the perceived time of the trance and the time that elapses in the physical world. There is not always a clear relationship between cause and effect.

The shaman's experiences often include highly symbolic elements. This is because the mind can only understand things in terms of what it knows, and so when the shaman returns from beyond the veil, the shamanic experience can only be understood in terms of earthly symbols and references. There are many things in the Otherworld our earthly minds simply cannot wrap themselves around except through symbols.

As to spirits, shamans usually find them to be much as they were in life, only expanded. Sometimes the more negative aspects of the personality have dropped away or lessened, and the spirits often seem to be fully in command of their soul's higher powers.

Shamanic experience agrees with that of the near-death experience in describing the Otherworld as a pleasant place with much going on, not a place of reward or punishment as posited by more primitive religions.

Voluntary crossing between the worlds was once a major component of European Witchcraft as well. Many once-important spiritual practices of ancestral Wicca have all but disappeared from modern practice. Drawing Down the Moon is one of the few widespread instances of the once-vital technique of channeling divine messages from God/dess and from the ancestors, and many temples today no longer even do or understand how to Draw Down the Moon.

For the Witches of Germany, the Hexen, crossing between the worlds was an extremely important aspect of their beliefs. The Hexen believed in THE WILD RIDE. In the Wild Ride, the Goddess or God of the Otherworld would lead the spirits of the dead in a great procession, often portrayed as a hunting party. This spirit procession would careen wildly through the countryside in the dead of night.

There were various beliefs about when this happened. Some said the Wild Ride occurred on nights of the full moon, some said it happened at the cross-quarter days (solstices and equinoxes), still others ascribed the Wild Ride to a series of holidays called the Ember Days. Some believed that the Wild Ride could occur on any night. But they all agreed that for a living person to encounter the Wild Ride was a very bad thing. It meant they were destined

to join the spirits soon, and would either die on the spot or within the year.

The exception to this was the Hexen themselves. The Hexen believed that they could go into trance, leave their bodies (a process often pictured as a the soul emerging from the body in the form of a white mouse, a theme touched upon in the *Vangello delle Streghe*), and go forth to join the Wild Ride as members. Here they would join the spirits of the Otherworld and communicate with them.

When they joined the Wild Ride, the Hexen could carry messages from the living to their loved ones in spirit and bring back messages in return. The Hexen might also ask the spirits about future events, be taught magic, or request favors from the spirits. Sometimes the Hexen would see the astral form of another living person in the Ride, and then they would know that person was either another Hexe or someone who would soon cross over.

The Wild Ride was described as a joyous and exhilarating event, led either by the Lord or Lady of the Otherworld. In the German Witch Trials, the Wild Ride was often described as being led by the Goddess Holda, Holle, or Hella. Despite the grim picture the Sagas paint of her, the transcripts of the Witch Trials describe Hella as a beautiful Goddess who rules over an Otherworld paradise of joy and delight, the same Otherworld scenario described by those who have had near-death experiences. In the trial transcripts, Hella was likened not to the Roman goddess Diana but to Venus, goddess of love and pleasure, and the Otherworld paradise was termed Der Venusberg.

As well as joining the Wild Ride, the Hexen also made it a regular feature of their practice to cross over into the Otherworld, Venusberg, to commune with the Goddess and the spirits of the ancestors. The Hexen described Venusberg as a scene of joyous feasting and revelry. Often this trance-induced trip to the Otherworld is confused in the trial transcripts with the idea of a physical sabbat. This same confusion arose in other countries, too; this is the source of the legend of Witches flying to the sabbat. Because they did not admit of an astral plane or astral body, Christians were unable to differentiate between a physical and an astral journey.

Both the shamans and the Hexen are examples of world walkers. A world walker is one who voluntarily crosses between the worlds, usually for the purpose of communicating or interacting with the beloved ancestors.

What does a world walker do? In addition to bringing back messages from the spirits, world walkers serve several other important functions. World walkers often help spirits who are stuck between the worlds to finish crossing over. They do this by locating the spirit and literally guiding them into the Otherworld, encouraging them and soothing their fears, if necessary. World walkers also help spirits to be reborn, a process vital to the full awakening of the soul. This is done in just the same way: the world walker must locate the spirit in the Otherworld and literally guide them to a favorable new incarnation. In this way, the spirit of an adept may be helped into an incarnation in which it will be recognized as such and from which it may pick up its work where it left off. In both of these processes, the world walker joins efforts with spirit guides who are actually in the Otherworld.

World walkers also sometimes act as spirit guides themselves, depending upon their level of expertise. In this capacity, they may assist either those who are in the Otherworld or others on this side of the veil whom they contact psychically. Sometimes a spirit may only receive certain kinds of healing from one who is in this world. It is said that this is because this world is the place of transformation, and that while those who are in spirit can grow and expand, they cannot necessarily transform without our help. For this reason, we should inaugurate as much positive transformation as possible during our time in the physical world.

The experiences of the world walkers agree with those of the shamans and the

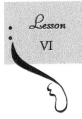

near-death experiencers that the Otherworld is a beautiful place of great joy to its inhabitants. There is much activity, especially learning, teaching, and healing, and there is much communication between the earthly world and the Otherworld.

· · · ·

What It Is Like to Be a Spirit

Though they perceive it as being much like this world, due to the limitations of the human mind, those who have experienced the Otherworld say that it is made of light—that is to say, energy. The spirits who inhabit the Otherworld do not have a physical body but rather an energy body, which is in essence quite different.

The spiritual body, composed of light/energy, does not speak as we do but rather communicates instantly through telepathy. Its method of communication is psychic, through feeling and knowing rather than through words. The spiritual body also has no concept of space, as we do. In the Otherworld, spirits move from one place to another by conceiving it and transporting instantly.

Yet what we might think of as physical sensations are extremely strong in spirit. Any person who has done serious work with magical energy will have some idea of what is meant by this, for energetic sensations are at least as strong as physical sensations, and often much stronger. Indeed,

when two spirits touch, even casually, the sensation is incomparable to anything in physical experience, except perhaps orgasm. This is why when a person in this world dreams of a communication from a spirit, it will sometimes be remembered as inappropriately sexual, as it is one of the few things the mind has to compare the sensation to.

We know that this is so because the most advanced among us have been able to perceive the Otherworld in this way when they have returned from it. For most of us, however, when we travel to the Otherworld and return, the memory we bring back will have been filtered through our conscious mind and rendered into more familiar terms. Thus the Otherworld is usually remembered as looking pretty much like this one, and the spirits of our beloved ancestors appear to us like their physical selves rather than as luciform energy bodies. This is both because our minds have little frame of reference for pure energy and also because of our emotional and mental attachments, which are benefited as well by the familiar frame of reference.

· · · ·

What If I Have Trouble Crossing Over?

It sometimes happens that the soul has trouble crossing into the Otherworld and becomes stuck between worlds. This happens when the soul is overwhelmed by doubt, emotion, or confusion. This can be caused by a traumatic death or by an inability to release earthly situations. It can also be caused by fear of what lies beyond.

When we have become stuck in this way, we usually perceive it in one of two ways: either as a dreamlike version of our earthly life that never seems to change or progress, or as a series of symbolic events or gateways that allegorize the process of releasing the blockage(s) holding us back.

This allegorical process of release is what the Egyptians are describing in their Book of the Dead, where the soul's internal blockages are externalized as a series of gates, or pylons, through which the soul must pass. The method the Egyptians used to ease this passage is equally symbolic. They used magical formulae designed to act as keys to the Higher Self, intended to help the soul release its blockages from a superconscious level. This method works perfectly well—to a point, anyway.

Thus, if in crossing over you find your way blocked by a gateway or a "guardian" of some sort, the externalization of an inner blockage, a ritual formula attesting to your purity of spirit, delivered with true belief, will usually be enough to open the way. This works in the same way as all magic spells, a seemingly "automatic" act that is, in fact, a key triggering a more complicated

internal process that we do not consciously perceive as it occurs.

In any event, whether you experience being stuck between the worlds as a stagnant replica of earthly life or an allegorical vision, there are specific things you can do to break free of whatever is blocking you and move on: 1) Stay calm. Look inside and meditate. When souls are unable to cross over fully, it is usually because of anxiety or fear. Release these, and the crossing can usually be completed with ease. 2) Listen for your spirit guides: they are still with you and will be trying to help you. Call for them and be open to their aid. Sometimes when a soul is stuck between the worlds, its guides will seek out a world walker to help reach the soul from this side of the veil. Sometimes a world walker can succeed where spirit guides fail, since those who are stuck between the worlds are often closer to this side of the veil.

And, of course, it is always good to pray. Ask the Goddess to come and help you across; as soon as you are able to receive her, she will.

. . . .

How We Can Help Those Who Are Crossing from This Side

Because those who have difficulty crossing over are frequently closer to this side of the veil than they are to the Otherworld itself, we can sometimes be of great help to them.

We have spoken of how a world walker can help to guide a spirit to the Otherside, and as Pagans we do well to take advantage of this skill. In the Correllian Tradition, we have always tried to assist the spirits crossing in this way, whenever we felt there was a need for it.

Other things we can and should do for our loved ones in spirit include sending them energy. We can do this in a variety of ways: through prayer and meditation, as well as focused acts of power. A very simple technique is to simply say a prayer and light a candle in honor of the spirit; the energy generated by the candle then benefits the spirit. Another technique is to visualize the spirit, then form a ball of white light, and send it to the spirit. The process of crossing over can sometimes be draining to the spirit, and sending them extra energy in this way can be very helpful.

Another thing we can do to help the spirit in its process of crossing over is to enact one or more ceremonies of soul retrieval to help release blockages. This is done by ritually calling forth the spirit, visualizing it strongly, and enacting the ceremony for the spirit's benefit.

It can also be important to make sure that the appropriate funereal ceremonies are observed—meaning those that were desired by the spirit during life. This may help the spirit to cross over by providing it a sense of closure on the life just ending.

Also, the appropriate ceremonies can help to focus the spirit for its eventual return. For the Highcorrells, it was always considered extremely important that the soul should return to the family to continue the family business.

. . . .

How Do I Return?

Return? How do I return? Isn't that taken care of on the Otherside?

Well, yes, it is. But we can help. Those of us who are adepts usually want to return to pick up our work where we left off. Indeed, when an adept is reborn, it sometimes happens that there is scarcely a break for the new life to take shape before the work is picked up again. This is called *conscious incarnation*. I have lived this and know it to be true.

There are many things which those on this side can do to help a spirit return. But of course the most important part is up to the spirit.

When an adept is dying, they must try to stay focused on the concept of a swift return in a suitable incarnation. The world walkers can help the spirit by staying in contact with it once it has passed to the Otherside and by making sure it has a swift passage.

Once on the Otherside, the adept must remain focused on the idea of return and must choose parents for the new incarnation that will be conducive to its purposes, i.e., resumption of magical training and activity. Often these will be found within the family of the previous incarnation or among friends or associates from the previous incarnation. Sometimes, however, the new parents will come from some entirely different origin, yet still are within the same soul group.

In the case of a focused adept, the world walkers assist rather than guide this process, but sometimes the world walkers must actually guide, for it does not always go as smoothly as all that. The spirit may lose its focus and need to be reminded of its original intentions. Sometimes the spirit will simply change its mind, and the process will end there. Usually, however, the spirit will allow itself to be guided back to the original plan and a suitable rebirth.

Once born, the conscious incarnate can be identified in a number of ways. The world walkers who have assisted the spirit will sometimes be able to identify the new parents; usually it is not that simple, though. Often psychic means can be employed to narrow down the field, and clairvoyant messages, divination, and astrology can all be used to help locate a conscious incarnate. When the child as whom the ancestor has returned is old enough, it can be tested; the child's dreams, past-life memories, and ability to identify people or objects connected with its last incarnation can greatly help to identify it as a conscious incarnate.

This is, of course, the same process that has been used by the Lamas of Tibet to identify a *tulku*, the Tibetan term for a conscious incarnate.

By identifying the conscious incarnate (commonly termed an incarnate for short), the child's education can be geared toward using the major strengths of its spirit and toward continuing the work started in the preceding incarnation. In this way the break between incarnations is bridged, and instead of experiencing many short lives, we begin to build one long one with brief interruptions.

Lesson
VI

. . . .

Exercises

In Lesson V we dealt with exercises that should be done occasionally, rather than as part of our daily routine. That will also be the case in this lesson.

At this point, your daily sequence of exercises should now begin with the Ohm exercise, then open the chakras with balls of colored light, changing the balls of colored light to balls of white light, changing the balls of white light to balls of purple light, changing the balls of purple light to balls of silver stellar light, and then filling your aura with silver stellar light. Next, change the balls of silver stellar light to balls of golden stellar light, then fill your aura with golden stellar light. Finally, change the balls of golden stellar light to balls of amber light, and fill your aura with the amber light. Now, from each chakra, call forth its personified form, and imagine it before you. You would then do Exercise 11 or any other of the occasional exercises at this point. Remember to close the chakras and clear and release when finished.

You have been using this routine for some time now, and there is a reason for that, as you will learn in Lesson VIII. It is necessary for the chakras to be strong and well exercised in order to make the next jump in the daily routine.

In this lesson's exercises, we will continue working with our personified chakras.

One of the many reasons for working with the personified chakras is to be able to better relate to and assess the condition of your chakras. Exercise 11 will show you one way to use the personification of your chakra to strengthen or heal it.

Exercise 11

It is probably best to do this exercise right after the daily routine, at least while learning it. Later you will be able to do it at any time, without going through the whole routine.

You will work with the personified chakras one at a time in this exercise. You may want to do them all at one time or over several days. It is probably best to start

with the root chakra and work your way up through the other chakras in sequence.

Go all the way through the daily routine until you have opened each personified chakra. Now you will want to focus on just the one personified chakra you are going to strengthen and heal.

Begin by assessing the general condition of the chakra. How does it look? How does it feel to you? Does it seem healthy? Well balanced? Take note of anything that seems to indicate a problem: is the image murky, the colors dull, the form of the personified chakra unhealthy-looking?

Now ask the personified chakra itself what kind of condition it is in, and let it answer. The answer may come in words or symbols.

If the chakra is in good condition, then this exercise will serve to strengthen it. If there is any problem, then this exercise will help heal it.

Once you have assessed the chakra's condition, make an incantation to declare your intent to strengthen and heal the chakra; you may wish to ask Deity to help you. You might make a declaration like this:

"Behold, there is one power in the universe, and I am a perfect manifestation of that power, and as such I call upon the divine power within me to strengthen this chakra

*and heal it of anything which
ails it. Divine Mother Goddess,
divine Father God, lend me your
aid in this undertaking, I pray
you! By my will, so mote it be!"*

Now imagine a ball of white light above your personified chakra. From that ball of light see a shower of light descend, filling the personified chakra—clear, shining light going into every part of the personified chakra. See the personified chakra filling with light, glowing with light as if a sun were within it, light shining out in all directions. See the light force out any negative energy, see the light heal any imperfection, and focus your intent on strength and healing.

As you do this, you may expect to see a change in the image of the personified chakra. Some of this you will cause consciously. You should address any aspect of the chakra's appearance that you noted as unhealthy and deliberately change it at this point. A murky image should become sharp, muddy colors should become clear, and the personified form should appear healthy and happy. Continue flooding the image with light until any such issue is addressed.

You may also see changes beyond those you consciously cause: the chakra may seem to grow larger or its appearance may alter. Eventually the personified chakra

will display signs of pleasure or delight, as smiling, laughing, dancing, etc. Sometimes they seem to sprout wings and fly around. This is when you know you are done. Sometimes this will come quickly, sometimes it can take quite a while.

When your personified chakra reaches the stage of showing pleasure, it is as full of light as it can be. Let the image of the shower of light cease. Thank the chakra, and talk with it for a while if you like. You can then either close the chakra or continue working in some other capacity.

You should do this for each of your chakras. Again, you can try to do them all in one session, but it is probably best to do them one a day. Remember that this is a special exercise, not meant to become a permanent part of the daily routine. It is a technique you can and should use periodically, however, to help keep your chakras in good running order.

When you have thus strengthened and healed all of the personified chakras, you are ready to move on to Exercise 12.

· · · ·

Spell for Lesson VI
Working with Spirit Guides

In keeping with our subject for Lesson VI, our spell for this lesson deals with death and the spirit realm. As in Lesson V, this spell is not so much a spell as a technique that should become a regular practice.

In the lesson we speak of spirit guides, and indeed we have spoken about spirit guides throughout these lessons. But how do we go about establishing communication with our spirit guides?

Everyone has spirit guides. As a rule, people have approximately five guides, of which one will be predominant. People who do a great deal of spiritual work may have many more spirit guides than this. Sometimes guides will be ancestors, but this is not always the case. Sometimes someone you have known in life who subsequently dies will become a guide to you. However, in all cases, your guides are spirits with whom you have had a preexisting spiritual connection.

If you have never worked with guides before, then you should start simply. Like so many other things in spiritual practice, the skill of communicating with spirits is one that is built through practice.

The best way to begin working with your guides is to make them regular offerings. The simplest offering is a lit candle. Because candles help to generate energy, even if you are making other offerings you should always include a candle. A good general offering is one of water and flour or cornmeal, along with a lit candle, though anything can be used for an offering. The offering, of course, is symbolic, but remember that symbols are keys and so can be very important.

Make your offering preferably around the same time each day, and address the guides. Ask them to accept the offering, and thank them for all their help you have received, whether you are aware of it or not. State that you wish to work with them more regularly and to learn to receive messages from them.

Then sit with a piece of paper and a pen, or better, with a partner who is also working on building better communication with the guides so that you can take notes for each other. Get comfortable. Clear and release. Close your eyes, and relax your mind.

Do not think; this does not mean that nothing will come into your mind but that you will not grab onto words or images that come to you. You want to do this passively: to receive messages. But don't clamp down on your mind either, or you won't be able to let the messages in. Whatever comes into your mind, write it on the paper or say it to your partner. Even if it seems trivial, record it, and do not judge it. Do not worry about whether it is "real or imagination" at this stage. If you have never done it before, you wouldn't necessarily be able to tell the difference anyway, although you will later. Rather, accept whatever comes to you uncritically. You can evaluate it afterward and indeed should take it with a grain of salt.

When you first do this, what you get may make little sense or have little relevance. This is natural. As you practice, this should change. You will also notice that as you practice, you will be better able to identify the physical sensation that accompanies messages. If you do this daily, within a few weeks your messages should become clear and have meaning. This is because it takes a while to establish a channel for communication; like a muscle, the skill increases with use.

Even then, you must at no point set aside common sense. Take everything with a grain of salt, and be skeptical. Assess your messages based on what you know of the situation and on track record. If you get a message telling you to sell everything you own and spend the proceeds on lottery tickets, don't do it. Usually your messages will be correct, but you must never forget that the information must come through your brain in order to be received, and in so doing, the information may sometimes be warped. No matter how skilled you become, it is always possible to warp the message.

As you become more skilled with talking to your guides, you should be able to "see" them. If you have been doing your exercises right along with the lessons, this should be relatively easy, because you will have built up the necessary skill with visualization. To see the spirits, you only need to relax

and allow yourself to do so, and trust what you get. The process is the same as receiving any other kind of information. In all areas of clairvoyance, the issue of trusting what you receive is of paramount importance, because if you second-guess what you are receiving, you may freeze up and stop the process. You can look at the information critically after you have brought it through, but not while doing so.

To see the guides, allow their image to come to you; have no preconceptions of what they should look like. Let them show you the face they need to. Even if you have seen a given spirit guide many times, there will be occasions when they may assume a different form for some reason, usually in order to emphasize some aspect of the message they are giving.

Obviously, the more you work with your guides, the better your connection will be. At first, it is likely that the communication will consist of messages dealing with mundane situations, but the guides are likely to provide direction in spiritual development as well. When the connection becomes strong enough, they may ask you to sit for energy work and do energy healing for you. This is a very interesting experience and can sometimes be quite intense.

This spell is only a brief introduction to working with guides, and if you continue your studies to Third Degree you will learn much more about them. Though it is very

basic, by practicing the above-given technique, you will be able to establish a strong relationship with your guides, which will form the basis for much later work.

. . . .

Glossary

Akashic—*Akasha* is a Hindu term for Spirit, the element from which the other four elements arise. The Theosophists taught that every feeling, thought, and action is recorded in Akasha, forming the Akashic Records, which may be accessed through trance. There are many other terms for the Akashic Records, including *Collective Subconscious*.

Amida—Amida Buddha is the central figure of Pure Land Buddhism, the Pure Land being the Otherworld, or afterlife. Amida is the Buddha of Everlasting Light. In Pure Land Buddhism, Amida is regarded as a previous incarnation of Gautama Buddha, who as a bodhisattva deferred enlightenment in order to confer eternal life in the Pure Land paradise on anyone who called upon him. This promise on the part of the bodhisattva was termed the Original Vow. Pure Land Buddhism arose out of Mahayana Buddhism in India, spread to China, where it was very popular, and ultimately spread to Japan. In Tibetan, Amida is known as Amitabha, and in Chinese as Amitofu; Amida is the Japanese form.

Book of the Dead—The Book of the Dead is a series of chapters intended to assist the deceased in the Afterworld through invocations, spells, and what we today might term visualizations. The Book of the Dead developed steadily throughout the history of ancient Egypt, ultimately totaling some 200 chapters, though each copy of the book was individual and no one known copy contained all 200 chapters. The earliest known chapters of the Book of the Dead come from the walls of pyramids dating to the fifth and sixth dynasties—very early indeed, though the Egyptians made the claim that they were already ancient then. The Book of the Dead is intended to guide the deceased to Amentet, the Blessed Land of the god Osiris and goddess Isis. Along the way, the deceased must pass many tests and avoid many monsters, which might be regarded as externalizations of spiritual blockages that must be cleared before the spirit can advance. In Egyptian, the Book of the Dead is called the *Peret Em Heru*, or "Coming Forth in Light."

brain death—Brain death occurs when the brain ceases functioning. People are often said to "die" when their heart ceases functioning, even though the

Lesson VI

brain is still working; this is perhaps better termed "near death." People often return from near-death experiences and tell similar tales of their experiences in the spirit world, but it is said that no one has returned following brain death. Whether this is true or whether it is only true that no one has been shown to have returned to life following brain death is open to speculation.

deified—The Pagan idea of "deification," whereby a person is looked upon more or less as a deity, is widely misunderstood. It is rooted in the idea of Deity as the diamond of many facets; because all things that exist reflect Deity, anything that exists can be a personal form of Deity, no less an ancestor than an allegorical idea. The beloved ancestors are looked on very much as one might look on a patron deity, and looked to for advice, teaching, and assistance just as one might look to a patron deity in this regard. Particularly important ancestors are sometimes looked upon as patrons of a whole group of people or of a given activity—again, just as one might look at a patron deity. A famous example of this is the deified Roman emperor Augustus, who was looked on as a patron deity of the state, or his deified wife Livia, whom we would regard as the patron of long-range plans.

There are those who would look at such deceased Pagan religious figures such as Om Seti or Lawrence Durdin-Robertson in a similar manner. Such persons are referred to as beloved ancestors and are very similar in character to Christian saints or Buddhist bodhisattvas.

Highcorrell, Mable—Mable Highcorrell was the youngest daughter of Caroline Highcorrell and the second Head of the Correllian Tradition. Born 24 January 1499 Pisces (AD 1899), Mable was the only one of Caroline Highcorrell's three daughters to survive her mother, succeeding as Head of Tradition in 1539 Pisces (AD 1939). Lady Mable was strongly influenced by Eastern philosophies and by theories of the nature of reality and illusion. A gifted medium, Lady Mable worked extensively with the ancestors and spirit guides. She also worked extensively with time magic and the manipulation of probability. The exercises used for psychic development in these lessons come largely from Lady Mable. Lady Mable died in February of 1566 Pisces (AD 1966), leaving her daughter LaVeda as the family's last matriarchal heiress of unbroken lineage.

Lamas—A Lama is a monk of the Lamaist school of Mahayana Buddhism. Lamaist Buddhism is a form of

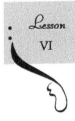

Buddhism traditionally based in Tibet that contains elements of the preexisting Bon religion as well as elements of Indian origin not always thought of as Buddhist. Lamaism is known for its advanced spiritual and energetic practices and techniques. Lamaism is also known for the practice of conscious incarnation, whereby spiritually advanced adepts, known as *tulku*, return to the same job through a succession of lifetimes, forming in essence a single very long life with brief interruptions.

Otherside—The *Otherside* is a term for the Spiritworld or Afterworld: where we go between lives. It is perceived as being on the "other side" of the veil, obscured from normal human perception.

spirit guides/guardian angels—*Guardian angel* is another term for a *spirit guide*—a spirit who aids and protects an individual through life. Some people interact with their guardian angels/spirit guides consciously, seeking their advise and assistance, while others have no conscious interaction with their guardian angels/spirit guides but are helped and assisted by them anyway. As a rule, *guardian angel* is a term that tends to be used in Judeo-Christian circles, but the term is not limited to these and is sometimes used by Wiccans as well. Some Judeo-Christians think of guard-

ian angels as beings that have never been physically incarnate, while others perceive them as the souls of the blessed dead, like Clarence in the movie "It's a Wonderful Life."

Wild Ride—In certain ancient mythologies, most notably Germanic, the spirits of the dead were believed to ride out in a great procession on certain nights. Some said this ride took place on nights of the full moon, others said it was only on certain festivals. Often the ride was characterized as a "hunt." It was believed that the living could join in this "ride" through astral projection. This was the basis of the German school of Witchcraft known as the Hexen, and is well attested to in trial transcripts from the Burning Times. Sometimes the Wild Ride was said to be led by the Crone Goddess. Sometimes the leader of the Wild Ride was the Horned God. There are many interesting descriptions of this Wild Ride in old literature. Odin, Herne the Hunter, Herlichinus (afterwards Harlequin), and a variety of other forms of the Horned God were said to lead the Ride. The hunt of Diana and her nymphs is sometimes seen as a version of the Wild Ride as well.

world walkers—A world walker is a person who walks between the worlds; that is, through trance and magic they are

active in the Spiritworld. World walkers assist spirits during the process of
death, between incarnations, and toward
rebirth. They also work with powerful
healing techniques and can act in the
same manner as spirit guides. World
walkers are particularly important in
the process of conscious incarnation, as
they assist the incarnate in remaining
focused between the end of one life and
the beginning of the next.

Lesson

VI

Lesson
VII

Sex Magic

In writing about sex magic, it is not our intention so much to instruct you in its performance as to familiarize you with the ideas and principles behind it and to show how sex and sexuality are viewed in Pagan religion.

One of the cardinal differences between the Pagan and the book religions is how they view gender and sexuality.

In the book religions, sexuality is viewed as shameful and is connected to ideas of weakness, dominance, and submission. Sexuality is blamed for the supposed FALL OF MAN and is believed responsible for all manner of evil in the world. One sees in the book religions a rejection of sexuality and consequently also of creativity, spontaneity, and self-acceptance. Moreover, this rejection of sexuality is also a rejection of the role of women, who are suppressed as a group and as individuals. This suppression of the female is known as PATRIARCHY, and though not unique to the book religions, it is strongly identified with them.

In Pagan religions, sexuality is revered as both a normal and desirable part of life and as an important manifestation of divine energy. Sexuality is seen as a source of strength rather than weakness, an important aspect of self-acceptance and spiritual integration.

Note that the acceptance of sexuality is not the opposite of its rejection. The book religions always fear that acceptance of sexuality means a sexual indulgence as extreme as their own repression. This is not the case. Rather, acceptance of sexuality aims for a healthy sexuality within a balanced life. Some individuals may choose extremity in their sexual expression, and that is theirs to choose, but it is not the definition of sexual acceptance. Similarly, MATRIARCHY is not the opposite of patriarchy, with females rigidly oppressing males, but rather is a balanced system that allows an important role for both genders.

Acceptance of sexuality exalts both genders, especially the female as the bearer of life. Indeed, the acceptance of sexuality is the acceptance of life as a good and holy state, while the book religions' rejection of sexuality is based upon a conception of earthly life as EVIL.

In most Pagan religions, the union of Goddess and God, Spirit and Matter, Yin and Yang, is a central element of the religion, and this is normally portrayed in terms of romantic/sexual union. This is described as the Divine Marriage, or HIEROGAMOS, and it figures in Pagan thought at a number of levels, including the cosmic level, where the union of Goddess and God creates and sustains the universe, and the personal level, where the union of Spirit and Matter, and the interaction between them, holds the key to personal spiritual growth. This is the nature of the ALCHEMICAL MARRIAGE, the Wiccan Great Rite, and a host of other traditions that depict the union of the lower (physical) self with the Higher (spiritual) Self in sexual terms, and that identify this internal process and the individual with the cosmic forces.

· · · ·

Sex Magic in the Ancient World

In many ancient cultures, this idea of divine marriage as a personal union with Spirit was enacted literally. The kings and queens of many ancient cultures included the hierogamos as a central feature of their ceremonial duties. The king would gain or renew his spiritual mandate by symbolically wedding the Goddess, embodied by the queen or a priestess. By so doing, the king identified himself with the God. The children that resulted from the ceremony were often considered to be simultaneously the children of the royal couple and also of the divine powers they had embodied during the ceremony.

A famous series of murals from the Temple of the Eighteenth Dynasty Pharaoh HATSHEPUSITU at Deir el Bahri shows the story of her divine conception and birth as the daughter of the Egyptian god Amon, presumably through such a rite, in which her mother, Queen Ahmose, took the role of Goddess, and her father, Pharaoh Tehutmose I, took the role of Amon.

This was one of the premises upon which many ancient kings claimed to be divine, their mystical identification with the god. But the practice of hierogamos was not limited to royalty. In many ancient cultures, hierogamos was practiced by the priestesses of the Mother Goddess who initiated ordinary men into the sexual mysteries. In some societies, all women were expected to spend a brief period before marriage studying and practicing the sexual mysteries and the hierogamos, some making a lifetime vocation of it. The book religions castigated these priestesses as prostitutes, calling them SACRED HARLOTS, and indeed in later ages the sexual mysteries did sometimes degenerate into mere sex, but in its proper form it encompassed all of the aspects of sexual magic that will be discussed below.

The hierogamos is the basis of the Wiccan Great Rite, in which priestess and priest are identified with and spiritually embody the Goddess and God and celebrate the divine union. In ritual, this is ordinarily performed symbolically by uniting the athame with the chalice. However, the Great Rite is sometimes celebrated privately in a more literal form by a married or otherwise involved couple.

Often a child conceived as a result of hierogamy is described as being of divine birth or of virgin birth. In both cases, the premise is that the physical father is not present at conception but rather the god whom he is embodying. This does not necessarily cancel out the physical father though, as often both the physical father and the god are looked upon as simultaneously being the parent. Thus, Hatshepusitu was simultaneously the daughter of Tehutmose I and the god Amon, while Alexander the Great was simultaneously the son of Philip of Macedon and Zeus, and Augustus Caesar was simultaneously the son of Octavius and Apollo. Though the mother embodies the Goddess in the rite, the Goddess is not normally reckoned as the mother because the mother's role extends far beyond the conception; however, there are exceptions to this, as AENEAS being considered the son of Venus, or Achilles the son of Thetis. Presumably both Aeneas and Achilles were sons of priestesses who embodied the relevant goddess during hierogamy.

It should be noted that hierogamy can occur in other forms besides symbolic and literal enactment. Hierogamy can be

enacted on the astral plane or through a dream or vision. This sort of hierogamy is usually spontaneous and unexpected. It was in this way that the Lady Atia, mother of Augustus Caesar, claimed Apollo as the father of her child, because he had come to her in a dream when she slept at his temple.

. . . .

Sex Magic in India

When people think of sex magic, they often think of India. The Indian sexual yoga, often termed *tantra*, is a highly developed practice for both Hindus and Buddhists.

The term *tantra* actually refers to a scriptural form in which spiritual concepts are expounded on in the guise of a dialog between two deities, usually a goddess and a god. There are tantra dialogues on almost every spiritual subject, not only sexual yoga, but in the West, the term has become associated with all manner of sexual magical practice being applied to Taoist and Western practices as well as Hindu and Buddhist ones.

It should be noted that sexual tantra is an esoteric practice in India, as elsewhere in the world, and is not necessarily well regarded by Orthodox Hindus.

All tantric practices are aimed at spiritual development and personal enlightenment—that is, union with Deity. The primary spiritual difference between Hindu

and Buddhist tantra is that the Hindus perceive the ego as a function of the soul, and thus an immortal self, while the Buddhists perceive the ego as a function of the mind, which is discarded through spiritual growth. The principal physical difference between Hindu and Buddhist tantra is that in Hindu tantra the male practitioner ejaculates, while in Buddhist tantra he does not. Both view sexual yoga as the most effective means of bringing about spiritual enlightenment, by reason of the tremendous capacity of sexual excitement to arouse psychic energy, which can then be directed toward spiritual development.

There is considerable debate as to which of the two schools of tantra is older, Hindu or Buddhist. Because Buddhist tantric writings are older than Hindu tantric writings, most scholars believe that Hindu tantra developed out of Buddhist tantra, which may have been based upon Taoist tantra from China. However, it is the nature of things that they must exist first before they can be written down, and sometimes they exist long before being written (as Wiccans, of all people, should know), so the antiquity of written materials is not the only consideration. A minority of scholars hold that Hindu tantra was already developed before Buddhism developed out of Hinduism, and in fact, goes far back into Indian prehistory; to support their position, they cite the existence of

Lesson VII

images from the Harrapa Era, which seem to directly correspond to modern Hindu deities and practice.

Like Wicca, tantra (Hindu, Buddhist, and Taoist alike) perceives the world as being created and sustained by polar forces, represented as feminine and masculine. Also like Wicca, tantra teaches that worldly problems are created by not moving in sync with the flow of the polarities. The goal of tantra is to bring about the union of the polarities within the *Tantrika*, or tantric practitioner, and thus transcend worldly difficulties and achieve enlightenment, or oneness with Deity.

In Hindu tantra, the polar powers are primarily envisioned as Shiva and Shakti. Shakti is the Mother Goddess, who has many forms, including the gentle Parvati and the fearsome Kali. In the body, Shiva is identified with the crown chakra, while Shakti is identified with the KUNDALINI serpent who lies curled up near the root chakra. The two are said to be one when the kundalini serpent arises and travels up the spine to unite with the crown chakra.

In Hindu tantra, the feminine is thought of as the active power, and it is Shakti who empowers Shiva with her boundless energy. In Buddhist and Taoist tantra, it is the masculine power which is thought of as active, while the feminine energy must be awakened by it. This reveals a difference in thought as to whether it is Matter which awakens Spirit or Spirit which awakens Matter.

In Buddhist tantra, the masculine power is associated with the head, while the feminine power is associated with the solar plexus (the root and second chakras are often downplayed or ignored in Buddhist tantra, and are absent altogether from Taoist tantra, as shall be discussed below).

The central practice of all forms of tantra is ritual sex. This can be practiced by an individual, couple, or even a group. In this ritual sex, the woman is identified with Goddess, source of spiritual energy, and the male seeks to unite with the Goddess as a form of hierogamy and to be spiritually empowered by her. In some branches of tantra this union is symbolic, in others it is literal. Some Tantrikas, to curry favor with Christians, have claimed that the sexual element in all tantra is always symbolic, but this is not true.

In India, those branches of tantra which practice symbolic sexual yoga are said to follow the "right-hand path," while those who practice literal sexual yoga are said to follow the "left-hand path." That the terms "right-hand path" and "left-hand path" have come to carry a connotation of "good" and "evil" in the West is due to the anti-sexual bias of certain Christian and Christian-influenced mystics of the fifteenth century Pisces (AD nineteenth century). In tantra, these terms merely

refer to ritual form. In all tantric ritual, the woman begins seated to the right of the man—in tantra that follows symbolic practice, she remains there throughout the ceremony, and in tantra that follows literal practice, the woman moves to the left side of the man (her natural power side) when the sexual part of the rite begins, thence the terms *right hand* and *left hand*.

All tantra is concerned with the chakras, which have had different names in different cultures, of course. This is especially true of Hindu tantra, whose chakra workings are the most advanced. Hindu tantra recognizes seven major chakras, the ones you are familiar with, while most other systems recognize only three. A few systems work with more than seven major chakras. Our Correllian position on this, as stated in the First Degree lessons, is that chakras develop with use, and that while everyone has an equal number of (thousands of) minor chakras, these only become activated as major chakras as the soul develops them through many lifetimes of effort.

In Hindu tantra, the chakras are thought of as rising up the center of the body, along the spine. In addition, Hindu tantra posits two additional energy pathways, known as the ida and the pingala. The ida is lunar and feminine, and arises on the left side of the spine. The pingala is solar and masculine, and arises on the right side of the spine. Beginning at the root chakra, the ida

and pingala wind upward, criss-crossing at each of the next five chakras, to unite at the crown chakra. The pattern formed by the ida and pingala as they ascend the spine is said to be the origin of the CADUCEUS.

In tantra, sexual energy is regarded as embodying the life force, what we have called psychic energy. This energy reposes in the lower chakras as the kundalini, and can be made to rise upward by means of sexual excitement. By channeling the energy upward through the chakra system, it is made to undergo a spiritual evolution. This process is experienced as physical ecstasy. As the energy enters the solar plexus, it is magnified by the inner sun, and negativity is burned away. The solar plexus is said to embody the sixty-four purifying flames of the goddess Saraswati, which are expressed through the sixty-four arts of classic Hindu culture (elaborated upon in the famed *Kama Sutra*). Purified, the energy then travels upward along the three pathways (spine, ida, and pingala) to the crown chakra, where enlightenment occurs. This is said to bring a spiritual ecstasy beyond words. This process is achieved through a long period of spiritual exercises, very similar to the exercises that have accompanied these lessons.

Buddhists describe this process in somewhat different terms, closer to the Taoist version that will be discussed below, but in each case it is the same process, with a slight variation in perception.

Tantrikas feel that the practice of sexual arousal accelerates their spiritual development. An individual yogi or yogini does this with masturbation; however, in the tantric view, when a couple performs the exercises together, along with ritualized sexual congress, they in fact unite and consequently magnify their psychic energy well beyond what either could do individually. Whenever two or more psychically open people come together, in fact, their psychic powers are magnified, for they empower each other. This is one reason why group ritual can be important.

When a couple engages in tantric intercourse, their energetic systems unite as if in a single system, the same energies flowing through both partners. This creates a more powerful vortex for transformation and spiritual growth, enriching both partners.

• • • •

Sex Magic and "Chakras" in Chinese Tradition

Sex magic, which we shall continue to loosely term tantra, is an important feature of Taoism, as well as Hinduism and Buddhism. Some scholars feel that tantra originated with the Taoists and was transmitted by them to the Buddhists and thence to the Hindus.

Taoism is said to have been created by the sage Lao-tzu around the year 700 Aries (c. 500 BC). In reality, however, Taoism is much more ancient, arising out of the ancient Pagan practices of China's prehistory, though it was Lao-tzu and his followers who gave it its formal definition.

The Tao is the movement of the universe, created and sustained by the interaction of yin and yang. The goal of Taoism is to move in synchronicity with the Tao. This is identical to Wiccan thought, yin being Goddess, yang being God.

In Taoist tantra, as in Buddhist tantra, the feminine (yin) is thought of as a passive but inexhaustible spiritual power that must be awakened by the masculine (yang). In Taoist thought, all things contain both yin and yang energy, but as a rule women are associated with yin and men with yang. Moreover, while women's spiritual yin energy is inexhaustible, men's temporal yang energy is more limited. Taoist (and Buddhist) tantrics apply this idea literally, identifying sperm with vital yang essence and viewing it as a limited quantity. As a result, men who practice Taoist or Buddhist sexual tantra do not as a rule ejaculate as part of their tantric exercises, but rather practice various disciplines that allow for orgasm without ejaculation. This is the primary physical difference from Hindu practice.

Taoists use sexual tantra to develop a stronger life force and increase their longevity, and some believe that it can even bring about temporal immortality.

Taoism posits three main energy centers in the body, which it terms *cauldrons* (Tan T'ien). These are located in the lower abdomen, roughly equivalent to the second chakra; behind the navel, equivalent to the lower solar plexus chakra; and in the head near the pineal gland, equivalent to the third eye.

Each of the three cauldrons is associated with a different kind or quality of energy. Ching, or sexual energy, is associated with the lower cauldron. Chi, or life—force energy, is associated with the middle cauldron. And Shen, the energy of the individual persona, is associated with the upper cauldron. In artwork, these three are represented by the image of a triple spiral.

These three cauldrons are used to unite and transform these energies in a process different in form but identical in concept to the Hindu process described above. To the Taoists, this process was conceived in alchemical terms. Sexual energy, spurred by masturbation or intercourse, and assisted by techniques of deep breathing and visualization, is made to ascend upwards from the lowest cauldron to the middle cauldron, where it is held to be transformed to "lead," or physical force. It is thence made

to ascend up the spine to the upper cauldron in the head, where it is transformed into "mercury," or spiritual force. It is then circulated back through the energetic system through a rather complex discipline that eventually renders it "gold," giving enlightenment. There are a total of twelve stages in the process, each of which is identified with one of the I CHING hexagrams. In this way, Taoist sages believed that they created the Elixir of Immortality within their own bodies.

As in Hindu thought, Taoists hold that this process is greatly helped along when performed by a couple, who magnify each other's energy, creating a more powerful vortex.

. . . .

"Chakras" in Celtic Thought

We mentioned earlier that while Hindu thought works with seven major chakras, most other ancient systems used only three. This is true of the Taoists described above and also of the ancient Celts.

The Celtic ideas about the chakras are related through ancient Celtic poetry. The famous Celtic shamanist Caitlin Matthews has done a great deal of work researching this, and it is from the works of Caitlin and John Matthews that I derive my knowledge of the Celtic chakra system, specifically *The Encyclopedia of Celtic Wisdom*, published by Element Books, Ltd.

Like the Taoists, the ancient Celts conceived of three energy centers in the body, which they also termed *cauldrons*. These were the *Coire Goiriath*, or "Cauldron of Heat;" the *Coire Ernmae*, or "Cauldron of Vocation;" and the *Coire Sois*, or "Cauldron of Knowledge." The Celts believed that whether these cauldrons were upright, sideways, or inverted—that is, fully open, partially open, or closed—determined the person's talents and capacities. The alignment of the cauldrons could be changed by emotionally or spiritually charged experiences.

The Coire Goiriath is located in the abdomen and is equivalent to the solar plexus chakra. Like the solar plexus chakra, the Coire Goiriath is considered the source of the body's energy. The Coire Goiriath is upright in all people.

The Coire Ernmae is located in the chest and is equivalent to the heart chakra. The Coire Ernmae is associated with creativity and talent. In people with no particular skills, the Coire Ernmae is said to be inverted. In people who are creative and skilled, the cauldron is said to be sideways, pouring out its contents. In people who are extremely skilled, the cauldron is said to be upright.

The Coire Sois is located in the head and is equivalent to the third eye. The Coire Sois is associated with spiritual enlightenment. The Coire Sois is inverted in most people. In the wise the Coire Sois is said to be sideways, and in the spiritually enlightened it is said to be upright.

. . . .

Sex in the Astral

It is to be noted that sexual relations can also be had in the astral plane as well as in ordinary consciousness, and that hierogamy is also practiced in this way.

You will remember that the astral plane is the level of existence at which physical life is given shape by the soul and also by the consciousness. When we rise to our Higher Selves, we are entering astral consciousness. When the soul travels outside of the body, it is said to be traveling in the astral. When the soul is traveling in this way, it can unite with other souls in a way that we often perceive as being sexual. As suggested previously, this is because sexual energy is the only thing in the physical world that is comparable to the intensity of feeling that is experienced through the touching of souls in this manner. One can experience this sort of soul touching with other incarnate persons while both are astrally traveling or with discarnate spirits. If you have ever had a dream in which you seemed to be having sex with an unlikely partner (such as a parent or grandparent, for example), this was most likely the touching of your two souls, which your mind has translated in a sexual manner because nothing else is as equally intense.

Some people deliberately seek out this sort of union with spirits and deliberately perceive it in a sexual way. This can be considered a form of hierogamy. A union thus achieved is energetic in nature, rather than sexual, per se, but it is usually perceived in sexual terms by the physically incarnate partner. A famous example of this is the vision of the Christian mystic Theresa of Avila, where she described her encounter with an ANGEL in this way: "In his hands I saw a great golden spear, and at its iron tip there appeared to be a point of fire; he plunged this into my heart... and left me utterly consumed by a great love of God." Though the images in Theresa's vision are symbolically rather than literally sexual, it is still obvious that her reaction is a sexual one.

It should be noted that the touching of souls that produces such ecstatic feeling is a deeper communication and more prolonged than the casual touching of souls that produces the famous shiver effect so well dramatized in the movie GHOST.

The most extreme example of astral sex magic are the practices of the famous Church of Carmel. A French Roman Catholic splinter sect founded by Eugene Vintras and later led by the defrocked Christian Priest Boullon, the Church of Carmel taught that people could achieve spiritual growth through sexual relations with more developed spirits. These more developed spirits included angels as well as ancestors such as Helen of Troy and Cleopatra. Sexual union was achieved through meditation/visualization and masturbation, or by physical intercourse in which one or both partners embodied a more advanced spirit. An interesting footnote to the history of the Church of Carmel is the exotic death of its second leader, Boullon, who supposedly died as the result of a magical battle with a rival order called the Kabalistic Order of the Rose-Croix.

. . . .

Sex Magic and Wicca

One of the principal differences between the book religions and the Pagan religions is how each one views the body and sexuality. To the book religions, the body (and all other physical manifestation) is evil, and sexuality is terribly negative and polluting. To the book religions, anything touched by sexuality is obscene, and sexual expression is permissible only in very narrow circumstances or through very repressed forms.

The Pagan religions, on the other hand, view the body as being good and holy, a perfect creation of Deity and a beautiful home for the soul. The body is an emanation of the soul, not unlike a snail's shell; it takes its form from the characteristics and experiences of the soul, which is one reason why physiognomy works as it does. Like the soul it emanates from, the body is a reflection of Deity and of the divine plan, and it is therefore itself a key to spiritual growth and cosmic understanding. As for sexuality, it is an expression of love and joy that is meant to uplift and enrich the soul. The expression of sexuality is neither damaging nor polluting, but rather is a holy thing, a normal and natural part of life, as well as an expression of the divine love of Goddess and God in microcosm.

Sexuality holds an honored role in Wiccan culture. The exact nature of that role varies widely, however, from one tradition to another. Some Wiccan traditions are highly sexual in their practices, others almost prudish. This is because the different Wiccan traditions began at different times and in different places, and often have very different backgrounds. In the past, they were united by being predominantly hereditary traditions with a Pagan theological base and a number of shared customs. Until Gardner, many of what would today be considered Wiccan traditions did not necessarily recognize each other as kin, and indeed, many refuse to do so even today, leading to all manner of argument and controversy over who is and is not Wiccan and what "Wiccan" is. These arguments greatly damage the Wiccan community both internally and externally, but they continue because too often the Wiccan leadership are concerned only about personal power or the power of their

own tradition. They fear putting an end to this fighting because they enjoy a level of power in the fractured community, which they might lose in a more mutually tolerant one. As long as we are fighting over who is and is not Wiccan and the different traditions remain isolated behind their political positions, particularly "modern" versus "hereditary," their leaders remain big fish in small ponds.

One aspect of Wiccan respect for the body and sexuality is the practice of skyclad worship. We discussed skyclad worship briefly in First Degree's Lesson VIII. Skyclad worship, an ancient custom well attested in history, is still important in Wicca today: that is, the practice of nude worship. Skyclad practice can be found at some level in most religions. Hindu and Jain mystics often practice skyclad or nearly so. There have been a variety of Christians who practice skyclad worship, including the Adamites of the Reformation period in Europe, some of the Flagellants of the late Medieval period, and of course the Greco-Romans of the Classical period had a great reverence for nudity, which included some practice of skyclad worship, such as the Lupercii Priests of Rome. European peasants, including hereditary Witches, also often had skyclad observances of various sorts, and in some Wiccan traditions, skyclad practice is extremely important, even today. Skyclad practice recognizes the

holiness of the body and its connection to the natural world as well as the divine.

We have spoken earlier of the importance of the Great Rite, or hierogamy, to Wicca. The Great Rite is a ritual reenactment of the union of Goddess and God, which is also the union of Spirit and Matter, and the union of the soul with Deity. In some traditions, this is enacted in a physical manner, with priestess and priest uniting in intercourse while embodying the energies of Goddess and God. In most traditions, including the Correllian, this sort of physical hierogamy is only enacted privately as part of a couple's personal practice, and the Great Rite is performed in ritual by the conjoining of the athame and chalice.

The Great Rite might be thought of as the highest ritual act in Wicca. It is a physical enactment of the yin-yang principle, the conjunction of the polarities whose union creates and sustains physical life. In a manner of speaking, the Great Rite is also enacted whenever a high priest/ess embodies the energies of the divine to bring through an oracle or a blessing, the central role of the Third Degree.

Some traditions, especially the Gardnerian, are highly sexual in practice. Most Wiccan traditions are not, especially the hereditary traditions, for obvious reasons. Physically enacting the Great Rite doesn't work when your co-religionists are parents and siblings. The late Wiccan leader Sybil Leek had a theory about this pronounced difference between traditions. Lady Sybil, whose tradition is today called the Horsa Tradition, taught that when the ancient Pagan religions came under persecution and their priesthoods went underground, the different groups of priesthood chose different aspects of their religions to focus on, thus some groups concentrated on saving the herbal mysteries, others concentrated on saving spellcraft, and some focused on the sexual mysteries. Today we know that it was not as cut and dried as this. The different traditions did not have a single origin, nor did they have mass organization. But Lady Sybil's teaching is still very relevant, because, in fact, different Pagan groups both did and do often concentrate on specific aspects of the religion for which they have greater aptitude: thus one temple may focus more on healing, another on divination, etc., according to the skills of their leadership and members.

. . . .

Correllian Views

Because the Correllian Tradition is hereditary in origin, our views reflect a hereditary sensibility. We honor the idea of skyclad practice and venerate the spiritual beauty of the body, but as a rule we do not practice skyclad ritual except in private. We consider the sexual mysteries to be holy and honorable, but also a matter for private practice. It is not that we disapprove of either of these things; on the contrary, both are very positive, liberating, and uplifting aspects of our religion. Rather, it is that we are a familial tradition and observe a difference between public and private sensibilities.

Socially, our views on sexuality are simple. Sexuality is a very subjective and personal thing. In practice, we have always held that whatever consenting adults want to do is their own business and not really anyone else's to judge. Beyond adulthood and consentuality, there really are no other legitimate issues for society to poke its nose into the bedroom. An exception to this is the presence of marital or other vows affecting one's sexuality and one's right to "consent," but that is a matter between the interested parties and not society. This is also why we favor the use of a marital contract, in which the marital parties can spell out their expectations so as to avoid misunderstandings.

Love (and also passion) is a function of the soul, while reproduction is a function of the body. The soul is neither male nor female, and has many lifetimes as both during its long existence. Consequently, each individual has elements of both polarities within them—within the yin there is always some yang, within the yang there is always some yin. These are balanced differently in different people, and

so must be allowed differing expressions. If there is a sexual ideal, it would be bisexuality, as this would be the full expression of the soul's range; however, ideals are part of the world of ideas. In the world of reality, each person must express their sexuality as they feel is appropriate to them.

Because of this outlook, we have no problem, as a tradition, with issues of sexual orientation or gender identification. We support same-sex marriage. We are okay with polyamory and open marriage. These are all matters of individual choice. They are right for some people, not right for others, but they are not harming anyone, so do as you will, so to speak.

• • • •

To Sum Up

Sexual magic is basically the use of sexual energy by an individual, couple, or group to intensify spiritual exercises and growth. Sexual energy is identified with the kundalini, or lunar energy circuit, and is made to arise through the chakras, uniting with the crown chakra in order to fully energize the person. This sexual energy can be raised by pure meditation, masturbation, or intercourse. When practiced by more than one person, each person's energy magnifies the whole. Because each person has both yin and yang energy within them, sex magic may be practiced with equal efficacy by anyone of any sexual orientation.

Sexual magic is very sacred and requires considerable practice and patience to perfect. Sexual magic is practiced for spiritual rather than sexual reasons, though it can have sexual as well as spiritual benefits.

Sexuality itself is holy and positive, and is an expression of the spirit and thus ultimately an expression of Deity. How people express their sexuality is their own business, so long as they observe the Wiccan Rede, "An it harm none, do as you will."

· · · ·

Exercises

In this lesson, once again we will be dealing with an exercise that serves a special purpose, and thus should be done occasionally rather than as a part of the daily routine.

Your daily routine of exercises should still consist of the Ohm exercise, then opening the chakras with balls of colored light, changing the balls of colored light to balls of white light, changing the balls of white light to balls of purple light, changing the balls of purple light to balls of silver stellar light, and then filling your aura with silver stellar light. Next, change the balls of silver stellar light to balls of golden stellar light, then fill your aura with golden stellar light. Finally, change the balls of golden stellar light to balls of amber light, and fill your aura with the amber light. Now, from each chakra, call forth its personified form, and imagine it

before you. You would then do Exercise 12 or any other of the occasional exercises at this point. Remember to close the chakras, clear, and release when finished.

Exercise 12

Exercise 12 is very similar to Exercise 11, except that instead of your chakras, we will be working to heal fears or spiritual wounds. This actually is a kind of chakra working, since these things lodge in the chakras as blockages, but it can be easiest to address them by externalizing them.

You should probably do this exercise right after the daily routine when you first try it. Later it can be done independently.

Begin by imagining yourself in a hallway; the hallway is long and on each side are many doors. Make it a point to notice what this hallway looks like. Is it dark or bright? Is it dirty or clean? How does it make you feel to look at it? Are the doors sturdy or flimsy?

The hallway represents your subconscious, and if it's dark or dirty, or makes you uncomfortable, take a moment to change it. Imagine it differently. See any mess disappear, create more light, redecorate it, make the doors stronger, if you choose. Make the hallway a place you are comfortable with.

Now walk along the hallway and look at each door. Behind each door is a fear or a spiritual wound, though you will not see them yet at this point. You do not need to know what the fear or wound is exactly to work on it in this way; sometimes it will be apparent and sometimes not.

One door, somewhere along the way, will be marked with an X or with some other sign that it is the one to enter. When you come to the marked door, go in.

Take note of the room; is it large or small, light or dark? In the room will be a fear or wound needing healing. These can appear in many different ways. Often they appear to be "monsters," but sometimes they may be wounded people or other things—always the meaning is symbolic. It is not uncommon for the personified fear or wound to be quite hideous, since this represents the amount of pain associated with them, but they can also sometimes be abstract or comical. Be aware that you may experience fear at this point, but do not be put off by it, as you are here to heal this.

If you find more than one in a room, it means that they are associated with each other, and you should heal them one at a time.

Declare your intent to heal the personified fear or wound. Again, you might ask God/dess to help you. We recommend a form like this:

"Behold, there is one power in
the universe, and I am a perfect
manifestation of that power,

and as such I call upon the
divine power within me to bring
healing to this part of myself.
Divine Mother Goddess, divine
Father God, lend me your aid
in this undertaking, I pray you!
By my will, so mote it be!"

Open a ball of white light above the personified fear or wound. Imagine a shower of light falling upon it, filling it with shining white light just as you did the personified chakras in Exercise 11. As the personified fear or wound fills with light, the negativity will be transformed, and you will see it change before your eyes. Focus on this, imagine it changing, and will it to change, becoming whole and healthy and beautiful as you watch. See the light transform it. The light will heal it, making it whole and healthy and happy. It may take a while, but as you focus more and more light into the personified fear or wound, it will transform into something beautiful and radiant; like the personified chakras, it will show signs of pleasure and delight when you near completion. Put as much light into the personified fear or wound as possible.

Let the light fill the room as well, transforming it to make it bright and healthy too.

In doing this, you have essentially used a technique of visualized externalization to

Lesson
VII

217

heal an energetic blockage in your chakric system.

Now thank the personified fear or wound, which has become healed and beautiful, for all that it has brought you (for in its origin it served a good purpose, which has merely become outdated within you), and assure it that it need never bear such pain again.

Come back out through the door you entered, and walk back up the hallway. Has the hallway changed since you began? You may find that it has.

As you come back up the hallway, let the image fade and return to your body.

Use this technique any time you feel the need.

. . . .

Spell for Lesson VII
Riding the Dragon

The dragon is a powerful symbol of strength and energy. Analogous to the serpent, the dragon represents psychic power and divine energy. At a cosmic level, the dragon represents the flow of the universe, what the Chinese call Tao. At an individual level, the dragon represents personal power and attunement to the universe.

Unlike the previous spells, this and the ones that follow are less spells than techniques. But they are techniques that you should be familiar with, and this seems as good a place as any to put them.

Begin by clearing and releasing.

Put yourself into a comfortable position and relax. Close your eyes.

Now go inside yourself. For some people this is very easy, and they need only shift their consciousness inward. Other people need an image, such as walking through a door, pushing through a barrier, or climbing a staircase with a set number of stairs (ten or thirteen is good) to illustrate the transition and assist them in making it. Use whatever technique works best for you to make that shift in order to do this or other similar meditations.

Now imagine that you are in a hallway, a long hallway, with many doors along both sides. Allow the hallway to appear in whatever way it needs to; have no preconceptions about its appearance. The hallway may be old and dusty, dark and foreboding, or bright and cheerful. It will be whatever it needs to be. The hallway represents your inner self, and its condition can help to tell you how you are feeling inside.

Imagine yourself walking along the hallway. As you go down the hallway, look at the doors on either side. Do they all look alike? Is each one different? How do they make you feel? One door will be different from all the rest—perhaps it will be marked with an X or perhaps you will just know it's the one.

Open this door and step through it. You will find yourself in the place you need to be. Usually it will be out-of-doors, though not always. Look around. Acquaint yourself with this place. What do you see? What are the qualities of this place? How does it feel to you?

Explore the area. Somewhere here is a dragon. Not just any dragon—it is a dragon just for you, your special dragon. You may have to hunt for the dragon, or the dragon may come to you. When you encounter the dragon, give it a warm greeting. Be friendly.

Pay attention to what the dragon looks like. Is the dragon colorful? Is it inspiring? Does it seem healthy? How does it react to your presence?

The dragon represents your personal energy, and your connection to Spirit and ability to feel and attune to the movement of Spirit.

If your dragon seems weak or unhealthy, or if it is angry or hostile, take a moment to send it healing.

Make a ball of light in your heart chakra—clear, white light full of healing energy and love. Then, from your heart, send healing energy to your dragon. See the dragon receive the healing energy and become healed and healthy. See the dragon shining with light and strength and health.

Embrace your dragon. The dragon is your friend.

Ask the dragon if it has anything to say to you. The dragon may have a message, or it may not. If it does speak, listen carefully, for it will be something you should hear.

Ask the dragon if you may ride it. It will usually say yes. If the dragon says that you may not ride it, ask why this is; address whatever issue the dragon raises. Then ask again, and the dragon will probably say yes.

Now climb upon your dragon's back. Take a firm seat and hold on. Imagine the dragon rising up and beginning to fly. Perhaps it has great leathery wings that begin to flap, raising it up into the sky, or perhaps it is wingless and propelled by magical power alone. Imagine riding upon the dragon's back as it leaves the ground behind.

Let the dragon carry you forward. Imagine it flying through the air. Let the journey take you anywhere that it needs to. Below you, on the ground, you may see forests or rivers, oceans or mountains, or even farms and cities.

As you continue to ride the dragon, imagine yourself becoming one with it. Feel its energy, its muscles, and imagine that they are yours. Become the dragon. Instead of riding it, imagine that you have become it, and fly where you will. Imagine the dragon's power within you, and let it carry you forward.

Lesson
VII

When this has continued for a time, allow yourself to become separate from the dragon again. Be the rider of the dragon once more, and allow your dragon to land. Thank the dragon for the ride. Perhaps it will wish to speak to you again, in which case listen carefully and thank the dragon for its message.

Now retrace your way to the door from which you entered. If you cannot find it, simply make it appear before you. Go through the door, back into the hallway. Walk back up the hallway, and as you do so, return to yourself.

Doing this meditation regularly will help you to attune to the flow of the universe and can lead to many interesting adventures.

• • • •

Glossary

Aeneas—A legendary figure in Greco-Roman mythology, Aeneas was a prince of Troy, the son of Anchises and the goddess Venus. Aeneas escaped from Troy during its defeat, carrying his lame father on his shoulders and the sacred palladium under one arm. The palladium was a particularly holy and very ancient (even then) statue of Athena, which was considered a primary treasure of Troy. After escaping from Troy, Aeneas had many adventures, including a love affair with Queen Dido of Car-

thage (based upon the historical Queen Elyssa), which ended in the queen's suicide. Eventually Aeneas would settle in Latium, founding the bloodline from which Romans would descend, becoming the ancestor of the legendary twins Romulus and Remus. The powerful Gens Julia, which produced Caius Julius Caesar and became Rome's first imperial family, claimed descent from Aeneas' son Iulus. According to Virgil, Iulus was the same person as Aeneas's son Ascanius, whose mother was the Trojan Creusa. Livy, however, held that Iulus and Ascanius were different persons, Iulus's mother being Aeneas's Latin wife Lavinia.

alchemical marriage—Alchemy is the art of personal transformation in order to achieve spiritual enlightenment, allegorized as transforming lead (the ordinary, conscious self) into gold (the enlightened self). The term *alchemical marriage* refers to the union of spirit and matter, or more specifically to conscious union of the waking mind and the Higher Self, i.e., Enlightenment. This is allegorized as the union of sun and moon, or Red King and White Queen, and is the same concept found in Wicca and most Pagan religions.

angel—*Angel* is a term used primarily but not exclusively by Judeo-Christians to describe an advanced spiritual being. In common Christian belief, angels are the spirits of the blessed dead, who are given jobs helping the living—the view can be readily seen in everyday Christian culture and is exemplified by movies such as *It's a Wonderful Life*. In this sense, they are exactly cognate to the idea of spirit guides. Other Judeo-Christians hold that angels have never been physically incarnate and regard them as something closer to faeries or devas. Angels are very important in some branches of Ceremonial magic, where they are treated more or less as personal forms of Deity. As a rule, the term *angel* is not favored in Wicca, but some Wiccans do use it—especially as a synonym for spirit guide.

caduceus—The caduceus is the sacred staff of Mercury, which is taken as an allegory of existence. The caduceus is composed of two serpents intertwined around a staff, sometimes surmounted by wings. The two serpents are taken to represent Goddess/yin and God/yang forces, and their intertwining represents the dance of life and death. The two serpents are also taken to represent the ida (yin) and pingala (yang) energy currents ascending the spine. The caduceus is also used as a symbol for the medical profession.

evil—The idea of evil is a misguided attempt to take the subjective experience of something unpleasant or painful and make it into an absolute quality. That experiences can be subjectively good or bad no one would argue, but from the point of view of the immortal soul, even the worst experience must be viewed as transitory and experientially enriching to the soul, which requires experiencing all sides of existence. For this reason, we would say that evil does not exist in a cosmological sense, as it is conceived of in some other religions.

Fall of Man—In Judeo-Christian mythology, the Fall of Man refers to the idea that humankind was originally perfect and immortal, but because of disobedience to Deity "fell" into imperfection and death. Often this is extended to the idea that humankind is getting progressively worse with time and can only be made better by joining whatever church the speaker belongs to. This point of view runs counter to Correllian theology, which teaches that evolution is an upward spiral, and that humankind is becoming progressively better as it develops further.

***Ghost* (the movie)**—The film *Ghost*, made in 1590 Pisces (AD 1990) and starring Whoopi Goldberg, Patrick Swayze, and Demi Moore, is noted for its realistic

Lesson
VII

221

depiction of certain aspects of the after-life experience, and if the "shadows" that overtake the villain are understood to be guilt and regret rather than external forces, the film is essentially accurate from a Correllian perspective in its portrayal of a spirit caught between the worlds. Other films that afford a relatively accurate depiction of afterlife issues include *The Others*, with Nicole Kidman and Fionnula Flanagan, Year 1 Aquarius (AD 2001), again depicting spirits caught between the worlds, and *The Adding Machine*, with Milo O'Shea, Phyllis Diller, and Billie Whitelaw, 1569 Pisces (AD 1969), which shows a most interesting and essentially accurate version of the Otherworld paradise as it might be perceived by the characters in the story.

Hatshepusitu—The name Hatshepusitu, more commonly rendered Hatshepsut, means "Preeminent Among Noble-women" or "Preeminent Noblewoman." Hatshepusitu was the daughter of Pharaoh Tehutmose I and Queen Ahmose. Hatshepusitu married her half-brother, Tehutmose II, who was the son of Tehutmose I by a lesser consort named Mutnofret. Tehutmose II reigned three or four years before dying, his only child being the future Tehutmose III, son of his own lesser consort Aset. Upon the death of Tehutmose II, Hatshepusitu made herself pharaoh and reigned in this capacity for some fifteen years, among the most peaceful and prosperous reigns of Egypt's Eighteenth Dynasty. Hatshepusitu had one child, the Princess Nofret, who is thought to have predeceased her mother. After Hatshepusitu's death in 1243 Taurus (1558 BC), she was succeeded by her nephew and half-son Tehutmose III. It used to be thought that Tehutmose III bitterly resented Hatshepusitu, and upon ascension to the throne began immediately defacing her memory; now it is thought that they had an amicable relationship, and that his celebrated defacing of her memory followed only after he had been on the throne for many years and was motivated by political rather than personal considerations. Hatshepusitu's primary monument is her magnificent mortuary temple at Deir el Bahri, one of the greatest achievements of Egyptian architecture.

hierogamos—The term *hierogamos* refers to divine marriage, an idea which has meanings at many levels. In the simplest terms, hierogamos is the embodiment of Spirit in Matter: the divine marriage is that of Goddess/Spirit/Yin and God/Matter/Yang, which creates and sustains the universe. Everything that exists is a microcosm of this union, because everything that exists has both a spiritual and a material aspect, even when these are not readily apparent to the uninitiated eye. The term *hierogamos* also refers to the process of Enlightenment, by which the conscious mind and the Higher Self come into union, and the physical life becomes a vehicle for the soul's higher purposes. At another level, the term becomes more literal: in Pagan religion, the union of Goddess and God is often enacted ritually, sometimes in symbolic form and other times quite physically. In many ancient cultures, the ruler was ceremonially married to the region's tutelary Deity in a very literal ritual version of hierogamos: the queen or a priestess would embody the Goddess through trance and the king would embody the God. A similar rite was practiced in temples, the idea being that by thus channeling the divine energy, one was moved closer to full union with the Higher Self. The fullest flowering of this practice can be seen in Hindu tantra. Finally, the term *hierogamy* can also be used to refer to the act of channeling divine energy.

I Ching—The I Ching, or Book of Changes, is a very ancient form of divination created in China. The I Ching is said to have been created by the semi-legendary King Wen, founder of the Chou dynasty, while he was imprisoned. King Wen's son, the Duke of Chou, is said to have created the first commentary on the I Ching around 200 Taurus (1000 BC). Many other Chinese sages wrote commentaries on the I Ching, notably Confucius himself. The I Ching is a divinatory system incorporating sixty-four hexagrams, the total number of possible combinations of the eight sacred trigrams (ba gua). Sacred in both Taoism and Confucianism, the I Ching is considered one of the five classics of Confucian thought. The five classics, or Wu Ching, include the I Ching (Book of Changes), the Shu Ching (Book of History), Shih Ching (Book of Poetry), the Ch'un Ch'iu (Spring and Autumn), and the Li Chi (Book of Rites).

kundalini—The term *kundalini* is used to refer to the kind of energy that is used in the lunar energy circuit. In Hindu thought, the kundalini takes the form of a serpent that sleeps at the base of the spine. When activated, the kundalini serpent rises through the seven major chakras, uniting them to form a kind of "super chakra." Through this technique, very high levels of manifestation are possible.

matriarchy—Matriarchy is a system of rule in which the mother is the head of the family, and women are preeminent

in society. Matriarchy is not an opposite of patriarchy; in matriarchal systems, relations between the sexes tend to be fairly egalitarian and are not marked by the subjugation of males to females. As a rule, matriarchal societies tend toward racial equality, tolerance of diversity, acceptance of the body and sexuality, and an emphasis on the rights of the governed.

patriarchy—Patriarchy is a system of rule in which all power is in the hands of the father, with other family members having no right to oppose his will. Similarly, in patriarchal societies all power is held by the government, with the people having no right to question or oppose it. Patriarchy is marked by a strict social and racial hierarchy, rejection of the body, and an often ruthless enforcement of law. The chief proponents of the patriarchal system today are the book religions. Wiccan religion, on the other hand, follows a matriarchal, or mother-centered, principle (see above entry on matriarchy).

sacred harlots—*Sacred harlot* is a term applied to priestesses who used hierogamy as a spiritual discipline—that is to say, they practiced tantric sexual ritual. In some parts of the ancient world, this was a common practice. The priestesses of Ishtar are particularly famous for this practice, but it was quite widespread, in the Middle East especially. In many places, it was a requirement that young women serve at temple in this capacity prior to marriage, so that they did not come to marriage ignorant of the ways of sexuality and of the world. In such societies, virginity at marriage was considered a very bad omen, for the bride had not been blessed by embodying the Goddess in a ritual setting. Some priests, such as the transsexual priests of Cybele or of Hercules, may also have practiced hierogamy in this way. The practice of sacral harlotry declined as women's position in Middle Eastern society worsened and female sexuality became more excoriated and repressed. The term *harlot* is said to come from a title of Ishtar. The book religions tend to view sacred harlotry as being no more than prostitution practiced in order to raise money for the temple, but while it may have degenerated into this in some times and places, the actual idea of sacred harlotry is quite elevated.

Lesson

VIII

Magical Calendars

In writing this lesson, it is not our purpose to familiarize you with every possible magical calendar or every possible magical use of a calendar. Rather, it is our hope to familiarize you with the idea of magical calendars and provide a few specific examples.

Magical calendars are calendars that are used for purposes of divination. The divinatory qualities of a year, day, or hour are used to shed light on the personality, strengths, and weaknesses of people born on that date, as well as what actions the date is most favorable toward. This is commonly termed "calendrical astrology." By studying the divinatory qualities of years and months, we can better align ourselves to their energies and take best advantage of them, swimming with the flow of the universe rather than against it.

We will begin by discussing the development of the calendar in the West and how it relates to natural time, i.e., the movement of sun and moon. We will then examine several magical calendars, specifically the Chinese Hsia calendar, the Aztec calendar, and the Witches' Calendar of Years.

. . . .

Development of the Western Calendar

The earliest calendrical notations that exist are carved into a portion of reindeer antler found in the Dordogne region in France and dated to 30,000 years ago. They show a record of the moon's cycle tracked over several months, as well as the position of the moon each night upon the horizon. It must, of course, normally be assumed that a practice must have existed for some time before being committed to record, even more obviously, at such an early time as this, when making a record was a much harder task than it is now. So we can assume that while this is the earliest "calendar" to survive, it is surely not the earliest one made and represents a well—established practice of lunar reckoning of time.

We have always known that the earliest calendars were lunar, because this was still the practice at the dawn of written history and long after, and indeed is still commonly used in liturgical calendars by many people even today. But it was a revelation that people were keeping records of the moon's lunations, presumably for use as a calendar for future lunations, at such

an early date. Indeed, it was a bit of a revelation that people were keeping records of anything at all so early.

You no doubt already know that the lunar and solar calendars do not coincide. The sun takes 365¼ days to complete an orbit of Earth. During this same time, there will be 12⅓ lunar months of 29½ days each, with twelve lunar months forming a lunar year of 354 days or thirteen lunar months forming a lunar year of 383½ days, depending upon practice. Because of this, the lunar and solar calendars are out of sync with each other, coinciding only rarely. Often the thirteenth lunar month is an intercalary month added to keep the solar and lunar calendars more or less in alignment.

The ancient Egyptians began their history with the lunar calendar, presided over by the moon god Thoth (as well as lesser local moon gods like Khonsu). The Egyptians normally thought of the moon as masculine until the Ptolemaic period introduced Hellenistic ideas. The sky was thought of as feminine.

By 200 Aries (1000 BC), the Egyptians had developed and implemented a solar calendar consisting of twelve months of thirty days each, and five epogamenal days. They continued to use the lunar calendar as a liturgical calendar, while the solar calendar became the civic calendar used for everyday activities.

The five epogamenal days were considered to form a period between the end of one year and the beginning of the next, and were said to be the birthdays of five of the most important deities. No work was done during these days, which were considered to be "a time outside of time."

The Egyptians had three seasons, each of which had four months.

The first season was Akhet (the Flood), which lasted from roughly June 21 till October 21. Akhet began with the entry of the star Sirius (representing Isis-Sothis) into the sign Canis Major at the summer solstice. This signaled the rise of the Nile flood upon which the Egyptian agricultural year was totally dependent. It also commemorated a legend that a tear shed by Isis-Sothis, searching for the body of her husband Osiris, started the cycle of the Nile's yearly inundation. This is still a major festival in Muslim Egypt today, under the name of *Aid* or "the Tear."

Akhet included the months of Payni (June-July), Epiph (July-August), Mesore (August-September), and Thoth (September-October).

The second season was Proyet (Emergence), which lasted from roughly October 21 October until February 21.

Proyet included the months of Phaophi (October-November), Hathyr (November-December), Choiak (December-January), and Tybi (January-February).

And the final season was Shomu (Summer), which lasted from roughly February 21 till June 21.

Shomu included the months of Mechir (February-March), Phamenoth (March-April), Pharmouthi (April-May), and Pachon (May-June).

The five epogamenal days fell between the end of Shomu and the beginning of Akhet.

The Egyptians were great mathematicians and correctly calculated the solar year to 365 days, but they missed the extra quarter day, so that in time their solar calendar began to fall out of sync with the actual solar year. After 1,460 years, the calendar had became so out of sync that it was practically useless; to rectify this, the Egyptian mathematicians added a special intercalary year, which pulled the calendar back into line with the natural year. This proved crucial to the history of the calendar in the Western world, because just as they were conquering the Mediterranean world, the Romans were inspired by this Egyptian achievement to reform their own terribly out-of-sync calendar.

The earliest Roman calendar began the year at the spring equinox, a system still in place in astrology, where the year begins with Aries, and in some branches of Wicca whose origins are Mediterranean rather than northern European. At first, this calendar had only ten months of twenty-

Lesson
VIII

227

nine or thirty days each, for a total of 304 days, the remaining sixty-one days of winter being unnamed and unnumbered. The great reformer King NUMA POMPILLIUS (c. 550 Aries/650 BC) added two months to the calendar so that it included the winter period and had a total of twelve months but only 355 days, which of course was totally out of sync with the actual solar year.

The original months of the Roman calendar were Martius (Mars), Aprilis (Opening), Maius (Maia: Venus), Junius (Juno), Quintilis (fifth), Sextilis (sixth), September (seventh), October (eighth), November (ninth) , and December (tenth), followed as stated by an uncounted period of winter. King Numa added February (Februus: Dis Pater), and January (Janus), which were later reversed. In the early empire, the senate changed the month of Quintilis to July to honor Julius Caesar, and Sextilis to August to honor his successor Augustus, thus creating the modern month system we use in the West today.

As their 355-day solar calendar became more and more out of sync with the 365¼–day solar year, the Romans responded by adding an intercalary thirteenth month, consisting of twenty-two or twenty-three days to every other year, and an additional intercalary month every twenty-four years. As might be expected, they could not keep up with this rather complex system, and it soon became a mess again.

Another great reformer, Julius Caesar, took on the issue of this unwieldy and almost useless calendar. Seeing how the Egyptians had fixed their calendar problem, Caesar called in an Egyptian mathematician, Sosigenes, to help Rome with its calendar.

Sosigenes correctly calculated the year to 365¼ days and thus created a 365-day year with a leap year every fourth year. This made for the most accurate solar calendar so far, and it became standard throughout the Roman empire and its descendants under the name of the Julian calendar.

However, Sosigenes made one minor error, miscalculating his year by eleven minutes. Over time, the eleven minutes added up, and by the 1100s Pisces (AD 1500s), the Julian calendar was about ten days off from the actual solar year. Pope Gregory XIII (R. 1172–1185 Pisces/AD 1572–1585), then paramount high priest of the Catholic Tradition of the Christian religion, made the final alteration to the Julian calendar, arranging that centenary years (1600, 1700, 1800, etc.) would not be counted as leap years unless divisible by four. Thus was created the Gregorian calendar used by most of the world today.

Meanwhile, in Asia, an entirely different form of calendar was developing, which we will discuss below, and in the Americas the native peoples had developed their own complex calendar system, also discussed below.

Dating Systems

We have now discussed at length the development of the solar calendar in the West. However, how these peoples dated events varied considerably. The Egyptians and most other ancient peoples dated events according to the reign of monarchs; for example, "The fifth year of King Djoser," or "The thirteenth year of King Amenhotep III." Consequently, they spoke more easily in terms of the number of years past rather than of dates as we know them.

The Greeks commonly dated from the First Olympiad in 424 Aries (776 BC), while the Romans dated from the foundation of the city of Rome in 447 Aries (753 BC). However, these were not fully institutionalized and often varied locally. Moreover, under the Roman empire, the Greeks were unwilling to assimilate its dating to the Roman custom, so that dates were handled differently, depending upon where in the empire you were, giving rise to some confusion. After the empire came to be dominated by Christians, they addressed this issue by imposing a dating system based upon the birth of their founder, Jesus (b. 1200 Aries), which superseded both the Greek and Roman dating systems, and became standard throughout the Christian-dominated Western world.

As Pagans, of course, this system of dating, based upon Jesus, is not necessarily suitable to us. Also, the larger part of history predates Jesus's birth, imposing an awkward "BC/AD" split that requires backward dating of events preceding Jesus's birth and gives an effect of disconnection from pre-Christian history. In recent years, many Pagan scholars have attempted to create a new dating system relevant to Pagans, but most of these have been such extreme revisions as to be unworkable in the real world. It was to address this situation that the Correllian calendar was created, with its 1,600-year zodiacal ages so timed as to coincide for practical use with the Christian dates, yet distinctly different. But we have discussed the Correllian calendar in depth in First Degree's Lesson III and so will only comment here on our opinion that it is a logical Pagan answer as the next step in calendrical dating.

And now that we have gone through the dry, boring stuff, let us get on to the fun stuff: magical calendars and how to use them!

Lesson
VIII

Magical Calendars: Calendrical "Astrology"

In Lesson II we discussed astrology as it is most commonly thought of: the study of the divinatory meaning of the perceived positions of stars and planets relative to a particular place and time, especially but not exclusively a person's birth. We also discussed the fact that while astrology appears and is generally considered to be based on the positions of stars and planets as they appear from Earth, this is in fact not so. The precession of the equinoxes has long since changed the actual position of the stars used in astrology, whose positions were unique to specific places on the planet anyway. Consequently, even astrology as we normally encounter it is based not on any actual positioning of the stars and planets, but on measurements of time that have been marked and are represented by those essentially symbolic positions. This is to say that astrology is actually about time, mathematical notation, and numerology, and not really much about stars at all. Stars are just the symbols the ancients used to represent the patterns in time they were observing, because at the time they appeared to coincide.

This does not matter too much in relation to astrology when spoken of in the ordinary sense. But there are many other forms of astrology beyond the one we would consider ordinary that have little or no relationship to the stars or planets. We are all familiar with the Chinese form of astrology, which is often found in simplified form on placemats in Chinese restaurants but is, in fact, an ancient and complex system, one that is clearly based on patterns in time rather than the perceived position of stars. Chinese astrology reckons the divinatory nature of a

given day and hour not by any positioning of stars but by the movement of temporal cycles. The Aztec calendar, familiar to all from the famous Sun Stone or Calendar Stone that is often featured on placemats in Mexican restaurants, functions in the same way, interpreting dates according to their place in the temporal cycle.

This is also true for the Correllian calendar, which—while it does not appear on anyone's placemats (yet)—is also based on the study of patterns in time revealed through numerology, rather than having any relationship to the stars, though it does use zodiacal terms to symbolize these patterns.

Understanding this idea—that with any form of astrology, we are really looking at an analysis of patterns of time—will help us to see why the term *astrology* is applied to magical calendar systems such as the Asian or the Central American "zodiac," even though at first they appear quite different in structure from what we might consider ordinary astrology.

The magical uses of calendars have been important all over the world and at all times. These purposes include both divination, especially as applied to birth date, but also the selection of appropriate times for important rituals and personal events. In the paragraphs below, we will examine several magical calendrical systems from around the world. We will begin with the best known: the Chinese Hsia calendar.

Chinese Hsia Calendar

The Chinese system of calendar-based astrology is by far the best known. Though it has its origins in China, it is in fact used through most of Asia. Almost everyone is familiar with at least some aspects of it, though most know only the animal signs that make up the so-called earthly branches.

The Chinese calendar is a lunar calendar based upon twelve lunar months of twenty-nine or thirty days, plus an intercalary thirteenth month added every three years to keep the lunar calendar relatively in line with the solar year. Each year begins with the first new moon in Aquarius.

The Hsia calendar was the official calendar of the empire of China until the revolution of 1512 Pisces (AD 1912).

According to Chinese legend, the calendar was invented approximately 4,700 years ago (103 Taurus/2697 BC) by the astronomers Hsis and Ho at the order of the legendary Chinese emperor Yao.

At first, the calendar was used to regulate the agricultural and ritual year, but over time it came to be used for divinatory purposes as well. By the time of the Tang Dynasty (218–507 Pisces/AD 618–907), the process of calendrical divination had become formalized and written up in a definitive treatise available throughout China.

The Chinese calendar is composed of two parts, the ten "heavenly stems" and the twelve "earthly branches." Each year is governed by both an earthly branch and a heavenly stem, which form a combination. This is not normally mentioned on the placemats we noted earlier, but it is an extremely important detail. Both the heavenly stems and earthly branches run through their sequence and repeat, but because they have different lengths they do not form the same combination, rather a series of five variations over the course of a sixty-year cycle. This sixty-year cycle forms a "century," in a manner of speaking, and traditionally the Chinese reckoned their history in sixty-year cycles, just as the West used hundred-year cycles.

Both the heavenly stems and the earthly branches are important in many other aspects of Chinese thought as well, much like the planets and signs of Western astrology, whose applications also go far beyond horoscopes.

The ten heavenly stems are: Chia, Yi, Ping, Ting, Mou, Chi, Keng, Hsin, Jen, and Kuei. The heavenly stems are associated with the five elements of Chinese thought in groups of two, and may be regarded as yin and yang expressions of each element. Chia and Yi are associated with wood. Ping and Ting are associated with fire. Wu and Chi are associated with earth. Keng and

Lesson
VIII

231

Hsin are associated with metal. Jen and Kuei are associated with water.

The earthly branches are the twelve animal signs that make up the Asian zodiac. Each animal sign rules one year and is influenced in that year by one of the elements. These are Rat (Tzu), Ox (Ch'ou), Tiger (Yin), Rabbit (Mao), Dragon (Ch'en), Snake (Szu), Horse (Wu), Sheep (Wei), Monkey (Shen), Rooster (Yu), Dog (Hsu), and Pig (Hai). Sheep is also sometimes termed Ram or Goat. Each of the twelve animal signs appears five times during the sixty-year cycle in a slightly different form, depending upon its elemental influence for that year.

Below follows a discussion of the twelve earthly branches, as well as the five variations caused by their interaction with the ten heavenly stems during the sixty-year cycle. The corresponding years ruled by each sign are provided in parentheses and have been given in Gregorian rather than Corellian dates for ease of calculation. The qualities described pertain to both the year itself and also those born in it.

Remember that the Chinese year begins with the new moon in Aquarius, and so the first month or so of the Western year is considered part of the previous year in the Chinese system. Thus we see that the Beloved First Elder Gloria was born in 1527 Pisces (AD 1927), which was the Year of the Fire Rabbit/Rabbit Watching the Moon, but as Beloved Lady Gloria was born on 1 January, she was actually a Fire Tiger/Tiger in the Forest because the Year of the Rabbit had not yet begun (it began February 2 that year).

Rat (Tzu)

Ambitious, determined, persistent, and marked by keen intelligence and strong emotional drives, Rat can also be quite charming and sociable. Rat does well in creative pursuits.

Prince Charles is a Rat.

Chia Tzu—"Rat on the Roof": (Years 1864, 1924, 1984, 2044, 2104) Highly intelligent but also impatient and easily distracted. Self-sufficient and great at starting new things, but poor on follow-through.

Ping Tzu—"Rat in the Field": (Years 1876, 1936, 1996, 2056, 2116) Energetic, ambitious, and competitive. Careful and good with details, but demanding and sometimes impatient.

Mou Tzu—"Rat in the Storehouse": (Years 1888, 1948, 2008, 2068, 2128) Pleasant, socially adept, and optimistic. Adaptable but insecure with matters of affection. May be overprotective of loved ones.

Keng Tzu—"Rat on the Beam": (Years 1900, 1960, 2020, 2080, 2140)

Strong organizational skills, good judgment, and common sense. Loyal and dependable, supportive of others. Strong willed and able to see below the surface of situations.

Jen Tzu—"Rat in the Mountains": (Years 1912, 1972, 2032, 2092, 2152) Energetic, responsible, and self-reliant. Too often keeps their problems to themself.

Ox (Ch'ou)

Sensible, cautious, and strong willed, Ox is extremely stable and reliable. Ox may be very intelligent and often shrewd, but as a rule is not especially creative.

Yi Ch'ou—"Ox in the Sea": (Years 1865, 1925, 1985, 2045, 2105) Inquisitive and innovative, always learning new things. Charming, dependable, and a good friend.

Ting Ch'ou—"Ox in the Lake": (Years 1877, 1937, 1997, 2057, 2117) Sympathetic, humanitarian, and generous. Loves to help others and tends to put own interests last, but usually comes out okay.

Chi Ch'ou—"Ox Within the Gate": (Years 1889, 1949, 2009, 2069, 2129) Hard worker, dependable, independent but works well with others. Honest to a fault and sometimes overly blunt.

Hsin Ch'ou—"Ox on the Way": (Years 1901, 1961, 2021, 2081, 2141) Sensible, diplomatic, avoids conflict whenever possible. Pleasant, adaptable, handles others well.

Kuei Ch'ou—"Ox out of the Gate": (Years 1913, 1973, 2033, 2093, 2153) Tends to be a late bloomer. Patient, perseverant, hard-working, pursues goals doggedly until they are achieved.

Tiger (Yin)

Intelligent, courageous, and talented, Tiger is a natural leader. Ambitious and energetic, Tiger can also be restless or impatient. As a rule they are lucky, and though they are loving by nature, they are sometimes slow to trust and open to others.

Ping Yin—"Tiger in the Forest": (Years 1866, 1926, 1986, 2046, 2106) Intelligent, quick-witted, easily bored. Confident and assertive, skilled in many areas. A loyal friend.

Mou Yin—"Tiger Crossing the Mountain": (Years 1878, 1938, 1998, 2058, 2118) Strong willed, emotional, restless. Loves challenges but dislikes surprises. Prefers to be in control.

Keng Yin—"Tiger Descending the Mountain": (Years 1890, 1950, 2010, 2070, 2130) Proud, moody,

but gets over moods quickly. Energetic, generous, supportive of loved ones.

Jen Yin—"Tiger Passing Through the Forest": (Years 1902, 1962, 2022, 2082, 2142) Responsible, deep-thinking, and sincere. Very outspoken and "tells it like it is," often to the chagrin of others. Takes duties very seriously.

Chia Yin—"Tiger Standing Still": (Years 1914, 1974, 2034, 2094, 2154) Cautious and slow to take action, but once committed is a serious and determined worker and a loyal friend.

Rabbit (Mao)

Rabbit is caring and nurturing toward others. Rabbit prefers constructive action and so tries to avoid unnecessary conflict, but can be brave when confrontation is necessary—Rabbit may seem timid, but has big rodent teeth to bite with. Rabbit is often financially lucky, though not necessarily rich.

The Correllian Tradition was founded in the Year of the Rabbit. The present Correllian Chancellor Reverand Don, former First Director Reverand Ed, and the beloved Regent LaVeda are all Rabbits.

Ting Mao—"Rabbit Watching the Moon": (Years 1867, 1927, 1987, 2047, 2107) Great endurance and determination. Psychically receptive and tends to pick up feelings from others. Must be at pains to stay clear.

Chi Mao—"Rabbit Running Out from the Forest": (Years 1879, 1939, 1999, 2059, 2119) Loves security, dislikes ambiguity or unfamiliar ground. Prefers clear-cut roles and clear expectations. Prefers to carry out decisions rather than make them.

Hsin Mao—"Rabbit in the Burrow": (Years 1891, 1951, 2011, 2071, 2131) Prefers safe, familiar people and places, dislikes challenges or innovations. Very loyal, sincere, and emotionally strong but guarded.

Kuei Mao—"Rabbit Running into the Forest": (Years 1903, 1963, 2023, 2083, 2143) Optimistic and lucky. Always looks on the bright side and takes advantage of situations, learning from them and turning them to the better.

Yi Mao—"Buddha's Rabbit": (Years 1915, 1975, 2035, 2095, 2155) Compassionate, honorable, devoted to justice. Well organized, determined, but modest and often puts others first.

Dragon (Ch'en)

Attractive, confident, proud, and willful, Dragon usually gets its way. Determined and persistent, Dragons often succeed where others fail. This strong personality wins dragon both friends and enemies. Dragon is often associated with magic and psychism.

Abraham Lincoln was a Dragon.

Mou Ch'en—"Yielding Dragon": (Years 1868, 1928, 1988, 2048, 2108) Enigmatic and attractive, accommodating and compassionate. Often dominates situations by force of character but prefers to avoid conflicts.

Keng Ch'en—"Angry Dragon": (Years 1880, 1940, 2000, 2060, 2120) Proud, dramatic, confident. Strong sense of self-worth but difficulty in handling other people's feelings.

Jen Ch'en—"Rain Dragon": (Years 1892, 1952, 2012, 2072, 2132) Courage and strength of character. Determination. Often has problems to overcome early in life.

Chia Ch'en—"Happy Dragon": (Years 1904, 1964, 2024, 2084, 2144) Just, honorable, good judge of character. Hard worker but devoted to family. Tends to keep work and family strictly separate.

Ping Ch'en—"Dragon Flying": (Years 1916, 1976, 2036, 2096, 2156) Restless, energetic, loves variety and new experiences. Dislikes feeling caged in or held back in any way.

Snake (Szu)

Intelligent, deep-thinking, and insightful, Snake has a reputation for wisdom. Determined, methodical, and fastidious, Snake is usually successful and resents failure when it occurs. Snake is jealous, possessive, and usually quite alluring.

John F. Kennedy was a Snake.

Chi Szu—"Fortunate Snake": (Years 1869, 1929, 1989, 2049, 2109) Good judgment, insight, and understanding. Hard-working, careful, determined. Usually successful.

Hsin Szu—"Snake Hibernating Through Winter": (Years 1881, 1941, 2001, 2061, 2121) Keen intelligence, curiosity, and originality, a love of new ideas and places. Dislikes boredom or sameness. Ambitious but scattered. Tends to have a hard start in life, followed by stability later.

Kuei Szu—"Snake in the Grass": (Years 1893, 1953, 2013, 2073, 2133) Quick-witted, quick-acting, and adaptable. Keen judgment of people and situations. Tends to be bad with money due to overconfidence in own abilities.

Yi Szu—"Snake Coming Out from Its Hole": (Years 1905, 1965, 2025, 2085, 2145) Well-liked but self-effacing. Dislikes the limelight and shies away from attention but sometimes resents the lack of it. Must learn to accept credit for achievements.

Ting Szu—"Snake in the Fishpond": (Years 1917, 1977, 2037, 2097, 2157) Ambitious, courageous, determined. Decisive and single-minded, willing to do whatever is needed to achieve the goal.

Horse (Wu)

Horse is intelligent, hard-working, and independent. Horse is perfectionistic and detail oriented, with good management skills, but hates to take advice or follow directions. Horse often has many romantic misadventures.

Keng Wu—"Horse in the Palace": (Years 1870, 1930, 1990, 2050, 2110) Honest to a fault, outspoken, and sometimes tactless. Devoted to loved ones, dedicated, and selfless to the point of self-sacrifice.

Jen Wu—"War Horse": (Years 1882, 1942, 2002, 2062, 2122) Energetic, independent, and hard-working. Stable, somewhat frugal, yet enjoys a good time. Keeps private life private and does not allow interference by others.

Chia Wu—"Horse in the Clouds": (Years 1894, 1954, 2014, 2074, 2134) Loving, compassionate, thoughtful. Generous and charitable, with strong friendships. Optimistic and trusting in providence.

Ping Wu—"Horse on the Way": (Years 1906, 1966, 2026, 2086, 2146) Enthusiastic and emotional, with many personal entanglements. Energetic and determined but often unfocused.

Mou Wu—"Horse inside the Gate": (Years 1918, 1978, 2038, 2098, 2158) Intelligent, inquisitive, and wide-ranging. Warm-hearted, gentle, and helpful. Loved by many.

Sheep (Wei)

Sheep is sensitive, gentle, and creative. Sheep is adaptive and optimistic, avoiding problems through luck and flexibility, but tends to lack willpower. Sheep is compassionate, caring, and known for consideration and good manners.

Hsin Wei—"Fortunate Sheep": (Years 1871, 1931, 1991, 2051, 2111) Compassionate, trusting, and forgiving, sometimes to a fault; should sometimes be more cynical. Strong ideals but not always practical.

Kuei Wei—"Sheep of the Flock": (Years 1883, 1943, 2003, 2063, 2123) Charitable and generous with

Lesson VIII

both time and effort. Caring and given to helping others, yet also sometimes tactless or brutally honest.

Yi Wei—"Honored Sheep": (Years 1895, 1955, 2015, 2075, 2135) Honest and hard-working, successful and respected. Conscientious and well-organized, a self-starter who resents confinement.

Ting Wei—"Lonely Sheep": (Years 1907, 1967, 2027, 2087, 2147) Seeks to understand the reasons behind things. Can be moody, emotional, strongly affected by surrounding events. Less thought and more action will serve to steady the emotions.

Chi Wei—"Sheep in the Mountains": (Years 1919, 1979, 2039, 2099, 2159) Honest and outspoken, but also charming and persuasive. Good at negotiation and debate, skilled in communication.

Monkey (Shen)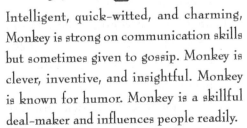

Intelligent, quick-witted, and charming, Monkey is strong on communication skills but sometimes given to gossip. Monkey is clever, inventive, and insightful. Monkey is known for humor. Monkey is a skillful deal-maker and influences people readily.

Beloved Caroline Highcorrell, founder of the Correllian Tradition, and Gerald Gardner, founder of the Gardnerian Tradition, were both Monkeys.

Jen Shen—"Pretty Monkey": (Years 1872, 1932, 1992, 2052, 2112) Sociable and outgoing but moody. Seeks security but can be impractical, will sometimes spend more for a bargain than is saved by it.

Chia Shen—"Monkey in the Tree": (Years 1884, 1944, 2004, 2064, 2124) Charming, witty, persuasive. Emotionally private, determined, and steadfast.

Ping Shen—"Monkey Climbing the Mountain": (Years 1896, 1956, 2016, 2076, 2136) Excellent judgment of people and situations. Sees below surfaces and makes astute deductions. Strong sense of self and rarely ever deceived.

Mou Shen—"Lonely Monkey": (Years 1908, 1968, 2028, 2088, 2148) Impatient, restless, inquisitive. Intelligent and thorough but easily distracted. Quicksilver moods change suddenly and often.

Keng Shen—"Monkey in the Fruit Tree": (Years 1920, 1980, 2040, 2100, 2160) Intelligent, forceful, shrewd. Very aware of appearances and usually attractive. Can be bluntly honest and sometimes reacts too quickly.

Rooster (Yu)

Rooster is outgoing and sociable, honest to a fault, and extremely confident. Rooster is deeply intelligent but often impractical. Rooster is persuasive, trusting, and often quite lucky. Rooster is optimistic and takes both success and failure in stride.

The present Correllian First Priestess Lady Krystel is a Rooster.

Kuei Yu—"Rooster in the Hen House": (Years 1873, 1933, 1993, 2053, 2113) Energetic and enthusiastic. Outspoken and sometimes given to gossip. Resilient and self-sufficient, a good negotiator and able to talk their way out of most anything.

Yi Yu—"Singing Rooster": (Years 1885, 1945, 2005, 2065, 2125) Buoyant and optimistic, always expecting the best. Trusts in providence. Sometimes acts too quickly.

Ting Yu—"Lonely Rooster": (Years 1897, 1957, 2017, 2077, 2137) Sentimental and emotional. A good communicator, sociable, and outgoing—makes friends easily and everywhere. Tends to have a rocky start in life but better situations later. Lucky.

Chi Yu—"Rooster Heralding the Dawn": (Years 1909, 1969, 2029, 2089, 2149) Extreme honesty and chaotic emotions make for difficulty in relationships, but luck and financial good sense provide financial stability and success.

Hsin Yu—"Rooster in a Cage": (Years 1921, 1981, 2041, 2101, 2161) Ambitious, enthusiastic, energetic. Loves a challenge and loves new ideas. Always ready to take on something new, usually quite successfully.

Dog (Hsu)

Loyal, honest, and reliable, Dog is a good and steady friend who can always be counted on. Dog is determined, caring, and a champion of good causes. Dog is sometimes pessimistic and may worry too much about others.

Zsa Zsa Gabor was a Dog.

Chia Hsu—"Guard Dog": (Years 1874, 1934, 1994, 2054, 2114) Enjoys activity, competition, debate. Determined; does not give up or back down, but also serious and inward-looking on occasion.

Ping Hsu—"Sleeping Dog": (Years 1886, 1946, 2006, 2066, 2126) Supportive, nurturing, skilled at helping others with their problems. Does not do well with rigid structure or with stress.

Mou Hsu—"Dog Going into the Mountains": (Years 1898, 1958, 2018, 2078, 2138) Intuitive, em-

Lesson VIII

pathic, far-sighted, and generous toward others. Independent and self-reliant.

Keng Hsu—"Temple Dog": (Years 1910, 1970, 2030, 2090, 2150) Contented, makes the best of any situation. Strong character and determination. Humanitarian, concerned for others, and angered by injustice.

Jen Hsu—"Family Dog": (Years 1922, 1982, 2042, 2102, 2162) Generous and loving, with many friends and supporters. Too generous to hold on to money, but always finds help when it is needed.

Pig (Hai)

Trustworthy, easygoing, and caring, Pig is a good friend. Slow to make a decision, Pig is steadfast and determined once the decision is made. Almost always succeeds at what they try to do. Pig loves the good life and is devoted to family.

Beloved Lady Mable, second matriarchal head of the Correllian Tradition, was a Pig.

Yi Hai—"Pig Passing By": (Years 1875, 1935, 1995, 2055, 2115) Honest to a fault, outspoken, and opinionated. Unwilling to accept arbitrary rules or blockages. May have problems with elders or with authority. Becomes more settled with age.

Ting Hai—"Pig in the Mountains": (Years 1887, 1947, 2007, 2067, 2127) Enthusiastic, likes challenges, sees potential in unusual situations. Works hard but puts family first.

Chi Hai—"Temple Pig": (Years 1899, 1959, 2019, 2079, 2139) Optimistic, adaptive, able to make the most of all situations. Often faces unexpected circumstances but is able to take them in stride. Lucky.

Hsin Hai—"Pig in the Garden": (Years 1911, 1971, 2031, 2091, 2151) Independent, confident, self-contained. Does not interfere in other people's business unless asked. Prefers to focus on home and family.

Kuei Hai—"Pig in the Forest": (Years 1923, 1983, 2043, 2103, 2163) Determined, perseverant, obstinate. Very loyal and supportive to friends, and a great help in time of trouble.

• • • •

It should be noted that to do a proper Chinese horoscope involves not only the year of birth, as Westerners sometimes think, but also additional elements such as the month, day, and hour. Because the months in question are reckoned by a lunar calendar and thus change each year, we will not comment on them, as the calculations necessary to convert a birth date from the Western solar calendar to the Chinese

Lesson VIII

239

lunar calendar are too much to include here. This is also true for the days, because they are dependent on the lunar months they fall in. However, we will comment upon the hours.

Each Chinese hour is the equivalent of two Western hours and is ruled by an animal sign, the same signs that rule the years. They are interpreted according to the same qualities described above. The list below tells which sign rules which hours.

11 PM–1 AM Tzu/Rat

1 AM–3 AM Ch'ou/Ox

3 AM–5 AM Yin/Tiger

5 AM–7 AM Mao/Rabbit

7 AM–9 AM Ch'en/Dragon

9 AM–11 AM Szu/Snake

11 AM–1 PM Wu/Horse

1 PM–3 PM Wei/Sheep

3 PM–5 PM Shen/Monkey

5 PM–7 PM Yu/Rooster

7 PM–9 PM Hsu/Dog

9 PM–11 PM Hai/Pig

Aztec Calendar

Like the Chinese calendar, the Aztec calendar will be most familiar to many readers from placemats in Mexican restaurants. The magnificent CUAUHXICALLI or "Eagle Bowl," more commonly termed the Calendar Stone or Sun Stone, is a major symbol of Mexican culture and pride, but few people understand what all it represents.

Engraved upon the Cuauhxicalli in intricate detail is the complicated Aztec calendar, surrounding the face of TONATIUH, the sun god of the present age. Like many other peoples, the Aztecs thought of the world in terms of successive ages that marked new beginnings for the world.

Like the Egyptians with their lunar liturgical calendar and solar civil calendar, the Aztecs used two simultaneous calendar systems. These were the Tonalpohualli (Reckoning of Days), a liturgical calendar of 260 days, and the Xiupohualli (Reckoning of Years), a civil calendar of 360 days, plus five epogamenal days called Nemontemi (empty days).

The Tonalpohualli was very ancient and long predated the Aztecs, having been used by many Mesoamerican peoples before and beside them, notably the Maya, who knew it as the Tzolkin. It seems to have originated when people noted that the sun passed a specific sacred spot near the Mayan city of Copan every 260 days. This 260-day year was then divided into twenty months of thirteen days each (*trecena* in Spanish), which were numbered.

The Tonalpohualli was recorded in a book called the *Tonalamatl*, which was consulted whenever a child was born, so that a horoscope could immediately be laid out. If it was considered that the child was born on an unlucky day, the horoscope would not be read until the following day in the hope that by thus fixing a different "official" birth date, the bad luck could be avoided.

In addition to astrological divination, the Tonalpohualli was also used to set the dates for religious ceremonies and select auspicious dates for important events.

The Xiupohualli, on the other hand, was a civil calendar based on the solar year. The Xiupohualli had 360 days, which were divided into eighteen months of twenty days each (called *veintenas* in Spanish). The months were further divided into four five-day weeks.

The addition of five epogamenal days made a 365-day year. The Aztecs called their epogamenal days Nemontemi, or "empty days," and regarded them as being between the year preceding and the year following, a "time out of time" similar in flavor to Samhain and reserved for religious activities alone.

While the Tonalpohualli was used for religious purposes and the Xiupohualli for civil ones, the two calendars came together for divinatory purposes. The twenty day names used in the solar Xiupohualli calendar were combined in sequence with the thirteen numerical day names of the Tonalpohualli calendar. Like the heavenly stems and earthly branches of the Chinese, the Tonalpohualli and Xiupohualli were of differing lengths; consequently, the combination of day names and numbers did not repeat exactly but rather in a series of unique variations. This continued in a cycle of 18,980 days, or fifty-two years, during which no two days had exactly the same name and number. This fifty-two-year cycle was considered extremely important and magical by the Aztecs, and like the Chinese sixty-year cycle, it was used as we use centuries, and in fact is often referred to as the "Mesoamerican century."

The end of each fifty-two-year cycle was marked by a twelve-day ceremony called Xiuhmolpilli, or "Binding up of Years"— this was the most important ceremony of the Aztec religion.

The Aztecs believed that the end of each fifty-two-year cycle was potentially the end of the world, and that the world must be revived and renewed in order to continue. The Xiuhmolpilli festival began with the extinguishment of all fires to mark the end of the old cycle. Days of fasting and abstinence followed. On the twelfth day, the appearance of a specific star signaled

that the world had been renewed and a new fifty-two-year cycle begun, a new fire was ceremonially struck in the temple, and every home relit its own fires from it.

Aztec Day Names

Below is a list of the twenty Aztec day names used in the Xiupohualli. Each one maybe interpreted according to the qualities of its symbol.

Each name was combined with a number, one through thirteen, from the Tonalpohualli, which affected its interpretation. The twenty day names repeated in sequence during each of the eighteen solar months, but obviously took different numbers each time, changing their meaning in numerological ways.

Not only was a child named according to the date of its birth, but each *trecena* (thirteen-day period) and each solar year was named according to the day they began upon.

A sample date is 31 January Year 3 Aquarius, which translates (using the Alfonso Caso method of correlation) to Year 4-Acatl (4-Reed), Trecena 1-Calli (1-House), Day 6-Tochtli (6-Rabbit).

1 **Coatl:** Snake

2 **Cuetzpallin:** Lizard

3 **Calli:** House

4 **Ehecatl:** Wind

5 **Cipactli:** Crocodile

6 **Xocitl:** Flower

7 **Quiahuitl:** Rain

8 **Tecpatl:** Flint

9 **Ollin:** Movement

10 **Cozcacuauhtli:** Vulture

11 **Cuauhtle:** Eagle

12 **Ocelotl:** Jaguar/Ocelot

13 **Acatl:** Reed

14 **Malinalli:** Grass/Herb

15 **Ozomatli:** Monkey

16 **Itzquintli:** Dog

17 **Atl:** Water

18 **Tochtli:** Rabbit

19 **Mazatl:** Deer

20 **Miquiztli:** Skull

Aztec Months

Below is a list of the eighteen twenty-day months of the Xiupohualli, or Aztec civil calendar. The Nemontemi brought the Xiupohualli to a total of 365 days.

1 **Atlacacauallo:** "Rain's End" (February/March)

2 **Tlacaxipehualiztli:** "Flaying Time" (March)

3 **Tozoztontli:** "Lesser Vigil" (April)

4 **Hueytozoztli:** "Greater Vigil" (April/May)

5 **Toxcatl:** "Dry Season" (May/June)

6 **Etzalcualiztli:** "Corn and Beans" (June)

7 **Tecuilhuitontli:** "Lesser Feast of the Nobles" (June/July)

8 **Hueytecuihutli:** "Greater Feast of the Nobles" (July)

9 **Tlaxochimaco:** "Birth of Flowers" (August)

10 **Xocotlhuetzin:** "Fruit Falls" (August/September)

11 **Ochpaniztli:** "Cleansing the Roads" (September)

12 **Teoleco:** "Return of the Gods" (October)

13 **Tepeihuitl:** "Feast of the Hills" (October/November)

14 **Quecholli:** "Precious Feather" (November)

15 **Panquetzaliztli:** "Raising the Flag" (December)

16 **Atemoztli:** "Rain Falls" (December/January)

17 **Tititl:** "Stretching" (January)

18 **Izcalli:** "Rebirth" (February)

Nemontemi: "Empty Days" (Five epogamenal days: February)

Witches' Calendar of Years

There is also a form of calendrical astrology associated with certain branches of Wicca. This system is based upon the number 9 and relates to the natural world and its phenomena.

Like the Chinese calendar, each year is assigned a ruler: these are Sun, Moon, Earth, Air, Fire, Water, Animal, Plant (Vegetable), and Stone (Mineral). Each year has specific qualities, and the cycle repeats in sequence. Again, years are provided below in Gregorian rather than Correllian notation for ease of reading.

The system reflects a Mediterranean base as it reckons each year as beginning at the spring equinox, which is traditional for some branches of Wicca, though less frequently encountered today than it once was.

I was taught this system by my mother, beloved LaVeda, who represented it as being traditional. I cannot say for certain where she learned it, but I believe I recall her saying she got it from *The Witches' Almanac* sometime in the early '70s. Who wrote it and where it actually originates I have no further idea.

I have found the system to be relatively accurate, but as we have said, God/dess will use any system that you believe in to speak to you, and so all divinatory forms are accurate in theory.

Lesson
VIII

The qualities given pertain to both the year itself and the people born in it. Remember that the first quarter of the year actually belongs to the previous year, since the system uses the spring equinox as New Year.

I have always thought whichever sign rules the first and ninth year of a decade also colors the whole period, as for example Earth rules the '60s and Air the '70s.

Sun

(Years 1922, 1931, 1940, 1949, 1958, 1967, 1976, 1985, 1994, 2003, 2012)

This year is marked by pride, ambition, and large-scale plans, but also generosity and loyalty. Egos are liable to be inflated, and people must be careful not to lose their sense of proportion.

Moon

(Years 1923, 1932, 1941, 1950, 1959, 1968, 1977, 1986, 1995, 2004, 2013)

This year is marked by emotionality, compassion, and humanitarianism, but also oversensitivity and moodiness. People may find themselves feeling vulnerable and sometimes seek refuge in rigidity as a result. Psychic and spiritual issues are strong.

Earth

(Years 1924, 1933, 1942, 1951, 1960, 1969, 1978, 1987, 1996, 2005, 2014)

This year is marked by a desire to be in tune with natural cycles and with the earth—a desire to set aside masks and get to the heart of things. Freedom, independence, and growth are accented, as is impatience with restriction. Honesty and truth are regarded as of paramount importance, but they are not always kept in perspective.

Air

(Years 1925, 1934, 1943, 1952, 1961, 1970, 1979, 1988, 1997, 2006, 2015)

This year is marked by new ideas, new directions, insight, and innovation, breaking with the past. Mind and intellect are strong but not always practical in approach. There is much restlessness, and it is hard to focus on just one thing.

Fire

(Years 1926, 1935, 1944, 1953, 1962, 1971, 1980, 1989, 1998, 2007, 2016)

This year is marked by passion, ambition, and drive. It is a time of focus, determination, and clear-cut goals. It also tends to be self-centered, even selfish, with difficulty in considering the needs of others.

Water

(Years 1927, 1936, 1945, 1954, 1963, 1972, 1981, 1990, 1999, 2008, 2017)

This year is marked by an easygoing, compassionate, and adaptable nature. Water is flexible and always seeks out the

best way to get where it is going. Plans are fluid, changing where necessary; practicality is important, but not at the expense of humanity. Psychic issues are strong.

Animal
(Years 1928, 1937, 1946, 1955, 1964, 1973, 1982, 1991, 2000, 2009, 2018)

This year is marked by passion, commitment, and willingness to fight for one's ideals. Courage and determination are strong, but self-satisfaction and overconfidence can be problems.

Plant
(Years 1929, 1938, 1947, 1956, 1965, 1974, 1983, 1992, 2001, 2010, 2019)

This year is marked by growth in all directions, prosperity, and an emphasis on personal pleasure. Experimentation, new ideas and directions, novelty and innovation are important. Sensuality and self-centeredness can be an issue.

Stone
(Years 1930, 1939, 1948, 1957, 1966, 1975, 1984, 1993, 2002, 2011, 2020)

This year is marked by examination of how things work, why they work (or don't), and attempts to make them work better. It is a conservative time, concerned with security, structure, and organization. Thoroughness and hard work are emphasized.

. . . .

Exercises

In Lessons V, VI, and VII we included exercises that were to be done occasionally rather than as a continuation of the daily routine.

At this time, your daily routine should begin with the Ohm exercise, then opening the chakras with balls of colored light, changing the balls of colored light to balls of white light, changing the balls of white light to balls of purple light, changing the balls of purple light to balls of silver stellar light, and then filling your aura with silver stellar light. Next, change the balls of silver stellar light to balls of golden stellar light, then fill your aura with golden stellar light. Finally, change the balls of golden stellar light to balls of amber light, and fill your aura with the amber light. Now, from each chakra, call forth its personified form, and imagine it before you. You might then do any other of the various occasional exercises at this point. Remember to close the chakras, clear, and release when finished.

We have been doing this daily routine for quite some time. This is so that the chakras will be strengthened for the next variation in the routine, which comes now with Exercise 13. Exercise 13 changes the daily routine considerably; you may find it difficult at first, but because you have been strengthening your chakras for so long, you should master it fairly quickly.

Lesson VIII

245

Exercise 13

Begin as usual with the Ohm exercise. Then open your chakras as usual with balls of colored light.

Now, instead of changing the color of the balls of light as we have been doing, we will add a new step. Begin with the root chakra. Open a second ball of colored light in the root chakra, so that one ball of light is in the middle of your body, the second in the front. Continue with each chakra until you have two rows of balls of colored light all the way up your chakras, one row at the front of your body, one in the center.

Now close the chakras, clear, and release as usual.

When you can do this exercise easily, you are ready for Exercise 14.

Exercise 14

You will probably not be surprised by Lesson 14.

Begin with the Ohm exercise. Then open one ball of colored light in each chakra. Then open a second ball of light in each chakra, as in Exercise 13. Now go through and open a third ball of colored light in each chakra, this one at the back of your body. This will give you three balls of colored light at each chakra: one at the front, one in the middle, and one at the back of your body.

Now close the chakras, clear, and release as usual.

When you can do this easily for each chakra, you are ready to progress to Exercise 15.

Exercise 15

Exercise 15 might be regarded as a variation of Exercise 14. This time, however, we are going to open all three balls of light in each chakra at once.

Begin with the Ohm exercise. Now, starting at the root chakra, open three balls of colored light: one at the front, one in the middle, and one at the back of the body. Do the same for each chakra, until all seven major chakras each have three balls of colored light open.

Now close the chakras, clear, and release as usual.

When you can do this exercise easily, you are ready to move on to Exercise 16.

Exercise 16

Before you begin Exercise 16 you should be able to open three balls of colored light in each chakra easily. Now we are going to return to the sequence of colors we had been using prior to Exercise 13.

Begin with the Ohm exercise. Now open three balls of colored light in each chakra, as we have been doing in Exercise 15.

Now go through each chakra and change all three balls to white light. Then go through each chakra and change all three balls of light to purple light.

Then go through each chakra and change all three balls of light to silver stellar light, and having done so, fill your aura with silver stellar light.

Now do the same with golden stellar light, changing all three balls at each chakra to balls of golden stellar light, and then filling your aura with the golden stellar light.

Finally, go through and change all three balls of light at each chakra to amber light, and fill your aura with that.

If you wish, you may now call forth the personified form of your chakras, but that is not necessary on a daily basis, as you have now learned how to work and interact with them. You may also do any other of the occasional techniques you have learned or other sorts of psychic work.

When finished, close the chakras, clear, and release as always.

At this point, you have begun preparation for interacting with the chakras at the level you will learn in Lesson IX.

····

Spell for Lesson VIII
Bonding with Trees

They don't call us Pagans tree-huggers for nothing, and this spell will prove that.

In this spell, we are going to discuss how to establish an energetic relationship with a tree or other plant. By doing this, you essentially are creating an energetic pathway between yourself and the tree, which can be used for healing, communication, or magic.

There are a variety of situations in which you might want to establish such a relationship. You will notice that many spells call for placing or burying things at the foot of a tree. Also, if you place the remains of offerings out-of-doors after ritual, you might place them at the base of a tree. In either case, it can be nice to use the same tree and develop a special relationship with it.

Also, some people like to talk to trees. That is to say, they are suited by talent or temperament to communicate psychically with plants. In this case, too, using this technique can be useful in establishing a good relationship with the tree or plant you wish to communicate with.

Obviously this technique can also be useful for trees and other plants that you may be trying to grow. It will create a strong rapport between yourself and the plant, as well as establish a ready pathway through

Lesson
VIII

which strengthening or healing energy may be sent to the plant when needed.

The technique is very simple. Begin by greeting your tree. Speak to it aloud or silently, but be clear in your focus. Be gentle and friendly—trees like that.

Tell the tree that you wish to establish a friendship with it and build an energetic pathway between the two of you. Explain that you would like it to help you with acts of manifestation, and that in return you will be happy help it if and when you can.

Ask the tree if it will accept this. Usually the answer will be yes; this is because if you are drawn to a tree, it is likely that the tree is also drawn to you. Allow the tree to answer. You may get the answer as a feeling or a clairvoyant message. Or you might use a form of divination such as a pendulum. If the tree's answer is positive, then proceed.

Place one hand on either side of the trunk. Imagine a ball of white energy between your hands, in the middle of the trunk. See the ball of light as clearly as possible. Imagine the energy as being very pure and strong, and without mottling or occlusions.

Now imagine a second ball of white energy in your heart chakra. Imagine this ball of light very clearly too. Imagine your heart chakra full of love, strength, and healing energy.

Finally, imagine a third ball of white energy above your head, see it clearly, and feel its energy above you.

From the ball of light above your head, imagine a shower of light descending on you. Let the light fill you, especially your heart chakra.

Focus the light entering from the top of your head through your heart chakra, and send it forth in a beam to the ball of light in the center of the tree trunk. Fill the light with love and healing energy as you send it forth.

Imagine the beam of light entering the tree through the ball of light in the trunk and moving upwards and downwards through the tree, up the trunk and out into the branches, down the trunk and out into the roots. Let the light fill the tree, and with it the love and healing you have sent.

Continue to do this until it feels like the tree can accept no more energy. Then let the beam of light fade.

Now ask the tree if it will send you energy. Imagine a beam of light coming out from the tree to your heart chakra. Receive energy from the tree through this beam. Let the energy fill your heart chakra, then spread throughout your body, going down into your arms and legs. Let the energy fill you completely.

Now thank your tree. Let the image of the various balls of light fade. Finally, clear and release.

You have now established a special relationship with your tree. You can use this same technique to send the tree energy in the future. Remember to be alert in case it needs anything, and try to help it as you have asked it to help you.

Now you can use the tree in spells or as a place to release offerings made in ritual, and feel a special bond with it. You may find yourself having communication with it as well. Sometimes a tree bonded with in this manner will act as a kind of spirit guide.

. . . .

Glossary

Cuauhxicalli—The Cuauhxicalli, better known as the Aztec Calendar Stone or the Sun Stone, is a huge, circular carving nearly twelve feet in diameter, three feet thick, and weighing twenty-five tons. *Cuauhxicalli* is a Nahuatl term variously translated as "Eagle Bowl" or "Heart Bowl." The Cuauhxicalli shows Tonatiuh, the sun god of the present fifth age, surrounded by the months and days of the Aztec calendar. The Cuauhxicalli was carved from olivine basalt around 1079 Pisces (AD 1479), during the reign of the sixth Aztec monarch, Axayacatl. The Cuauhxicalli was part of the Temple of the Sun in the Aztec capitol Tenochtitlan, and it was buried in the general destruction that followed the conquest of the Aztecs, only to be rediscovered in 1390 Pisces (AD 1790).

Numa Pompillius—Legendary second king of Rome, after Romulus, Numa is said to have ruled from 485 Aries (715 BC) to 527 Aries (673 BC). Numa established many Roman cultural institutions, especially regarding the Roman religion. Numa regulated the Roman liturgical calendar, established religious festivals, and created the office of *flamen,* or arch priest—one for each of the major Roman gods, most notably the flamen Dialis for Jupiter, whose life was surrounded by many taboos. The wives of the flamens served as *flaminias,* or arch priestesses. Numa also established the Salian Priesthood and the Vestal Virgins. Legend says he was married to the goddess Egeria, who transformed him into a sacred well in the forest of Aricia when he died.

Tonatiuh—The Aztecs believed that there had been successive ages of creation and destruction, each with their own sun and their own characteristic race. Tonatiuh was the sun of the fifth and current age. According to Aztec mythology, as related by the Spaniard Bernardino Ribera de Sahagun, after the fourth age had ended and all was destroyed, the gods had gathered at Teotihuacan to create

Lesson
VIII

249

the world anew. A new sun and moon had to be created, but these could only be created if two gods would sacrifice themselves for the purpose. A god called Tecucistecatl undertook to become the new moon, but no god could be found to become the new sun, for they were all afraid. At length, a humble and disfigured god called Nanahuatzin agreed to become the new sun. After extensive rituals of purification, a great bonfire was built, into which both Tecucistecatl and Nanahautzin were to throw themselves—but Tecucistecatl lost his nerve, so the humble Nanahautzin went first. Then, inspired by Nanahautzin's example, Tecucistecatl followed. Nanahautzin was reborn as Tonatiuh, the sun, while Tecucistecatl became the moon, and thus the fifth age began. Tonatiuh ruled an Otherworld paradise called Tollan, which was reserved for warriors who died in battle and for women who died in childbirth.

Lesson

IX

Advanced Chakra and Energy Working

This lesson is based upon the works of PETER BINDER, who has devoted his life to the study of the chakra system in minute detail. Binder describes his system for interacting with the chakras as astral physics. Binder taught me this system many years ago and gave me permission to teach it as well. I have found it an invaluable source of knowledge in dealing with the inner workings of the chakras.

We have discussed in the First Degree materials how the body is said to have seven major chakras but that there are also many thousands of minor chakras. Many of the minor chakras may be studied through systems such as acupuncture, which have mapped out meridians between them for purposes of medical treatment. However, in addition to the minor chakras found in every part of the body, there are also many levels and aspects to each of the major chakras as well.

As you have learned, there are three major energetic systems in the body: Mable Highcorrell, second matriarchal head of the Correllian Tradition, described these as the solar energy circuit, lunar energy circuit, and stellar energy circuit. Binder calls these same three energetic circuits the temporal system, existential system, and foundational system; for each of the three systems, he describes differing aspects of the major chakras.

Not all of the chakras have the same configuration, especially the crown chakra, which is unlike all the others, especially in that it does not have separate aspects for the three systems. Most of the chakras, however, have the same basic structure. Each of the major chakras has seven levels within it. At each level, there are three points: the primary chakra point and a right and left companion. In addition, some of the chakras, namely the temporal, solaris, and heart chakras, have a pronounced difference between the right and left sides of the central chakra point.

In addition to the major chakras in the three systems, I am including Binder's assessment of present, past, and future chakras, which regulate our interactions with the perception of time. Though time seems to be a very concrete thing to most people, it is, in fact, an illusion we generate that allows us to give order to our experiences so that we can more easily understand and learn from them.

In Lesson VII, we discussed the different way in which Hindus and Buddhists traditionally look at chakras, i.e., Buddhists usually omit the first and second chakras. You will notice in reading over this lesson that Binder has been influenced by primarily Buddhist studies. Hence, the root chakra and second chakra are not examined in this system. Based on study of the rest of the system, I would say that these first two chakras would probably deal with what we would regard as automatic systems, which serve to create and maintain the body, such as breathing, blood flow, generation of tissues, etc.

You will also notice that a lesser amount of information is included with each successive system discussed, the temporal chakras receiving the most attention. This is because the existential and foundational chakras are associated with a higher level of working, which requires more care and discipline than the temporal chakras. Indeed, of the foundational chakras we provide only a brief overview in this lesson. There is no need, nor is it necessarily wise, for deeper study of the existential and foundational systems before mastering the temporal system. The information provided gives you the knowledge you need for the level of interaction that should be attempted at a Second Degree level of study.

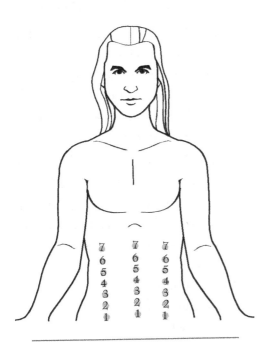

The seven levels of the solaris (solar plexus) chakra

Temporal Chakras

The temporal/solar chakras deal with issues of existence in the physical world and with the creation of our conscious being as an emanation of the soul. They are called temporal chakras because they deal with the world of time and space in a way that the existential and foundational chakras do not.

Solaris

The solar plexus chakra, called the solaris here, is by nature reactive. The most general interpretation is that it reflects how we interact with others and with the world; here we will examine it more specifically. We will see how the solar plexus chakra deals with instinctive response and with unconscious or semiconscious impulse.

Solaris Level One

The first level of the solaris is primarily concerned with instinctive and unconscious reactions to situations and people.

Right Side: This aspect of the chakra generates imagined reactions to situations and extrapolates potential consequences of action. This gives the ability to learn from situations and to associate specific consequences with specific causes. It is not to be

Lesson
IX

confused with conscious and intentional planning of situations, which has its primary seat elsewhere in the system.

Left Side: This aspect of the chakra stimulates unconscious physical reaction to situations based on instinct and self-preservation. For example, if a car is speeding toward you, the right aspect of the level one solar plexus chakra assesses the potential danger, and the left aspect of the level one solar plexus chakra motivates you to move out of the way.

Right Companion: This aspect generates a basic need for sex as a form of self-expression and derives satisfaction and grounding from sexual activity. If blocked, it can lead to sexual repression or frigidity, and consequent feelings of anger and disconnectedness. If overdeveloped or unbalanced by a blockage of the left companion, it can lead to sexual obsession.

Left Companion: This aspect generates a need for meaningful connection to other people through romantic or other forms of love and derives satisfaction and grounding from this emotional connection. If blocked, it can restrict the ability to feel or express love and affection toward others.

Solaris Level Two

The level two solaris is primarily concerned with the sense of humor and the pleasure taken from activity. This level of the solaris will be seen to govern the first level of learning—that is, play—causing us to first find delight in our environment, then to investigate and finally study it.

Right Side: This aspect of the chakra generates an ability to find humor in our surroundings and experience a sense of joy and fun. This aspect of the chakra is reactive and finds its humor in external events.

Left Side: This aspect of the chakra gives us an ability to find humor within, independent of external events, and to generate a sense of well-being and joy without external stimuli.

Right Companion: This aspect gives a sense of playful mischievousness and a desire to amuse others. It causes us to react positively to other's pleasure.

Left Companion: This aspect gives a serious interest in and desire to study things that give us pleasure. This companion is involved in phenomena such as science fiction fandom, the famous *Book of World Records*, stamp collecting, and other detailed studies of essentially lighthearted things. It is also involved in the seri-

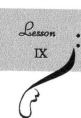
Lesson

IX

ous study of art and music, also essentially lighthearted things. This companion finds and develops real worth from activities whose primary quality is joy.

Solaris Level Three

The level three solaris has to do with sexual identity and relations with others. Ideas and ideals about love and sex, and about connections forged to others through these, are governed here.

Right Side: The right aspect of this chakra generates our sexual ego, our need to have sexual fulfillment, and how we feel about our own sexuality and sexuality in general. It gives a drive and a sense of duty to our sexual self.

Left Side: This aspect of the chakra governs our sexual self-image—whether we consider ourselves attractive, whether we regard sexuality as empowering or damaging, etc.

Right Companion: This aspect deals with familial love and is concerned with our attitude toward family and our connection to both ancestors and descendants and how we relate to them. Blocked, it gives a sense of estrangement from family and difficulty in forming close relationships. More serious blockage can create incestuous situations.

Left Companion: This aspect has to do with our sexual ideals, ideas about love, and how we express these outside of specifically sexual situations. The locker room braggart, the constant coquette, and the outspoken prude are all examples of blockage in this chakra.

Solaris Level Four

The fourth level of the solaris has to do with issues of self-preservation, how we react to new or dangerous situations, and whether or not we can tell the difference.

Right Side: This aspect deals with self-preservation and survival instincts, and it motivates reactions to dangerous or destructive situations.

Left Side: This aspect deals with curiosity, the desire and need to learn new things, the spur to experience the unexplored, to take chances and leave safe situations on the prospect of growth or gain. This aspect gives a desire for adventure and also a sense of acquisitiveness, a need to expand and embrace the new and different. This is also the seat of the so-called hunting instinct.

Right Companion: This aspect deals with issues of self-defense—evasive action in the face of a dangerous situation or threats, the ability to move

Lesson
IX

255

out of harm's way. This chakra also deals with the desire not to repeat dangerous situations, which may take the form of either a desire to avoid or to destroy what has caused danger or pain to us in the past. A blockage here can give a desire for retribution and revenge against those who are perceived as having harmed us and/or a tendency to make preemptive strikes as a means of avoiding danger.

Left Companion: This aspect gives the ability to react to danger with action, to counter threats and stand up against enemies. This companion manifests courage and ambition, giving us strength in the face of opposition. It is also the seat of the impulse to attack and destroy; if the solar level four left side is the seat of the hunting instinct, it is the solar level four left companion that makes the kill. Obviously, a blockage here can create either a very aggressive person or a very timid one.

Solaris Level Five

The fifth level of the solaris deals with our relations with other people, especially how we communicate and express ourselves.

Right Side: This aspect of the chakra gives us a need to make ourselves heard, to express our ideas and feelings, to affect others and make a mark in the world. It causes us to connect to others in an active way, through verbal or nonverbal communication.

Left Side: This aspect allows us to connect to others in a passive way, causing us to react to the behavior and actions of others even when it does not affect us directly. It gives an emotional reaction to others and causes us to form a "gut feeling" response to them and to their actions. A blockage here can make one overly sensitive to others, having no feeling of distance from them, or conversely, it can leave one with no emotional connection to other people, seeing them merely as objects to be manipulated.

Right Companion: This aspect has to do with our relationship with Deity and our Higher Self, and consequently our self-esteem and confidence as relative to others; specifically, it has to do with the extent to which we are secure in ourselves or feel controlled from outside. When well-developed, this companion allows us to understand that the acts of others do not inherently affect or control us, and that our self-worth is an internal value not affected by anything that

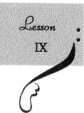

happens outside of ourselves. When blocked, this companion becomes inordinately concerned with what other people are doing and the idea of "divine justice" to punish them for real or imagined wrongdoing. Blockage here can cause great self-righteousness and a pretense of superiority that covers a feeling of inferiority.

Left Companion: This companion deals with the external expression of our relationship to Deity and our Higher Self. This can take a number of forms, the most basic of which is self-esteem and tolerance of others, which is only possible when we have a strong spiritual connection and the self-confidence and inner balance that comes from it. Tolerance, charity, compassion, willingness to help others—all of these are manifestations of a strong connection to Spirit. More ritualistic expressions of spirituality also have a seat here. When this companion is blocked, the person may confuse external expressions of piety for internal spiritual connection. Blockage here can also cause miserliness, intolerance, and contempt for things outside the self.

Solaris Level Six

The sixth level of the solaris has to do with how well we relate to our own Higher Self

and to others, how we become energized in relation to ideas and activities, and our ability to judge the consequences of our actions.

Right Side: This aspect has to do with our reaction to our soul's needs and purposes. This often manifests as issues of personal fulfillment, creativity, and expression, all of which are related to heeding the voice of the soul within ourselves. A blockage here can make us second-guess or ignore the inner voice that is the voice of our Higher Self telling us what we need. Listening to the inner voice leads us to fulfill our soul's needs and to become energized from within.

Left Side: This aspect is responsible for our becoming energized through external excitement. Through this aspect we gain energy from immersion in pleasurable activities and get excited when exciting things are going on around us. Obviously, a blockage here can make one dependent upon external stimulation for energy.

Right Companion: This aspect allows us to predict the emotional reactions of others. This allows us to anticipate how others will react to possible actions or to situations. A blockage here can cause us to have seriously mistaken ideas of others' feelings

Lesson
IX

and motivations, and serious misjudgments as to what actions are desirable or undesirable.

Left Companion: This aspect allows us to anticipate the emotional consequences of our actions to ourselves or others. The right companion allows us to assess how others will react emotionally to a situation, but the left companion tells us the emotional effects of the situation.

Solaris Level Seven

The seventh level of the solar plexus chakra deals with our long-term relationships with others and how we build them.

Right Side: This aspect gives a desire to improve our lives and the world around us. It gives devotion to ideals and a desire to help others and enhance the over-all quality of life. This aspect makes us want to build, to improve, and to perfect the things that are important to us.

Left Side: This aspect allows us to imagine the long-term effects of our actions and to formulate plans for long-term projects. If the right side of the solar plexus level seven chakra causes us to see what we want to do, the left side causes us to see how to do it. A blockage here can make for a lack of concern with outcomes or

for seriously bad misjudgments of outcome.

Right Companion: This aspect deals with our goals, ideals, and sense of duty to ourselves and others. It gives us a sense of situations worth working for, a higher purpose greater than the gratifications of the moment.

Left Companion: This aspect focuses on long-term survival issues, self-preservation in the long haul. This gives us concern with future situations and makes us feel the need to plan for the future. At one time, this was the companion that told us to move on when the grazing lands were depleted. Today, it is this companion that makes us worry about things like cholesterol or retirement funds.

. . . .

Heart

The heart chakra serves primarily to motivate action based on emotional response to situations. Unlike the solaris, which deals with situations at a basic level, the heart chakra views situations through a lens of conscience and moral ideals. Where the solaris assesses events mainly through a sense of success or failure, the heart sees things through a sense of right and wrong.

Heart Level One

The first level of the heart chakra is where we make moral assessments of external and internal situations, including our morals themselves.

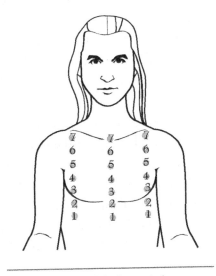

The seven levels of the heart chakra

Right Side: This aspect is where we assess how well we are fulfilling our moral duty to ourselves and our ideals. Are we answering the call of our soul? Are we doing the things we need to fulfill our physical, emotional, and spiritual nature, or are we neglecting our duty to ourselves? When ignored or blocked, this aspect of the heart chakra gives us the feeling that we are somehow behind where we should be, that we are constantly racing to catch up, never being good enough or moving fast enough.

Left Side: This aspect allows us to assess people and situations and render a judgment on the desirability of potential interaction with them, a "gut feeling." This is where we assess the character of others relative to our perceptions of what is right and wrong. If blocked, it makes one judgmental and prejudiced, having knee-jerk reactions; conversely, a blockage here can leave one overly trusting and naïve, a poor judge of character.

Right Companion: This aspect is where we assess the accuracy of our

moral perceptions and conceptions of right and wrong. This companion causes us to reflect on and refine our understandings of our moral relationship to ourselves, Deity, and the world about us. It is this companion that allows us to move from the simplistic view that what gives us pleasure or success must be "right" to the more complex idea of abstract values of right and wrong.

Left Companion: This aspect assesses whether actions or situations are in accordance with our perceptions of what is right and wrong. It examines our own and others' actions and renders a moral judgment. It should be noted that while this companion assesses the perceived rightness of situations, it does not in any way assess the correctness of the standards it is judging by.

Heart Level Two

The second level of the heart chakra regulates our emotional attachments: our loves and hates, likes and dislikes, attractions and repulsions.

Right Side: This aspect generates our desire for situations that cause us emotional pleasure and our desire to avoid situations that cause us pain. This is where we get our motivation

to seek out or manifest beneficial situations, as well as our desire not to deal with things that cause us hurt.

Left Side: This aspect generates our emotional reaction to the circumstances we encounter: it reacts with pleasure or pain, love or hate. This aspect of the chakra does not assess the "correctness" of its response in any way, it only registers the feeling.

Right Companion: This aspect logically assesses our attachments (loves and hates, likes and dislikes, etc.), to see whether they are of benefit to us or not. While the main body of the level two heart chakra relates to situations based on emotional attraction to or repulsion from them, without assessing the reasons for these, the right companion examines these feelings for their accuracy and currency. This is what allows us to let go of our emotional attachments when they are no longer relevant to us. It allows emotional growth through constant emotional assessment. A blockage here can make it impossible to let go of past emotions and move on, leaving us frozen in the past.

Left Companion: This companion generates an attraction to or repulsion from people, places, or situations based on their energetic qualities.

Have you ever met someone and said, "Ewww, they have icky energy"? If so, it was the heart level two left companion that caused you to recognize it. It should be noted, however, that it is not necessarily that the other person or place has "icky" energy per se, as much as that it reacts badly with your own. This is also true when you are aware of someone's "really great" energy. This companion pulls you to people/places/situations because of your compatibility with their similar or different energy (remember, opposites also attract), and repels you from those with whom your energy reacts badly. This companion also attracts or repels you from people/places/situations with which you have karmic ties.

Heart Level Three

The third level of the heart chakra gives us a sense of emotional relationship to time, and an ability to learn from our past experiences and apply that knowledge in present or future circumstances.

Right Side: This aspect gives us an innate reaction to time, a sense of entropy or decay that causes us to take action and to assess the results of action in relation to the results of time. It causes us to feel the limitations of time and to struggle against these. Of course, time is an illusion created by physical manifestation and by the intensity of focus and effort brought to the continual manifestation of the physical world, but this knowledge does not register at this level of the energetic system, where the illusion of time is perceived as a very concrete thing.

Left Side: This aspect gives us the ability to use time to our benefit, to plan and carry out long-term projects. This aspect of the chakra assesses the lessons of past experiences and projects the results into the future, overruling short-term needs in favor of long-term potentials. It gives us determination and perseverance, the ability to work long hours or endure sacrifices to fulfill our long-term goals—in short, the ability to focus on the far future even at the cost of discomfort in the near future. A blockage here gives an obsession with instant gratification and an inability to look ahead.

Right Companion: This aspect assesses past experiences and actions for their effectiveness, and studies and analyzes their results. This companion allows us to learn the lessons of our experiences. A blockage here can

result in repeating the same mistakes over and over again.

Left Companion: This aspect generates a sense of pride in past achievements, whose purpose is to help us recall lessons learned in the past. It gives a sense of attachment to the past, and if blocked, can cause us to either ignore the past or become trapped in it.

Heart Level Four

The fourth level of the heart chakra is the seat of our impulse for revenge and also forgiveness. It deals with our emotional reactions to people and situations, and the long-term consequences of them.

Right Side: This aspect assesses past experiences in order to determine potential dangers or threats in present or future situations. Ideally, it takes the lesson of past situations, but lets go of the emotion; thus, it is the center of forgiveness. If blocked, it clings to the emotion and becomes vengeful and bitter, never able to forgive or forget, or conversely becomes completely self-abnegating, losing its sense of self-preservation.

Left Side: The left aspect of this chakra assesses past situations in order to determine the best ways to interact with people or situations in the present or future in order to achieve de-

sired results. If blocked, this chakra can become manipulative or callous, making the desire for results its sole motivation and reducing people to mere tools.

Right Companion: This aspect makes long-term plans regarding specific people or situations based upon what has been learned through past interactions with them.

Left Companion: This aspect generates a desire to move on from the past, to forgive and forget, to leave the past behind and move into the future unencumbered by past attachments. This companion motivates us to forgive, to be in a state of balance and of love with all things.

Heart Level Five

The fifth level of the heart chakra deals with our relationship to Deity and how we consciously (or, more often, unconsciously) evaluate all things in relationship to it.

Right Side: This aspect causes us to project our feelings about our relationship with Deity onto our relationship with the world, in keeping with the concept of "As above, so below." Thus, if we have a good relationship with Deity and feel that Deity loves us, we are likely to treat others with love. If we feel punished

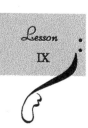

or persecuted by Deity, we are likely to punish and persecute others. Blockages here cause us to feel estranged from Deity and that there is something wrong with us or with the world, and to view the world darkly as a result.

Left Side: This aspect engenders a desire for a good relationship with Deity and with the world. It gives us a desire to be in or return to a state of balance and peace, to forgive and move on, to make things better. Here the concept of "As above, so below" is translated into a knowledge that our actions draw a natural consequence, violence begets violence while love begets love. If the right side of this level sees other people and situations in light of the relationship to Deity, the left side sees action in terms of relationship to Deity.

Right Companion: This aspect assesses one's life as an extension of one's relationship to God/dess. The right companion causes us to view our past and our future in light of our relationship to Deity: as a wonderful journey or a vale of tears. Blockage here makes one pessimistic about life and the future.

Left Companion: The left companion projects our attitude toward our relationship to Deity into our behaviors toward others. When unblocked, this manifests as compassion and love for others, and gives a desire to do good for the sake of it; blocked, it will make one "holier than thou" and often makes people confuse "divine justice" with their own personal desire for retribution or vengeance.

Heart Level Six

The sixth level of the heart chakra deals with our sense of destiny and our desire to play a role in the divine plan. It helps us to find our place in the universe and to align more fully with the needs and purposes of our Higher Self.

Right Side: This aspect helps us to have a sense of the greatness of the universe/Deity, an appreciation and awe of the endless diversity of creation and existence. It gives us a sense of our spiritual potential—how much there is to learn, do, be, and become.

Left Side: This aspect facilitates interaction with higher spiritual beings, usually unconscious but sometimes conscious. Here we feel the protection of our guides, for example, or sense the presence of a spirit or ghost. This is not a seat of communication per se, as this is found higher

Lesson
IX

in the system, but rather of a more emotional level of interaction.

Right Companion: This aspect reminds us that we have a higher purpose in life. It pulls us toward destiny and the fulfillment of the soul's needs and purposes. When functioning properly, this companion gives us a sense that there is a special role for us in life, as there is for all people. When blocked, it leaves us feeling that our life has no higher meaning.

Left Companion: This aspect assesses our future in terms of the soul's purposes and our own relationship to God/dess. If the right companion gives us a desire to play a role in destiny, the left companion actively pursues it. Here we seek to take part in things greater than ourselves and to make a mark in the universe.

Heart Level Seven

The seventh level of the heart chakra has to do with our feeling of oneness with Spirit and our ability to shape things through magic.

Right Side: This aspect has to do with issues of external manifestation, creating magically in the outside world through our connection to Deity and our Higher Self. This aspect gives us a sense of well-being and confidence

in the universe that is an aspect of a strong connection to Deity and that allows us to create magically, with or without conscious knowledge. Magic is a constant, ongoing process in our lives, usually unconsciously; though this chakra governs the process, it does not critically assess what is being manifested. This is how we sometimes trip ourselves up by manifesting what we focus on rather than what we consciously want. A blockage here can also leave us feeling fearful and powerless toward the universe in general. This chakra also has to do with how we feel about magic and the ability to manifest; when this aspect of the chakra is blocked, we may be suspicious or distrustful of magic, which is really a distrust of our inner, Higher Self.

Left Side: The left side of this chakra has to do with issues of internal manifestation, or how we create our body and its health. Our body itself is an act of magic, a constant and usually unconscious magic; this is true of our health as well. Our body is a manifestation of our soul, and thus ultimately a manifestation of Deity. Because it is a manifestation of our soul, our body reflects the state of our soul, and emotional

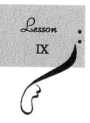

and spiritual blockages in our inner self register in our outer self as well ("As above, so below"). Often this takes the form of sickness and poor health. More conscious control of our health can be taken through this chakra. This chakra also has to do with how we feel about our body and our relationship to it. When this aspect of the chakra is blocked, we may have a poor physical self-image or we may reject the body as an unworthy vehicle for Spirit—but this is really a rejection of Spirit, since the body only reflects it.

Right Companion: This aspect generates a sense of oneness with eternity, a sense of timelessness that, when tapped into, allows us to transcend all worldly concerns and gain peace within ourselves.

Left Companion: This aspect generates a sense of oneness with God/dess, which manifests as spiritual elation or ecstasy. This is the feeling (akin to orgasm) that we feel in certain kinds of trance and when we touch souls. It is the divine ecstasy that people mean when they refer to feeling joy in "the presence of God."

· · · ·
Throat

The throat chakra levels deal with primarily mental/conceptual energies—with ideas, ideals, and issues of conscience.

Unlike the solaris and the heart chakras, the throat chakra levels do not have a distinct difference between the right and left sides of the central chakra. There are still distinct right and left companions, however.

Throat Level One

The first level of the throat chakra deals with shared ideals and group icons. This aspect of the chakra gives us a desire to be part of the group, to be with others of like mind, and to find strength in numbers. This level of the chakra causes us to find things appealing or desirable because our peers do, and to reject things that our peers reject. At its best, it helps us to have a healthy attachment to others and enables us to share ideas and values with society. A blockage here can lead to cliquishness, conformism, and prejudice, or conversely to misanthropy and rejection of others.

Right Companion: This aspect assesses others in relation to the extent to which they conform to our preconceived ideals and ideas about right and wrong. At its best, it helps us to associate with persons of like mind and to spot and avoid people whose

Lesson
IX

265

actions are harmful or destructive. Blockage here makes us judgmental of other's beliefs and self-righteous about our own.

Left Companion: This aspect analyzes the results of following the crowd, and in particular whether or not the actions of the group are in accordance with our own conscience. This companion assesses our self-worth versus the value we place on the group, and weighs individuality versus conformity. Blockage here can lead to self-abnegation at one end and extreme egotism at the other.

Throat Level Two

The second level of the throat chakra deals with issues of personal integrity. This aspect of the chakra gives us a desire to always act in accordance with our ideals and conscience, and generates a loyalty to abstract ideas of right and wrong, success and failure. It does not, however, in any way assess the correctness of our perceptions regarding these concepts, only our attachment to them.

Right Companion: Here we examine our behaviors and motivations in light of our ideals and beliefs. This is very much an aspect of self-analysis and of the need for consistency in thought and action. It is also an as-

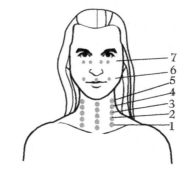

The seven levels of the throat chakra

Lesson

IX

pect of conscience. It is here that we determine if we have departed from our perceptions of right and wrong. A blockage here can lead one to self-delusion and an inability to connect cause and effect in our behaviors.

Left Companion: The left companion deals with our ability to assess compatibility: to seek like minds, to learn from others, and to seek out compatible people and situations. If blocked, it can be gullible at one extreme, snobbish at the other.

Throat Level Three

The third level of the throat chakra deals with issues of projecting our ideas and conceptions onto others. Here we assess people and situations according to the efficacy of our own past behaviors, judging their intellectual worth and potential success or failure on the assumption that what has worked well for us must work equally well for others. At its best, this allows us to assess others' ability to follow through successfully on their intentions and representations and to make a realistic judgment of the extent to which we can trust them and anticipate their acts. A blockage here can make us prejudiced and dismissive of others when they depart from our perception of the best way of doing things.

Right Companion: This aspect helps us to have emotional distance from people and situations in order to assess them in an impartial manner. It allows us to rise above our own emotions and desires to see the "big picture" beyond our personal needs.

Left Companion: This aspect allows us to set aside preconceptions and view things with an innocent eye, taking them only for what they are, without reading in additional meaning. The left companion allows us to appreciate things in the moment, seeing them for what they are, without relating them to ourselves and our experience. This allows us to view them analytically rather than anecdotally.

Throat Level Four

The fourth level of the throat chakra also deals with issues of projecting our ideas onto others. Where the throat level three deals with intellectual judgments about people and situations based on the idea that what has been successful for us in the past must be successful in general, the throat level four deals with emotional and moral judgments about people and situations based on our perceptions of right and wrong. At its best, this is a function of self-defense, allowing us to avoid people and situations that are hurtful or destructive. A blockage here, however, can make

us self-righteous, bossy, and overly concerned with the actions of others.

Right Companion: This aspect allows us to transcend emotional concerns in order to view situations logically in terms of their direct effects on us. This companion allows us to assess situations in a detached and intellectual manner that is not swayed by emotional attachments like love or hate, or by established behavior patterns. A blockage here can cause us to lose emotional perspective and intellectual distance, to think the actions of others affect us far more than they really do, becoming overly sensitive or aggressively defensive; or conversely, it can make us oblivious to concerns that really do affect us.

Left Companion: This companion generates a view of the self wholly separate from external concerns and based on our inner life, perceptions of our connection to Deity and to eternity, and the integrity of our belief systems.

Throat Level Five

The fifth level of the throat chakra helps us to have an awareness and appreciation of our life's purposes and of the lessons we learn through living. When well developed,

this chakra helps us to understand what we have learned from the experiences of our lives and to assess all events in light of the soul's purposes. A blockage here tends to make us fatalistic, to give a feeling that life is meaningless, even cruel.

Right Companion: The right companion gives us a sense of destiny and of our soul's purposes, a desire for constant growth and development: a sense of being more than we consciously perceive and the desire to grow into our potentialities.

Left Companion: The left companion gives us a perception of the divine plan and the fact that we each have a place in it. This aspect gives us a sense of karma, of our connections to all things and the hand of Deity in our lives. This companion helps us to see others as aspects of the divine and to understand that each has a role to play. When well developed, this companion helps us to see and accept that all things happen for a reason, that problems can really be lessons, and to adopt a "live and let live" attitude. When blocked, it gives a sense of insularity and an obliviousness to the spiritual causes of situations.

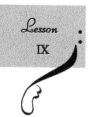

Throat Level Six

The sixth level of the throat chakra generates internal visual images and assigns meaning to them. It is here that many of us translate spiritual energy into color and perceive psychic energy as "light." This chakra also gives us the ability to visualize and "see" psychic images. This chakra gives us the power to generate such images, while the inner eye's level two left companion actually makes use of them.

According to Binder, the throat level six chakra is related to the "dreaming attention center" of CARLOS CASTANEDA. A fuller discussion of the dreaming attention center follows the section on the crown chakra.

> **Right Companion:** This aspect allows us to extract meaning from visual images, whether physical images that we see or astral images that we "see."

> **Left Companion:** The left companion assesses the usefulness of our visual symbols and our ability to interpret them, and motivates us to update and expand our understanding of these.

Throat Level Seven

The seventh level of the throat chakra is also the first level of the inner eye chakra; here, the throat and inner eye chakras run together into one.

Inner Eye

The inner eye chakra, commonly referred to as the third eye or spiritual eye, deals with how we interact with the astral plane, the plane on which we create the circumstances of the physical world. As you learned in First Degree, Lesson 1, we create the world unconsciously in every moment of existence.

It is not uncommon to find these chakras underdeveloped in many people.

Inner Eye Level One

Level seven of the throat is also the first level of the inner eye. It brings us an awareness of the astral plane, the plane on which we create the circumstances of the physical world. As you learned in First Degree, Lesson 1, magic is the result of shaping energy through thought and emotion; this process happens in the astral plane and then takes form in the physical world. It is the throat level seven/inner eye level one chakra that begins this process, and it is here that we can become aware of it and begin to take conscious control of it.

> **Right Companion:** This aspect serves to create imaginings of the soul's needs and potentials, those things that enhance our being and facilitate its creativity, learning, and growth. In imagining these things, the companion begins the process of creating

them through the astral, though it requires sustained focus to bring them into being.

Left Companion: The left companion is concerned with finding solutions to problems and ways to facilitate growth. It seeks ways to overcome obstacles, to surpass limitations, to eliminate difficulties. By thus envisioning these things, the left companion begins the process of creating them in the astral.

Inner Eye Level Two

The second level of the inner eye chakra deals with issues of imagination and fantasy: creating fantasy scenarios about extant or potential situations in our life and envisioning possible ways in which they might develop. In this way, it explores the directions in which these situations might be developed and begins the process of creating their future.

Right Companion: This aspect regulates our emotional connection to our fantasies and imaginings throughout the whole system. Ideally, it gives us enough of an emotional connection to spur the process of spiritual creation without blurring the line between extant reality and potential. A blockage here can cause our fantasies to have too little emo-

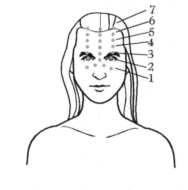

The seven levels of the inner eye chakra

Lesson

IX

270

tion, thus stunting them and making us overly passive in our relation to life and creation, or can deliver too much emotion, causing us to place fantasy above extant reality and perhaps lose touch with reality.

Left Companion: This aspect regulates the content of our fantasies and our psychic visions. The left companion assembles a lexicon of ideas, words, and images that we fill our imaginings with and that are also the language through which we translate psychic messages. We can never understand a psychic message that we do not have terms to understand, and the process that translates the pure energy of psychic messages into images that have meaning to us is centered here. A blockage here can make it difficult either to fantasize or to translate psychic messages, due to a lack of material from which to facilitate either process. Inability to visualize might also be due to a blockage of this chakra.

Inner Eye Level Three

The third level of the inner eye, or third eye, is concerned with clairvoyance and the reception of psychic information regarding present and near-future events. The ability to translate clairvoyant energies into a form understood by the conscious mind is controlled by the inner eye's level three left companion, and can be expanded by enlarging the body of symbols and ideas available for it to work with. This aspect of the chakra has to do with clairvoyant assessment of what we or others are creating in the astral, and messages received here can be addressed at that level.

Right Companion: This aspect assesses the efficacy of our past actions in terms of our soul's purposes and our need for spiritual advancement; this gives us a need to discard behaviors that hold us back spiritually and cultivate behaviors that will help us to move forward spiritually. This is the place where we address bad habits and self-defeating behaviors. The third eye's right companion is also the second level of the past chakra, to be discussed below.

Left Companion: If the right companion assesses the value of our habits and established patterns, seeing the need to adopt or discard a specific behavior, it is the left companion that actually implements this. The left companion builds behavior patterns and also breaks them. When it is well-developed, it builds patterns based on perceived benefit; of course, the benefit level changes as we grow

and our needs vary, requiring the patterns to be changed or discarded over time. When this companion is blocked, we become stuck in old patterns because we are mentally or emotionally so attached to them that we cannot move forward.

Inner Eye Level Four

The fourth level of the inner eye, or fourth eye, allows us to receive clairvoyant information regarding the farther future. Where the third eye sees what is being created in the immediate future through the astral, the fourth eye draws its information more from the soul level and reflects the soul's purposes. The most immediate difference here, beyond the distance each eye is capable of seeing, is that the visions of the third eye may be readily addressed at the astral level and are subject to great possibility of change. The visions of the fourth eye, dealing with the needs of the soul and the life's purposes, are much less likely to change and require very deep inner work to alter. The famous seer Jeane Dixon described this idea as the difference between "prediction" and "prophecy," the former being more fluid and subject to potential change from the conscious level, the latter being more certain and difficult or impossible to change.

Right Companion: This aspect gives a sense of the need to care for ourselves, to maintain ourselves and our resources, and to provide for our needs. This is, in fact, a function of the companion's connection of our soul-level purposes, as the companion seeks to ensure the body's continued ability to fulfill the soul's needs. If blocked, this companion can lead to either extreme self-indulgence or self-mortification.

Left Companion: This aspect assesses our level of well-being at all levels and generates a feeling of discomfort when any aspect of the being is blocked or out of proper alignment. This is a function of the companion's connection to the soul-level purposes, just as was the case with the right companion. The companion seeks to maintain our well-being so that the soul may express itself and pursue the purposes of the life through the body.

Inner Eye Level Five

The fifth level of the inner eye, or fifth eye, integrates the higher consciousness of the soul into the physical body. It facilitates the process by which the body is created as an emanation of the soul (a process similar to that by which a mollusk creates its shell

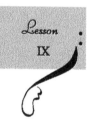

or an insect its exoskeleton) and allows for the expression of the soul's consciousness through the body. Like all other aspects of the physical, the body is created at the astral level, and it is at the fifth eye level that we may affect the body through astral workings. Here, too, the extent of connection between higher and lower consciousness is controlled. It is the seat of the magical shift of consciousness, and when expanded through exercise, it allows for ever-greater oneness with the Higher Self. Through the fifth eye, the ego, or lower self, transcends itself to become one with the soul. This is the primary chakra in our ability to create magically.

Right Companion: This aspect allows us to see the potential of creation— to know that all things are possible, and that nothing need hold us back. This companion gives us the sense of our ability to shape things through magic—that is, the conscious application of thought and emotion to shape energy at the astral level. The relative strength of this chakra is very important to the extent of what we can create at the astral level. A blockage here can make us feel that we are powerless and unable to affect anything, at one extreme, and at the other can make us feel that we can jump straight to magical proficiency

without the need to work on developing it.

Left Companion: This companion gives us focus and direction in our ability to create at the astral level. It is here that we fine-tune our creations, and here that we bring the soul's purposes into the physical through the astral. This companion is detail-oriented and works with the finer points of astral creation to bring the astral stirrings created throughout the chakra system into concrete creation.

Inner Eye Level Six

The sixth level inner eye or sixth eye integrates monadic consciousness into the physical being. The monad, you will recall, is the microcosm of God/dess through which souls are formed. God/dess has nine monads, each of which is a separated microcosmic aspect of Deity; each monad has many souls, and each soul has many lives. As we are part of our soul, our soul is part of our monad. Connection to the monad gives us a sense of eternity and universality, and an ability to recognize spiritual connections and patterns at a high level. The more highly developed the sixth eye, the more we are able to access the monadic consciousness.

Right Companion: This aspect integrates the soul's purposes into the

Lesson
IX

273

physical being. Each soul has certain purposes for each life, i.e., lessons to learn, skills to acquire, and experiences to have. So, too, each monad has basic patterns and purposes that are unique to it and to all of the souls and lives that are part of it. Here we connect to the soul's and monadic purposes and work to fulfill them.

Left Companion: This aspect facilitates the creativity through which the soul's energy is integrated into the being, and through which the being is created and itself creates.

Inner Eye Level Seven

The seventh level inner eye gives us an understanding of God/dess as All That Is. Here we can connect to a feeling of oneness with all things and appreciate the ties that connect all of creation. Here we feel divine purposes in which the soul is but one part.

Right Companion: This aspect connects us to the divine plan: destiny, karma, and the web of being. All things connect and interlink at this level, and through the seventh eye right companion we can feel this and navigate our place in the web.

Left Companion: This aspect serves to anchor the divine energy that is the ultimate source of life into the

physical being. It directs the divine energy throughout the system to all the places it is needed, subtly transmuting it in the process.

· · · ·

Crown

Binder calls the crown chakra the "inner ear" because it receives and reacts to energy and vibrational frequency. The crown chakra is the most complex of the chakras, and we will only briefly discuss its aspects here. The chakra is, in effect, a psychic antenna that draws energy into the body. In particular, the crown chakra draws in divine energy, from which all else is created. The chakra also picks up on many other kinds of energy, including the psychic energies sent from spirit guides as well as other beings (such as fellow people). This is how we receive channeled messages and energies. The chakra also picks up on ambient energies found in our environs. The crown chakra is particularly susceptible to sound, or vibration, and the magical uses of sound interact directly with the crown chakra, just as the magical uses of visual images interact with the inner eye.

Although we include it with the temporal chakras, the crown chakra is, in fact, the same for all three systems. That is, while the solaris, for example, has temporal, existential, and foundational aspects associated with the front, middle, and rear

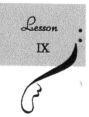

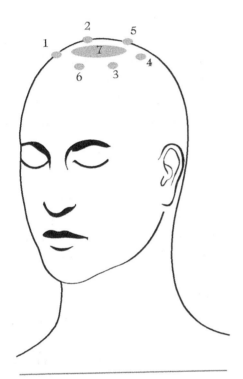

The seven levels of the crown chakra

of the body respectively, the crown chakra is beyond these aspects and interacts with all three systems at once.

Crown Level One

The first level of the crown chakra connects us to the divine plane and receives and interprets information and messages regarding our place in it. This chakra is located at the top right of the forehead, in the same place as the temporal inner eye's seventh level right companion.

Crown Level Two

The second level of the crown chakra helps us to assess the best possible courses of action in order to advance the soul's purposes in the physical life. It uses divine energy to create new and different ideas and patterns of action. This chakra is located at the top right side of the back of the head, in the same place as the existential inner eye's seventh level right companion.

Crown Level Three

The third level of the crown chakra serves to direct and integrate divine energy throughout the being. This level is responsible for routing divine energy and making sure it is available. This divine energy is the energy of God/dess that is the "spark of life" within all things. This chakra is located at the top left forehead, in the same

Lesson
IX

275

place as the temporal inner eye's seventh level left companion.

Crown Level Four

The fourth level of the crown chakra uses divine energy to create and implement solutions to problems. It is original and innovative in nature and outlook, creating new patterns of action. This chakra is located at the top left side of the back of the head, in the same place as the existential inner eye's seventh level left companion.

Crown Level Five

The fifth level of the crown chakra generates the "inner voice" that guides us from within and whose advice we can always trust. This "inner voice" is actually the "voice" of the soul, which knows our higher purposes because it sets them. It is a conduit of soul consciousness into physical consciousness. This chakra is located in the same place as the existential inner eye's seventh level primary chakra.

Crown Level Six

The sixth level of the crown chakra helps us to understand and be one with Deity, to appreciate the connectedness of all life as manifestations of God/dess. Here we have a sense of oneness with Deity. This chakra is located at the top center of the forehead, in the same place as the temporal inner eye's seventh level primary chakra.

Crown Level Seven

The seventh level of the crown chakra is the primary entry port for divine energy as well as stellar energy into the body. Here messages are received from Deity as well as from spirits and spirit guides. These messages are interpreted primarily through the inner eye system. Here, too, massive amounts of energy enter the body on a regular basis, especially during advanced spiritual workings. This chakra is located approximately two inches above the very top center of the head.

• • • •

In addition to this brief discussion of the structure of the crown chakra, a number of lesser aspects may be added. Each level of the crown chakra has two lesser points that connect into the past chakra system, as well as two lesser points connecting to the future chakra system. Four points exist for each level, making a total of fifty-six connections into the past and future chakras.

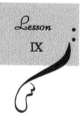

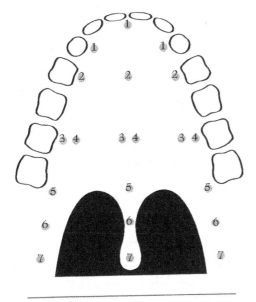

The seven levels of the dreaming attention center (DAC)

• • • •

The Dreaming Attention Center

The dreaming attention center (here shortened to DAC) is a chakra located in the upper mouth and related to the throat's level six chakra. The DAC generates dreams and visions, creating images through which spiritual knowledge from above the level of conscious understanding may be translated to the conscious mind. People who have difficulties with visualization can address those issues by working with this chakra. Apparently, the DAC is extensively discussed in the works of Castaneda; however, I am pretty sure that this represents a different take on it.

DAC Level One

The first level of the DAC produces a sense of our own energetic movements. It helps us to direct and focus energy through visualization. This chakra also translates our ability to use energy into symbolic images, such as walking or running, or conversely the image of hitting a wall when a blockage is encountered.

DAC Level Two

The second level of the DAC allows us to sense vibrational frequency and to translate it into visual or aural images. Here we may perceive the "sound" of energy or the music of the spheres.

Lesson
IX

277

DAC Level Three

This aspect allows us to perceive our own energetic nature, and as such is instrumental in all forms of inner working.

DAC Level Four

This aspect allows us to assess the qualities of energy according to its "texture" by likening it to physical textures. For this reason, an energetic blockage might be perceived as rocks or mucous, symbols that help us to interpret the energy in question.

DAC Level Five

This aspect allows us to perceive minute details of images and dreams, and provides the finer points of psychic images. This chakra gives a sense of stability and realism to our images. This chakra translates psychic energy into complex "human-made" images such as buildings, books, and even words as such.

DAC Level Six

This aspect allows us to perceive the qualities and motion of energy. When we assess the nature of psychic energy, healing energy, cleansing energy, nurturing energy, etc., we are engaging this chakra. Here, too, is the mechanism that allows the actual translation of dream images into meanings.

DAC Level Seven

The Seventh Level of the Dreaming Attention Center generates symbols for fantasies, dreams, and visions in the form of animals, landscapes, and other natural phenomena. This chakra allows us to perceive complex subjects in simplified visual form. Though the images are generated here it should be noted that their meaning and use is directed elsewhere in the system, namely the Throat and Inner Eye chakras. This is also where we assign a visual dimension to Spirits and to psychic energy, whose true nature is without physical form in the sense we are familiar with.

· · · ·

Past Chakras

Past Chakra Level One

This level gives us a sense of the passing of time, without assessing its effects or the changes that have come through time. It regulates our ability to perceive time, and a blockage here can cause us not to perceive time and become lost or trapped at a specific period, unable to move forward.

Past Chakra Level Two

Here we perceive the differences between the past and the present. This allows us to understand that changes happen with the passage of time, though this chakra does not assess the value of those changes. A

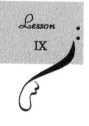

blockage here can leave us feeling that change is our enemy and is something to be feared and avoided.

Past Chakra Level Three

This level allows us to assess the nature of the changes that have come through time. This allows us to differentiate experiences in terms of their benefits and to learn from them accordingly, and it is also crucial to our ability to extrapolate the effects of our actions in the future.

Past Chakra Level Four

This level allows us to perceive and understand the far past, before our present life, and to assess our place in a longer process of existence. Here we see how we have been affected by past generations and assess how our actions affect future generations.

Past Chakra Level Five

Here we gain a sense of time beyond the world we know: eternity. Here we perceive the patterns and cycles of time, and gain a sense of time far beyond ourselves. In this level, we see that we represent a point of consciousness in a much larger continuum of being, and we gain a sense of just how much else has already gone before.

Past Chakra Level Six

This level helps us to perceive existence outside of time, to transcend time and view existence from the soul level rather than from our conscious level. Here we see that time does not truly bind existence, as we have thought, though it is elsewhere in the chakric system that we learn to operate outside of time.

Past Chakra Level Seven

Level seven of the past chakra helps us to assess the nature of existence beyond physical form. This helps us to have a sense of the nonphysical world and of the higher aspects of our being. Also, this chakra helps us to perceive our existence before this physical life and have a sense of what will follow.

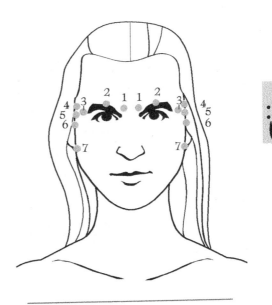

The seven levels of the past chakras

• • • •

Future Chakras

Level One

The first level of the future chakra gives us an awareness of and helps us to assess the effect of the past on the self. This chakra allows us to understand the process of growth and development through time. It also helps us to assess our place in time relative to our soul's development.

Level Two

The second level of the future chakra generates desires and plans for the short-term future. This chakra allows us to focus on details at hand without concern for the future, which allows for deep learning and deep involvement in situations.

Level Three

The third level of the future chakra generates precautionary imaginings about the future for the purpose of generating practical plans. Here we assess potential problems or challenges that we might encounter in the future and plan accordingly.

Level Four

Here we assess the role of cause and effect upon the future, both in practical and, more

especially, in karmic terms. This is fundamentally a chakra of personal responsibility, for it shows us the effect of our own actions and prevents us from blaming others. A blockage here often makes us feel that life is unjust and Deity is cruel, since the blockage inhibits the understanding of the causes of unpleasant events.

Level Five

This level of the future chakra generates imaginings of future interactions with other people and their effect on the self. Often this chakra focuses specifically on romantic situations, but not always. A blockage here can cause obsessions with romantic situations or with the actions of others.

Level Six

This level helps us to assess the far future in terms of growth and transformation. This allows us to see that growth is a journey made up of many steps. When well-developed, this chakra assesses growth and transformation in terms of the journey; when blocked, it focuses only on the destination, seeing value only in outcomes and conclusions rather than the process of growth. A blockage here can create

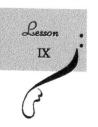

Lesson

IX

an obsession with milestone events, such as one's wedding, retirement, or death. The main aspect of this chakra is located roughly on that part of the earlobe that people commonly pierce, and that in many cultures is associated with wisdom, which certainly comes from an understanding of the nature of growth.

Level Seven

The seventh level of the future chakra deals with the illusory nature of time, which exists to organize experiences to make them easier for us to learn from. Few people have this chakra well-developed, as it allows us to move beyond the constraints of time, though it will be found open and well-developed in adepts of time magic. For most people, this chakra functions at a rudimentary level and allows us only to glimpse glitches in time, as when a specific period of time is being repeated. (For example, have you ever been certain it should be Friday but found it is only Thursday? And then found that you are not the only person with a sense that it should actually be the following day? In this case, you have used the seventh-level future chakra to detect that the day is being repeated.)

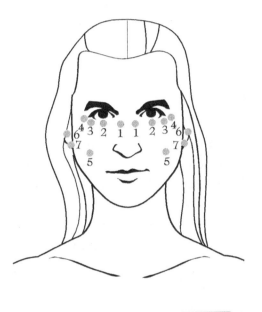

The seven aspects of the future chakras

. . . .

Present Chakras

The present chakras, not surprisingly, help us to operate in present time. Their primary purpose is to establish our understanding of the present moment in relation to time and generate a response to it. The present chakras always ask us, "Who am I, and what do I do NOW?"

The present chakras are closely interrelated with the sense object chakras, a description of which follows the present chakras.

Level One

The first level of the present chakra assesses our actions and experiences in relation to a period of centuries, a century being roughly the upper limit allowed for a human lifespan. This level of the chakra assesses our position relative to a century previous or a century following: "How am I better off than my ancestors were a hundred years ago? How will my actions affect my descendants a hundred years from now?"

Level Two

The second level of the present chakra assesses our current position relative to a period of thousands of years, which is beyond our immediate ancestry and posterity and into the realm of history. This gives us a sense of perspective regarding our own actions within a much larger context.

Level Three

The third level of the present chakras deals with the idea of millions of years. Here we can appreciate the cycles of time and the fact that whole worlds have and will exist beyond our experience, and that future and past are without limitation. Here we assess just how personal and subjective our actions are relative to the universe.

Level Four

The fourth level of the present chakras assesses our present moment and our actions in the face of eternity. Here we appreciate the eternal re-creation of the universe and the long-term existence of the soul. Here we see the eternal dance of God/dess and the wheel of karma in an existential sense, always moving forward. A blockage here causes fear of the end of the universe.

Level Five

The fifth level of the present chakras assesses our current position relative to God/dess. Here we perceive the oneness of all things and how each affects the others because they are all part of a whole. Here we perceive the meaning of the present moment and whatever may flow forth from it in a purely existential sense, beyond the illusion of time and space.

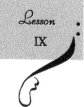

Lesson

IX

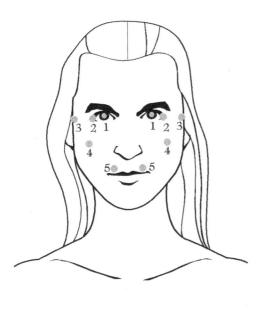

The five levels of the present chakras

Sense Object Chakras:
Nose

Level One

The nose's level one chakra assesses energies left behind by previous activities in physical space. This chakra generates positive or negative reactions to people and occurrences in a given location, based on their energetic effects. This chakra also helps to pick up déjà vu, ghosts, and past—life memories.

Level Two

The nose's level two chakra gives us an emotional sense of the far past. This helps us to pick up on past lives and karmic patterns from the far past, but it also tends to romanticize the past and to project present or future issues onto it.

Level Three

The nose's level three chakra gives us a sense of eternity, periods of millions and billions of years. This chakra generates a sense of awe in the face of time, and also a sense of emotional connection to the possibility of existences before or after our own. Here fantasies of the far past and far future are created of worlds other than our own, which also have their astral effects.

Lesson
IX

283

Level Four

The nose's level four chakra helps us to make an emotional connection to the cycles of time, to cosmic beginnings and endings. If well-developed, it gives us a sense of the universe's constant regeneration. If blocked, it gives a fear of the end of the world.

Level Five

The nose's level five chakra gives us a sense of transcending time, of Nirvana, of being beyond all limits of any sort.

. . . .

Eyes

The eye chakras are connected with our ability to unite with and draw upon higher energies. In magically advanced cultures, the eyes are often ornamented with cosmetics that serve to enhance the area of the eye chakras. This is especially true of the Egyptians and peoples influenced by them.

Level One

The eye's level one chakra helps us to perceive the spirit world and the existence of things beyond our physical perception. This chakra helps us to unite with the spirit realm.

The five levels of the nose chakras (note each level contains three chakra points)

Level Two

The eye's level two chakra helps us to perceive other universes, other time probabilities, and parallel lives, to sense the infinite potentialities of life. This chakra helps us to unite with all aspects of the universe.

Level Three

The eye's level three chakra helps us to understand how much there is in creation—how many universes, parallels, probabilities, variations, etc.—and to assess our relationship to the created world. This chakra helps us to unite with all of creation.

Level Four

The eye's level four chakra helps us to perceive guides and ascended masters. This chakra creates a desire for communication with guides and ascended masters and facilitates that communication. It helps us to unite with all ascended masters.

Level Five

The eye's level five chakra governs our understanding that we are manifestations of Deity and our ability to assess what that means. This chakra creates a desire to connect with God/dess and helps to facilitate the connection. This chakra helps us to unite with God/dess.

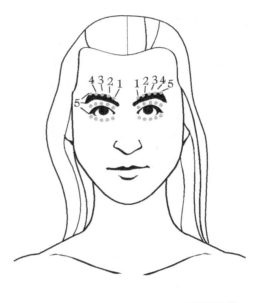

The five levels of the eye chakras (note each level contains three chakra points)

Lesson
IX

285

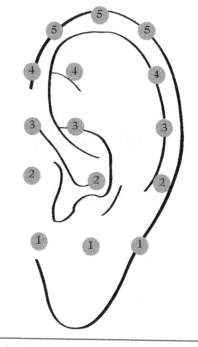

The five levels of the ear chakras

Level One

The ear's level one chakra provides the most basic experience of timelessness, the ability to lose oneself in pleasurable activities such as art, music, or sex. This is the sense of timelessness that comes from complete focus on something outside of oneself.

Level Two

The ear's level two chakra gives a sense of the limitation of time. This is needed to budget time in order to accomplish our goals. If in balance, this chakra gives a sense of "everything in its right time." If blocked, it tends to develop either a desire to procrastinate or a tendency to feel constantly behind and need to work to catch up.

Level Three

The ear's level three chakra regulates time concerns according to external forces. Originally this served to attune us to the rhythms of nature. Today these stimuli include the work day, set times for tasks, etc. This chakra gives us a desire to order our time and our lives.

Lesson

IX

Level Four

The ear's level four chakra governs our ability to focus on tasks to the exclusion of time or bodily needs. It can help us to transcend time, as through meditation, as well as to set aside discomfort to accomplish a goal. If blocked, it can lead to self-abnegation and such habits as regularly working (or playing) to exhaustion.

Level Five

The ear's level five chakra causes us to comprehend the cause-and-effect nature of time management. This gives us an understanding of the need to work to produce or create, as well as the need for delayed gratification in the face of long-term goals.

. . . .
Mouth

Level One

The mouth's level one chakra senses the cycles of life, birth, youth, age, death, and assesses our own, as well as others', position in the cycle. This is also true for places and situations. All things have their beginning, development, decay, and end, and it is through the mouth's level one chakra that we get a sense for it. When this chakra is highly developed, a person may be able to sense an unknown pregnancy or an imminent death.

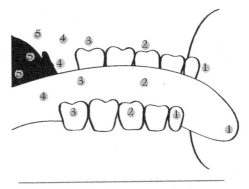

The five levels of the mouth chakras

Lesson
IX

Level Two

The mouth's level two chakra senses whether or not a given thing is alive or dead, and whether an inanimate object has ever been alive in the ordinary sense. This chakra senses the inner nature of physical structure and helps us to tell the difference between what is animate and inanimate, what is animal or vegetable or mineral. When well-developed, this chakra allows us to attune to all these differing kinds of structure.

Level Three

The mouth's level three chakra provides the ability to assess whether a thing is edible. It also has an innate sense of the food chain and our karmic place within it. This chakra detects what is safe versus what is poisonous, both physically and energetically, and generates an appropriate reaction.

Level Four

The mouth's level four chakra deals with issues of immunity and the ability to resist biological threats. These biological threats may be viewed as a physicalization of spiritual imbalances. This chakra has to do with the integrity of the soul/body system as a whole and its ability to withstand pressure.

Level Five

The mouth's level five chakra provides joy in self-expression and communication. This chakra also finds joy in attunement to music and sound vibration. This chakra allows for an energetic reaction to hearing or creating sound.

• • • •
Existential Chakras

If the temporal/solar chakras deal with issues of time and of past/present/future, the existential/lunar chakras are beyond issues of time altogether, and they deal rather with issues of existence. This is the kundalini system, which we use for the highest reaches of manifestational magic.

Binder terms this system the Grainne Mhael (*Grah-nyah Whale*) system.

As with the temporal chakras, each of the existential chakras has seven levels, each of which has distinct properties. As with the temporal chakras, each of the existential chakras also has a right and left companion; however, we will not discuss these here, as working with them is somewhat beyond what we would consider a Second Degree level.

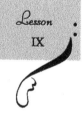

• • • •
Existential Solaris

The existential solaris is focused on creating successful outcomes to the situations we face and eliminating obstacles or difficulties.

Level One

The first level of the existential solar plexus generates and directs physical energy in the body. When we describe the solar plexus as being the inner sun and the source of the body's energy, it is the first level of the existential solaris that we are referring to.

Level Two

The second level of the existential solaris generates a psychic connection to other people, places, things, and even situations. The second level existential solaris reaches out, not unlike a psychic hand, and attaches to things that have provoked a strong response in it. This level of the existential solaris forms "cords" that connect it to things it has experienced and that form patterns of interaction with those things; these cords should be periodically "cut" so that old patterns may be left behind. Symbolically, this is related to the umbilical cord, which is a physicalization of it unique to the birth process.

Level Three

The third level of the existential solar plexus chakra assesses the survivability of situations and generates an emotional response to this. This is the seat of the fear response, which exists to protect us from dangerous situations. Here, too, is the seat of the sense of excitement that comes from taking and surviving risks.

Level Four

The fourth level of the existential solaris generates a self-concept based on the relationship between soul and consciousness. The reason for this is to keep us in line with our soul's purposes. This has three parts: how we feel about ourselves, how we see ourselves, and how we idealize ourselves. This is the seat of our self-esteem and our soul's emotional reaction to who we are in this incarnation.

Level Five

The fifth level of the existential solaris generates a physical reaction to emotional, mental, and psychic stimuli. This is what allows us to have a "gut feeling" in the literal sense, or to have our "hair stand up" in the presence of spiritual energies, etc.

Level Six

The sixth level existential solaris generates an emotional reaction to success or failure. Pride and shame both have their origins here and are based in the extent to which our actions fulfill our image of ourselves.

Lesson
IX

289

Level Seven

Level seven of the existential solaris generates a sense of selflessness, an ability to rise above personal concerns for the sake of others.

. . . .

Existential Heart

The existential heart chakra has to do with our relationship to our soul purposes. It has to do with how well we fulfill our life lessons and our relationship to these—whether or not we are "on track."

Level One

The first level of the existential heart chakra assesses and generates a physical reaction to how well we use our time and actions to fulfill our soul's needs and purposes, and whether or not we are following our true purpose in life. Here we are compelled to do the things that nourish our soul or risk becoming unhealthy because of not doing them. Here we are compelled to learn our life lessons or we risk developing phobias, neuroses, or even physical illness because of blocking their energy in our lives.

Level Two

The second level of the existential heart chakra generates an emotional reaction to our surroundings. We have an innate need for our external circumstances to be in sync with our soul purposes, and when these diverge, the second level existential heart chakra calls our attention to the fact with a sense of emotional disquiet. This level requires a sympathetic relationship with the environment in which one lives in order to feel at peace and feel good about life.

Level Three

The third level of the existential heart chakra generates a conscientious reaction to the people around us. Do these people serve our soul purposes? Are we in sync with them? Just as the second level assesses our synchronicity with our environment, the third level of the existential heart chakra assesses the level of synchronicity we have with the people we deal with. The existential heart's third level generates emotional fantasies to display to our consciousness the extent to which the people in our lives fulfill our soul purposes and impel changes when needed.

Level Four

The existential heart chakra's fourth level generates an emotional reaction to the extent to which we are integrating our soul's purposes and energies into our physical life. When well-developed, it generates a sense of well-being and personal responsibility. A blockage here can cause us to blame others for imperfections in our life.

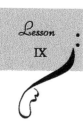

Lesson
IX

290

Level Five

The fifth level of the existential heart chakra generates a feeling of love for those things that help us to fulfill our soul's purposes in life and that bring us closer to Deity. This is also the seat of that sort of love that is not so much about emotion as about "rightness," the Divine Love whose opposite is fear.

Level Six

Level six of the existential heart chakra generates a sense of gratitude and thankfulness for the good things we receive, both at a physical and a spiritual level. Here we get a sense for divine providence and of the importance of our connection to God/dess and to our soul's purposes in order to have happiness and balance in life.

Level Seven

The seventh level of the existential heart chakra generates a sense of respect and awe for things we perceive as being greater than ourselves, as well as a desire to emulate and assimilate the qualities and/or behaviors that cause us to perceive them as greater. This chakra is the seat of the impulse to worship.

. . . .

Existential Throat

The existential throat chakra is focused on creating successful outcomes to the situations we face and eliminating obstacles or difficulties. It does this by assessing our circumstances and taking the appropriate actions to avoid problems and take advantage of benefits.

Level One

The level one existential throat chakra generates spiritual sounds that reflect the qualities and state of our soul—our own spiritual sound as opposed to the external music of the spheres. Sound, of course, is vibration, and so it is also an assessment of our vibrational rate. Most people hear this as an occasional low hum, though it is different for everyone.

Level Two

The second level of the existential throat chakra generates a sense of intuition about the value of new circumstances. It creates a feeling that we have done the right thing—or conversely, that we have made a mistake. In either case, it prompts the appropriate reaction. A blockage here may cause us to be constantly second-guessing our judgment.

Level Three

The existential throat chakra's third level provides a need to explore all possibilities of a new circumstance from a view to their usefulness and practicality, in order to assess all potential benefits of any given circumstance.

Level Four

The level four existential throat chakra provides a need to assess new circumstances from a view of any potential danger, whether physical or emotional, and generates a reaction to these. In all cases, the reaction is based on avoiding damage from the perceived threat and eliminating the threat. Sometimes this takes the form of an angry emotional reaction, other times of a cagey mental reaction, depending in part on how well-developed the chakra is. When poorly developed, this chakra reacts with temper tantrums or with rage; when well-developed, it reacts with well-thought-out strategies based on a realistic assessment of potential problems.

Level Five

The fifth level of the existential throat chakra forms an emotional response to others based on how well they can be interacted with toward fulfilling the soul's needs and purposes.

Level Six

The sixth level existential throat chakra deals with visions or fantasies whose nature we may be uncomfortable with because it seems to be at odds with our perceptions of right and wrong or with our own soul purposes. Here is where we make sense of seemingly senseless situations, such as natural disasters, early deaths, etc.

Level Seven

The level seven existential throat chakra deals with visions and fantasies that relate seemingly unconnected circumstances to our soul's purposes. This is where we see that "As above, so below" applies to all things, and that our soul's purposes are part of the divine plan, in which all other things also have a place.

• • • •

Existential Inner Eye

The existential inner eyes are arranged differently from the temporal inner eyes in that they fall into three subgroups. Levels one and two form one group. Levels three, four, and five form a second group, and levels six and seven form the final group.

Levels One and Two

Levels one and two of the existential inner eyes help us to have a sense of what is around us even if we cannot see it visually. This is where we sense the presence or movement of physical entities beyond our range of vision. For most people, these chakras are not well-developed and give only occasional information, but in earlier ages, when their function was more important to our survival, these chakras were usually more highly developed than they are now.

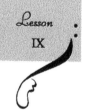

Lesson

IX

Levels Three, Four, and Five

Levels three, four, and five of the existential inner eyes all work together to generate all manner of internal and external expression via words. As a rule, however, it cannot do both at once, so actual physical speaking and imagined internal dialogues cannot normally be engaged in at once, though persons with these chakras highly developed can carry on mental and physical conversations at the same time.

Levels Six and Seven

Levels six and seven of the existential inner eyes work together to generate potential solutions to problems, though they depend on other aspects of the chakric system for the actual implementation of the solutions they come up with. When unblocked, these chakras form an aspect of the "inner voice" and are always right, though blockage can warp the chakras' abilities and cause false answers.

. . . .

Crown

As has been previously observed, the crown chakra is a single construct shared by all three energetic systems. Consequently, there is no separate existential aspect to the crown chakra.

. . . .

Foundational Chakras

The foundational/stellar chakras allow for development of long-range plans and projects without concern for personal circumstances of gain, loss, or even personal survival. This system is solely focused on the "greater cause," whether that is Deity, family, country, business, or whatever else the individual may be attached to. These chakras deal with survival issues not relative to the self but relative to things the self cares about. When the existential system is well-developed, these causes are, in fact, the goals and work of the soul, of which the conscious mind may or may not be aware. The primary purpose of this, which is little understood by most people, is to allow for multigenerational projects that require many lifetimes for the soul to complete. The foundational chakras connect the work of past lives with the present life and jointly focus on the soul's work.

One aspect of this is that the foundational chakras work with the soul/Higher Self, with the spirit guides, and with Deity, in order to make sure that the soul's work is addressed during the life. For this reason, the foundational chakras are connected with the reception of spiritual messages and channeled information.

For most people, these chakras are among the least developed.

Solaris

The foundational aspect of the solaris looks below surfaces and senses the foundations of things. It senses our connections to the physical universe and to the earth in much the same way as other parts of the system sense connections to people, and it interacts with place in a highly personal fashion, which the conscious mind has little or no awareness of. Here, also, is the seat of the ability to dowse for substances below the surface of the earth and to sense the currents of energy in the ley lines and vortices of earth and sky, as well as (eventually) outer space.

Heart

The foundational aspect of the heart chakra senses currents in time and motivates responses to them. This is how we sometimes find ourselves "in the right place at the right time." Here we sense social movements, imminent disasters (like earthquakes or tornados), and other large-scale agitations in the fabric of space and time. From this, we are able to derive a sense of timing that allows us to move at the best time to accomplish our soul's purposes.

Throat

The foundational aspect of the throat chakra deals with our mental understanding of our soul and its purposes, giving us

a sense of fate and/or karma, and helping us to regulate our actions in accordance to them. Here we also sense the long-term consequences of our actions relative to the soul's purposes.

Inner Eye

The foundational inner eye deals with the foundational aspects of our connection to Spirit—that is to say, our soul's purposes and place in the divine plan. The foundational inner eye brings through spiritual energies and messages to keep the soul's business being worked on. Here we sense currents in fate/karma and adapt ourselves to them, not transcending but rather taking a more active role in our own destiny. Here we work with our spirit guides on issues pertaining directly to our soul's purposes and life plans, and integrate these into our physical life.

Crown

And as with the existential chakras, there is no specific foundational aspect to the crown chakra, which interacts with all three systems from its single aspect.

. . . .

Exercises

Your daily sequence of exercises should now begin with the Ohm exercise, then open three balls of colored light in each chakra, changing the balls of colored light to balls

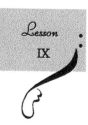

of white light, changing the balls of white light to balls of purple light, changing the balls of purple light to balls of silver stellar light, and then filling your aura with silver stellar light. Next, change the balls of silver stellar light to balls of golden stellar light, then fill your aura with golden stellar light. Finally, change the balls of golden stellar light to balls of amber light, and fill your aura with the amber light.

Exercise 18

Go through the daily routine as usual.

When you have filled your aura with amber light, turn your attention to your crown chakra.

Consider what you have learned about the structure of the crown chakra in this lesson—that it is a central point surrounded by a circle of six lesser points.

Imagine seven small (one—to three-inch) balls of red light, one at each of the seven levels of the crown chakra. There will be a central ball of light at the very top center of your head and six balls forming a circle around it. Imagine the balls strongly, and have the image clear in your head. Hold the image for a time. You can then go on to do other work, or close your chakras, clear, and release.

When you can do this easily, you are ready for Exercise 19.

Exercise 19

Exercise 19 begins just the same way as Exercise 18. Do the daily routine as usual; after filling your aura with amber light, open seven small balls of red light in the crown chakra, a central ball of light surrounded by a circle of six more.

Now change the seven balls of red light to balls of white light. Hold the image for a few moments, then change the balls of white light to balls of purple light.

Now change the balls of purple light to balls of silver stellar light. Hold the image for a few moments, and then change the balls of silver stellar light to balls of golden stellar light.

Finally, change the seven small balls of golden stellar light to balls of amber light.

When you can go through this sequence easily, you are ready for Exercise 20.

. . . .

Spell for Lesson IX
Energetic Constructs in the Chakras

In keeping with the subject of this lesson, advanced chakra working, this installment will deal with chakras.

In this spell, we will be working with the idea of energetic constructs in the chakras, a subject touched upon briefly in this lesson, with the warning that you should not attempt to create such constructs without a high degree of psychic openness and skill.

We are not going to be discussing the creation of them, however, but the regulation of existing constructs in the chakras.

Chances are that if you are on this path, you will have one or more energetic constructs in your body. The origins of these constructs are spiritual. They may have been set up by your spirit guides in this or previous lives, or they may have been created by you in previous lives. Rather like skills and talents, they carry over from one life to the next.

Energetic constructs work rather like similar physical constructs. Hearing aides help us to hear, glasses help us to see, a pacemaker helps regulate heartbeat; chakric constructs do the same kind of things energetically. A construct in the third eye may help with clairvoyance, for example, and a construct in the heart chakra may help with emotional issues and also with certain kinds of healing. They are like little engines that help to improve performance, and they are also a tool we have used in the process of evolution to stimulate the growth of new abilities. Such constructs are not always in the major chakras; they may be placed in the minor chakras as well, for either spiritual or physical reasons.

It is to be kept in mind, however, that such energy constructs sometimes get dirty and must be cleaned. Sometimes, too, they become outgrown and must be updated or discarded.

To discover if you have such constructs, you must examine your energetic body. This is a simple enough process.

Get into a comfortable position. Begin by clearing and releasing excess energy.

Now open clairvoyantly to your body. Look for the body's energetic grid, the network of lesser chakras and meridians that runs throughout the body. This will appear to you as a mass of connected lines not unlike veins, except it is likely to appear in a clear, bright color such as a glowing white, laser red, or computer-grid green. Exactly how the grid will appear to you is individual to you; it depends on how you are able to receive and interpret the information, which in turn depends on your own inner language of symbols.

The process of seeing the energetic grid is much the same as seeing spirit guides in Lesson VI's spell and the dragon in Lesson VII's spell; allow it to come to you as it needs to, without preconceived notions that limit it. Let it take the form that is right for you, the form you will be best able to interpret.

Now examine the grid. It is highly reactive: it will highlight whatever you are looking for. You can find many things about your personal energetics by examining the grid in this manner. It will show you blockages and potential blockages. It will also show you energetic constructs you may possess, even though you may not have been aware of them.

In this case, we are looking for constructs. The grid will show you any constructs that are present. As a rule, they look like little or not so little machines. Often they are highly geometric in character, the various geometric shapes each having their own specific energetic qualities and effects. Geometric magic will be discussed in Lesson X, and this will give you an idea of how such things may be interpreted.

Sometimes constructs will appear in other, more symbolic forms, clockwork perhaps, or images drawn from the natural world that have meanings to you that are relevant to the qualities of the construct. The form in which you perceive the construct is not really relevant, except insofar as it may help you to understand its nature.

When you find a construct, remove it. Imagine lifting it out of the body, rather as you learned to remove energetic blockages in First Degree, Lesson X. Hold the construct up, and examine it clairvoyantly. What does it look like? Does it appear old?

Ask your Higher Self if you still need the construct. If the answer you receive is no, then dissipate the energy of the construct: see it shrink down smaller and smaller until it disappears, then symbolically blow it away. If, however, the answer

you receive is yes, you do still need this construct, and you must clean it and return it to its place.

Blow on the construct as if you were blowing dust from it, and as you do so, imagine it being cleaned. Imagine any blocking energy being removed from the construct and blowing away.

Now fill the construct with white light. Flood the construct with light until it is suffused and glowing with white light shining out in all directions. This may cause a change in its appearance. Do not be surprised if the construct alters its color or its form while you are doing this; this shows that it is being revitalized.

Now, when you have filled the construct with light until it can receive no more, put it back into your body in the same spot you found it.

You should do this for any constructs you find. You can do them all at a sitting or on different days, depending on your preference.

If you find no energy constructs in your energetic grid, this is okay, too; not everyone has them.

If you continue your studies to Third Degree, you will learn more about these kinds of energetic constructs, including how to build and place them.

There are many other ways that you can use your energetic grid. As stated, it can show you blockages and other problems

Lesson
IX

in the energetic system. It can also be personified and interacted with in the same manner that you have learned to personify the chakras.

Obviously you can also do this with other people, examining their energetic grid as a healing technique. Remember that the grid will respond to where you put your attention, highlighting blockages, constructs, even physical illness. You can use the grid as a guide to what needs healing, then heal it energetically.

. . . .

Glossary

Binder, Peter—Peter Binder is the creator of an advanced system for developing the chakras that he titles "astral physics" but which is more widely known as "the Binder system." The Binder system addresses in great detail the many levels and aspects within each of the major chakras. Binder teaches his system through live classes, primarily in the Chicago area, and is the author of the book *Astral Physics*, which he self-published in the late 1590s Pisces (AD 1990s). Peter Binder developed his system through first-hand experience and experimentation; however, he acknowledges the teachings of the Order of Bards, Ovates, and druids, and the works of author Genevieve L. Paulson, as being seminal to his works.

Castaneda, Carlos—Carlos Castaneda is the author of several books on metaphysics, in which he describes his apprenticeship under the Yaqui mystic Don Juan Matus. The Castaneda books deal with issues of perceived reality, psychic development, and manifestation. Castaneda's works include *Journey to Ixtlan*, *A Separate Reality: Further Conversations with Don Juan*, *The Art of Dreaming*, *The Teachings of Don Juan: A Yaqui Way of Knowledge*, and *The Fire From Within*. The first of Castaneda's books, published in 1568 Pisces (AD 1968), emphasized drug use as a technique of spiritual opening and will be forever associated with the '60s. Questions have been raised concerning the identity of Don Juan Matus, and it has been suggested in recent years that he may be either completely imaginary or a composite of several persons. This may or may not be true, but inconsistencies in Castaneda's books certainly fuel speculation. Don Juan's teachings are said to be very different from what are normally thought of as traditional Yaqui teachings—however, there is no inherent reason to think that all Yaquis think and teach exactly the same thing, and it is entirely possible that the teachings could simply be highly individual. Some people feel that they discern Hindu and Buddhist elements in Don Juan's teach-

ings, but a Native American is as capable of studying and being influenced by these as anyone else. Castaneda is not the only person to claim to have studied under Don Juan Matus—author Merilyn Tunneshende makes the same claim. However, it should be pointed out that the spiritual teachings in Castaneda's books do not necessarily require Don Juan to have been a real person to have relevance; the relevance of any given spiritual technique rests simply on its efficacy and importance to its followers. Carlos Castaneda died in 1598 Pisces (AD 1998).

Lesson

IX

Lesson

X

Ley Lines

Called *Lung Mei* or "dragon lines" in China, ley lines have been known and used by practitioners of FENG SHUI for millennia in Asia. Their history in the modern West is much shorter.

The first person in the modern West to identify the existence of ley lines was Alfred Watkins, a British amateur antiquarian. In 1521 Pisces (AD 1921), Watkins discovered that many ancient archeological sites appeared to be arranged along a network of straight lines.

The monuments that Watkins studied included the very ancient monuments of the Mesolithic peoples, who built Stonehenge, Newgrange, and other great stone monuments as much as 5,000 years ago (though they were thought to be considerably younger at the time), as well as other sites dating from as late as the Medieval period (primarily churches). Watkins and many other scholars believed and still hold that many medieval churches were built on sites that had been sacred long before the later structures were built, and so Watkins felt that even these later structures actually marked more ancient Mesolithic sites.

Watkins was certain that this geometric relationship between monuments, widely separated by both distance and time, could not be mere chance, but he did not perceive the ley lines (a term he coined) to be energetic in nature; rather, he thought he had discovered the existence of a series of extensive ancient trading routes.

The ley lines Watkins mapped out ignored the topography of the land, running in perfectly straight lines, thence the term "Old Straight Track," which Watkins also coined to describe them. Often they ran over difficult terrain or hills, which might argue against their having been roads, but Watkins theorized that the positioning of many of the connected monuments on hilltops was so that they could be used as landmarks, visible from far away.

In 1522 Pisces (AD 1922), Watkins published *Early British Trackways*, followed in 1525 Pisces (AD 1925) by *The Old Straight Track* and the *Ley Hunter's Manual* in 1527 Pisces (AD 1927). During these same years the Old Straight Track club was formed, which further helped to popularize Watkins' theories.

The perception of ley lines as ancient roadways was seriously altered in the following decade by the great occultist DION FORTUNE, whose 1536 Pisces (AD 1936)

novel *The Goat-Footed God* described ley lines as "lines of power" known only to Witches (who were not portrayed particularly sympathetically) who had handed the knowledge of them down from Mesolithic times. After this, ley lines were increasingly thought of as being energetic and magical in nature.

Interest in ley lines remained high until the advent of the Second World War, which caused something of an eclipse of the spiritual-magical revival that had been a major social force for decades preceding it. During and after the war, interest in magical and spiritual matters dropped before reviving again in the '60s and '70s.

By the '60s, ley lines were equated with the dragon lines of Chinese feng shui and perceived as energetic meridians linking vortices of earth energy. John Mitchell's *The View Over Atlantis* was published in 1569 Pisces (AD 1969), becoming something of a definitive statement on the subject.

Thus the modern understanding of ley lines took shape.

• • • •

What Are Ley Lines?

Ley lines are thought of as being currents of the earth's energy. You will often find them described as MAGNETIC; this is because, in the older sense of the word, *magnetism* was one more term for "psychic energy." The earth's "magnetism" is thought

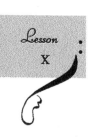

to react with the ANIMAL MAGNETISM of living things in a way that is unconscious and instinctual.

Birds, animals, insects, and bacteria are believed to use ley lines as a guide in their migrations across great distances, as presumably did early humans. It was by their instinctive psycho-physical reaction to the presence of ley lines that ancient peoples were able to identify their location long before having an intellectual understanding of them. This is also how we identify ley lines today, through an instinctive reaction manifested through clairvoyance or through DOWSING.

The point where two or more ley lines meet is usually the site of an energy vortex. There are thousands of such vortices, just as the body has thousands of minor chakras. And just as the body has a few highly developed major chakras, some of the earth's vortices are much more developed than others. Ley lines have the same connection to the earth's vortices that meridians have to the body's chakras.

. . . .

The Dragon and the Tiger

The Chinese call ley lines *Lung Mei* or "dragon lines." Lung Mei are perceived as being of two types: yang lines, represented by the blue dragon, and yin lines, represented by the white tiger. The intersection of the two, balancing yin and yang,

is perceived as a power center—that is, a vortex.

This same duality is increasingly perceived in the West as well.

Yang ley lines are normally perceived as being at the surface and just below the surface of the earth. They are straight lines that form geometric shapes, especially triangles, when they cross each other, which they often do. Yang ley lines give a feeling of high energy that is sometimes described as invigorating or electric. They tend to increase physical energy, and when very strong, they can produce an ungrounded effect. This is why when too many ley lines intersect in one spot, it is often impossible for life to thrive there.

Yin ley lines are perceived as being deeper in the earth and are normally associated with underground water, subterranean rivers and springs. Unlike the straight yang ley lines, yin ley lines are circuitous and curvilinear. Yin ley lines give a feeling of heavy, slow energy sometimes described as calm and peaceful. They tend to dampen physical energy but heighten psychic energy and meditative states. It is difficult to live over a yin ley line because it creates a passive atmosphere in which it can be very difficult to function on an everyday level.

When these two kinds of ley lines intersect, a powerful energy is formed that partakes of the qualities of both, though not

always in equal measure. Indeed, the qualities of each vortex are unique to it.

The idea that there are both yang and yin ley lines, and that both are connected with the ancient megalithic monuments, is supported by the work of dowsers M. Louis Merle and Reginald Allender Smith. Just as Watkins demonstrated a relationship between ancient monuments and straight ley lines during the '20s, during the '30s, Merle and Smith demonstrated a similar relationship between the ancient monuments and the presence of underground water sources, and frequently of freshwater springs—that is to say, yin ley lines.

. . . .

Origins

We usually think of vortices and ley lines in the same way as we think of our chakras and meridians: as being natural formations we have played no role in shaping. This is not necessarily so, however.

Energy develops according to its use. Our chakras and meridians are more or less highly developed, depending on how much we work or have worked with them in this and previous lifetimes. If we work with certain chakras more than others, or with aspects of a given chakra more than others, then these will be more developed. We learned in Lesson IX just how complex chakras can be. In examining chakras,

you may find that one person has stronger development in their fourth level solaris chakra, while another has the solaris most highly developed in the sixth level, and both the perceived location of the chakra and its qualities will vary accordingly.

Moreover, advanced energy workers often create energetic constructs to improve or strengthen the functioning of certain chakras. These often appear as geometric forms within or adjacent to the chakra. Sometimes these energy constructs amount to synthetic chakras in themselves.

This is also the case with the vortices and ley lines of the earth. Not only natural vortices and ley lines exist, but also synthetic vortices and ley lines created through the habitual movement and/or magical workings of people and animals. This is why temples often become the center of a vortex even though there was no vortex present when the temple began. Similarly, the presence of a large number of people continually moving along a specific road can create a ley line even though the road was not originally constructed upon a ley line. This can also be true for shorter but extremely traumatic experiences, such as the Cherokee Trail of Tears, whose route has the properties of a yin ley line.

How can you tell the difference between a natural and a synthetic vortex or ley line? You can't necessarily tell the difference,

nor does it inherently matter. You would deal with both natural and synthetic forms in the same way. Over time, synthetic vortices and ley lines become integrated into the natural system and eventually are simply part of it.

The Correllian Tradition has worked a lot with ley lines over the years, both in cleansing and strengthening existing ley lines and in adjusting or constructing synthetic ley lines. These synthetic ley lines, which will be addressed in greater depth below, serve a number of purposes, including creating an energetic environment to help carry forward the work of the tradition, a major part of which is assisting the transition of the age.

• • • •

Other Types of Ley Lines

So far we have discussed ley lines of the earth, yang lines on or near the surface and yin lines farther beneath the surface. But ley lines and vortices are found in all parts of space and time, and not only the earth but the air and the waters have ley lines. These tend to be very curvilinear in form and are rarely worked with except by weather Witches. Outer space, too, has ley lines, and Earth has ley lines that serve to connect and integrate it with space. These ley lines are both straight (yang) and curvilinear (yin) like those of the earth. Because

the Correllian Tradition believes strongly in the need to interact with space, we have sometimes worked with these ley lines to help strengthen the energetic bonds between Earth and space, and to develop potential future routes into space.

The Correllian Tradition holds the view that humanity has not developed the ability to leave the planet by accident; rather, as we are part of the integrated life form which is the planet, this ability to leave the planet must accomplish a purpose of the planet itself. We have long held the view, developed by Rev. Ed Hubbard, that the ability to leave the planet is, in essence, a method of reproduction developed to ensure the continuation and expansion of Earth-based life forms, as natural in its way as a plant dropping a seed or a bacteria sending out a spore.

Lady Bitterwind has further developed a view that our ability to leave the planet is a form of self-defense on the part of the planet—that after being hit with meteors to the considerable detriment of its ecosystems, the planet consciously created a life form capable of leaving the planet's surface in order to prevent any similar catastrophe ever happening again.

For both these reasons, we are strongly in favor of space travel. Thus we have an interest in it and have worked with the ley lines of space.

Lesson
X

Temporal Ley Lines

The final type of ley line we will discuss is the temporal ley line—that is, ley lines in time. Time, like space, has ley lines of its own. Working with these can help facilitate long-term projects by creating an energetic path for the projects to follow, which helps to focus and energize the project in the present and project it into the future.

INCARNATE souls can use temporal ley lines to find their way back to a project generation after generation. There are many such multigenerational projects undertaken at a soul level; as a rule, the conscious mind has no knowledge of them, though that is changing as humanity develops further spiritually. The Correllian Tradition is such a project, as its aims are tied to the turning of the age and the shaping of the New Age, especially the continuing spiritual development of humanity. As humanity moves from being primarily centered in the third (mental) plane to being increasingly centered in the fourth (astral-magical) plane, our psychic and magical abilities will increase in depth and scope and become much more common and widespread.

We will not go further into the nature and use of temporal ley lines in this lesson, as it is not really Second Degree work, though it is important for you to know they exist. We will discuss time and time magic much more in our Third Degree studies.

How to Locate Ley Lines

In order to do anything with a ley line, you first have to find one. Although we have spoken of ley lines in the air and water, in space and also in time, we will only address the issue of working with the ley lines of Earth, as this is what is most commonly done, though in many cases the techniques described are equally applicable to the other sorts of ley line as well.

There are several ways to locate ley lines; all would be considered methods of dowsing.

Dowsing may be accomplished either through pure clairvoyance or the use of any of several tools. The most traditional tool for dowsing is the forked stick. One can also use copper dowsing rods or a pendulum.

Copper dowsing rods are short, straight rods mounted on handles in such a way that the handle is stable but the rod may swing freely. They are held one in each hand, pointing forward to start.

A PENDULUM is a token suspended from a string or chain. It is held by the chain and allowed to swing freely, its movements being interpreted. The most famous traditional example of a pendulum is a wedding ring suspended from a single hair, often used to predict the sex of unborn babies, but anything that can be suspended from a string can be used as a pendulum, and today pendulums are often specially made,

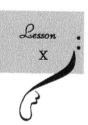

Lesson

X

frequently using one or more stones to beautify and add energy to the pendulum. Pendulums are most commonly used to ask yes or no questions, the answer being determined by the direction of its swing (there is no specific rule on which direction means what—you determine this by first asking the pendulum questions to which you know the answers, and see how it answers, or by setting the rule yourself). Pendulums can also be used with a sheet of letters written around a circle to spell out messages, the letter being shown when the pendulum swings in its direction. But it is the pendulum's use in dowsing that we will examine now.

All of these dowsing methods work in basically the same way. The dowser relaxes their mind and shifts to a magical state of consciousness. Then the dowser walks over the land in question, having set their intent to find the ley line (or other substances, such as subterranean water or metals) and when they are over it, the tool gives a signal. The forked stick will jerk downward or sometimes upward, the copper rods will cross, the pendulum will begin to swing forcefully, and in the case of clairvoyance a "knowing" will come, or a special feeling or signal (depending on the clairvoyant) will make clear that the spot has been found.

In all cases, the most important thing is to relax the mind, to not think in the ordinary sense but to shift consciousness and open to psychic stimuli. The pendulum, forked stick, and dowsing rods all work in the same way; they move in reaction to the unconscious muscle movements of the dowser, which are triggered by psychic stimuli.

In addition to the kind of dowsing described, which is to say on-site dowsing, one can also dowse from a remote location by means of a map. This is usually done with a pendulum but can also be done with dowsing rods. If using a pendulum, one can either ask yes or no about specific areas as the pendulum is held over them, or one can move the pendulum slowly over the map. It will begin to swing vigorously over the location of the ley line (or whatever else one may be dowsing for). If using the dowsing rods, they are held over the map and allowed to swing. The point where they cross each other will indicate the location of what you are dowsing for.

Finally, a clairvoyant can locate a ley line not only by the method earlier described—walking over the ground and "feeling" it—but also by clairvoyant messages, which can reveal the location of ley lines of all sorts.

• • • •

Working with Ley Lines

Why do you want to be able to find a ley line, anyway?

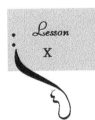

Lesson
X

307

Well, for one thing, it helps to locate energy vortices that may be useful for psychic development or for ritual centers.

It can also explain energetic problems that may be afflicting a specific area; as said, living or working on top of a yang ley line can sometimes cause ungroundedness, and living at the intersection of several can be very detrimental to health and well-being because of the effect of continual high energy on the system. Living or working on a yin ley line can cause sluggishness and inertia or contribute to disturbing psychic phenomena, such as retention of emotional energies, especially traumas, or hauntings. The extent of these phenomena in either case depends, among other things, upon the strength and character of the individual ley line in question. By locating the ley line, one can determine in advance if a location may be unfavorable for habitation, or one can adjust the energies to make a location more favorable.

How do you "adjust" the energies of a ley line? Psychic cleansings may be employed to decrease the amount of energy and make a location more habitable. The creation of energetic constructs may also be helpful, or the infusion of counterbalancing energy. As a rule, we use geometric forms for this sort of working.

• • • •

Geometric Magic

In the Correllian Tradition, we make much use of geometric forms in the creation of energy constructs. This is especially true in terms of working with ley lines, where the base of our practices is geometric. Energy is focused through geometric constructs. The constructs impart their own qualities to the energy and are also sometimes used to act as generators, continuing to create and project the desired energy long after the working has finished.

This lesson's spell describes the process of this in greater detail through the example of a simple ceremony for working with ley lines. More complex examples of this sort of work will be discussed elsewhere, but to help you get a feel for it, we will discuss the various geometric shapes and how they are used in this context.

When we use geometric forms in magic, we use a three-dimensional image of them, created through visualization and intent to focus and shape energy. Thus we use a sphere rather than a circle and a pyramid rather than a triangle. It is very important for you to understand this, even though it may take you some practice to be able to fully imagine the three-dimensional form.

Sphere: the sphere is considered the perfect form, because it is the same from all angles. The sphere is perhaps the most common energetic con-

struct, and one with which you will have a great deal of experience if you have been doing the exercises regularly. The sphere generates a smooth, steady energy flow that tends to be fairly self-contained. It is especially useful for generation of energy, but is usually not so useful for direction of energy.

Line or Beam: More commonly termed a *beam*, a line is a very focused construct intended to deliver energy to a tightly defined destination. The beam, because of its restricted narrow form, intensifies the energy, creating an effect not unlike a laser. Beams are used in many ways, and you have used them in the exercises quite a bit already: they have special application to advanced techniques of psychic healing.

Tetrahedron: The tetrahedron is a three-dimensional triangle, having three triangular sides and a triangular base. Use the tetrahedron for transformative energy, energy whose purpose is to induce change. The tetrahedron induces movement, development, and growth. The tetrahedron is one of the five PLATONIC SOLIDS, which are the five perfect polyhedrons the Greeks used to represent the air, fire, water, earth, and spirit. The tetrahedron represented fire and the qualities associated with fire, such as action and movement.

Pyramid: The pyramid is similar to a tetrahedron except in that the pyramid has four triangular sides and a square base. This gives energy focused through a pyramidical construct a greater stability but reduces its transformative power.

Cube: The cube is a three-dimensional square having four square sides as well as a square top and a square bottom. The cube is a form that promotes stability and focus. Use a cube when you want to make an energy flow more steadily or you need to anchor energy very securely. The cube is resistant to change and also tends to slow energy. The cube is also called a hexahedron and is one of the Platonic solids used by the Greeks to represent earth and the qualities earth corresponds to, such as solidity.

Octahedron: The octahedron has eight triangle-shaped sides. Visually, the octahedron resembles a double-sided pyramid or a diamond design. The octahedron partakes of the transformational nature of the triangle, the stability of the number four, and also the intensity of the number eight; thus, it gives an intensified but still

Lesson

X

309

stable transformative energy very much like the pyramid doubled. The octahedron is most useful as a long-term construct meant to disperse energy over an extended period. The octahedron is one of the Platonic solids and was used by the Greeks to represent air and the qualities associated with air, such as thought and inspiration.

Decahedron: The decahedron has ten triangle-shaped sides and gives the effect of a three-dimensional pentagram/pentagon. The decahedron is similar to the tetrahedron in that its energy is transformational and promotes growth and change, but the influence of the number 10 gives it a regenerational power as well, which serves to constantly revitalize its energy. The energy of the decahedron is adaptive as well as transformational, and it tends to re-create itself as needed. Because it renews itself, the decahedron is more durable than the tetrahedron, and—like the octahedron—is used for constructs that are meant to last for a long period of time.

Dodecahedron: The dodecahedron has twelve pentagon-shaped sides. As such, it partakes of the transformational qualities of the five-

sided pentagon as well as the idea of completion often associated with the number twelve. Use the dodecahedron for a construct that is meant to lead to the completion of a specific goal, as opposed to simply imparting a certain kind of energy or a certain effect. The dodecahedron has a very focused quality that will help to hold the construct on course for its duration. The dodecahedron is one of the Platonic solids and was used by the Greeks to represent Spirit and the qualities associated with Spirit, such as unity and providence.

Icosahedron: The icosahedron has twenty triangle-shaped sides and may be most familiar to the modern reader as being the shape of the twenty-sided dice used in role-playing games. The icosahedron, associated with change and adaptability, is best used for long-term projects where the construct may be subject to changing conditions, as the icosahedron is more flexible and adaptable than most of the other geometric constructs. The icosahedron can also be used to create a stable emotional atmosphere in a location where this might be needed, or to help stabilize a person or situation that is prone to emotional instability. The icosa-

hedron is one of the Platonic solids and was used by the Greeks to represent water and the qualities associated with water, such as fluidity and mutability.

. . . .

It is to be noted that although the geometric forms are often used individually, they are also often used in combination, though combining them should only be attempted after first becoming familiar with the basic forms.

The same geometric forms that are used in this context to influence ley lines and vortices can also be used in psychic healing to influence the body's chakras and meridians, where they can be used to modulate the flow of energy or affect it in various ways. As we have commented, advanced energy workers sometimes create energy constructs in this way, which are placed in the chakras or even become synthetic chakras. But this is a more advanced level of working than using them to interact with ley lines and should not be attempted without a high degree of psychic openness.

. . . .

The Crystal Web

The Correllian Tradition has worked with both natural and synthetic ley lines in a number of ways. Our most notable project has been the ongoing construction of the Crystal Web. The Crystal Web is a synthetic vortex and ley network whose principal purpose is to heighten psychic communication, as well as create a system along which magical energy can travel. The Crystal Web is specifically attuned to the Correllian Tradition and is worked with primarily through the geometric magic described above.

The Crystal Web is so named because it is facilitated through quartz crystals, which, as you may recall from your First Degree studies, have the natural property of transmitting energy. Other stones are also used in the web to impart specific qualities. The web began in the Chicago and Vermilion County regions of Illinois and has been slowly spreading out as the tradition has grown.

The Crystal Web is centered at Chicago's Cricket Hill. A secondary center exists at the original location of the Under-The-Hill estate in Vermilion County, though this site has not been accessible for some time.

One of the central tools used in dealing with the Crystal Web is the ULUNSUTI, or Eye of UKTENA, a unique crystal that is said to be the eye of the great dragon Uktena. The ulunsuti is used in the ceremonies of the Correll Mother Temple to focus energy into the web, among other purposes. This is especially true in the lustration ceremonies, where the ulunsuti is used to bless the water used in the ceremony, attuning it

to the crystalline frequency, so that as the blessing travels outward, toward the four quarters, it can be anchored into the lines of the web and thus made more stable.

As the tradition continues to grow, the use of the web in tradition-wide ceremonies and attunements will probably become more prominent, as this is what the web is designed for. So far as we know, it is a fairly unique metaphysical construct.

• • • •

Vortices

As a final comment on the subject of ley lines and vortices, we offer a partial list of what are considered major vortices of the earth. The list is by no means complete or definitive, and reflects our own perspective and experience. There are, of course, vortices all over the earth, and it should be remembered that individuals do not always react to the same vortex in the same way.

The major vortices include Athens, Greece; Avebury, UK; Ayers Rock, Australia; Bimini, near Florida; Easter Island, Pacific; Calgary, Canada; Cairo, Egypt; Chicago, US; Lake Titicaca, Peru; Kathmandu, Nepal; Machu Picchu, Peru; Magaliesburg Mountains, South Africa; Mount Shasta, US; Osaka, Japan; Rome, Italy; Sedona, US; Santo Domingo, Dominican Republic; Smokey Mountains, US; and Lhasa, Tibet.

• • • •

Exercises

Exercise 20

Begin your daily routine with the Ohm exercise, then open three balls of colored light in each chakra, changing the balls of colored light to balls of white light, changing the balls of white light to balls of purple light, changing the balls of purple light to balls of silver stellar light, and then filling your aura with silver stellar light. Next, change the balls of silver stellar light to balls of golden stellar light, then fill your aura with golden stellar light. Finally, change the balls of golden stellar light to balls of amber light, and fill your aura with the amber light.

Now open seven small balls of red light at the crown chakra, one at each of the seven levels of the crown chakra—that is, a central ball surrounded by six others. When you see the seven balls of red light clearly, change them to seven balls of white light. Then, when you see the seven balls of white light clearly, change them to balls of purple light. Now go on to change them to seven balls of silver stellar energy, and then go on to change them to seven balls of golden stellar energy. Finally, change them to seven balls of amber light.

When you clearly see the seven balls of amber light, send up a slender beam of red light from the central ball. Play with this beam as you have done with similar

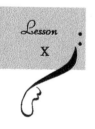

Lesson

X

beams of light in earlier exercises: move it around, write with it, draw pictures, practice using it. When you can do this easily, you are ready for Exercise 21.

Exercise 21

Exercise 21 begins just the same way as Exercise 20. Go through the whole routine, just as you did for Exercise 20, until you have raised a beam of red light from the center of your crown chakra.

Now, one at a time, send up a slender beam of red light from each of the other six crown chakra points, so that the first beam of light is encircled by a ring of six others. If you cannot manage all six the first time, that is fine; try again the next day. Take as long as you need.

Once you have raised all seven beams of light, begin to move and play with them as you have already been doing with the central beam. Become accustomed to the idea of directing and moving the beams. Have fun with it.

When you can do this easily, you are ready for Exercise 22.

Exercise 22

Exercise 22 begins where Exercise 21 leaves off. Go through the full daily routine as usual, until you have opened seven beams of red light from the crown chakra. Now, instead of just playing with the beams of light as you have been doing, use them

in more focused ways. One at a time, direct each beam of light in a specific direction: straight up, on a diagonal or out to the side, shooting it out in any direction. Play with the length of the beam of light: make it shorter, then longer, then shorter again. Practice curving the beam, so that instead of being straight it bends at a ninety-degree angle. Direct the beam to the ceiling or wall, and write with it. Do this, one at a time, for each of the beams of light.

When you can do this comfortably, you are ready for Exercise 23.

. . . .

Spell for Lesson X
Chakra Dowsing

In magic, it is often the case where techniques that appear simple, even childish on the surface, can have unexpectedly deep and effective results.

This is because in magic we work through our Higher Self, and our Higher Self is very responsive to symbolic keys, as we discussed way back in First Degree, Lesson 1, and with keys, simpler is often better.

In this spell, we will be discussing just such a simple but effective technique for cleansing the chakras by means of a pendulum and water. The pendulum is used to monitor the state of the chakra, while the water is used to convey negativity away from it.

Lesson
X

313

For this technique we will need:

- A large bowl or pitcher filled with water
- A large bowl or pitcher to receive water after it has been used
- A cup
- A pendulum
- A partner to work with, who will act as the subject

As you will see, this is not a technique you can do for yourself, but rather a type of healing you would do for another person. Therefore, you will need a partner.

This sort of chakra cleansing is always good, and we need not be especially blocked to benefit by it. As you will recall from your First Degree studies, chakras naturally build up blockages all the time, as the result of various stimuli, and consequently need regular cleansing. I would recommend using this technique every few months, if not more often.

You might think that the more we advance in metaphysics, the less often we would have to cleanse our chakras; not so. In fact, the more we advance, the more sensitive we become to energetic blockages. This may give the impression that we actually have to cleanse our chakras more often as we become more magically proficient, though in fact it is simply a matter of being more aware of the importance of energetic cleansing.

In working with this technique, you and your partner should each take a turn being the subject of healing, not only so that you each have the experience of doing the cleansing, but so that you each have the benefit of being cleansed.

You will need to select a pendulum. There are excellent commercially produced pendulums created especially for this purpose, but you can also use any object that can be swung on the end of a chain or string as a pendulum. It is very common to use a favorite pendant or ring for this purpose. A pendulum need not be fancy or expensive to work well.

The theory of the pendulum, of course, is that you keep your hand still, and the pendulum is moved by Spirit to answer your query. Many people work very hard to keep their hand perfectly still, and in so doing shut down the process by putting their concentration in the wrong place. Do try to keep your hand still, of course, but don't be tense and nervous about it. Let your hand be in a natural, relaxed state— not rigid, just still. As you work with the pendulum, you will see that its movement is not dictated by the hand, and perfect immobility is not required.

In ordinary practice, a pendulum is used to answer basic questions, normally yes or no questions, by the direction in which it swings. A pendulum may swing back and forth, side to side, or in a circular motion.

Before working with a pendulum to answer questions, we must first determine which type of swing indicates a positive or negative answer to our particular question.

Many people prefer to do this by asking the pendulum questions to which they already know the answer, in order to determine which kind of swing means yes and which means no. However, we can also program our pendulum to answer in a specific way, perhaps back and forth for *yes*, side to side for *no*, and circular for *maybe* or *no answer at this time.*

To program the pendulum, you would hold it in your hands and tell it with a clear intent what you want it to do. You might also focus white light into the pendulum as you program it, which will strengthen the effect.

For the purposes of chakra cleansing, however, we will program our pendulum a bit differently. Hold the pendulum in your hands and charge it to tell you the state of the chakras it will be exposed to; a clockwise motion will indicate a chakra that is unblocked, a counterclockwise motion will indicate the presence of a blockage in the chakra.

In addition to the pendulum, you will need two large bowls or pitchers, one full of water, one empty. Tap water is fine for this. You will also need a cup. It does not matter what these items are made of—glass

is very nice and may give a more magical mood, but plastic works just as well.

Now, have your partner lie down in a comfortable position on a floor, sofa, or bed. Hold your pendulum in one hand—as a rule, whichever hand you write with—and the cup in the other. Have the full bowl and the empty bowl both close at hand.

Begin with the root chakra. Hold the pendulum directly above the lower pelvic region, concentrating on the root chakra.

Observe the swing of the pendulum. Does it go clockwise or counterclockwise? If the pendulum swings clockwise, it means that the chakra is fine, and you can go on to the next chakra.

If the pendulum swings counterclockwise, it means that the chakra is blocked. In this case, you must cleanse it. Take your cup and dip it into the bowl of water, filling the cup. Now place your fingertips into the water in the cup and continue to dowse with the pendulum. Keep your fingertips in the water until the pendulum stops swinging counterclockwise and begins swinging clockwise. When the pendulum begins to move clockwise and assumes a good, strong swing in this direction, then you are done and should empty the used water into the empty bowl. Be careful not to confuse the two bowls, as the used water now has a negative charge.

Sometimes you may need to use two or more cups of water before the pendulum

will start going clockwise; this is fine, it just means that the chakra is very blocked. In this case, just dump the used water into the used water bowl, take up more clean water, and continue.

Move upward through the seven major chakras, one at a time. As you dowse each chakra, the pendulum will either go clockwise, in which case you go on to the next chakra, or it will go counterclockwise, in which case you fill your cup and cleanse the chakra as we have just described.

Sometimes if the pendulum moves clockwise but in a slow or very narrow circle, an incipient blockage is indicated. In this case, treat the chakra as if it were already blocked. Fill your cup of water, place your fingertips in it, and continue until the pendulum swings freely in a wide clockwise circle.

Continue this through all seven major chakras.

The subject will feel the energy while you are dowsing their chakras to a greater or lesser extent, depending on their degree of psychic openness. Some subjects will feel the energy very strongly, some not so strongly, and some may not know how to recognize it, but the degree to which the subject feels the process does not indicate the strength of the cleansing but rather their own sensitivity to energy. This can be very interesting, because often what the subject feels may be in a different part of their body from the chakra you are dowsing at that moment, but this is because the chakras connect to all parts of the body. Sometimes, too, the subject may have images come to them that deal with the nature of the blockages, often through symbols; however, this is not necessary for the cleansing to be effective.

When you have cleansed all seven major chakras, take a break. Both you and your partner should clear and release. Dispose of the used water; I recommend flushing it. The negative charge will dissipate fairly quickly, but you may wish to imagine the used water filled with violet light to transmute the negative charge immediately.

Then you and your partner should change places so that you can be the subject and get a feel for both sides of the practice.

Like everything else, the more you use this technique, the better you will get at it. Don't expect your first attempt to be perfect, but be prepared to practice. You will find your practice well rewarded.

Variation

As you might expect, the technique can also be used with the minor chakras as well, which are everywhere in the body. The process is the same but can be applied to any area you might be concerned about.

Glossary

animal magnetism—*Animal magnetism* is an old term for "psychic energy." The idea of animal magnetism is that all creatures have a spiritual energy field that affects and can be affected by other spiritual energy fields, whether those of other creatures, stones, metals, ley lines, etc. The term *animal magnetism* is particularly associated with Franz Anton Mesmer, who advanced the concept in the 1370s Pisces (AD 1770s). Mesmer thought of spiritual energy as a subtle fluid (a pretty good description in the era before electricity) and sought to influence it by the use of magnets and by force of will. Although Mesmer was denounced as a fraud and a charlatan, it will readily be observed that this is the same basic theory we use today under the term *psychic energy*.

dowsing—Dowsing is a means of psychically locating things that are underground or otherwise concealed from normal means of detection. The dowser walks over the area where something is being looked for, such as water or underground mineral deposits, and finds it by feeling the difference in energy where it is located. Often a dowser will use a handheld device, such as a forked stick or a set of dowsing wands, that will move automatically when they walk over what they are seeking. Other times dowsing will be done by the feel of the energy alone. Dowsing can also be done remotely, as with a pendulum over a map.

feng shui—This ancient Chinese art of geomancy is based on the directions and the Asian system of five elements. Feng shui is used to align the position of buildings, to decorate rooms, and in general to divine the most auspicious place to put things to allow for a free flow of chi (spiritual energy). Feng shui makes extensive use of the Chinese ba gua trigrams.

Fortune, Dion—Dion Fortune is the pseudonym of British occultist Violet Mary Firth. An encyclopedic author on metaphysics, Dion Fortune wrote many books on the subject, including *Training and Work of the Initiate, Psychic Self-Defense, Esoteric Orders and Their Work, Sane Occultism, Through the Gates of Death*, and *The Mystical Qabbalah*, to name a few. She also wrote a number of novels, including *The Sea Priestess, The Goat-Footed God, Moon Magic*, and *The Winged Bull*. The name *Dion Fortune* was taken from her motto "Deo Non Fortunis," meaning "Deity, Not Fortune." In 1529 Pisces (AD 1929), Dion Fortune founded her own spiritual order, the Community of Inner Light, which continues to function and is now known as the Society of Inner Light. In addition to

Lesson
X

317

work in metaphysics, Dion Fortune was also a practicing psychologist. Fortune's work is considered extremely influential in the development of the modern Pagan movement, and *Psychic Self-Defense* is considered to be the defining work on the subject of psychic attack and defense. Dion Fortune was born in Chelsea, UK, in 1490 Pisces (AD 1890) and died in 1546 Pisces (AD 1946).

incarnate—An incarnate is a person who is reborn into the same family or group as part of a multigenerational commitment, with many or most of their memories of previous lives accessible. Incarnates usually pick up where they left off in their previous life very early in the present life, so that they can continue the work their soul has chosen to do. The term is short for "conscious incarnate." The most famous example of incarnates of this kind are the Tibetan Tulkus, such as the Dalai Lama, who reincarnate repeatedly to continue the same work in the same office.

magnetic—In the sense used here, *magnetism* is another term for *psychic energy*. All things have an energetic field, and this field can affect and be affected by other energetic fields. In this sense, ley lines can be described as magnetic, and there is a belief that animals react to this magnetism, following the energetic current in their migrations.

pendulum—A pendulum is a pendant hung on a string or chain for use as a divining mechanism. One holds the pendulum by the chain so that the pendant hangs free, and asks questions. The answers are determined by how the pendant swings: back and forth, side to side, in a circle, etc. The meanings of the different swings vary with the reader and sometimes with the pendulum.

Platonic solids—The Greeks used geometry as a tool for representing and understanding the universe. Geometric forms carried metaphysical significance and were thought to reveal the processes of existence. A polygon is a two-dimensional shape bounded by straight lines. A regular polygon is a polygon whose edges are the same length and meet at equal angles, and the intersection of these angles is called a vertex. A Platonic solid is a perfect polyhedron whose facets are congruent regular polygons, with the same number of facets meeting at each vertex. There are only five such geometric shapes: the tetrahedron, composed of four triangles with three triangles meeting at each vertex; the octahedron, composed of eight triangles with four triangles meeting at each vertex; the icosahedron, composed of twenty triangles with five triangles meeting at each vertex; the hexahedron, or cube, composed of six squares, with three

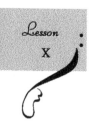

Lesson

X

squares meeting at each vertex; and the dodecahedron, composed of twelve pentagons with three pentagons meeting at each vertex. The great Greek philosopher Plato associated these five perfect polyhedrons with the four elements (elemental theory having been expounded a generation earlier by Empedocles), with the octahedron representing air, the tetrahedron representing fire, the icosahedron representing water, and the hexahedron, or cube, representing earth. The dodecahedron was used to represent the cosmos. Because they are so strongly associated with Platonic thought, they are termed the Platonic solids.

Uktena—The Uktena is the great dragon of Cherokee mythology. The Uktena has the body of a snake and the legs of a deer; it has large wings and great antlers upon its head. The Uktena's body is covered with beautiful, shining scales, although some say that it is a feathered serpent like those venerated in Mesoamerican tradition. The Uktena's body is marked by a beautiful pattern of circles along its length. Between the Uktena's antlers is the ulunsuti, or eye of Uktena; this is a powerful crystal that functions in effect as the dragon's third eye, allowing it to see the future and the past, and to focus its magical powers. In some myths, the Uktena is presented as beneficent, a world builder appointed by the Sun Mother to help create the world. In others myths, the Uktena is presented as a fearsome creature, embodying destruction and fear. Like all dragons, the Uktena ultimately represents the Tao, or flow of the universe, and how the Uktena is perceived depends in part upon one's relationship with that flow. The eye of Uktena is regarded as the most efficacious of all magical tools.

ulunsuti—The ulunsuti is the eye of the dragon Uktena. Traditionally it is said to be a clear crystal with a red streak inside. The red streak marks the dragon's pupil. The ulunsuti is said to confer great magical power, especially in terms of clairvoyance and prophecy. Sometimes the ulunsuti is described in other ways—some say that the whole crystal is red, others say that the streak will appear as either white or red, depending upon the observer, and some regard any crystal formation resembling an eye to be an ulunsuti: slices of colored agate, for example. The Correllian ulunsuti is a large clear crystal with a deep red streak, almost purple in color, at the crystal's center.

Lesson
XI

The Ba Gua
(Pu Kua)

It was in the years that I was editing *The Round Table Magazine* that I learned to spell correctly. Not that my spelling could not be understood before that, but it was fraught with misspellings, the result of a most well-intentioned circumstance. I learned to write in school, of course, but I learned to read in my parent's library. The library contained all manner of fascinating books, most in English, some in other languages. As a child, I had no idea—and I am not altogether certain to what extent my parents understood either—that the English language has two forms of spelling, British English and American English. The library and other libraries that I later learned to love contained many books from both categories. Consequently, I was exposed to both British and American spellings without knowing there was a difference, and my spelling contained a jumble of both. Add a heavy emphasis on

Shakespeare and his contemporaries, and you have some idea of the spelling complexities of my youth.

I tell this little tale because the same problem arises in this lesson, as in any other writing I undertake on Chinese subjects. There are two primary systems for transliterating Chinese words into English writing. The older system is called Wade-Giles and was developed by English-speaking MISSIONARIES in China, who based it on Cantonese pronunciations. Until the 1580s Pisces (AD 1980s), the Wade-Giles system was standard for rendering Chinese words into English. At that time, a newer system that had developed in the People's Republic of China began to become known and used in the West. This system is called Pinyin and is the dominant system today. As a rule, I do not know enough Chinese to know the difference between the two, and so they are all too apt to be jumbled awkwardly together in the lesson that follows. Where I do know both forms, I try to give them.

One reason for this is that I was taught most of what I know about Chinese philosophy and religion before Pinyin became popular, and so I know mainly Wade-Giles terms. Another reason, which I think you will readily agree with upon independent study, is that most books on Chinese eso-

terica will be found even today to be in the Wade-Giles system.

Being thus warned of the imminent pitfalls of my transliteration skills, let us proceed to our discussion of the *ba gua* (*pu kua* in Wade-Giles).

- - - -

The Ba Gua

The ba gua are the eight sacred TRIGRAMS that form the basis of much of Chinese religious and philosophical thought. So integral are the ba gua to Chinese thought that they are almost as emblematic of Chinese Taoism as the more famous yin/yang and often appear in combination with the yin/yang.

To understand why this is so, it may be helpful to think of the ba gua as the Chinese equivalent of our Wiccan quarter system. Like the quarters, the ba gua have many levels of interpretation and correspondence, from directions to archetypes. Like the quarters, the ba gua may be taken to represent the unfolding process of creation, though not in quite the same way.

According to Chinese mythology, the ba gua were created at the dawn of time by the legendary culture hero FU HSI. Fu Hsi and his wife NU KUA were credited with the invention of many of the arts of civilization, rather like Isis and Osiris in Egypt or Quetzalcoatl-Kukulkan in Mesoamerica.

In origin, Fu Hsi and Nu Kua were probably very ancient creator deities, and one of the most famous depictions of them shows them as being winged deities with the upper half of humans and the lower half of serpents, entwined together rather like serpents on the caduceus or the Hindu ida and pingala. Most depictions, however, show them in purely human form.

As a culture hero, Fu Hsi is said to have lived around the beginning of the Age of Taurus (2800 BC). Among the many inventions attributed to Fu Hsi is the use of writing, which is believed to have replaced an earlier system of recording by use of knotted cords, resembling the Inca QUIPUS.

Chinese writing is ideogrammatic in nature—that is, each symbol represents an idea, not a sound. The concept, rather than the word, is conveyed; thus, it is entirely possible for two people to communicate through Chinese ideograms without ever being able to speak each other's languages. The ba gua are said to be the earliest of these ideograms.

The ba gua are a series of eight trigrams, symbols composed of three lines each. The lines may be either straight or broken, as illustrated below. Fu Hsi is said to have gotten the idea for the trigrams from the markings on a turtle's shell, and you can get a feeling for this when you see the ba gua as they are normally arranged in a circle.

In Chinese thought, the polarities are called yin and yang, and may be thought of as rest and action. Yin and yang move in an eternal pattern; their interaction forms and sustains the universe. Each contains the seed of the other, so that they are not separate so much as they are two aspects of the whole. Yin goes as far into itself as it can before doubling back and becoming yang. Yang goes as far out as it can before doubling back and becoming yin. All things that exist contain elements of both yin and yang. This is the same idea as the Greek PROODOS AND EPISTROPHE or the Wiccan polarities of Goddess and God.

Of the eight ba gua, one is purely yin and one is purely yang; the rest are mixed in all the combinations afforded by use of three lines. The two polar forces united in every variety of combination is believed to reflect the inherent order of the universe.

Each ba gua has a distinct character unique to it. This is represented by a natural phenomenon; for example, Chen is "thunder." They are further characterized as a family, each being assigned a role that reflects its unique character. Earth, for example, is Mother, while Heaven is Father.

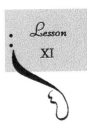

The eight ba gua are as follows:

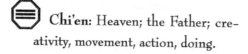 **Chi'en:** Heaven; the Father; creativity, movement, action, doing.

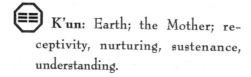 **K'un:** Earth; the Mother; receptivity, nurturing, sustenance, understanding.

Chen: Thunder; the Eldest Son; courage, excitement, growth, expansion, initiative.

Sun: Wind; the Eldest Daughter; gentleness, adaptability, fluidity, serenity.

K'an: Water; the Middle Son; the mysterious, the hidden, the subconscious, fears.

Li: Fire; the Middle Daughter; intelligence, illumination, clarity, thought.

Ken: Mountain; the Youngest Son; stillness, tranquility, meditation, introspection.

Tui: Lake; the Youngest Daughter; joy, delight, satisfaction, balance.

• • • • The Yi Jing

The most significant use of the ba gua is the basis for the Yi Jing (*I Ching* in Wade-Giles). The Yi Jing is very ancient. Not only is the Yi Jing one of the oldest forms of divination still in common use, but it is by far the most ancient written book of divination to remain in continuous use, being approximately three thousand years old. In the Yi Jing, the eight ba gua are arranged in combinations of two, forming hexagrams—that is, symbols formed by six lines. There are sixty-four hexagrams in the Yi Jing.

According to legend, it was King Wen, founder of the Zhou Dynasty, who created the Yi Jing while imprisoned by his overlord, the Emperor Shang Zhou Wang. In his cell, the king had a vision of the ba gua and was led to arrange them in combinations and interpret meanings from this. After King Wen was freed, he began the overthrow of the Shang Dynasty, a task which would be completed by his son Zhou Wu Wang, founder of the Zhou Dynasty. Another of King Wen's sons was the Duke of Zhou, Zhou Gong Don, who set about elaborating on the meanings his father had ascribed, creating the first commentary on the Yi Jing. This was in approximately 200 Aries (1000 BC).

In later centuries, many others wrote commentaries on the Yi Jing, the most notable of these being KUNG FU TZU (Confucius, b. 449 Aries/551 BC). Founder of Confucianism, Kung Fu Tzu is considered one of China's greatest philosophers (along with his contemporary, Lao-tzu, who founded Taoism as a formal movement). Although later Confucians sometimes attacked it as superstitious, Confucius himself said of the Yi Jing, "If I had fifty more years to live, I would devote them to the study of the Yi Jing and become perfect and without fault."

The Yi Jing is and has always been popular for divination, but it is also considered a philosophical text. Many devotees of the Yi Jing, in fact, study it only as philosophy and do not make use of its magical properties. The ancient commentaries on the Yi Jing contain much elevated thought related in enigmatic and sometimes obscure language, which rewards deep reflection on their inner meanings. That will not be especially apparent in this lesson, however, as we have chosen to focus on the Yi Jing as a divinatory tool, rendering its meanings into very modern form. We feel that this will better serve the Wiccan practitioner by offering an easily understandable introduction to the concepts, which can be very hard to understand in more ancient and less familiar language.

As has been the case through most of our Second Degree lessons, we seek here to provide you with a basic understanding and a working acquaintance with our subjects. More in-depth knowledge can be gained by independent study.

• • • •

How to Read the Yi Jing

Traditionally, the Yi Jing is taken very seriously as a divinatory device; that is to say, it is not a plaything but a sacred undertaking that should only be approached with respect. Don't do it just for fun. Don't ask silly questions you don't really care about. Do not ask a question again after you have already gotten one answer. It is traditionally believed that in any of these cases, the oracle will be offended and the answers given will be unreliable.

Is this true? Well, if you believe it, it will be true. Remember that divination is a way of communicating with Deity through an agreed-upon language of symbols. Be clear in your mind of what you believe, and that is what you will get. Divinatory tools need not be temperamental, but if you expect them to be so, they will.

There are several ways in which the Yi Jing can be consulted. The simplest way is to close your eyes and randomly select a hexagram. This simple form of BIBLIOMANCY has been used around the world with many different sacred books, from the AENEID of VIRGIL to the Judeo-Christian Bible.

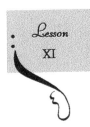

More commonly, however, the hexagrams are not chosen but built line by line. In a traditional setting, incense will be offered, prayers said, and the question will be stated directly to the Yi Jing before using one of two methods to build a hexagram line by line, then looking up the hexagram in the book.

The older and more traditional way to build a hexagram is by the use of twenty-four slender sticks of yarrow wood. The twenty-four sticks are divided into six groups of four sticks each. Each group of six sticks is marked to represent one of the four kinds of lines that may be used to construct a hexagram: changing yang, fixed yin, changing yin, and fixed yang (changing lines are explained below). The sticks are thrown on a flat surface repeatedly, the uppermost stick on the resulting pile being taken by its marking to indicate one line for the hexagram. If no one stick is uppermost, then they are thrown again. At length, six lines will be determined.

The more common modern way to build the hexagram uses coins instead of sticks. Three coins are used, the obverse side being reckoned as having a value of three and the reverse being reckoned to have a value of two. People often prefer to use special Chinese coins for this purpose, but any coin may be used. The coins are

shaken and tossed onto a flat surface. The number value of the sides facing upward are added together and interpreted: if the visible side of the three coins adds up to six, it represents the changing yang. If it adds up to seven, it represents fixed yin. If it adds up to eight, it is the changing yin, and if it adds up to nine, it is fixed yang. The coins are tossed six times to determine six lines of the hexagram.

In both cases, the hexagram is built from the bottom upwards. Each set of three lines is a ba gua, and the two ba gua form the hexagram. The number of the hexagram formed may be determined from this chart by lining up the top and bottom ba gua of the hexagram with the number marking their intersection. Thus, Earth/Mother over Heaven/Father will be seen to be number eleven, while Heaven/Father over Earth/Mother will be seen to be number twelve.

Having found the number, you then look up the meaning of your hexagram.

If your hexagram includes changing as well as fixed lines, then you will end up with two hexagrams. Changing lines are counted according to their name in the first hexagram; changing yin lines are yin, changing yang lines are yang. But in addition to the hexagram thus arrived at, a second hexagram is formed by changing the

lower \ upper	☰	☷	☵	☶	☷	☴	☲	☱
☰	1	34	5	26	11	9	14	43
☷	25	51	3	27	24	42	21	17
☵	6	40	29	4	7	59	64	47
☶	33	62	39	52	15	53	56	31
☷	12	16	8	23	2	20	35	45
☴	44	32	48	18	46	57	50	28
☲	13	55	63	22	36	37	30	49
☱	10	54	60	41	19	61	38	58

The Yi Jing hexagram numbers.

changing lines to their opposite polarity: changing yin changing to yang, changing yang changing to yin. The second hexagram is taken as a commentary on the first.

Below are the sixty-four hexagrams of the Yi Jing. In writing this commentary, I have not attempted to quote the Chinese commentaries traditional to the Yi Jing but rather to explain their meanings. The traditional commentaries are very poetic and can be hard to interpret without knowledge of traditional Chinese society and ideas. There are many fine books detailing the traditional verses, and I recommend you seek them out, though I think that you will quickly see in doing so why I have chosen to interpret rather than to quote.

. . . .

The Sixty-Four Hexagrams of the Yi Jing

1. **The Creative:** The Father doubled; heaven of heavens; yang; the masculine polarity; god.

   Action will bring success. Do not delay but rather strike while the iron

is hot. Be bold and confident, reaching out to grasp your desired goal.

2. The Receptive: The Mother doubled; earth of earths; yin; the feminine polarity; goddess.

Do not force the issue. Listen and follow inner guidance. Patience and perseverance bring success. Allow the situation time to develop and think in the long term.

3. Difficult Beginnings: Middle Son over First Son; water over mountain.

The situation is still in its formative stages. Don't rush it. Like a seed that has been planted, the situation needs time to grow and flower. This may indicate new relationships, new projects or ventures, new directions—in any case, it is the opening stage of development.

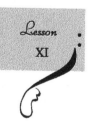

4. Inexperience: Third Son over Middle Son: mountain over water.

Be bold and decisive; strong, focused action is called for. Make your decision, and once made, stick to it.

Do not dither. In this way, you will go forward to success.

5. Patience: Middle Son over Father: water over heaven.

Sincere and persistent effort will bring success; stick to your principles. Remain true to your vision regardless of external circumstances, and pursue it with determination and patience. It may take a while.

6. Conflict: Father dominates Middle Son: heaven over water.

Be careful. Avoid sudden decisions or risky situations; play it safe. Think things through thoroughly and proceed only with caution.

7. Marshalling: Mother over Middle Son: earth over water.

You must be disciplined and organized in your approach. Without focus in thought and effort, your goals will elude you. Avoid dissipating your forces.

8. Unity: Mother supports Middle Son: water over earth.

Here you must give in order to later receive. You must be generous toward others in order to spur development and bring your goals to fruition. By offering your help to others, you will set energy in motion and loosen apparent blockages. You must grease the wheels, for the greased wheel turns when the ungreased wheel locks up.

9. Details: Eldest Daughter over Father: wind over heaven.

Attend to details: make sure of the fine print. Take nothing for granted, but be cautious and examine everything closely. Move carefully and with certainty. Take little steps.

10. Advancing: Father over Youngest Daughter: heaven over lake.

You have the resources to overcome whatever obstacles you may encounter; expect difficulties but expect also to overcome them. The road ahead holds challenges but also success.

11. Peace: Mother over Father: earth over heaven.

"Union of heaven and earth." Good luck and blessing. Success, joy, harmony. Much happiness. An excellent situation and many benefits coming from it.

12. Stillness: Father over Mother: heaven over earth.

Confusion, misunderstandings, possibly deceit; things are not as they appear. Take nothing at face value. Try to look beyond appearances, for there are things here you do not know that can cause you problems. Your understanding of this situation is incorrect. Be cautious and avoid risk. Be wary of the advice of others at this time, as they will be either innocently wrong or deliberately guileful.

13. Fellowship: Father over Middle Daughter: heaven over fire.

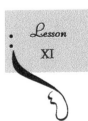

Lesson

XI

Think first of others rather than yourself. In this situation, you must look to the larger picture rather than your own needs; self-centered action will bring difficulties. Attention to duty, compassion, and openness of spirit are called for.

14. Control: Middle Daughter over Father: fire over heaven.

In this situation, it would be wise to seek the advice of others with greater experience than yourself; their advice will be of benefit. You must make your own decisions, but the advice of others will give you greater perspective in doing so.

15. Self-Restraint: Mother over Youngest Son: earth over mountain.

Chill out. Do not act from impulse or emotion. Be calm. Look within and act from your Higher Self. Swim in the deep water rather than the shallow water. Be guided from what is within you rather than reacting to what is around you.

16. Enthusiasm: Eldest Son over Mother: thunder over earth.

The current situation is too much for you to handle successfully, but if you seek help from others and approach it together, all will go well. Alone, you cannot do it, but together it will be easy. The needed help is there if you look, otherwise you would not be advised to seek it. Be sure that you are clear on what is needed, however, and avoid miscommunications.

17. Adaptation: Youngest Daughter over Eldest Son: lake over thunder.

Do not push to the front, but be comfortable in the shadows. Let others lead and follow along for now. It would be premature to try to take a leading role at this point. It would be too much difficulty and would bring sadness. Bide your time for now.

18. Restoration: Youngest Son over Eldest Daughter: mountain over wind.

So you have a mess on your hands. How did you come to this point? Well, it doesn't really matter: turn your attention to extracting yourself from difficulty. Be practical, avoid making decisions out of emotion or out of fear, and address your situation step by step. By dealing with it rather than trying to avoid it, and being prepared for patient but focused effort, you can return to a good position. Do not be afraid. Do not be angry. Do not wallow in the situation. Do not run from the situation; overcome the situation by applying good sense and consistency.

19. Approach: Mother over Youngest Daughter: earth over lake.

Things may seem still, but new situations are developing below the surface. Consider what you want to see take shape and focus on it. Focus on the positive, eliminate the negative. Soon enough the changes that are stirring will flower into being; shape them consciously.

20. Study: Eldest Daughter over Mother: wind over earth.

When you run in the dark, you are liable to injure yourself. You do not see clearly in this situation. You do not know all you need to know. Meditate; look within for guidance. Allow Spirit to show you the way.

21. Regeneration: Middle Daughter over Eldest Son: fire over thunder.

You may feel blocked or held back, unable to move or advance as you would like. But this apparent dead-end is an illusion. There is a way to proceed if you look for it and take action. You must break the barriers that seem to limit you. Do not permit yourself to be held back. Seek a new path and use it.

22. Grace: Youngest Son over Middle Daughter: mountain over fire.

Be gracious and accommodating toward others. Do not cause friction; "play the game," as they say. This is a time for diplomacy and caution. Follow rules, be very honest in your dealings, avoid upsetting others; in this way, you will avoid unnecessary problems.

23. Erosion: Youngest Son over Mother: mountain over earth.

Wait for the right moment; it isn't now. Be patient. Be calm. Do not rush. With the present situation, you will find that timing is everything. Wait for the correct moment—you will know it—and do not act until the time is right.

24. Return: Mother over Eldest Son: earth over thunder.

It is important at this time to get rid of the "deadwood" that is holding you back. You are giving too much energy to people or situations in your life that are not helping you—things that take your time, effort, or money but are not really your responsibility and from which you derive nothing but difficulty. Examine everything in your life, and ask yourself about each, "Is this helping me?" If it is not helping you, it is hurting you by taking time and energy away from what you really need to deal with, and it should be eliminated.

25. New Experience: Father over Eldest Son: heaven over thunder.

At this time, you must have a healthy sense of selfishness. You must identify and insist upon getting what you need from your situation. If you do not insist upon getting what you need from the situation, no one else will get it for you. Do not be patient. Do not assume that you will be taken care of. In this circumstance, it is your responsibility alone to pursue your needs, and you must do so, otherwise your efforts will be unrewarded.

26. Making Useful: Youngest Son over Father: mountain over heaven.

Make connections, schmooze. Get out among people and take an active part in society. Avoid the temptation to stay at home and withdraw from the community. You must be active, you must stay busy; if you do, then soon things will move your way.

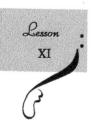

27. Nourishing: Youngest Son over Eldest Son: mountain over thunder.

"Don't sweat the small stuff." Prioritize your concerns and focus on the big ones. Pay attention to what matters most, and avoid trivialities and minor detours. A red herring never yet made anyone a good meal.

28. Excess: Youngest Daughter over Eldest Daughter: lake over wind.

There is much happening around you, and many changes will ensue. It is easy to be overwhelmed or distracted and forget what matters to you; do not allow this. Be at pains to keep your focus, no matter what the distractions. Maintaining a steady, sustained effort will pay off in the end.

29. The Abyss: Middle Son doubled: water of waters.

Be stubborn. Stick to your principles, do not allow others to sway you from what you feel is right. This is not the time to compromise. Though there are difficulties and it is tempting to give in, you must hold to your position against all attempts to move you; later you will be glad you did.

30. Consuming: Middle Daughter doubled: fire of fires.

Do not be overly ambitious; accept your limits, and work with what you have. It is easy to get carried away with enthusiasm and try to do too much at once. The potential of your situation is great, but it must be handled in a practical manner and cannot all be done at once. Focus on the small steps first, and you can take the big steps later. Try to take the big steps now and you will simply fall.

31. Attraction: Youngest Daughter over Youngest Son: lake over mountain.

It is a good time. Good fortune and happiness attend you. Pleasures abound. But do not allow your abundance to overwhelm your good sense. Be like the ant rather than the grasshopper, and make good use of this time, for it is transitory. Do not be caught unprepared when this pleasant time passes.

32. Endurance: Eldest Son over Eldest Daughter: thunder over wind.

Success will come through sustained effort. Be persistent, persevere. Although you face difficulties, do not lose faith in your plans and goals but pursue them despite opposition. Expect it to take a while, but patience and determination will see you to your success.

33. Retreat: Father over Youngest Son: heaven over mountain.

"Run away! Run away!" It is sometimes the case that the better part of valor is knowing when to get out of the fight. You're not going to win this battle, but you don't have to lose it either, and a prudent retreat now may allow you to win another day. Withdraw from confrontation, back away, and bide your time.

34. Greatness: Eldest Son over Father: thunder over heaven.

You are in a good situation. You know what you need to do and have all that you need to do it. Now you need only carry it out. Do not second-guess yourself, give in to fear, or complicate the matter with games of "what if"—just do what you know is needed, and you will have success. If you think you don't know you are wrong, do not miss the obvious.

35. Progress: Middle Daughter over Mother: fire over earth.

Spread the joy. Your situations are doing well and will only improve. Take advantage of this to improve situations around you. Be generous. Use your good fortune to build others up. Repair what is damaged and nurture what is growing. Later you will be glad of this, as you will be able to rely on those whom you have helped.

36. Repression: Mother over Middle Daughter: earth over fire.

Lock your door, go back to bed, and pull the covers up over your head. Don't do anything. Don't talk to anyone. Take no action. Whatever you are asking about, this would be a very, very bad time to do it. Be very

quiet. Do not call attention to yourself. Wait for a better time.

37. Family: Eldest Daughter over Middle Daughter: wind over fire.

It is imperative that you fulfill your obligations in this situation: loyalty, duty, and responsibility. Pay strict attention to these at this time. It is tempting to ignore what is required of you, but if you do, it will work against you later.

38. Opposition: Middle Daughter over Youngest Daughter: fire over lake.

Seek compromise. Though you are opposed, your opponents have no malice against you but rather honestly disagree with you. They are reasonable people and should be approached accordingly. Diplomacy, willingness to negotiate, the hand of friendship—these will serve you better than fighting against your opponents.

39. Blockage: Middle Son over Youngest Son: water over mountain.

You cannot go forward in the way you wish. You should back off and regroup. Rethink your plans; consider other ways of handling the situation. Seek help from others.

40. Liberation: Eldest Son over Middle Son: thunder over water.

The path seems blocked, but the obstacles can be overcome by bold, swift action. Do not delay and do not overthink; rather, take simple, quick steps to cut through whatever is holding you back. Remember Alexander and the GORDIAN KNOT. Do not worry about the staid opinions of others; here, audacity and courage will serve you best.

41. Decrease: Youngest Son over Youngest Daughter: mountain over lake.

It is easy to get carried away by enthusiasm and dissipate your energies at this time. This would not be good. Instead, make it a point to exercise self-discipline and restraint. Keep your mind on your goal, stay focused, and act prudently.

Lesson XI

42. Increase: Eldest Daughter over Eldest Son: wind over thunder.

It is said that success comes from seeing a need and filling it best. In the same spirit, it is said that to rule is to serve. In this situation, you will prosper by finding out what others want or need and being the one to help them get it. Be indispensable and you will never be dispensed with.

43. Determination: Youngest Daughter over Father: lake over heaven.

Be resolute and determined. Do not be turned aside from what you know you must do. An issue of principle is at stake. Pay no attention to other's actions, but focus on your own task at hand and see it through to completion, no matter the opposition. What needs doing must be done.

44. Encountering: Father over Eldest Daughter: heaven over wind.

Trust your own judgment. Others may want to help, but their advice is skewed or even deceptive. Make your own decision and stick to it, even if others criticize; they are in error, not you.

45. Gathering: Youngest Daughter supported by Mother: lake over earth.

This is a time to ask for assistance. Do not try to do it all yourself, for this will not prove practical; rather, seek help from others with more experience or greater strength.

46. Arising: Mother over Eldest Daughter: earth over wind.

Circumstances are changing quickly; all is in a state of flux. Be flexible. Adapt to changing situations. Be prepared to move quickly when opportunity arises, for the window of opportunity may be small. Do not hesitate to seek advice or aid if needed.

47. Difficulties: Youngest Daughter over Middle Son: lake over water.

Things are not going your way. You may feel held down and blocked.

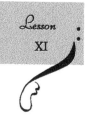

It is a difficult time, and you must draw on inner strength to persevere. Be patient. Hold back. Make the best of things and wait for better times.

48. The Wellspring: Middle Son over Eldest Daughter: water over wind.

Look to the past for guidance in present situations. The knowledge you need you already have, for you have faced similar things before. Reflect on past events and how you handled them. Adapt what worked then to the present situation; avoid repeating mistakes. Consider historical examples as well. The past is not always a guide to the future, but it is in this instance.

49. Change: Youngest Daughter over Middle Daughter: lake over fire.

Be open to new ideas. Seek new and innovative approaches. Situations are changing, and what worked in the past will not be enough for the future. Adapt to the times; do not fight against them.

50. The Cauldron: Middle Daughter over Elder Daughter: fire over wind.

Slow and steady development is called for here. Be cautious, circumspect. Avoid sudden changes. Stick to the tried and true, play it safe, and keep a low profile. Do not choose this time to take risks.

51. Arousing: Eldest Son doubled: thunder of thunders.

Sudden or unexpected developments may threaten to knock you off course. Do not allow yourself to be overwhelmed by them. Seek inner balance; remain stable in yourself, and you will be able to ride out the situation.

52. Introspection: The Youngest Son Doubled: mountain of mountains.

All seems calm and still. You have achieved your past goals and are in a good position. But do not be deceived: this is not the end of the road, but merely a resting place between journeys. Take this time to

Lesson
XI

reflect and consider where you wish to go from here. Make plans. Use this peaceful time wisely.

53. Gradual Progress: Eldest Daughter over Youngest Son: wind over mountain.

Move with slow but steady steps. Take things one at a time. Allow things time to develop. Avoid haste. Do not rush into things or make rash decisions; take your time. Be careful about giving guidance or advice at this time, and be sure you have considered matters thoroughly.

54. Subordinate: Eldest Son over Youngest Daughter: thunder over lake.

Be careful in your dealings with persons who have authority over you or who wield greater influence than yourself. Be diplomatic with superiors, avoid arguments or confrontations. Fulfill any obligations and avoid giving cause of criticism. This is a moment for placation of the powerful, for your own position is a vulnerable one.

55. Prosperity: Eldest Son over Middle Daughter: thunder over fire.

Rejoice. You are in a position of abundance and prosperity. Good luck and success attend you. All bodes well for you; go forward, therefore, in confidence.

56. Gypsy: Middle Daughter over Youngest Son: fire over mountain.

Change brings you into new and unknown circumstances. Be circumspect, get the lay of the land. Be patient and familiarize yourself with the new conditions you face before trying to act. Keep your eyes and ears large, your mouth small, and proceed with caution until you know all you need to know. Advance with care.

57. Penetration: Eldest Daughter doubled: wind of winds.

Move slowly but thoroughly. Be ubiquitous: surround rather than confront the situation. Expand by small steps but in all directions. Make yourself a factotum, and you cannot fail to have influence.

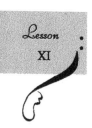

58. Joy: Youngest Daughter doubled: lake of lakes.

Listen to your heart. Success will follow happiness. If you do what you are drawn to do, all will go well. Forsake your own happiness for outside concerns and all will go badly.

59. Dispersion: Eldest Daughter over Middle Son: wind over water.

You must work with others to move forward; you will not succeed alone. Be cooperative, genial, unselfish. Generosity and flexibility will serve you well. Rigidity, self-centeredness, and hard-heartedness will bring disaster.

60. Limitation: Middle Son over Youngest Daughter: water over lake.

You can only do what you can do. You face many limitations and frustrations. You would like to clear them all and move forward, but that is not within your power. Work with what you've got. Change what you can change, accept what cannot be changed. Make the best of what you have.

61. Truthfulness: Eldest Daughter over Youngest Daughter: wind over lake.

Be true to yourself. Trust your inner guidance and walk your path. Do not allow external situations or other people to make you doubt yourself or reshape yourself to their wishes. You are not here to please them but to fulfill the purposes of your Higher Self and God/dess. Trust in yourself and walk on.

62. Precision: Eldest Son over Youngest Son: thunder over mountain.

Focus on details. Attend to the small things. Careful, precise effort brings success. This is not the time for major changes but for small yet specific adjustments. A small leak may sink a ship. The lack or imperfection of a needed part may wreck the whole.

63. After Completion: Middle Son over Middle Daughter: water over fire.

Success crowns your efforts, and this is wonderful. But the successful completion of a goal is not the end of life. A new goal always follows. Just because you have done well does not mean that you should stop trying. Instead, continue forward, building upon the success you have. This is not the time to rest on your laurels, as it were—it is not an ending but, in fact, a new beginning.

64. Before Completion: Middle Daughter over Middle Son: fire over water.

Your situation is almost at a successful conclusion; do not relax your efforts now. There is only a little way more to go, but though well in sight, it still remains to be done. The racer must not stop to nap before the finish line, even if tired. Soon enough you may rest, but not yet. Remain focused until the situation is complete, or you may grab failure from the jaws of victory.

• • • •
Feng Shui

The Yi Jing has been known and used in the West for a long time. But it is only one use of the ba gua. Another equally important art based on the ba gua has only recently become popular in the West. This is feng shui, or Chinese geomancy.

Today, feng shui is very commonly seen among non-Chinese, if not so commonly understood. Not long ago, there were few practitioners outside of Chinese communities. We have already learned about Wiccan geomancy in our First Degree lessons. Feng shui is very similar in that it seeks to align to the natural qualities of energy, or chi, as interpreted through direction.

Feng shui is not nearly as old as the Yi Jing. By comparison, it could almost be called a modern science, since hundreds of years separate the codification of the Yi Jing by King Wen and Duke Zhou and the codification of feng shui. The ideas on which feng shui is based, however, are very ancient.

The first mention of feng shui principles is from the time of Confucius. In the LI CHI (or Book of Rites, one of the Chinese Five Classics), it is remarked that the dead are always buried with head toward the north because the north was associated with yin energy, death, and the spirit world, and the south was associated with yang energy, life, and the world of the living.

Books on feng shui first appear during the Han Dynasty (993–1420 Aries/207 BC–AD 220), including the Chia Ching, or Book of Dwellings. Although feng shui was attacked by the philosopher WANG CH'UNG as early as 1320 Aries (AD 80), feng shui became increasingly popular.

Feng shui became codified and standardized over a long period stretching from the Three Kingdoms period (beginning 1379 Aries/AD 221) through the end of the Sung Dynasty (879 Pisces/AD 1279). During this period, the definitive texts of feng shui were written, including the Kuan Shih Ti Chih Meng (Master Kuan's Geomantic Indicator) and the Tsang Shu (Song of Geomancy), credited to the famous philosopher-poet Kuo P'u (who actually lived several centuries earlier).

As with most of our Second Degree subjects, feng shui is a huge and complicated art, having developed over many centuries. A full discourse on its principles is more than we can hope to do in this space. However, here we will attempt to briefly familiarize you with its basic ideas.

· · · ·

Chi

If you remember First Degree, Lesson 1, you will recall that one of the world's many names for psychic energy is chi. The principal concern of feng shui is the flow of chi. When chi flows freely, it creates a bright, uplifting, positively charged environment. When chi is blocked, it moves slowly and becomes negative energy, which can have an enervating effect on those who live in its vicinity.

One of the principal concerns of feng shui is the movement of chi in the open landscape and the auspicious placement of buildings relative to the landscape and to each other. We touched upon this in Lesson X when we discussed ley lines and will say no more about it here except that feng shui has complicated rules to determine auspicious locations.

Another principal concern of feng shui is the movement of chi within a building. This is the more common use for feng shui in the West, and it is this that we will focus on here.

As a general rule, chi is perceived as moving in gentle spirals, rather like wisps of smoke. Chi normally enters a house through the front door and flows through the house with a spiraling movement. Chi can also enter and exit through windows and secondary doors. The chi can be slowed down and blocked by a number of factors, including poorly placed walls and other architectural features, as well as clutter or inauspiciously placed furniture that block its flow, creating negative energy. A variety of tools are used to adjust the flow of chi, including mirrors, wind chimes, crystals, and miniature fountains.

☰ *Ch'ien* Heaven/Father Northwest Teachers/benefactors	☵ *K'an* Water/Moon–Middle Son North Career	☶ *Ken* Mountain/Younger Son Northeast Education and learning
☱ *Tui* Lake/Younger Daughter West Creativity		☳ *Chen* Thunder/Elder Son East Family and Health
☷ *K'un* Earth/Mother Southwest Love and marriage	☲ *Li* Fire/Sun–Middle Daughter South Fame and recognition	☴ *Sun* Wind/Elder Daughter Southeast Wealth and prosperity

The ba gua in feng shui

Lesson
XI

The Ba Gua in Feng Shui

The ba gua are used in feng shui as the quarters are used in Wicca: to determine what energies are in sympathy with which directions. In feng shui, it is believed that the rooms of a house should reflect the organization of the ba gua, as should the features of each individual room. Both buildings and rooms are preferably square, to emphasize stability and also to allow each ba gua equal space.

The North is ruled by K'an, the Middle Son. K'an is water: the depths of the sea and the moon. North is the place for career and business issues.

Northeast is ruled by Ken, the Younger Son. Ken is the lofty mountain: stillness and reflection. Northeast is the place for education and learning.

The East is ruled by Chen, the Elder Son. Chen is thunder: ferment and fertilization. East is the place of family and health.

The Southeast is ruled by Sun, the Elder Daughter. Sun is wind: gentle, expansive, and penetrating. Southeast is the place for things that pertain to wealth and prosperity.

The South is ruled by Li, the Middle Daughter. Li is fire and the sun: ardent, enthusiastic, and forceful. South is the place for issues of fame and recognition.

The Southwest is ruled by K'un, the Mother. K'un is the earth: stable and enduring, nurturing and sustaining. Southwest is the realm of love and marriage.

The West is ruled by Tui, the Youngest Daughter. Tui is the calm lake: happy, joyful, and well-balanced. West is the place for creativity and also for children.

The Northwest is ruled by Ch'ien, the Father. Ch'ien is the expansive heavens: creative, dynamic, and vital. Northwest is the area for issues dealing with teachers, friends, and benefactors.

By aligning to these energies, it is believed that one attunes to the natural focus of the universe and is thus assisted and carried forward by the universe's own natural flow. A chart of the ba gua as used in feng shui is on the opposite page.

. . . .

Exercises

Exercise 23 is an exercise you should do as part of your daily routine until you become proficient at it, while its variant, Exercise 24, is a technique you should use any time you feel the need. For me, this somewhat odd and incongruous technique is one of the most effective I have ever learned. Of course, like everything else, its effectiveness grows with practice.

When I was first taught this technique, I thought it was very weird, and I imagine

you will agree, but you can't argue with success.

Exercise 23

By now you should be fairly proficient at raising and directing beams of light from your crown chakra. Begin by going through your daily routine as you have been doing for Exercise 22, until you come to the point where you raise the beams of light. Before you raise the beams of light, first take a moment and think of something you wish to manifest. Start small; maybe you would like a favorite movie you haven't seen in a long time to play on TV sometime in the next few days. Maybe there is something you have lost and wish to find. Make sure it is something small that you believe can happen.

Make a brief incantation. I usually say the following (my favorite and trusty all-purpose standby):

"There is one power in the universe,
and I am a perfect manifestation
of that power. And as such, I will
(whatever you are manifesting)
Behold: I will it,
I draw it to me,
I manifest it ..."

Now, open your seven beams of light all at once; shoot them upwards like arrows or shooting stars. See the seven beams of red light soar upwards. Imagine your wish as some simple abstract form off in the astral, and aim the beams for it. Use the seven beams to grab the abstract image of your wish and pull it back to you and into your crown chakra.

Finish the incantation:

"Behold: I accept it,
I receive it,
and I give thanks for it.
With harm toward none,
so mote it be."

Now close your chakras, ground, and release as always.

Think no more about what you have manifested. Wait for it to happen, but do not worry about it. Usually it will show up fairly soon, but when not expected. If for some reason what you have asked for does not manifest, do not get discouraged—it most likely means that you need more practice. Practice makes perfect, as they say. Or it may be that some aspect of yourself has not accepted what you manifested, and that you should examine your feelings on the matter.

Do Exercise 23 as part of your daily routine only until you can do it easily; after that, use it only as needed.

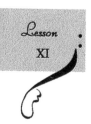

344

Exercise 24

Exercise 24 is the same as Exercise 23, except that it is a technique meant to be done wholly independently of your daily exercises.

Consequently, you will not begin with your normal routine of exercises. Instead, you will use the technique whenever you wish to do a quick manifestation.

Begin by focusing on what you wish to manifest.

Make an affirmation:

"There is one power in the universe,
and I am a perfect manifestation
of that power. And as such, I will
(whatever you are manifesting)
Behold: I will it,
I draw it to me,
I manifest it ..."

Now, open your seven beams of light and let them shoot upwards. Imagine the seven beams of red light speeding toward the abstract image of your wish. Grab the abstract image of your wish with the seven beams of light and pull it back to you, into your crown chakra.

Finish the incantation:

"Behold: I accept it,
I receive it,
and I give thanks for it.

With harm toward none,
so mote it be."

Then clear and release as always.

. . . .

Spell for Lesson XI
Crystal Web Ritual

The purpose of this ritual is to allow you to access the energies of the Crystal Web. The Crystal Web is an energetic construct created over the course of the last several decades. The web uses buried crystals and other stones to form a giant network, which can be used as a battery or to facilitate earth healing or spiritual communication.

First you will need to select a crystal. For the purposes of this ceremony, it should ideally be a clear quartz crystal, though this technique can be used with other crystals and stones at other times for other purposes.

The details of the stone are not terribly important, whether it is large or small, clear or cloudy, etc. What matters is that it feels right to you. Select a crystal that speaks to you. You may just have a knowing of what crystal is correct to use, or you may use the technique of running your hand slightly above a number of crystals and using the one that feels different from the others.

Of course, if you have only one crystal available to you to use, you should assume

that it is the right one for the job, since it is there.

In the event that you have tried but cannot get a quartz crystal, you should take it as a sign that you are meant to use another sort of stone for some reason, and select a stone from whatever may be available. The Goddess will make sure you get what is needed. Though we regard that it is best to use a quartz crystal, one must be sensitive to the will of Deity, and if Deity wishes you to use a different kind of stone and expresses this by an absence of available quartz crystals, then by all means use what Deity provides.

Now you will need a place to bury your crystal. The crystal must be buried in the earth, and ideally it should be a place that has special meaning for you. It is not necessary that the crystal be buried directly on a ley line; rather, the crystal will be used to form a remote link.

Dig a hole in which to bury your crystal; a garden trowel will prove an excellent instrument for this, but any digging tool may be used. Depending on the level of privacy, you may wish to use your athame, since this is a sacred act. The hole does not need to be large but should be somewhat deep so that the crystal will not be easily exposed by the elements or by digging animals. In this sense, the deeper the hole, the better.

Now you are ready for the actual ritual.

Dig your hole first so that this is done and ready.

Now cast a circle. Since you will be outdoors and may not be burying your crystal in a private place, you may want it to be a very simple circle. You can do it entirely in your head, imagining the circle around you, then silently calling the quarters and imagining them as pillars of white light. You may silently invoke Goddess and God.

Of course, if you are in a more private place or are comfortable being observed casting a circle, you may do the circle as elaborately as you choose.

Hold your crystal in both hands. Above the crystal, imagine a three-dimensional triangle of white light. Take a moment to imagine this fully. Then imagine the triangle spinning clockwise.

Become aware of your heart chakra. Imagine a ball of white light in the heart chakra, and when this is clear in your head, imagine sending a beam of green light from the heart chakra into the spinning triangle.

As the green light enters the triangle, it will change its shape, becoming a cube (still spinning clockwise). Imagine this transformation fully. Fill the cube with green light from your heart chakra.

Once the spinning cube is filled with green light, the flow will reverse, and green light will return from the cube to your heart. Imagine the green light filling your heart, then your chest, then your whole body, as well as the crystal held in your two hands. Let the crystal become full of this light so that it is glowing with green light and shining out in all directions, like a green sun.

Let the image of the spinning cube fade, but continue to imagine the crystal filled with green light. Place the crystal into its hole and cover it.

Place both hands directly over the now-covered hole and focus white light down into the earth and the buried crystal.

Now charge the crystal to link into the Crystal Web. This may be spoken aloud or done silently. You might say something like:

"O crystal, I charge you to link
into the Crystal Web, becoming
one with its energies. Through you
I gain access to the web, which
links my Correllian family."

Now imagine a beam of white light coming from the crystal and shooting off in one or another direction, underground; this is the crystal linking into the web. You may or may not be able to see what direction the beam goes in; this is all right, it is not imperative that you know just now. This will not be the only time you will use the crystal, and if you don't see exactly how

it links in this time, you may next time. If you are good at visualization, however, you may find that you see not only the link created by your own crystal, but perhaps the whole web itself.

Now that your crystal is linked, you are finished and should take down your circle, then clear and release.

To use this crystal in the future, follow these steps:

Imagine the buried crystal within a cube of white light. Imagine the cube spinning clockwise. Focus a beam of green light from your heart into the cube, and imagine it changing into a triangle, still spinning; the crystal will then be open and may be interacted with. When finished, allow the image to fade.

· · · ·

Glossary

Aeneid—The *Aeneid* is an epic poem composed by Publius Virgilius Maro (Virgil) at the urging of Caesar Augustus, which tells the story of the founding of Rome by Aeneas. Aeneas was a Prince of Troy, son of the goddess Venus by the mortal Anchises. When Troy fell, Aeneas managed to escape, carrying his aged father on his shoulders. The *Aeneid* tells the legend of his wanderings and eventual founding of the city of Rome. The poem is in twelve books/chapters, with many sub-plots, including a love affair

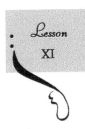

between Aeneas and Dido, founder and queen of Carthage (the historic Queen Elyssa). For the Romans, the poem took on a sacerdotal character similar to that of the *Iliad* and *Odyssey*, which were looked upon by Greco-Romans rather as Christians look upon the Bible.

bibliomancy—Bibliomancy is the art of divination by book. The most common form is to open a book randomly in the belief that whatever page you thus turn to has a message for you. Another variation is to close your eyes, open the book at random, and thrust your finger blindly on the page—the word or sentence thus indicated is the message or answer sought. Any book can be used for bibliomancy, but in the past, books such as the *Iliad*, *Odyssey*, and *Aenead*, or the Christian Bible, were commonly used for the purpose.

Fu Hsi—Fu Hsi is a Chinese culture hero/god. In early Chinese mythology, Fsu Hsi and his wife Nu Kua taught humankind all of the arts of civilization. Among many other things, Fu Hsi created the ba gua, which are so important in ancient Chinese culture. In some images, Fu Hsi is shown as a dignified gentleman in primitive clothing; in others, he is shown with a serpent's tale and wings, a kind of dragon-man.

Gordian knot—The Gordian knot was a knot created by the Phrygian King Gordias with the prediction that whoever could untie it would rule all of Asia. Many people attempted to untie the knot and failed. Alexander the Great, presented with the knot, drew his sword and cut it in half, thus untying it—and then went on to conquer all of Asia.

Kung Fu Tzu—Kung Fu Tzu, better known as Confucius, is one of the greatest philosophers of China and founder of the Confucian school of thought. Confucius was born Kung Chiu in the state of Lu in 649 Aries (551 BC) to a noble family who had recently fled from the state of Song and had fallen on hard financial times. Confucius's father, a District Commander in Lu, died when the boy was only three, but his mother worked hard to see that her children were educated and brought up well, despite their poverty. Confucius married at the age of nineteen and had one son and two daughters. Confucius had a number of jobs as a young man, but after his mother died in 674 Aries (527 BC), he settled into his career as a teacher. When Duke Zhao of Lu fled into exile after a disastrous war with a neighbor, the young Confucius accompanied him as a retainer, returning to Lu after the duke's death. Confucius

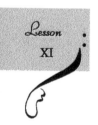

Lesson
XI

348

wanted very much to have an office in the government and declared that he would take pretty much anything he was given, but though he received occasional appointments he never really made a career in politics. He did receive a position as a ducal counselor around the age of fifty, but it was pretty much an empty title and he was not really consulted. But his fame as a teacher and philosopher grew. In his late fifties, Confucius left Lu to travel around China with his students, and much of his legacy is based on this period and the experiences he and his students had abroad. He returned to Lu at the age of sixty-seven and died there at age seventy-two, having outlived his son and several of his most loved students. The primary record of Confucius's teachings is the Annalects, composed by his students after his death. Confucius's teachings deal with virtue and right action, respect, and treating others decently. His ideas became almost universal in China, and indeed east Asia, and served as a basis for social interaction and good government.

Li Chi—The Li Chi, or "Book of Rites," is one of the Five Classics of Confucian thought. The Five Classics, or Wu Ching, include the I Ching (Book of Changes), the Shu Ching (Book of History), Shih Ching (Book of Poetry), the Ch'un Ch'iu (Spring and Autumn), and the Li Chi itself. The Li Chi is a collection of very ancient rites and ceremonies, said to have been compiled by Confucius himself, and was used as a moral guide in such matters.

missionaries—Religious missionaries are people who believe that they have a duty, a "mission," to spread their religion to others. Missionaries are usually thought of as being a Christian phenomenon, but in fact many religions have had and still have missionaries. Some missionaries are decent people who are actually trying to do good works and attract people to their religion by example, but others are aggressive and offensive proselytizers—that is, they try to coerce or force people into joining their religion. Some churches have organized missionary campaigns that send waves of missionaries into an area to try to force its conversion. In the 1400s Pisces (AD 1800s), missionaries were often used to help subdue non-European cultures as part of a strategy of conquest: the missionaries would convert large numbers of indigenous people to Christianity, teaching them to be pacifists and telling them that all Christians were nonviolent, honorable, and trustworthy; when troops from European colonial powers

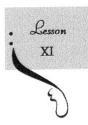

were subsequently sent in, these converts were completely unprepared for the reality of their situation, in which none of these values had meaning and all that they had been taught about Christianity proved to be false.

Nu Kua—Nu Kua is a Chinese creator goddess and the wife of Fu Hsi. In some stories, it was Nu Kua who created humankind, modeling them out of clay and baking them. Some the goddess was very careful with, and these became fine, upstanding people of high character. But the goddess became bored and began to hurry her work, so some of the later people came out very flawed as a result.

proodos and epistrophe—In Neoplatonic thought, proodos and epistrophe are the currents of the universe, roughly equivalent to yang and yin. Proodos is the advancing and epistrophe the turning-back. It was felt that proodos came forth from Spirit into matter, and reaching the fullest extent of matter became epistrophe, turning back and ascending to Spirit. Here we see that proodos is the active element, which like the God or yang energy advances into the physical as far as it can. Reaching the limit of physicality, it must turn back toward the spiritual Goddess/yin energy. There were and are different schools of thought and interpretations of proodos and epistrophe, but this is the basic principle.

quipus—Quipus comprise a system of notation used by the Incas in Peru. Quipus are made from string of various colors, knotted in special ways. The color of the string and the number and position of the knots have special meanings that enabled them to be "read" by special scribes. The quipu is among the most unique forms of "writing" ever created. Sadly, no one today can read them—although attempts are being made to decipher them. *Quipu* means "knot" in the Quechua language used by the Incas.

trigrams—The Chinese trigrams are symbols made up of three lines each—hence the name. In Chinese, they are termed ba gua or bagua. There are a total of eight ba gua: Chi'en/Heaven, K'un/Earth, Chen/Thunder, Sun/Wind, K'an/Water, Li/Fire, Ken/Mountain, and Tui/Lake. These eight trigrams are the basis of an extensive system of correspondences, much like that of the quarters in Wicca. The ba gua are important in feng shui and are the basis of the I Ching system of divination. The ba gua are often used as a symbol of Taoism, arranged around the yin/yang.

Virgil—Celebrated by the Romans as their greatest poet, Virgil also enjoyed a reputation as a great sage and sorcerer in later ages. Publius Virgilius Maro was born in Gallia Cisalpina, in northern Italy, on 15 October 1130 Aries (70 BC). Son of a wealthy Celtic family, Virgil received a top-rate education and became a man of letters, acquiring Roman citizenship in 1151 Aries (49 BC). Between 1158 Aries (42 BC) and 1163 Aries (37 BC), Virgil wrote a series of pastoral poems, known variously as the *Eclogues* or *Bucolics*. He also wrote the *Georgics*, an extensive treatise on agriculture. After the rise to power of Caesar Augustus, Virgil enjoyed imperial patronage and moved in court circles. Augustus pressed Virgil to write a Roman epic comparable to the Greek *Iliad* and *Odyssey*, which had a standing in Greco-Roman times comparable to the Bible for Christians. Virgil responded with the *Aeneid*, an epic about the founding of Rome by the Trojan Prince Aeneas. The poem was still unfinished at Virgil's death in 1181 Aries (19 BC), and the poet left orders for it to be destroyed—but the emperor intervened and had the *Aeneid* published. The poem became a classic, and the Roman public did, in fact, accept it as comparable to the *Iliad* and *Odyssey*, establishing Virgil with a reputation comparable to Homer's for many centuries thereafter.

Wang Ch'ung—The great Chinese philosopher Wang Ch'ung was born in China in 1227 Aries (AD 27) and died in 1300 Aries (AD 100). Wang Ch'ung was a Taoist but drew upon Confucian ideas as well in his philosphy. His primary works attacked what he saw as superstition—including feng shui. Wang Ch'ung taught that all things happen spontaneously: he believed that Deity does not take direct action in the physical world and that events happen from chance and not divine plan. He denied the idea of the soul and life after death. Wang Ch'ung also held that theories must be supported by experimentation and objective proof. He was never very well received in China, but his ideas were rediscovered and celebrated by Western rationalists long after his death. Wang Ch'ung is also known as Wang Chong.

Lesson
XII

Group Dynamics

We began our Second Degree studies with a commentary on the meaning and duties of the different degrees of clergy. It is only fitting that as we come to the end of Wicca 201, we return to this subject with a deeper discussion of the nature and duties of Second Degree clergy and the challenges you may face as a Second Degree cleric.

As we said at the beginning of these studies, the Second Degree priest/ess normally pursues a more focused role than First Degree priesthood. This is true for the solitary and especially true in the temple: while the First Degree cleric may assist in ritual and sometimes in teaching, perhaps acting as a MENTOR under Third Degree guidance, the Second Degree priest/ess is more often called upon to lead or take an important role in ritual, to take a specific job in the temple or shrine, and generally to take a more active and responsible role.

Where the First Degree tends to be quite general, the Second Degree priest/ess

often specializes their practice, concentrating on one or more skills in which they excel. Thus, a Second Degree may choose to become expert in herbalism, HERALDRY, psychic arts, community building, or any of many other subjects. Throughout the Second Degree lessons, we have been discussing various potential specialties at an introductory level. This is not to say that the Second Degree cleric always specializes, or that if a specialty is chosen that it should be pursued to the exclusion of other arts. A Witch should always make an effort to be well-rounded in their skills and interests. Nor is it expected that a Second Degree cleric should attempt to specialize at once. It may take quite a while to find a specialty, and once a specialty is chosen it may well be one of many.

In reading these lessons, you might assume that my own specialty is teaching, and that is true enough, but this only came after several years. My first specialty was theology, and then came ritual, and then I specialized in the psychic arts as well—all long before specializing in teaching. So specialization should not by any means be thought of as limiting oneself. Rather, it is the deeper study of specific skills.

For the Second Degree cleric following a solitary practice that is not part of a specific temple or shrine, specialization is the biggest potential difference from First Degree. It would be completely appropriate for a solitary Second Degree to become an expert in one or several areas and to enrich the tradition through their work in these areas either individually or as part of an order. We have a great need as a tradition for specialized work in many areas, including Pagan-oriented publication; event organizing; home and parochial schooling; community outreach; heraldry; liturgical artwork and skills such as metallurgy, glass-working, and lapidary; general and liturgical music, dance, and drama; and many others. Of course, in no case should a cleric become so specialized on one subject as to limit or exclude the full exercise of their skills. Ultimately, you should pursue deeper knowledge in all areas, not just one or two. But as we have said, issues of specialization have been dealt with throughout these lessons.

For temple and shrine clergy, however, Second Degree is a different matter. For temple clergy, the first order of business is always the smooth running of the temple itself. Second Degree status in a temple confers a certain amount of responsibility within the group, and often brings the cleric into increased contact with the wider Pagan community in a political context. We have not dealt with these issues so far, but this will be our focus now.

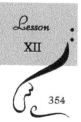

Temples,
Proto-Temples,
and Shrines

In this lesson, we will focus on temple structure, management, and procedure, and also on interaction, both as an individual cleric and as part of a temple or shrine with the wider world, Pagan and non-Pagan alike.

For the purposes of this lesson, we will, for the most part, make no distinction between a full temple, proto-temple, and a Witan shrine. However, let us first review exactly what a Witan shrine and proto-temple are.

A Witan shrine or proto-temple are temples-in-training, if you will. A Witan shrine is headed by a Witan shrine keeper, and the head of a proto-temple is a proto-temple head. Either one should be a Third Degree or a cleric under the imperium of a Third Degree sponsor. Witan shrines and proto-temples are considered probationary and have no representation on the Witan Council. If the Witan shrine successfully completes a probationary period of a minimum of one year, then it is eligible to be translated to proto-temple, which in turn has an additional probationary period of at least a year. After the successful completion of this second probationary year, the proto-temple becomes a full temple, and the head of the proto-temple becomes a temple head (if a Third Degree) or an acting temple head (if under imperium). Furthermore, only a fully seated temple head may represent a temple in the Witan Council.

The practice of asking all new temples to spend a probationary period before being accorded full temple status began as a response to the fact that running a temple is not as easy as it seems, and many people who wish to try it are not really suited for it. We believe in giving people every opportunity to serve the Goddess as she calls them, and we wanted a system flexible enough to allow prospective temples to form, even knowing that not all would succeed. The Witan shrine and proto-temple system allows time for the prospective temple to see if its members are comfortable in that role, and for both the prospective temple and the tradition to make sure that all will run smoothly.

We were inspired to create the Witan shrine after the collapse of two of our temples—both in their first year, though a few years apart—whose leadership proved unable to handle the pressures of running a full temple. At this time, the Witan shrine was also considered a proto-temple, and the total probationary time was only a year. Interestingly enough, and contrary to what many people might think, the temples that collapsed were not those run by people with less experience but were in

fact headed by experienced Third Degree clergy, who for the most part couldn't cope with the difficulties inherent in dealing with public and semi-public groups.

The Witan shrine and subsequent proto-temple status allows for such potential problems to come to light and hopefully be dealt with before full temple status is conferred. It is considered a bit of an embarrassment for a temple to collapse this way, but there is no embarrassment if a Witan shrine or proto-temple, after fulfilling its probation, does not go on to become a temple. There are several reasons why full temple status may not be conferred. The Witan shrine keeper may realize that the shrine is not ready to become a proto-temple or a proto-temple to become a full temple, or the tradition may feel the Witan shrine or proto-temple is not ready to take the next step forward. In either case, the Witan shrine or proto-temple that does not become a temple may either disband, request a second probationary period to address its problems and try again for temple status, or choose instead to become a formal or personal shrine.

In terms of structure and management, a Witan shrine or proto-temple is, for all intents and purposes, the same as a temple except for not having the title of temple head or acting temple head.

In the case of a formal shrine or a personal shrine, the structure is usually much simpler. A personal shrine, being in essence an expression of personal piety, usually has the shrine keeper as its only officer, though this need not necessarily be so. A formal shrine falls between the simplicity of the personal shrine and the complexity of the temple in its structure, depending on the purpose it was created for.

· · · ·

Temple Structure

As a general rule, the newer the temple, the simpler the structure. A small temple does not require many officers, and it is a mistake to appoint officers you don't need. A large and very active temple, on the other hand, may require a number of officers to facilitate its smooth running.

A new temple usually starts with just one officer, the temple head.

· · · ·

Temple Head

The most important officer in any temple is the temple head, who is the sole person responsible for the temple in the eyes of the tradition and who is chartered by the tradition specifically as temple head. Because the temple head is established by charter of the tradition, the temple head may not be changed except by charter of the tradition (this is discussed in greater detail below).

In most cases, the temple head will be either the chief priestess or chief priest,

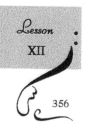

but in theory the temple head could be the chief director, if circumstances warrant.

In addition to running the temple, the temple head represents the temple in the Witan Council, which is the convocation of the tradition's temple heads, elders, officers, and other notables. The Witan is primarily an advisory body, without binding power, but issues are sometimes presented to it for a vote. In such a vote, only the fully seated head of a temple or their chosen proxy may wield the temple's vote.

As has been stated, one must be a Third Degree to be fully seated in the Witan (though in some cases an honorary Third Degree may be given to facilitate this). However, the tradition has a well-established practice of allowing First and Second Degree clerics to start temples under the imperium of a Third Degree sponsor, with the understanding that they must eventually achieve Third Degree status in their own right in order to become fully seated. People running temples under imperium in this way are called acting temple heads. An acting temple head may attend the Witan but does not become a voting member until being fully seated.

. . . .

Co-Head of Temple

The temple head may have a co-head, if they care to appoint one. Usually this would be the chief cleric of the opposite sex, but not necessarily. Appointing a co-head is entirely in the hands of the temple head, or in some cases (if the temple constitution specifies) the temple board of directors: they may appoint or dismiss a co-head of temple at will. This is because co-head of temple is an office considered internal to the temple and does not carry Witan seating. A co-head of temple may attend the Witan and may even address it, but only the head of the temple may be seated in the Witan and represent the temple with a vote.

The co-head of temple is considered to have equal standing with the acting head of a temple.

. . . .

Joint Head of Temple

A temple may also have a joint head, who has equal standing with the temple head. This is true for the Mother Temple and for Holy City Temple, as well as a few other temples. A joint head is a co-adjutant, sometimes appointed because of health issues or a possible geographical separation of the joint heads, or other duties which make it difficult for the temple head to fully fulfill their role.

As a general rule, the joint head structure is usually reserved for special circumstances and not necessarily encouraged. Like the temple head, a joint temple head is established by a charter from the tradition and assumes a role of responsibility

to the tradition for the smooth running of the temple.

A joint head of a temple has full status in the Witan, equal to a temple head, but the temple still has only one vote.

· · · ·

Chief Director

Other offices include chief director for the temple. All members of the board of directors may be described as directors, but one is given the office of chief director and the job of dealing with things like paperwork and legalities as needed. In many of our temples, at present, the temple head and chief director are the same person. However, it can be advantageous to separate the two jobs, since the skills that make for a good temple head and the skills that make for a good chief director are not necessarily likely to be held by the same person.

The chief director is appointed by the temple head or sometimes by the board of directors, depending upon the temple constitution.

· · · ·

Directors

As soon as possible, a temple should establish a board of directors. As a rule, the first directors will be appointed by the temple head. In some temples, this remains the case thereafter as well, while in other temples directors may be elected; this depends upon the temple constitution, which varies from one temple to another.

The board of directors is composed of three or more people, who usually hold other offices in the temple as well. The term *director* is usually only used to describe a member of the board of directors who holds no other office in the temple.

A common arrangement is for the board of directors to be composed of the temple head, co-head/joint-head (or pursuivant), and chief director. Where the acting head of a temple is under the imperium of a Third Degree sponsor, the sponsor would be considered a director of the temple as well.

How much power the directors hold depends upon the temple constitution. In some temples, the board of directors holds little or no real authority, existing basically to carry out the will of the temple head. In other temples, the board of directors may have considerable power and exercise it through voting.

As a rule, we discourage giving too much authority to the directors until the temple is well established, and encourage keeping the board of directors small. This avoids a number of potential problems. Having too many directors too soon is prone to destabilize a small or new temple, and may lead to personality-based in-fighting, which we abhor above all else. Nor should director status be given automatically with

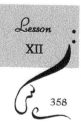

an office. If it is to be given with an office, then it should only be given after a probationary period has demonstrated that the officer is satisfactory in that role.

• • • •

Chief Cleric

The chief cleric is the highest-ranking priest or priestess in a temple.

Some temples have only one chief cleric, usually synonymous with the temple head. Other temples have both a chief priestess and a chief priest. In the latter case, one will most likely be the temple head, the other being simply chief priestess or chief priest—unless they should be appointed co-head of temple, which is by no means always the case.

It is perfectly respectable to simply be chief priest/ess.

When a temple has only one chief cleric, it is often because there are not enough experienced clergy of the opposite sex to have both a chief priestess and a chief priest, or at the other extreme it may be because there are too many experienced clergy of the opposite sex to fairly pick just one for the office. It is not uncommon for a temple to have considerably more members of one sex than the other. Also, if all the members of the temple are of the same sex (by choice or circumstance), then there will be only one chief priest/ess,

the next highest ranking being usually the pursuivant.

When there is only one chief cleric, for whatever reason, they will often appoint a pursuivant (maiden priestess/cadet priest), who will then be the second-ranking cleric for the temple.

We use the title chief priest/ess for this office in preference to high priest/ess because we consider all Third Degree priesthood to be high priesthood. An established temple sometimes may have a number of Third Degree high priest/esses in it; only one can be chief priestess and one chief priest.

• • • •

Pursuivant Priesthood

Another common office in a temple is that of pursuivant, normally called a maiden priestess or cadet priest. (As far as we know, the term *pursuivant* as a general term for maiden priestesses and cadet priests is one of those things that is pretty much uniquely Correllian.)

A pursuivant can be appointed by the temple head at any time they so choose. The pursuivant is often a person who is studying for the high priesthood (or has attained it) and who is expected to function as the second tier of temple clergy, after the chief priesthood.

There is no reason a large temple could not have several maiden priestesses/cadet priests, and it is also possible for a person

Lesson
XII

to be appointed to this office *pro tem* (that is, just for a specific event), which is what is commonly done by the Mother Temple at the lustration ceremonies.

. . . .

Other Offices

Other offices a temple might have include secretary, treasurer, guardian (usually ritual guardian, but may also deal with security issues when relevant), and herald (heralds are involved in making of regalia and ceremonial paraphernalia, and may also act as announcers and ushers at events). Secretary and treasurer are jobs usually filled by the temple head or chief director, but they need not be. In addition, other jobs may present themselves according to need.

As a rule, however, a small temple will not need all of these offices. Begin simply. I would advise against putting someone on the temple's board of directors simply because they have been given a temple office. After they have held the office for a while and done a good job, then maybe elevate them to director status.

. . . .

Changing Officers

As far as the tradition is concerned, the temple's officers are the temple's business and they may be filled and changed as the temple sees fit (usually specified in the temple's constitution or bylaws).

The exception to this is the temple head.

As stated above, temple heads are established by charter of the tradition and are viewed as the responsible party in a temple by the tradition. As far as the tradition is concerned, temple heads take precedence over boards of directors and temple officers. Temple heads cannot be voted out or otherwise removed by the board of directors, they can only be changed by charter.

One reason we take such a strong line on this is to avoid dissension in the temple. Sadly, it is sometimes the case that personal politics invade the sanctity of the temple, and personal ambition may sometimes lead to factionalism. If the office of temple head could be easily changed, then ambitious temple members might try to seize it through political means, which not only causes tremendous bad feeling but often splits or destroys the temple. We see this sort of behavior in many other Wiccan traditions. We will never permit it in the Correllian Tradition.

In the event that members of a temple cannot get along with each other or with the temple head, it is easy enough to either go to another Correllian temple or found a new Correllian temple themselves. This is always preferable to damaging the existing temple.

If it should come to pass that a temple head is accused of actual wrongdoing by

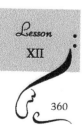

the temple members or the board of directors, as opposed to personal disputes, then the temple members should seek assistance from the office of the chancellor.

• • • •

Succession

In regards to succession, it is up to the temple head to choose their own heir and keep the tradition informed of their selection. However, this is usually not an issue until the temple is very well established. We also advise that temples follow the tradition's policy with regard to heirs and keep the succession secret, even from the proposed successor; that way, if the successor needs to be changed later, it can be done without hurt feelings. A temple head should never assume that their selected heir will not change over time. Any number of influences may bring this about, especially age. It is fine for a young temple head to have a young heir, but as time passes and age advances, an heir of the same age would be a potential problem.

If a temple head should die or leave office without an heir, the board of directors would probably be asked to select one.

Remember, too, that a temple head may leave office for reasons other than death. They may move to a new geographic area; they may move on to a higher office in the tradition, which may make actively heading a temple difficult; or they may choose

to retire in old age. These are all good reasons to have an heir chosen.

• • • •

What Temples Do

Of course you have a basic idea of what a temple does, even if you have never been to one. You know that temples are places of worship, and hold rituals for sabbats and esbats, and sometimes for other occasions as well. Temples are often the setting for rites of passage: Wiccanings, handfastings, or funerals. Also, many temples offer a variety of classes and study groups.

But there are also many other activities temples can engage in, and it is not uncommon for the Second Degree clergy to be involved in organizing or running such events. If you are in a temple or formal shrine, but also if you have a personal shrine, you may wish to consider some of the following ideas:

Social Nights

Many temples sponsor social nights. Social nights allow people to come together and get to know each other in a nonritual setting, which allows for a more casual interaction. Social nights are an excellent way to network with your local Pagan community and become acquainted with other nearby Pagans. Also, many temples use social nights as a forum for meeting and getting to know potential new members.

Social nights are commonly held in restaurants, coffee houses, or bars, depending upon the temperament of the organizers. To find a place to hold a social night, go to a variety of establishments and pick some that seem likely, then ask if they would allow you to hold your social night there. Be upfront about it being Pagan. You want to know from the outset if the establishment is Pagan-friendly or not. In most urban areas, this will not be an issue, although smaller towns may be hit or miss. Point out to the proprietor that social nights often attract a good number of people who can be expected to buy food or drink during the event, and who may become patrons of the establishment at other times as well.

Once you have a location, pick a date and let people know about it. Advertise the social night in the Pagan press, in local free papers, and on the Internet. The first couple may be small, but give it time to build.

As a rule, social nights are unstructured social time. You provide a place, and people mingle and get to know each other. It can be helpful, however, to prepare and casually introduce interesting topics of conversation if the evening gets off to a slow start.

Because social nights are very public events, they attract all sorts of people, not all of whom you will necessarily like, not all of whom will always like each other, and some of whom will be GOMERS (see below). Consequently, if you decide to be involved in running a social night, you should be prepared to be very tolerant of differing personalities and be willing to play peacekeeper if need be.

Book Clubs

Many temples also sponsor book clubs. Book clubs meet on a regular basis, usually monthly but sometimes weekly. At each meeting, the club agrees that each member will read a specific book, and at the following meeting the group discusses the book. This is an excellent way for temple members to get to know each other better as well as to investigate subjects in which they may have an interest but which the temple does not wish to teach, per se.

A book club might meet at the temple or it might be set up in a public place. You would go about this in the same manner as setting up a social night. Large bookstores with lounge areas are especially good places for holding book clubs and will often help advertise it on the premise that people who attend book clubs are people who will buy books as well.

Nature Walks

Another nice thing that a temple can sponsor in good weather is a nature walk. This can be held at a public park or on private

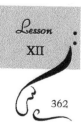

land. People assemble and walk together along a usually predetermined scenic route. If the temple has an herbalist, a discussion of wild plants encountered during the walk is especially entertaining.

A nature walk is also an excellent occasion for discussing respect for the earth and ways in which we can help our environment.

A nature walk would be advertised in the same way as a social night or a book club.

Nature Clean-ups

A nature clean-up is very similar to a nature walk, except that you choose a natural area that needs to be cleaned up. Beaches, forests, parks, even stretches of highway are perfect for nature clean-ups. Indeed, in many communities, it is possible to "adopt" a street or a stretch of road that the temple would periodically clean. A sign is usually posted at the area, crediting the group that has adopted it, which can be excellent and very positive publicity for your temple.

A nature clean-up might include just the members of the temple, or you might advertise it in the same manner as the other events we have discussed.

Fundraisers

There are a variety of fundraising activities a temple can take part in. A very com-

mon one is the making of craft items for sale at craft shows or rummage sales. This not only brings in funds, it can be a very enjoyable activity if the temple members are craft oriented. Indeed, even temple members who do not think of themselves as craft oriented may sometimes find that they really enjoy making craft items.

There are all sorts of craft items that temple members could make: beadwork, embroidery, ceramics, woodworking, or whatever the temple members have a talent and a taste for.

A temple can also sometimes raise funds through ticket sales to an event, such as psychic fairs, Witches' balls, expos, and plain old parties. But make sure you know your local legalities first, as some communities have unexpected rules about such things.

Witches' Balls

One of the best fundraisers is a Witches' ball. Witches' balls are normally held at Samhain and are usually costume parties. They may be held at a temple, but are more often held in rented rooms. Restaurants and bars, as well as community centers and sometimes parks, are good places to consider renting space for a Witches' ball. Hotels are also a good possibility but tend to be rather on the pricey side.

Temple members, local metaphysical bookstores, and sometimes general

bookstores can sell tickets for the event in return for a percentage (for the businesses). Tickets sold in advance should be slightly cheaper than tickets bought at the door; as a rule, tickets should not be expensive in any event. Advertising in local papers, the Pagan press, and online can get the word out.

At the ball itself, one or more temple members can act as emcee. Contests can make the evening more fun—costume contests, of course, but also novelty contests like Broom Riding (a perennial favorite at the Chicago Witches' ball)—give someone a broom and see what they can come up with for broom riding! Perhaps local metaphysical or other shops may be willing to donate door prizes.

Food should be simple; finger foods are best. As a rule, we advise against potlucking it. It is better to either provide food yourselves or hold the ball in a venue that sells food.

Witches' balls usually feature a Samhain ritual during the evening. We advise making it one of the first events and not offering alcoholic beverages until afterward. Of course, you may or may not want to feature alcohol at all, but that is up to you.

If your temple does decide to do a Witches' ball, it should start small. There's a lot to learn before you try to do a big one.

Witches' balls are a lot of work, but they are great publicity and a lot of fun, not to mention an excellent fundraiser.

• • • •

Some Important Things to Remember in a Temple

Avoid Defeatism

If there is anything a Wiccan should never be, it's defeatist. Wicca and magic are all about the infinite possibilities of what *can* be done, yet—sadly—many people who call themselves Wiccan limit themselves with worry and pessimism.

You are a perfect manifestation of the Goddess; the Goddess is within you. Therefore, all things are possible for you. Granted, we sometimes have to find the way to make the possible happen, but that is why we study magic.

Of course, we are all human, and as such, we sometimes lose sight of this. Worry, depression, fear—these come into our lives sometimes, and it is only natural. But as Wiccans, we should know better than to give in to them.

Nothing makes a thing impossible faster than believing that you can't do it. Maybe it can't be done in the way that you first think, but nothing is impossible for the Witch.

Why do I need to tell you this?

Sadly, many people in the Pagan community forget this. The Pagan community is notorious for its "poverty consciousness" and for feeling persecuted and powerless. Those Pagans who feel poor and powerless are often very annoyed with us Pagans who don't. When faced with optimism and confidence, they usually try to attack it. This is because they have often wrapped a lot of their ego around the idea of being powerless and feel threatened by the idea that the world just might be a good place after all.

Yet how can we be manifestations of the Goddess, skilled in magic, and be powerless? The Correllian answer is that a Witch is never powerless. Correllians have no fear because we know the Goddess is with us, within us. This can be very annoying to others who do not have faith in themselves or an equal faith in the Goddess.

Yes, a Witch may be poor, or have problems, or even be persecuted, but these are not limitations so much as challenges we must rise to. This is why we study magic, why we meditate and pray, so that we may overcome such things.

So if someone tells you "It can't be done" or "That could never work" or "The world is out to get you," *do not listen to them!* Listen to the Goddess instead. She loves you.

Avoid Spoilers and Gomers

This is closely related to the previous topic. In working with a temple, you will often find people who have problems. Sometimes you can help these people, but sadly this is not as often the case as one might wish.

All people, of course, have problems and idiosyncrasies. We wouldn't be people without them. And an enlightened person can deal with most idiosyncrasies, as long as they don't hurt anyone.

But there are two types of people whom one may encounter in a temple, and definitely in the wider Pagan community, who do tremendous harm. These are spoilers and gomers.

Spoilers are people who just cannot stand to see other people succeed. They may pose as friends and may even believe it themselves. But they will tear down everything you try to do. They will shoot down every idea, make problems where there are none, and generally be obstructionists, often while appearing to be backing the temple.

In the Pagan community, spoilers usually come in one of three types: the pessimist, the pedant, and the poohbah. The pessimist is completely defeatist, sees the world as a very unfriendly place, and will try to make everyone around them feel that way too. Often the pessimist is a conspiracy lover (though not all conspiracy lovers are pessimists) and may use "The Government," "The Great Secret Council," or "The Evil Space Aliens" as excuses to never attempt anything. The pessimist

cannot stand to see anything productive done because if a project were to succeed, it would challenge their self-image and view of the world.

The pedant, on the other hand, will try to stop others from doing potentially positive things by bringing up every possible objection they can about imperfect details. They will tell you that nothing should ever be done unless it is absolutely perfect and will look for any flaw to attack in the hopes of preventing any sort of action or progress. This is not caution or troubleshooting, both of which can be very wise, but is a political tactic usually aimed at maintaining a status quo in which the pedant has an interest.

But the worst kind of spoiler is the poohbah. The poohbah is the one who thinks they are the only one who should ever do anything. Some people just are this way. They think only they are smart or talented or just plain privileged enough to initiate any action. They will attack anyone who tries to do something independent of them. The favorite weapon of the poohbah in the Pagan community is gossip. They attack those who displease them with lies and innuendo, always behind the subject's back. You should never deal with these people, and above all, never listen to them.

You should be extremely careful of anyone who exhibits any of these characteristics, and as a rule, the farther you stay from them, the happier you will be. Granted, you may have to deal with them in the community, and you should always try to be civil in such cases, but the less you have to do with them, the better.

And then we have our friend the gomer. For me, the gomer is the hardest. A gomer is a person who appears to need and want help, and as spiritual people it is our natural inclination to give that help. But what makes a gomer a gomer is that while they ask for help (and often ask, and ask, and ask), they won't really take it. But they will take all the physical aid you can give them. A gomer can drain a temple's resources very quickly, but it never seems to help them because they refuse to actually address the causes of their problems.

When you are dealing with a gomer, you will often find that you are working much harder to solve their problems than they are.

My advice on gomers is this: give them a chance. Help them once. Help them twice. Even three times. But don't do more than that unless you see them actually improving their circumstance. Though sad and sometimes heart-wrenching in their plight, a gomer can eat a nice person alive with their unending and unnecessary needs.

Avoid In-fighting

Finally, the most important thing to remember about the tradition and its temples is that we are a family. Because of this, we must make every effort to support each other. This does not mean that we must always like each other or always get along with each other; members of a family don't always get along. But it does mean that while we may disagree, even argue, our bond of loyalty to each other must remain paramount.

Do you have to like everything a fellow Correllian does? Of course not. But we must respect each other's right to differing opinions and working styles.

One of the things most frowned upon in the tradition is in-fighting. We may sometimes find ourselves engaged in fights outside of the tradition, but within the tradition we must do everything possible to stick together.

Members of the tradition or any of its temples may from time to time disagree, even vehemently. Disagreement is natural, and it is useful because it exposes and allows the resolution of problems, which can sometimes be addressed in no other way. But we must never allow such disagreements to be more important than our common bond. Disagreements, even arguments, are common in families, yet in healthy families even serious arguments

do not disrupt the bond of love that holds the family together. It is even so in the tradition.

Whenever possible, we seek to resolve our disputes in a manner that preserves above all our common bond of love and loyalty to each other.

In this, we differ from many other Wiccan traditions, which as a rule have no way to handle disagreement.

Consequently, when disagreement arises, as it naturally does any time two or more humans work together for any length of time, it often leads to dire circumstances such as gossip and RUMOR MILLS, and ultimately the scourge of WITCH WARS. These circumstances we Correllians try to avoid at all costs.

If it should come to pass that a disagreement cannot be resolved between the disputing parties, then they must either agree to disagree and work separately thereafter or they should seek ARBITRATION from a learned high priest/ess. It is perfectly permissible for two Correllian clerics to have a serious disagreement that prohibits them from working together, providing it does not disrupt their work otherwise, but it is not permissible for them to permit their disagreement to disrupt the SERENITY OF THE TRADITION.

If it should come to pass that actual wrongdoing is involved, as opposed to a personal disagreement, then it should be

brought to the attention of the tradition leadership, who will appoint a DEEMSTER or a deemster's commission to look into the situation.

. . . .

Some Things to Remember When Dealing with Other Pagans

Here we have talked about some of the bad things that you should be careful to avoid. Now let us talk about some of the good things that you can do to get the most out of the Pagan community.

Despite the problems we have talked about, most people in the Pagan community are good, positive, highly spiritual people—a joy to know and a pleasure to work with. Here are some things that will help you to interact with them in the most effective ways.

Modesty

Whenever you meet new people, especially in the Pagan community but also from the outside, it pays to be polite and modest. Don't walk in the door and start listing your accomplishments. Get to know people first, and then let them find out about you in a natural manner. This is infinitely more successful in making friends.

As a rule, I have usually made it a practice when meeting new people to try to find out as much as I can about them and their interests. This is always good, but especially so when there is a political aspect to the situation, as there often is when leadership from two temples deal with each other. I try to get the lay of the land, so to speak, before jumping in; that way, I am less likely to be surprised. I tell them about myself when they ask or if it is appropriate to the conversation. As a rule, I understate rather than overstate things I have done.

One of the best things about modesty is that it allows you to get a clearer picture of the other person. If they are arrogant or rude, you will find out.

Respect for Others' Achievements

You should always assume and will usually be right that whatever someone has they have worked for. Whether it seems like much or little to you, it is important to them. Be respectful.

If you know that they are a Third Degree or have reason to think that they are (such as their heading a temple), be respectful. Don't go overboard, but treat them as you would any person you respect. Third Degrees are often called Lady or Lord, and if you see that this is the custom in a given temple, you should follow it.

If you go to an event someone is hosting, always be complimentary and pleasant. Even if it is not a very good event, they have probably worked very hard on it.

And above all, if you are in someone else's temple, especially if it is a temple from another tradition, remember that you are in effect an ambassador of the Correllian Tradition, and behave as graciously as possible.

Even if they are not gracious, you should still be as gracious as possible. This is a sign of self-confidence and integrity.

This is not so important for a First Degree, but remember that a Second Degree is a higher estate and a position of some responsibility, so people will look at you differently and have higher expectations.

Remember, You Aren't Going to Like Everyone You Meet

Not only will you not like everyone you meet, but you shouldn't expect to. People are people, and they come in all kinds. Just because someone may not make a good impression doesn't mean that they are necessarily a bad person. Do not mistake a personality clash for wrongdoing. And do not let this discourage you; there will be personality differences in every community. If you let that stop you from doing things, you will not be doing many things.

Avoid Gossip

Gossip is the bane of the Pagan community. We have spoken about spoilers above. Gossip is their favorite tactic. Because Pagans often have limited contact with each other, gossip is easily spread but hard to ascertain the truth of. This creates and sustains hard feelings and makes it needlessly difficult for people in the Pagan community to pull together when the need arises.

One reason gossip is so rife in the Pagan community is that people who prey on our community use it as cover. Sadly, we do have people in our community who prey on the weak and take terrible advantage of the foolish. By keeping all manner of outlandish rumors flying around all the time, it is easy for them to dismiss accusations of their own wrongdoing as being just rumors—personal dislike rather than serious issues.

We advise avoiding all gossip. It is best not to listen to it, but definitely don't spread it. Nothing hurts our community more than this.

Be Aware of Politics

If you are a solitary Second Degree cleric this is not so much the case, but if you are a Second Degree priest/ess in a temple, and especially if you are part of your temple leadership, it is important to realize that yours is a political position. At events and in networking, you must be mindful of the fact that people are not always what they seem. There are deep divisions between certain Wiccan traditions, and this is not something to be naïve about. You should

Lesson
XII

take people as you find them, but be aware that there may be deeper dimensions involved than appear on the surface. This is especially true in dealing with people who are in a position of leadership.

Try to get a feel for the politics of your local community. Then steer clear of them. Getting bogged down in this nonsense can only hurt you and your temple.

Within the Correllian Tradition, we frown on this kind of politics. Because of this, Correllians sometimes assume that all traditions do. Sadly, it is not always the case. Most Pagans, including most Pagan leadership, are great people—but not all. So keep an eye open for the bad apples, and do not get caught in their games.

. . . .

Some Things to Remember When Dealing with the Wider World

We have talked a bit about things to remember in dealing with the Pagan community—but how about the wider community? Some simple tips may help you to interact more successfully with non-Pagan organizations.

Be Credible

When you are dealing with the wider community, especially government or interfaith organizations, dress and act well. Be respectful, polite, and timely. Do not overwhelm them with eccentricity; they know you are Pagan, they want to see that you are also decent people. Or as my friend Novalla once put it, "Wicca is sensational, therefore I don't have to be a sensationalist."

Do Your Research

If you are looking to be involved in an organization, find out as much about that organization as possible before you contact them. That way you will show yourself to be a competent and knowledgeable person.

If you are accepted into such an organization, be helpful but not pushy. Assist them where they need assistance. If what they need is not what you want to do, then perhaps it is not the right place for you.

Making Complaints

If you encounter something that upsets you (in the media, for example) and wish to make a complaint, make sure you know the whole story first. Do not run off half-cocked. If after researching the matter you are still upset and feel the need to do something (write a letter, make a phone call, picket), do not do so in an emotional manner. Wait until you cool down and make your argument in a thorough and credible manner. You will be much more likely to succeed this way than by venting your anger.

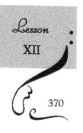

Avoid Christian Bashing

Some Pagans love to bash Christians. This is never a good idea, especially in front of Christians. For one thing, mainstream Christians are not our problem; radical right-wing Christians are. Most mainstream Christians are curious and friendly toward us once they have some idea of who and what we are. But lumping all Christians together and bashing them makes a really bad impression on the friendly Christians.

Beware of Labels

Labeling can be highly damaging to a person. Society marginalizes Pagans with labels that imply illegitimacy to our faith. Often we do not realize which labels are damaging.

For example, are we an alternative religion? If we are an alternative religion, it implies that another religion is more normal, more acceptable than ours. That view is fine for those who follow that religion, but we must not ourselves endorse it. We are not an alternative religion to ourselves and must not use this term. We follow our religion because it is right for us, not because we reject another religion and need an alternative to it.

Another very damaging term is *Neopagan*. Whoever hung the term *Neopagan* around our necks did us tremendous dam-

age. *Neopagan* makes a division between traditional Pagans and modern Pagans, cutting us off from our past and our natural allies. But if there were any way to add to the bad feeling that many Judeo-Christians have for the word *Pagan*, putting "Neo" in front of it is surely the way. Scholars may think of *Neo* in terms of Neo-Platonism and Neo-Confucianism, but ordinary people (who are by far the majority) do not. For most people, the term *Neo* is exclusively associated with negative groups: Neo-Nazis, Neo-Fascists, etc. Popular culture does not have a single positive connotation for "Neo" that I can think of.

So, not only because we don't approve of making unnecessary divisions between Pagan religions, and because we are of a familial origin, but because the term just plain doesn't help us, the Correllian Tradition very strongly frowns on the term *Neopagan*. We are not Neopagans, we are Pagans, and we seek to overcome the barriers between Pagans, not make new ones.

Remember Always That You Are An Ambassador of the Tradition

I know we said this already, but we can't say it enough. People will judge your temple and your tradition by your behavior, so set a good example.

In saying these things, we do not mean to overwhelm you or to imply that we expect a superhuman effort. We are all people. We all act foolishly or even badly sometimes, and we all make mistakes. But by keeping these things in mind, you will find that you can sometimes avoid pitfalls that others before you have made.

We hope that you have enjoyed Wicca 201 and will continue in your Second Degree studies. May the blessing be upon you!

. . . .

Spell for Lesson XII
Soul Retrieval

In this spell, we will be dealing with an important technique of deep healing: soul retrieval. Working with this technique will be a great help in moving forward and in deepening your personal practice.

The idea behind soul retrieval is that parts of our soul become caught, or "lost," because of strong emotions or traumatic experiences, and must be "retrieved" in order for us to be whole again. A better way to explain this is that when we go through a traumatic experience, a part of our consciousness becomes fixated on it and cannot move forward until it is dealt with; that part of our energy is "blocked," its natural flow interrupted, and its growth halted.

This is the same thing that happens to spirits who are caught between the worlds and unable to move on to the Otherworld, except on a smaller scale. An energetic attachment has been formed to an experience, which becomes a blockage because it is unresolved. Part of the self is "lost" because that part, attached to the past trauma, is unable to move forward. Because it is caught in a past trauma, it cannot be in the now.

Everyone has blockages of this nature, some more than others. Some people are so blocked in this way that very little of their consciousness is able to be in the present.

These blockages form as a natural result of our experiences in the physical world, and we must make an effort to heal them and to free ourselves from their effects.

The technique of soul retrieval is a very powerful way to free the blocked parts of the soul.

As a First Degree priest/ess, you should recognize this technique, as you will have seen it before. However, what you may not realize is that it can and should be used as often as needed. It can be used to heal blockages caused by events, and also emotions whose exact causes you may not know. It can even be used to heal outmoded beliefs. The process is the same for each, and it is simple enough.

You will need to be in a comfortable position.

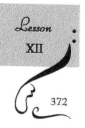

Clear and release before you begin, and again when you finish.

Imagine a ball of clear white light in your heart chakra. See this light as clear and strong and beautiful, filled with peace and love. This is the light of Spirit—the Goddess.

Let the white light expand outward from your heart chakra, filling your chest, expanding through your shoulders and abdomen, down into your arms and legs, and up into your head, so that you are filled with the white light of the Goddess.

Let the light move within you. Feel its strength and peace.

Now imagine the light expanding beyond your body, so that it surrounds as well as fills you. See the light form a circle around you, so that you are within a ball of white light. Imagine yourself floating weightless within the ball, supported gently by the light.

Now imagine the ball of light raising up, carrying your consciousness with it, but leaving your body behind.

Now float up through the ceiling, through the roof, and out into the sky. Imagine yourself floating among the clouds, gently buoyed by the light.

Let your soul float. Imagine yourself gently carried as if by the hand of Spirit. Imagine yourself floating through the atmosphere, out into the darkness of space.

See the stars shining around you as you float farther and farther out.

At length, you come to rest. Before you, you see the Goddess herself.

Have no preconceptions as to her appearance, but let her reveal herself to you in whatever manner is best.

Give greetings to the Goddess, and listen to see if she answers you. She may or may not.

Tell the Goddess that you are here for healing.

Now take a moment and think about what it is that you wish to have healed. This can be one thing or several. It can be the effects of a specific event or it can be an emotion, belief, or behavior that you wish to heal.

Now that you have made clear what you wish the Goddess to heal, think about all the things that are attached to it—the feelings, fears, beliefs, perceived limitations, everything that is connected to what is to be healed. Tell these, too, to the Goddess.

Do your best, but don't worry about whether you have thought of everything. Your Higher Self will put in your mind the things that need to be addressed at this time.

Now ask the Goddess to give you healing for all of these things.

Imagine a shower of golden light coming down on you from above, entering through the top of your head and washing

through you. Let it continue as long as it needs to. Tell yourself:

"I allow this healing,
I invite this healing,
I welcome this healing."

When the shower of golden light has finished, you are ready to continue.

It is not enough to receive the healing. You must also accept the healing.

Ask the Goddess to help you to have the acceptance of this healing.

Imagine the acceptance washing through you like a wave of energy, entering through the top of your head and passing through you. This is the power of the Goddess, helping you to fully accept the healing.

And, finally, you must integrate the healing and the acceptance into your being.

Ask the Goddess to help you to make this integration.

Imagine the integration pouring into your heart chakra like water pouring into a drain. Let this process continue as long as is necessary.

You have now had your healing, but you are not done.

Imagine all of the burdens you have carried because of that which has been healed. Imagine these burdens as packages, logs, or bricks, or in any other form that will symbolize burden for you. Imag-

ine taking these burdens out of your body and laying them before the Goddess. Dig as deeply as possible, and rid yourself of as many burdens as you can. You may find that there are more burdens appearing before the Goddess than you are aware of placing there—these are burdens that are connected to these things but of which you have no conscious knowledge.

Now ask the Goddess to take the burdens from you. Imagine the burdens glowing with purple light, becoming engulfed with the purple light, then disappearing. Sometimes this will appear as purple flame.

Thank the Goddess.

Now you must practice forgiveness. This can be the most difficult part of the ceremony, but it is the most important. This is you releasing what has held you back.

Begin by making a formal forgiving of every person who has anything whatsoever to do with what has been healed. Forgive them one at a time, and then forgive any others who do not come to mind or whom you are not conscious of. Now, forgive all of the circumstances and situations that pertain to what has been healed. Forgive, also, any actions of your own that have contributed in any way to any blockage you may have carried.

By practicing forgiveness, you are releasing any anger or fear that you may

have carried, and opening the blockages that come from these.

Do not forget to forgive yourself. Often it is ourselves whom we have blamed most and been most angry at.

And finally, forgive Deity. Forgive Deity in all of Deity's many forms, for any anger which you have harbored against her.

Ask the Goddess to help you make these forgivenesses as deep and complete as possible.

Now ask the Goddess to return to you the parts of yourself that have been lost because of these issues. Trauma, pain, anger—these cause us to cut ourselves off from parts of ourself, to "block" our own energy.

Imagine Goddess returning these lost parts of yourself to you. See them as glowing shapes of light that come into your body and return to their proper places.

Now ask the Goddess to give you healing for these lost parts of yourself. Imagine a golden light again raining down on you, passing through you, healing the lost parts.

Now ask the Goddess to help you have the acceptance of the healing of the lost parts of yourself. Imagine a wave of energy passing through you, helping you to accept.

And, finally, ask the Goddess to help you have the integration of the healing of the lost parts of yourself. Imagine the integration draining into your heart chakra.

Now thank the Goddess.

Finally, ask the Goddess if she has anything further to tell you. She may or may not choose to tell you something more at this time. If she does, the message may come in words, or she may show you a message in symbols. However she responds, thank her.

Now return to your body. Settle back into yourself and into the here and now. Cleanse and release all excess energy. You have completed your soul retrieval.

. . . .

Glossary

arbitration—Arbitration is the official or semi-official intervention of a third party to bring about resolution in a dispute that may otherwise spiral out of control. Arbitration of disputes between members of a temple is often necessary in order to prevent the dispute from disrupting the temple's operations. Such arbitration is usually carried out either by the temple head or by an outside party, such as a deemster appointed by the tradition for this purpose. Disputes between temples also sometimes require arbitration. In the Correllian Tradition, arbitration between temples is usually carried out by a deemster.

Lesson XII

375

deemster—A deemster is an investigator or a judge appointed by the tradition to resolve a dispute or allegation, or to oversee a process such as a temple making. A deemster may either be appointed for a specific duty or length of time, after the fulfillment of which they cease to be a deemster, or it may be an office of indefinite duration. Deemsters may be black handed (so called because of the sigil of the deemster's order) or red handed. A red-handed deemster is one who is empowered to render a judgment on their own authority, as opposed to black-handed deemsters, who can only investigate and advise. The term *deemster* is of Manx origin and means "one who deems" or makes judgment.

gomers—A gomer is a seemingly innocuous person who just needs a "little help." The distinctive feature of the gomer, however, is that no matter how much help is given, their problem is either never solved or immediately is replaced by another similar problem. The reality is that the gomer uses their apparently real problems as tools to structure their life and avoid deeper issues; consequently, they can never actually allow the problems to be solved. This is usually subconscious. The gomer readily asks for and accepts help but will not apply it or sabatoges it so that the problems can never, in fact, be resolved, which can take tremendous amounts of time, effort, and resources from those who try to help them. Often the gomer will experience the same problem again, and again, and again, because they are, in fact, using it to give shape to their lives. The presence of a gomer can seriously destabilize a temple or group. The term *gomer* originates in medical slang and is an acronym for "get out of my emergency room."

heraldry—Heraldry is the use of distinctive symbols for purposes of personal or group identification. Many different groups, including cultures, nations, religions, and private groups, have developed systems of heraldry to help them identify themselves and their members. The most famous type of heraldry, from which the term originates, is the European system of personal arms, developed by the old Knightly aristocracy. Many cultures the world over have used heraldry in one way or another, with Egyptian Nome heraldry being among the earliest examples. In the Correllian Tradition, heraldry is used in a variety of ways, most notably the distinctive sigils used to identify temples and orders, and also distinctive sigils used by individual members of the Witan Council.

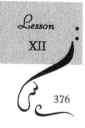

mentor—In the Correllian Tradition, a mentor is a peer counselor who assists with the learning process. Traditionally, only a Third Degree is allowed to teach and initiate as such, but a person of any degree may mentor—that is to say, help guide a student through the material, toward possible self-initiation. In practice, mentoring has displaced the older system of teaching.

rumor mills—A rumor mill is an informal and often shadowy system of people or groups who repeat or manufacture rumors. Often this is done as a form of entertainment, but equally often it is done for political advantage. Rumor mills exert tremendous power in the real-time Pagan community, and a great deal of politics is done by rumor. Because the rumor mills are essentially anonymous, the rumors spread cannot be easily proven or disproven, nor can the authors of false rumors be held in any way accountable, as they cannot usually be identified. This system allows for the easy dissemination of tremendous distortions of actual events, as well as the manufacture of outright lies in the pursuit of political advantage.

serenity of the tradition—The "serenity of the tradition" is the desired state of spirituality and civility that should characterize the tradition and the dealings of its members, especially internally. To disrupt the serenity of the tradition is to introduce contention or rancor, especially for political reasons. The Correllian Tradition values its serenity highly and has had a policy of ejecting those who violate it, especially anyone who attempts to start a Witch war within the tradition itself.

Witch wars—Witch wars are highly acrimonious political disputes between individuals, temples, or even entire traditions, which are identified by character assassination, politically motivated rumor-spreading, and a high level of bitter invective. Usually Witch wars arise out of personality conflicts and occasionally doctrinal differences, but rarely do they arise from anything that justifies the level of hyperbole with which they are prosecuted. As a rule, Witch wars tend to leave a great deal of bitterness and disillusion in their wake, and they often destroy one or both sides of the conflict. Witch wars are perhaps the greatest scourge of the Pagan community.

Lesson
XII

377

Well, here we are: the end of the book. In preparing the Second Degree lessons, it was my intention to give the student as wide an introduction as possible to the various arts employed by the Second Degree priesthood. Of course, this knowledge is only a beginning and must be built upon by personal practice, deeper understanding, and further study. These lessons give you a basic framework upon which to build further.

Not every Second Degree cleric will practice all of these arts on an ongoing basis, or even necessarily any of them. The Second Degree vocation is that of practical application of knowledge, which can take any number of forms in practice.

The Second Degree cleric may, of course, pursue their vocation as a solitary deepening of personal practice. However, within the temple and shrine setting, as well as the wider tradition structure, the Second Degrees do much of the practical work. For this reason, it is not uncommon for a Second Degree to specialize their

Conclusion

vocation in one or more areas, such as ritual, theology, or clerical counseling.

In Correllian terms, the practice of clerical counseling is limited to the practice of the psychic arts and the interpretation of theology, and it should never be confused with psychological counseling, which is not within our oeuvre. If one were to seek clerical counseling from a Correllian, one would expect to receive a tarot reading, an astrological consultation, a spell—or something along these lines. This is why the psychic arts are so heavily accented in the Second Degree lessons; they are an important aspect of the vocation for many Second Degree priesthood.

. . . .

Initiation

As is the case with First Degree priesthood, just because you have undertaken the study of these materials does not mean you are in any way obligated to seek Second Degree initiation; quite the contrary. It is perfectly all right to study this material for knowledge alone, and even though many people study these materials successfully, they may choose not to pursue the higher degrees of priesthood.

If, however, you do feel that you would like to pursue Second Degree initiation, please remember that it is a serious commitment—not so much a commitment to the Correllian Tradition (though it involves that) but a commitment to yourself. Do not do it thinking it is a meaningless ceremony or an empty rank, for it will work actual changes in your life, as all initiations do. Indeed, the Second Degree initiation is famous for bringing unresolved issues to the surface, where they must be dealt with.

We began these lessons with a discussion of the courses required to apply for Second Degree initiation. As you will recall, these requirements extend beyond this book and include other courses. This will be discussed more fully if you actually choose to apply for Second Degree initiation. To make such an application, go to www.correllian.com, follow the instructions found under "Applications," and you will receive assistance in moving forward.

However you proceed in this regard, I wish you all success and blessings.

May you blessed be,

Rev. Donald Lewis-Highcorrell

Comparative Religions

When the Second Degree program was originally designed, it included several components that were later dropped from the course requirements, as the main course proved to be so information-intensive. These classes were then put on the back burner, with the intention of returning them to the course requirements at a later time. Among these were Comparative Religion and World History.

I have always felt that these were important subjects for the student, because they help to put Correllian ideas into a larger context. Comparative Religion is also important because it helps us to understand people of other religions with whom we may find ourselves dealing.

Well, the "History of the World According to Don" is not finished—after all, it is a rather big subject. A Pagan-centric view of world history is a much-needed but daunting venture. However, I am very

Appendix

pleased to be able to finally return the Comparative Religion class to the Second Degree program.

This class on Comparative Religion is not universal but rather deals with a number of religious movements that I feel are of greatest relevance to the student. It will be noted immediately that all are Pagan religions. I have chosen them, in most cases, because I feel that they have directly influenced modern Paganism, especially Correllianism. I have also chosen them because each is either a living movement in its own right or an integral part of a living movement with which the initiate may well have occasion to interact in the wider Pagan community, and it behooves us to have some knowledge and understanding of our neighbors.

Each section is a brief overview of the religion in question. There are many more things that could be said in each case, and each of these movements is the subject of many books—but such books, however numerous, are in no danger of exhausting the subject matter. There are those who may argue that I have focused on the underlying similarities of these movements to our own and to each other at the expense of their differences; however, the differences between religions are all too easy to discover, while the similarities are sometimes more necessary to point out. Moreover, as clergy, it is the similarities

that mean the most to us, as it must be our constant desire to bring people together around their similarities if our world is to have its best hope for a future.

· · · ·

Shamanism

Shamanism is a name used to describe a wide variety of Pagan tribal religions, notably Native American, Inuit, Siberian, and Southeast Asian tribal religions. Many people believe that shamanism was once a universal human practice, the basis upon which all religious experience is built—a point of view with which the Correllian Tradition inclines to agree.

Some people believe that the ancient druids practiced a form of shamanic religion, from which European Witchcraft descended, ultimately trickling down to the Witchcraft revivals of the last two centuries and thence to modern Wicca. Certainly, medieval accounts of Witchcraft show strong shamanic elements, particularly in stories of flying, shapeshifting, and communication with animals and animal spirits.

The term *shamanism* comes from the Siberian word *shaman*, meaning "a Witch," or "Witch doctor," as it is sometimes called. The terms *shaman* and *shamanism* were popularized by the study entitled *Shamanism* by Mircea Eliade, published in 1551 Pisces (AD 1951).

Today, shamanism is enjoying a great revival among people of all backgrounds and walks of life. It has become very popular, in part because it tends not to be highly structured and is very introspective and internal in its practices.

What shamanic religions have in common is principally the practice of ecstatic trance and astral travel. During the trance, which may be light or very deep, the shaman's soul leaves the body to experience visions and have a variety of spiritual adventures.

Shamans use a number of means to induce trance, including meditation, music, and dance. Some use mind-altering substances as well, such as the famous PEYOTE mushroom, or hashish, but this is by no means the dominant practice, and some frown upon it.

Using trance, shamans travel between the worlds (i.e., through the planes of existence) to communicate with deities, spirit guides, and higher aspects of their own or others' souls. Among the spirit guides that shamans deal with are the ancestors: the spirits of the beloved dead. Shamans cross into the Otherworld to speak with the ancestors, to be taught by them, and to undergo initiatory experiences. They also interact with the spirits to practice healing and to gain knowledge of the future.

Shamans are also famous for working with animal guides. Animal guides are spirit guides who appear in the form of animals. It is a widespread belief among Pagan religions, especially but not only the shamanic ones, that there is no difference between humans and animals on the soul level, and that the species can communicate psychically or spiritually. This is illustrated by the numerous myths from around the world that describe animals removing their skins to reveal a "human" form beneath—that is, to reveal that their soul is the same as ours. The swan maidens of Russian myth, the fox maidens of Japan, and the bear and snake people of North America are only a few examples of this concept.

The influence of animal guides is often interpreted in light of the qualities associated with the animal in whose form it appears. For example, a spirit appearing as a bull or bison would have to do with issues of strength, an owl with wisdom, a frog with fecundity.

Shamans also frequently practice shapeshifting; that is, they assume animal shapes during their astral journeys. It is often claimed that this transformation can be so complete as to have a physical manifestation that can be perceived by others. This practice is believed to be the origin of the European stories of werewolves and African stories of wereleopards.

Shamans perceive these astral journeys in terms of nature-based symbology; they journey to the Underworld through holes in the ground or through wells or lakes. They fly through the air in magic boats, on spirit animals, or in the form of birds. Many people believe that this is the origin of the legends of Witches flying on brooms, eggshells, and magical animals.

Shamanic descriptions of Otherworld journeys vary, according to the shaman's cultural perceptions. Usually the Otherworld is perceived as resembling the shaman's everyday world but having a dreamlike quality to it. The laws of physics do not apply there, nor does time as we understand it. For this reason, the shaman may experience a time distortion between the perceived time of the trance and the time that elapses in the physical world. There is not always a clear relationship between cause and effect.

The shaman's experiences often include highly symbolic elements. This is because the mind can only understand things in terms of what it knows, and so when the shaman returns from beyond the veil, the shamanic experience can only be understood in terms of earthly symbols and references. There are many things in the Otherworld our earthly minds simply cannot wrap themselves around, except through symbols.

How one becomes a shaman varies from one place to another. In some cultures, psychically gifted youngsters are chosen by existing shamans and trained by the apprentice system. In other cultures, it is believed that shamans must be chosen by Spirit, a choice that is demonstrated through dreams, unexpected shamanic experiences, or in some cases by surviving serious illness.

It is often believed—and experience tends to confirm—that coming close to death heightens psychic ability. Many people who have had serious illnesses or accidents, especially when they are accompanied by near-death experiences, have become deeply spiritual or psychic afterwards.

The famous Iroquois FALSE FACE shamans were chosen in this way. It would sometimes fall that a person who was ill would dream of the False Face spirits; this was a summons from the spirits. The person would send for the False Face shamans, who would don their distinctive masks and conduct a healing ceremony and dance. If the person died, it was believed that the dream summoned them to the Otherworld. If the person lived, it was believed that they had been called to become one of the False Face shamans. With much reverence, they would carve a False Face mask from the trunk of a living tree—the mask was made in the image of the spirit whom the person had dreamed of and who was their special familiar. They would then be trained in the art of False Face healing.

• • • •

Animism

Like shamanism, animism is not so much a religion—though it is sometimes spoken of as such—as it is a group of related religions or an underlying principle of many religions.

Most Pagan religions are animist or animistic. Greco-Roman religion, Germanic and Celtic religion, most of modern Wicca—all are animistic religions.

Animism is the idea that everything existing is alive. From an animist point of view, everything that exists possesses an ANIMA, or soul. *Anima* is a Latin word meaning "life force," and from it comes such words as *animal* and *animate*—though the Romans, like other animists, certainly did not consider the possession of an anima to be limited to animate creatures. In animist thought, everything—houses, cars, tools, stones, plants, etc.—has a soul.

There is a famous example from Roman religion, often cited derisively by those who don't understand the nature of animism, which lists the spirits (animas) involved in the construction of a door, all of whom had to be propitiated during the process. These included the spirit of the door itself, as well as the spirits of the hinges, the spirit of the door-knocker, the spirit of the door-case, etc. It was believed that by connecting with and propitiating these spirits/deities, the work would go better, be more success-

ful, and last longer—an idea that should be familiar to you, since it is the same idea expounded upon in First Degree, Lesson XII, when we speak of working with a stone's spirit.

Another example of animism from European religion is the hero's sword, of which EXCALIBER is the most famous example. The magical blade with its own name and spirit, which when called upon gives the hero extra strength, is a feature of many European hero stories. The idea that a sword could have a soul or powers of its own is an example of animism.

This is the idea behind the naming of personal items: an acknowledgment of and contact with their souls. Thus the Witch who names her car "Broomhilda" and talks to "her" in traffic, or calls her computer printer "George" and encourages "him" to print faster, is following a very ancient and thoroughly Pagan practice.

Of course, animism also applies to plants and animals in basically the same ways as shamanism. Every plant has a spirit of its own: these are often personified as fairies or nymphs. Animals too have spirits, and the spirits of both plants and animals are portrayed as interacting with humans in the mythology of animist peoples. Thus in the story of Cupid and Psyche, when the goddess Venus in her Crone phase harshly tests Psyche to see if she is truly worthy of marrying Venus's son Cupid, forest animals and bees come to Psyche's aid to repay kindnesses she had earlier shown to their kind, just as later generations would portray talking animals coming to the aid of Snow White in the forest; it is the animal's Spirit or Higher Self that is referred to as interacting in this way.

Indeed, it is more than mythology, for by aligning with the Higher Self of any creature or artifact, we can build a connection to it that will allow for the sorts of interactions described above.

Moreover, the animist point of view applies not only to animals, plants, stones, and human-made artifacts, but also to the planet as a whole: to the animist, Earth too has a soul and is a living creature. This is the "Gaia Hypothesis," as some call it. In this view, the ecology and climatic cycles of the earth are the bodily processes of a living being. The winds and waters might be thought of as being like the earth's blood, the stone her bone, the plants her hair, and people and animals not unlike cells—all parts of an integrated being.

This same view can be applied to the universe, whose many galaxies might be thought of almost as organs within a single body.

This view should not seem odd to you, since it runs through all the Correllian writings.

Some animist peoples go even further and view certain activities as having a soul of their own, personified as a spirit or personal deity; thus in Rome we find such deities as Vervactor (the breaking of fallow ground), Redarator (the second plowing), Imporcitor (the furrowing), and so forth. Such deities or spirits of actions are also called AUGENBLICKGOTTER—gods of the blink of an eye. More modern examples might include the deity of writing, the deity of computer work, the deity of housecleaning, etc. These are extreme examples of personal deities—very personal images for Deity that help the individual to understand their interaction with Deity and with life in a personal way.

This idea that everything is alive underlies the philosophy of almost all Pagan peoples. You will certainly recognize the animist aspects of Correllian thought from the First Degree lessons. Animism is a very ancient concept, arising from the earliest times, and was probably universal among our ancestors. The followers of the book religions like to portray animism as "primitive," but it is actually quite subtle and profound.

• • • •

Ceremonialism

Ceremonial magic is sometimes confused with and has greatly influenced Wicca, though in fact the two systems are very different in both theory and practice.

Ceremonialism and Wicca have long and often related histories, and they share many common origins. There are important differences too.

One of the principal differences between the two systems is that Ceremonial magic is strongly influenced by the book religions, dealing with ideas of angels and demons, heaven and hell—ideas absent from Wicca. Moreover, the Ceremonialist often seeks to invoke these spirits with the idea of controlling or compelling them, and tends to take an almost adversarial role toward them.

Another major difference is that while Ceremonial magic was followed primarily by wealthy practitioners, Wicca—or Traditional Witchcraft, if you must differentiate traditional from modern Wicca—was primarily a movement of poor country people.

This difference is reflected in the ritual requirements of Ceremonialism: the importance placed upon exact ritual timing, the need for specific and often expensive ritual tools—these presuppose possession of extensive leisure time and disposable income on the part of the Ceremonial magician.

In Ceremonial magic, the tools used and the specifications of their construction are much more important than in Wicca—the form and materials of the tools being considered to be of importance in themselves by Ceremonialists. Ritual elements such as incense must be of the proper planetary correspondence and are looked upon not merely as keys to a shift in consciousness but as being of material aid to the Ceremonialist.

Ceremonialism, or Ceremonial magic, takes its name from the importance of ceremony in its practice. Ceremonies and rituals are very important, as is the manner in which they are conducted. Some Ceremonialists believe that missing or mispronouncing a word, or omitting a gesture, will ruin a ceremony and require it to be done over from the beginning. This is a very ancient idea and was widespread in the Roman empire; Roman priests and priestesses held the same view, as well as the idea that if any ill omen were seen or heard during a ceremony, it must be postponed or begun again. To combat this, Romans always performed rituals IN CAPUT VELATO—that is, with a veiled head—so that they could not see anything but the altar itself.

In Ceremonial magic, the magician works to align with and manipulate external forces: cosmic forces aligned with through astrology and correspondences, and spiritual forces influenced by ritual.

In Ceremonial magic, the forces of the universe are perceived as distinctly external—powers to control or be controlled by—though this attitude has changed

387

somewhat in recent generations due to the increasing influence of Wicca, which perceives the forces of the universe as being reached from within.

Traditionally, Ceremonialism concerned itself with the summoning and control of vast numbers of spirits, viewed as good or evil, depending on their qualities: legions of angels and archangels, devils and demons. These were compiled into long lists, which the Ceremonialist might choose from according to his need: a spirit for every occasion. Often—and increasingly in modern Ceremonialism—these spirits included the ancient Pagan gods, who were also called upon according to their qualities.

In the Renaissance and today, the Ceremonial magician would choose a spirit to summon and align all aspects of the ritual with the desired energy, including the timing, which would ideally be astrologically determined. Using a pentacle—a mystical symbol of the spirit in question—to help focus the ritual's energy, the magician would invoke the spirit and seek to either persuade or compel it to do his bidding. To do this, the magician would create a magic circle that he himself would stand outside of: the circle was to contain the spirit for the magician's protection. The magician would stand inside a triangle, which was intended to magnify his own power.

Wiccan-style magic circles are used in Ceremonialism as well, especially in modern times, with the magician inside the circle and the four guardians invoked for the quarters. But in Ceremonialism, the four guardians are archangels: Raphael, Michael, Gabriel, and Auriel. Significantly, the Ceremonialist regards this kind of circle as being for protection from external forces, while the Wiccan regards it as a tool of focusing energy.

Other Ceremonial means of invoking the powers of spirits include all manner of spells and amulets, often cataloged in GRIMOIRES, of which the most famous is the KEY OF SOLOMON, purporting to contain the magical secrets of Israel's King Solomon, supposedly a great sorcerer. These are not dissimilar to a Wiccan Book of Shadows, for which the term *grimoire* is also sometimes used.

Ceremonialism shares many of the same influences as Wicca: Hermeticism, alchemy, Greco-Roman and Egyptian religion and mysticism—all strongly influence Ceremonial magic as well as Wicca. However, Ceremonialism is also strongly influenced by ideas from the book religions, drawing heavily upon Judeo-Christian sources such as the Cabala, Gnosticism, and Roman Catholicism, which do not have a major influence in Wicca. Indeed, the greatest difference between Ceremonialism and Wicca is that Ceremonialism incorporates at its core key assumptions of the book religions, such as the idea of a universe divided between good and evil, and the concept of the divine as an external rather than internal element, which are ideas rejected by Wicca.

This difference is obscured somewhat by the increasing overlap between Ceremonialism and Wicca (as well as other Pagan religions). Many people practice both Ceremonialism and Wicca, or a fusion of the two. Indeed, Ceremonial leaders like Crowley and Wiccan leaders like Gardner deliberately worked to fuse elements of the two systems, a fact which does much to disguise the basic differences between them.

While this overlap between the two systems has had a profound influence on modern Wicca, it has also had a strong influence on Ceremonialism. Increasingly, Ceremonialists are adopting Wiccan ideas on the immanence of Deity, no longer seeking to control external powers but to draw upon powers from within. The practice of "Assumption of God-forms," wherein the magician embodies the deity (the ability that defines the Wiccan Third Degree), has become common, as has the concept of spiritual enlightenment rather than spiritual power as the goal of magical practice. Ceremonials are now more likely to work with goddesses and gods than with demons, though angels and archangels remain popular.

As to the influence of Ceremonialism on Wicca, the demarcation point between traditional and modern Wicca might be said to be the point, in the early years of the last century, that Ceremonial elements were introduced into Wiccan practice by reformers like Gardner. Prior to this, Wicca had been more concerned with philosophy and the practice of magic; its rituals were informal and spontaneous (at least by Ceremonial standards). This is partly because even then most Wiccans were solitary, and those groups that existed were small and kept small by both tradition and social pressure. However, the introduction of Ceremonial elements and the greater formalization of ritual sparked a systematizing of Wiccan thought and practice that brought about the demise of DECADENT PAGANISM (fragmentary Paganism mixed with Christian elements) and the return of Wicca as a major religion with a consciousness of its destiny and its role as a people.

. . . .

Isianism and Kemetism—Varieties of Egyptian Spirituality

Since ancient times, the religion and magic of Egypt has operated a fascination upon the minds of other peoples. Known from their earliest history as past masters of magic, especially in matters of the afterlife, the Egyptians have been and are enveloped by an aura of mystery and power that has always attracted others to study their beliefs. Even after the knowledge of how to read and write their distinctive hieroglyphs was lost, and with it most real knowledge of their civilization and its metaphysical beliefs, their artifacts were still regarded as supremely magical and sought after by other peoples for magical uses of their own—even the mummified bodies of the Egyptians themselves, which were ground into powder and used for "medicine" by medieval doctors and sorcerers.

The religion of ancient Egypt is, in a way, a perfect microcosm of Pagan belief, at least as regards structure and function. It is perhaps the most important of the ancient Western forms of Paganism for our modern priesthood to study, because the forces at work in Egyptian religion are so clear and uncluttered by the self-conscious intellectual glosses of later academics, which make it necessary to always read between the lines of Greek and Roman religion, or the general lack of information that makes it almost impossible not to read between the lines of ancient European religions.

The most important aspect of ancient Egyptian religion, which must be understood in order to make any headway in studying it, it that it was intensely local, with many hundreds of deities whose primary worship was confined to a specific area. Some, especially as Egyptian history progressed, were worshiped nationwide, but even these had once been of local provenance: for example, the great god Ptah was worshiped in Nopf (Memphis) and became nationally prominent only when Nopf became Egypt's capital and Ptah a patron of the ruling house. The same was true for mighty Amon, who was a god of the south, centered at Wast (Thebes), and whose worship became a national phenomenon only when Wast became the nation's capital after the end of the HYKSOS era.

Because of this intensely local nature, each area had its local deities who were dominant in the region and might not be known elsewhere, or if known might be thought of differently. These were basically the same deities repeated in hundreds of local variations: goddesses and gods of creation, of wisdom, of specific skills, of fecundity and prosperity, of birth and death and the Otherworld.

Thus, mighty Aset (Isis) was the Mother Goddess—but so was Hat-Hor, and so was winged Nuit, and in the south, the goddess Mut.

Everyone knows that Ptah was the Egyptian creator god, but this was not true for all Egyptians. For some, Knum was the Creator, or Khepera, or Temu, or Amon. Thehut (Thoth) was the god of the moon and of wisdom, but in Wast the moon god was Khonsu, son of Amon and Mut.

Consequently, you can never read an Egyptian text thinking that it is the sole expression of their theology. In Judeo-Christianity there was the Bible, which was the sole standard for theological expression with which in theory all Judeo-Christians must agree, even though they may interpret it differently. There are no similar books in the ancient Pagan religions, for such sacred scriptures as they produced, such as the *Peret Em Heru* (The Book of the Dead) express only one of a number of beliefs that vary widely and are subject to change and growth.

Even that most quintessential of Egyptian dieties, Osiris, the lord of the dead, was not the only lord of the dead, for Ptah, Sekher, and Sobek were also all gods of the dead worshiped in different regions.

Often two or more deities with the same general attributes were worshiped in the same area, overlapping each other. The Egyptians saw no problem with this: they were the SYNCRETISTS. Syncretism is the idea that all religions reflect the same truths, and consequently are cognate to each other. Syncretism is one of the main pillars of Pagan thought. Thus, when Ptah, Sekher, and Asar (Osiris) were all worshiped in the same region as lord of the Otherworld, the Egyptians—rather than fight about which was "right"—built a temple to Ptah-Sekher-Asar, as all three were obviously manifestations of the same deity.

When the followers of Amon and the followers of Ra both insisted that their god was the king of the gods, no problem: "Praise be given unto Amon-Ra!" And later, when the Greeks came, the same process brought about the worship of Zeus-Amon.

This deeply philosophical and utterly civilized way of looking at religion is the very essence of higher Pagan thought, as opposed to the book religions' sordid and eternal fighting over minor details. Unfortunately today some Pagans, making an outward conversion from the book religions without any real inner change, have begun to fight over minor details in just this way, and portray the ancients as being narrow-minded and hidebound as the worst Southern Baptists (which the ancients never were). This is an unworthy practice, which it is incumbent upon true clergy to discourage.

Perhaps the most important god of ancient Egypt was the "Good God"—that is, Pharaoh, the Divine King. Egypt was ruled by kings from the dim recesses of PREDYNASTIC history, and a good argument can be made for Egypt as the birthplace of kingship, although the prevailing view regards Mesopotamia as the birthplace of kingship.

From the start, the kings of Egypt held a role as much sacerdotal as political, being considered to have one foot in this world and the other in the Spiritworld.

The pharaoh was considered to be the physical embodiment of the spirit of the nation, and the chief intermediary between humankind and the divine, being himself part of both worlds.

The idea of the divine king is often misunderstood; the Egyptians were not stupid, nor were other ancient Pagan peoples who maintained the idea of divine kingship. No one believed that a pharaoh could work cosmologic miracles anymore than anyone really believed that King CANUTE could hold back the tide; rather, they believed that the divine king had a special connection to Deity, created and sustained through ritual, which allowed him or sometimes her to act as a kind of focal point between the human and the divine. For a pharaoh, this connection was the subject of frequent, even daily rituals designed to strengthen his role as divine intermediary.

The pharaoh received his status and his powers from the gods, who made him one of them; this connection was the subject of the coronation ceremonies and of the great SED, or Jubilee, ceremonies held to reaffirm and strengthen a pharaoh's rule. In theory, a pharaoh was the chief priest of every deity, and all the high priesthood of Egypt carried out their duties as stand-ins for him. AKHENATEN'S great religious "revolution" in many ways came down to little more than reasserting this ancient role of the pharaoh as the people's

principal intermediary to the divine. The coronation ceremony, the Sed ceremony, the many daily ceremonies that a pharaoh regularly performed in person—all stressed a pharaoh's relationship to the gods and his receipt from them of divine favor and power. When a pharaoh fell to coup or revolution, as pharaohs sometimes did, the Egyptians felt it was because he was not a worthy vessel of the divine favor and—as the Chinese put it, regarding their own divine emperor—the MANDATE OF HEAVEN passed to one who was worthy.

Serving all of these gods was a gigantic priesthood that grew progressively larger through Egyptian history. As has been said, the chief clergy served as intermediaries for a pharaoh, stepping aside when he performed the daily rites in person. Still, the chief clergy of Egypt were extraordinarily powerful, wielding considerable political clout in all periods and controlling the great wealth of the temples. Each god had his or her own chief cleric, who served in the god's main temple in their regional center. The most powerful in early times were the chief priest of Re in the city of On (Heliopolis) and the chief priest of Ptah in Nopf (Memphis). By the New Kingdom, it was the chief priest of Amon in Wast (Thebes) who was preeminent and enjoyed tremendous influence in the state. The chief priesthood of other deities, such as Isis and Osiris in Abtu (Abydos) or Bast in Per-bastet (Bubastis), were also very important in their region but had less influence in the government.

Below the chief priesthood, whose titles varied according to their deity, were many lesser priesthood, termed *Hem Neter* (Servant of the Deity), who served in the great temples, and minor priesthood carrying the title *Wab* (meaning pure or holy) who presided over the smaller temples and shrines of villages. In addition, there were a variety of specialized priesthoods including the funereal and mortuary priests called *Hem Ka* who served the ancestors.

The priesthood were under strictly enforced taboos regarding diet, dress, and sexual abstinence (complete celibacy was required)—but only when they were on duty. A priest or priestess usually served for a few weeks or a few months at a time, depending upon the temple and the period; the rest of the year they lived normally. Often the leading priesthoods were awarded to members of the royal family or officers of the court, and sometimes a person might hold several priesthoods in several temples, serving each in different times of year. The more important the priesthood, the more service was involved.

Often there was a loosely hereditary quality to the priesthoods, with children of previous priesthood tending to become priesthood as well, though the priesthood was not limited to these hereditaries. As time wore on and the power of the Egyptian Kingdom waned, this loosely hereditary quality became rigid, with the priesthood ossifying into a purely hereditary profession set apart from society and dominated by priestly dynasties—but this belongs to the late and decadent periods following the New Kingdom, when Egypt came to be ruled by foreign dynasties.

But by far the most famous aspect of ancient Egyptian religion are their beliefs about the afterlife and the elaborate mortuary ceremonies they undertook to ensure that afterlife. The magnificent tombs of Egypt's royalty and nobility are great works of art and one of our principal sources of information about their daily lives, and their MUMMIFIED bodies have been a source of fascination to other peoples for millennia.

Humankind has practiced ceremonial burial since Neanderthal times, and some Cro-Magnon burials were quite elaborate, so the Egyptian concern over the final resting place was nothing new. The early Egyptians buried their dead in unremarkable shallow graves at the edge of the desert that bordered their communities, along the narrow strip of fertile land created by the Nile's annual flood. This form of burial exposed the corpse to the hot and drying desert sands, and had the effect of naturally mummifying it. Observing this, the Egyptians came to feel that the idea of the body being preserved long after death was natural and desirable. As their civilization advanced and its prosperity increased, the Egyptians began to build larger and more enduring tombs, but this had the unexpected effect of preventing the body's natural mummification by shielding it from the sands. So the Egyptians began the long process of developing an artificial means of mummification. At first, they merely covered the body with a rigid shell of resin-soaked linen, so that its outer appearance was preserved even while the actual body decomposed within. But soon they learned to use drying agents to preserve the actual body to an extraordinary degree. Eventually they perfected a process of mummification, which took on average about three months to complete and included removing most of the body's internal organs and drying the flesh with natron (Het Jeryt), a sodium that absorbs moisture and acts as a natural antiseptic.

To receive the mummies that were so skillfully prepared, gloriously decorated tombs were created and stocked with articles from everyday life for the soul's enjoyment in the Otherworld. These might be the actual objects a person used in life, or they might be painted representations or miniature models of things they had possessed or wished they had possessed in life, the belief being that these would be magically animated in the Otherworld. In our terms, these paintings and models served as keys to the things they represented, so that the spirit could create and use them in astral form, having crossed over. Every good thing the family could afford would be included in full size or miniature in the tomb. In elaborate tombs, these might extend to miniature buildings, cattle, servants, and so on.

Most tombs included USHABTIS. An ushabti was a figure of a person shown in mummy form, intended to be animated in the Otherworld to serve the deceased in various ways—a kind of astral servant.

Great care was taken that the name and face of the deceased should be preserved, as this was considered essential to the soul's remaining as an ancestor. Sculptures were included so that if the mummy were damaged or destroyed, the soul would still have a likeness to connect to. The Egyptians believed that if the face were destroyed and the name forgotten, the soul would wither away—in our terms, that the soul would cease to act as ancestor, forget its old persona, and move on to other lifetimes. For this reason also—to preserve the soul as an ancestor—the Egyptians performed frequent mortuary rituals to maintain their bond with the ancestor and to show their regard for it. In these ceremonies, the soul would be called upon and offerings would be made, either directly by the family or by mortuary priesthood hired for the purpose.

The family would communicate with their ancestors in various ways, including writing letters to them, of which some examples have been preserved.

The Egyptians described the soul as having a number of constituent parts, some close to the physical persona and others more abstract. The Ka and the Ba were the parts of the soul that continued to have contact with the living. The Khu, the Sah, and the Sekhem were transcendental. The Khat, the Ren, and the Khaibit all began to decay if not tended to by the living. This same idea survives in our seven planes of existence and Higher and Lower Selves, the Higher Self being transcendent and eternal while the Lower Self decays after death, its experiences continuing on within the Higher Self, of which it was a manifestation.

In addition to the soul's existence as an ancestor, the Egyptians also believed in an Otherworld paradise to which the soul was admitted if it passed the *Psychostasia*, or Divine Judgment, of Osiris. In the Psychostasia, the soul (in the form of the heart, which the Egyptians considered the spiritual center of the body) was weighed against a feather, symbol of truth. If the person had lived a good life their soul would be light as a feather, and they would advance to Osiris's paradise. If they had lived a bad life, their heart would be heavy and they would be consumed by

Ammemit, a hideous (and somewhat silly looking) demon. To put this in our own terms, the soul could be held back by regret or guilt about the life just ended, and thus be unable to advance, devoured by its own self-judgment.

To reach the realm of Osiris, the soul required many magic spells in order to overcome a variety of tests it encountered on the way. These spells were provided to the deceased through the Peret Em Heru, or Coming Forth in Light, the book commonly known as the Egyptian Book of the Dead. The Peret Em Heru is a loose collection of spells and incantations found in several versions and highly variable in content. Parts of the Peret Em Heru dated from the earliest periods and refer to very ancient beliefs whose real meaning is lost to antiquity. Some chapters of the Peret Em Heru known as the Pyramid Texts were already in use as early as the Fifth and Sixth Dynasties (and presumably have their origin well before that), others are of much later provenance. At first the book seems to have been reserved to royalty, but by the New Kingdom it was in common use.

Egyptian civilization stretches over a period of at least four thousand years, beginning in the Predynastic period and extending till the rise of Christianity. During the last several hundred years of this period Egypt fell on hard times, being conquered by a series of foreign rulers. This caused Egyptian religion to turn inward and decay, becoming rigid and classicizing, looking only to preserve the past and ceasing to grow or innovate. Even during this twilight period, however, Egypt remained fertile religious ground, producing two major movements that still influence us today.

The Thirtieth Dynasty—the Greek Ptolemies who acquired Egypt in the wake of Alexander the Great's conquest of the Persians—saw Egyptian ideas exported into the Mediterranean as never before. The Ptolemies actively sought a syncretism of Egyptian and Greek religious ideas and patronized Egyptian deities who took on Greek aspects; chief among these were the goddess Isis and god Serapis (Osiris-Apis). The worship of Isis in this period became a distillation of earlier Egyptian thought, embodying Egyptian ideas of the Afterlife and the Egyptian sense of syncretism that caused the followers of Isis to see her as the inner nature of all deities everywhere: Isis of Ten Thousand Names. Thus the Isiac priesthood said "All goddesses are one goddess, all gods are one god" and preached a universality of Deity. Isis came to be worshiped throughout the Greek world, and then throughout the Roman world, as far north as Britain, and in time would prove to be the principal rival to Christianity as the Roman Empire drew to its sad close.

The second movement was centered in the use of magic. Egypt had always been known for its magic, but under the Ptolemies Egyptian and Greek magical ideas merged to create a vibrant magical revival centered in the Ptolemaic capital at Alexandria. Huge amounts of magical papyri have been preserved from this period and show the origins of the Hermetic and alchemical traditions that would flourish in the DARK AGES to come and leave such an impact on the magical community of today.

There are two main branches of Egyptian religion active in the world at present. The first are the Kemetans, the second the Isians.

Kemetans are RECONSTRUCTIONISTS who generally attempt to revive ancient Egyptian religion as it was in ancient Egypt. Their ideas, ceremonies, and customs are taken from the ancients with more or less variation. There are a variety of Kemetic groups, with a wide variation in outlook and practice. Some capture the open, confident, syncretic spirit of early Egypt, others tend toward the narrower, inward, more hidebound spirit of Egypt's twilight. The best Kemetans are majestic and spiritually encompassing. The worst Kemetans are narrow-minded and bigoted, rejecting all syncretism and believing variation sinful, and have more in common with Southern Baptists than with the very open-minded and eclectic Egyptians of Pharaonic times.

The second major movement of Egyptian inspiration active today are the Isians, embodied in the Fellowship of Isis. (Note: the ancient followers of Isis are termed Isiac, the modern followers of Isis are termed Isian.) The Fellowship of Isis was founded at the Spring Equinox of 1576 Pisces (AD 1976) by the most rev. Lawrence Robertson, Twenty-First Baron Robertson of Strathloch; his sister, the most rev. hon. Olivia Robertson; and his wife, Lady Pamela Robertson. The Fellowship of Isis is dedicated to the idea of Isis of Ten Thousand Names: that is, the idea that all deities reflect the same universal Deity which is within all things. The Fellowship of Isis is also dedicated to the veneration of the feminine aspect of Deity in all religions. As such, the fellowship builds upon the ideas of the ancient Isiac priesthood and the long traditions of Egyptian syncretism that gave rise to them.

The Fellowship of Isis is extremely open in its forms and makes use of a very wide-ranging liturgy, mostly written/channeled by Lady Olivia. The use of channeling, or oracles, is very important in Isianism, as are mystery plays, in which important points of doctrine are illustrated through drama. At present, the Fellowship of Isis has nearly 20,000 members in some ninety countries.

. . . .

Pythagoreanism

Pythagoreanism was one of the most important metaphysical schools of thought in the ancient world, and one which has had a profound effect on almost all later metaphysical movements. The ideas of Pythagoras and his followers are found in almost all contemporary Western Paganism and New Age spirituality, though the followers of these systems do not always realize the origins of the ideas. Here we provide a brief overview of Pythagoreanism to help familiarize you with its principles and with the role it played in the formation of modern spiritual attitudes.

Development of Pythagoreanism

Around 620 Aries (580 BC), a merchant named Mnesarchus and his pregnant wife, Parthenis, visited the ORACLE OF DELPHI while on a business trip.

The Temple of Apollo at Delphi housed the Oracle of Delphi, the leading oracular shrine of ancient Greece. The priestess of this shrine, called the PYTHIA, gave oracular messages while in a trance induced in part by chewing sacred bay laurel leaves. There were countless Pythias over the centuries, and no distinction is made between the various priestesses who held the title, but many of them produced strikingly accurate prophecies.

Sometimes the Pythia would be consulted on important matters of state by different governments from around the Aegean. But the Pythia was also available to be consulted by ordinary people as well. Mnesarchus and Parthenis had simple questions, ones that no one expected to produce earth-shaking answers: Will our trip be profitable? What future can we expect for our unborn child?

The Pythia answered that the trip would indeed be profitable, and that the child would be of great beauty, great wisdom, and great service to humanity. Parthenis was so impressed with this unexpectedly grand prophecy that she changed her name to Pythais (or Pythasis) in honor of the Pythia, and the child, when born, was given the name Pythagoras (*Pyth* in reference to the Pythia + *Agor*, meaning "spoke").

The child would grow up to be one of the greatest of all Greek philosophers, and arguably the greatest in terms of modern metaphysical thought.

Mnesarchus was a TYRIAN merchant who had delivered a shipload of grain to the island of Samos during a famine. The grateful Samians made him a citizen, and he settled among them, marrying the lady Parthenis (later Pythais), a descendant of Ancaeus, founder of the city-state of Samos. Mnesarchus was a wealthy and internationally well-connected gentleman of affairs who gave his three sons—Eunos-

tus, Tirrhenus, and Pythagoras—an excellent private education. He also took the boys on many of his wide-ranging business trips.

As was the custom of the time, Pythagoras and his brothers studied under various well-known philosophers to obtain their education. Such philosophers maintained private schools, which admitted the sons and sometimes daughters of primarily upper-class families. Pythagoras is said to have studied under the philosophers PHEREKYDES, THALES, and ANAXIMANDER, among others.

Each of these philosophers would have some effect on Pythagoras's own later teachings.

Pherekydes of Syros was a philosopher noted for his teachings about the immortality of the soul and the idea of reincarnation, or METEMPSYCHOSIS. Many later authorities, including CICERO, considered Pherekydes to have been the first Greek philosopher to have taught that the soul was immortal. Pherekydes was also known for his use of the pentagram as a symbol and as an allegorical teaching tool. Pherekydes' followers are said to have used the pentagram, which they called *pentamychos*, or "Five Chambers," to identify themselves, much as the Pythagoreans would do later.

Thales of MILETUS is said to have been the first Greek philosopher to question the origin of substances. Thales taught that water was the most important of the elements and that all things were ultimately derived from water—a point of view his successor Anaximander would expand upon and change. Thales also taught that Earth was round. Although most ancient sources say that Thales was of pure Milesian descent, a dissenting view held that he was, like Pythagoras, of Tyrian descent. Thales is also supposed to have studied in Egypt and is said to have advised Pythagoras to do the same.

Anaximander (Anaximandros) of Miletus was a student of Thales and successor as head of Thales' school of philosophy. Anaximander's most notable contribution to modern metaphysical thought is the idea that the four elements have their origin in Spirit, which Anaximander called APEIRON. Anaximander also taught that there were myriad parallel worlds that came into and out of existence in the universe. In addition, Anaximander is sometimes considered the first philosopher to teach the idea of physical evolution, holding that humanity evolved from an aquatic ancestor.

Mnesarchus is also supposed to have arranged for his son to study with the CHALDEAN priests of his native Tyre. These priests were particularly known for their excellence in astrology and interest in celestial cycles and patterns.

As an adult, Pythagoras took his place as a leading citizen of Samos but never lost his interest in learning. Not long after Polykrates became TYRANT of Samos in 662 Aries (538 BC), Pythagoras traveled to Egypt. At this time Samos and Egypt were allies, and there was a considerable Greek presence in the north of Egypt. According to some sources, Pythagoras came with a letter of introduction from Polykrates, while others hold that he was actually fleeing the Tyrant.

In Egypt, Pythagoras studied at a number of temples, including the Temple of ON (HELIOPOLIS), which at that time had a reputation for learning similar to that which would later attain to Alexandria in the Ptolemaic period, and the Temple at WAST (THEBES), where he became initiated as a priest.

In 675 Aries (525 BC), Cambyses II of Persia invaded Egypt following the death of Pharaoh Ahmose II, deposing the new Pharaoh Psametik III after a reign of only a few months. In this, he had the aid of Polykrates of Samos, who had abandoned his former alliance with Egypt and sent considerable naval support to Cambyses.

This invasion ended the Twenty-Sixth Dynasty—the last native dynasty to rule Egypt—and saw Egypt annexed to the Achemenid Persian empire. Psametik and many other prisoners of war were deported to Persia, where they met various fates:

Psametik himself was forced to commit suicide; Pythagoras, also a prisoner of war, fared rather better.

Freed relatively quickly, Pythagoras spent his time in Persia studying under the MAGI (or Magoi), the priests of the Persian Zoroastrian religion. At the time, the Magi enjoyed a preeminent reputation for magic; indeed, so much so that the term *magic* was developed from their own name.

The various different philosophers and priesthoods Pythagoras studied with over the years all had an impact on his later teachings, as did his own original thoughts. In addition to those already mentioned, sometime during his youth Pythagoras is supposed to have met and received some instruction from Celtic druids as well. The Celtic peoples had a strong presence in northern Italy at this time and so were not exactly remote from Aegean culture.

After being freed by the Persians, perhaps because of his Samian origin, Pythagoras returned to Samos. Here he founded his first school of philosophy, called the Hemicycle. He also apparently selected a cave outside of the city, which he used for teaching as well as personal meditations.

Polykrates of Samos had died in 678 Aries (522 BC), and the island had become part of the Persian empire. There was much unrest on the island, and Pythagoras found the area politically and philosophically unreceptive to his ideas.

Supposedly the Samians also found his allegorical methods of teaching difficult to understand.

Around 680 Aries (520 BC), Pythagoras moved his school to the city-state of CROTON in Calabria, Italy. Here the school flourished and attracted many students, while Pythagoras himself became prominent in Crotonian politics.

Around 690 Aries (510 BC), Croton went to war with its longtime rival city-state Sybaris. Sybaris was vanquished, but the government of Croton was destabilized and soon after overthrown. A democracy replaced the older oligarchic Council of One Thousand that had ruled Croton, and many of the upper class fled or were driven out.

A rejected student by the name of Kylon is said to have organized a political attack on Pythagoras's school, which obliged Pythagoras to flee to nearby Metapontum. It is not clear how long this exile lasted, but Pythagoras and his people apparently returned to Croton and once again prospered there.

Pythagoras was generally held to have lived to somewhere between the ages of ninety and 100, dying peacefully in old age. Many ancient writers held that he was a teacher of Empedokles, who was not born until c. 710 Aries (490 BC), which if true would suggest that Pythagoras was indeed around 100 at the time of his death. However, like his date of birth, Pythagoras's date of death is uncertain. Pythagoras was succeeded by THEANO, who was either his widow or his daughter—ancient sources differ.

After 700 Aries (500 BC), Pythagoreanism began to spread throughout Greece, and it also began to break into a number of different factions.

In 740 Aries (460 BC), there was a violent movement against the Pythagoreans that resulted in their suppression in a number of places. In particular, the Pythagorean school in Croton suffered badly, which may have led to the alternate story that Pythagoras died violently in an attack upon his school.

Pythagorean Beliefs

One of the problems in discussing the ideas of Pythagoras and his followers is the impossibility of saying exactly what Pythagoras's own ideas were, because the ideas of subsequent Pythagorean philosophers were, as a rule, ATTRIBUTED to him. This is a problem in discussing many early philosophical schools because it was—and in some cases still is—a common practice to attribute new works to earlier authors. This is not, as some rather priggishly style it, "forgery," but rather was thought of by these philosophical schools as an entirely appropriate homage to their founder or sometimes other early exponents.

To understand the thinking behind the idea of attributing a new work to a sometimes long-dead authority, consider the apple tree. If an apple tree bears fruit, we do not as a rule say that the third fork of the left branch has borne fruit, though that would certainly be more exact—we say that the tree has borne fruit. This is how groups such as the Pythagoreans looked at themselves, and why most every Pythagorean author attributed their own work to Pythagoras himself—even though Pythagoras's own teaching is said to have been entirely oral.

This creates a situation similar to what we might have if all books on modern Wicca were attributed to Charles Leland, rather than their actual authors; the individual contributions of people like GERALD GARDNER, ZSUSANNA BUDAPEST, GAVIN AND YVONNE FROST, etc., would then be indistinguishable from one another.

It is thus with Pythagoreanism. Over a span of centuries, authors signed the name of Pythagoras to their work, yet it is fairly certain that Pythagoras himself did not commit any of his ideas to writing. Moreover, the Pythagoreans to some extent observed rules of secrecy about their inner doctrines, which makes a full understanding of exactly what they believed difficult or even impossible.

Consequently, when we speak here of the ideas of the Pythagoreans or of the practices of the school of Croton, it must be understood that we are speaking to the best of our knowledge, considering the abovementioned hindrances.

The students at Pythagoras's school at Croton are said to have been divided into two groups: the Akousmatikoi, ordinary students who formed a sort of Outer Court, and the Mathematikoi, elite students who formed what might be considered the Inner Court. Both men and women were accepted into both grades and treated on an equal basis.

The Akousmatikoi, whose name means "those who hear," were students who lived in the surrounding area and followed an otherwise ordinary lifestyle but who studied philosophy at the school of Croton by attending lectures and discussions.

The Mathematikoi, whose name means "those who study," not only learned the ideas of Pythagoras's philosophy but also put them into practice as a lifestyle. The Mathematikoi were required to live onsite at the school, to forego private property and live in common, and were subject to a number of strictures regarding dress, diet, and behavior. The Mathematikoi formed an inner religious community, rather like the cloistered monks and nuns of later eras, and it is their behavior that later Pythagoreans would model themselves on.

The Mathematikoi were required to live abstemiously, dress modestly (ideally going barefoot), and practice vegetarianism. Their vegetarianism seems to have been based on their belief in metempsychosis and the idea that one could be reincarnated as an animal as easily as a person. Curiously enough, however, the Pythagorean idea of vegetarianism did not extend to the meat of ANIMAL SACRIFICES, which was considered acceptable to eat, having been sanctified. The Mathematikoi were also prohibited from eating any sort of bean, which together with their vegetarianism would seem to have given them a significantly restricted diet, considering the seasonal nature of food before the modern era of refrigeration and irradiation.

The Mathematikoi are also said to have followed a rule of silence, although since they relied so heavily on oral teaching and did interact with the wider society, this rule must have applied only in limited circumstances.

Similarly, we are told that the Mathematikoi were enjoined to pacifism; however, this too must have applied within limited circumstances, as Pythagoras's student MILO OF CROTON led the Crotonian armies against Sybaris, an action of which no one seems to have disapproved.

The ideas studied by Akousmatikoi and Mathematikoi included reincarnation and past-life studies. Pythagoras taught that the soul perfected itself by living many lives in many forms, including both human and animal. Consequently, Pythagoreans often studied their past lives using techniques similar to those we use today.

Pythagoreans also laid great importance upon the idea of polar powers, which they knew as apeiron (formless) and PEIRON (formed), and the interaction between these. Apeiron and peiron were looked upon much as we look upon goddess and god, yin and yang. Apeiron was the origin of all things, which was given expression and definition by peiron, to which it in turn gave essence.

The relationship between apeiron and peiron was maintained by HARMONIA. Harmonia was looked at as the flow of the universe; the "Tao," if you would. Harmonia was regarded as being in perfect balance, even if that balance could not always be seen from the temporal point of view. Harmonia was very similar in concept to our own ideas of fate, karma, and divine plan, all of which it encapsulates. The idea of Harmonia is very likely based upon or influenced by the Egyptian idea of Ma'at, or divine balance, and like Ma'at is often portrayed as a goddess.

But the most famous aspect of Pythagoreanism is, of course, its emphasis on numerology as the key to understanding the universe. Pythagoras and his people placed tremendous importance on the mystical understanding of numbers and upon the mathematical relationships between these—indeed, the Mathematikoi would give their name to the science of mathematics. To the Pythagorean, numbers could be used to define and gain insight to all aspects of creation.

It was Pythagoras who invented the earliest known MUSICAL SCALE, in an attempt to understand why certain music was harmonious and certain music was not. He did this by studying the intervals between harmonious sounds and the pattern created by these. Studying this pattern led him to postulate that similar mathematical patterns underlie all of existence, and consequently that all of existence can be analyzed and understood through mathematics.

The patterns of numbers and the individual qualities ascribed to each number were the key to understanding the higher nature of these mathematical patterns. All things were held to correspond to specific numbers, and each of these numbers were held to have specific qualities inherent to it, which could be used to study and gain insight into the inner nature of existence. You will learn more about the Pythagorean meaning and interpretation of numbers in the lesson on numerology included in this volume.

The TETRAKTYS triangle was used as the numeric diagram of creation, and was a symbol of paramount importance to the Pythagoreans.

The Tetraktys is a diagram of four lines, having respectively one, two, three, and four points. This reflects the single origin of all things in Apeiron, or Deity (One), which sets existence in motion by defining itself (Peiron) and becoming two. The interaction of these two is creative in nature and sets into motion Harmonia, or the Flow of the Universe (three); the interaction of Apeiron (one) and Peiron (two) is carried forward by Harmonia (three) to become the manifest world (four) created from the four elements and symbolized by the four directions, while the sum total of all the points together is ten, representing the furthest extent of creation, which, since ten reduces to one ($10 = 1 + 0 = 1$), is revealed to be reunion with Deity, the point of both origin and destination, alpha and omega.

The Tetraktys was so important to the Pythagoreans, symbolizing all existence as it does, that they used it to swear sacred oaths by, a practice originating with Pythagoras himself.

The other symbol strongly associated with Pythagoreanism is the pentagram, which they called the "pentalpha" or "five As" because it could be seen as a series of interlinking letter As. The Pythagoreans, who used the pentagram as an identifying symbol, inherited its use from Pythagoras's own teacher, Pherekydes, whose followers had also used it as an identifying symbol.

Pherekydes called the symbol *pentamychos*, or "five chambers," and used it as a teaching tool to illustrate his philosophy. As he had studied in Egypt, where the five-pointed star was already a millennia-old religious symbol representing magic and the Otherworld, it is reasonable to assume that Pherekydes acquired his use of the pentagram there.

Having discovered the idea that mathematical patterns interpreted in light of the mystical understanding of numbers formed the basis of existence because of his study of the musical scale, Pythagoras quite naturally associated the idea of number with sound. Thus Pythagoreans believed that specific tones corresponded to specific numbers, which corresponded to archetypal cosmologic forces. From this they developed the theory of the Music of the Spheres, which we addressed in our First Degree materials. They also developed systems that used sound to effect spiritual and physical healing, much like today's "toning."

The Pythagoreans were an extremely important philosophical school in their own right in the ancient world. However, they are equally important for the influence they have had on other schools of thought: Platonism, Hermeticism, alchemy, Cabala, Ceremonialism, and Wicca are all deeply influenced by Pythagorean ideas, and all can be thought of as descendants of Pythagoreanism.

....
Confucianism, Taoism, and Buddhism

The religious history of China is particularly interesting to the modern Pagan because of the way in which several essentially distinct religions were treated and interacted with at once.

Famously, the three major religious movements—Confucianism, Taoism, and Buddhism—developed a symbiotic relationship that allowed most Chinese to have recourse to all three without feeling any kind of contradiction. Although certainly some favored only one of these three dominant religious systems, many went to each for its own specialty—seeking moral guidance from Confucianism, spiritual guidance from Taoism, and turning to Buddhism for the higher development of the soul.

Although there was a "state religion" from earliest times built around the sanctity of the emperor and an official pantheon of deities, this is usually thought of within the context of Taoism, though it embraced all systems. For example, Confucius and Lao-tzu were both regarded as deities within the state system, as was the Buddhist Kwan Yin.

Because of this, Chinese Paganism—very much like modern Western Paganism—embraced a plurality of religious ideas at once. Whatever contradictions may arguably have existed between these systems were simply regarded as another way of looking at the whole.

Granted, this had not always been the case—this religious symbiosis developed over centuries, some of which saw great religious strife—but it certainly marks the apotheosis of Chinese religious thought.

Of these three systems—Confucianism, Taoism, and Buddhism—the first two are native to China, while the third was imported from India. All three, however, arose at roughly the same time: the seventh century of the Age of Aries (sixth century BC).

Buddhism, based upon the teachings of Prince Siddhartha Gautama, of what is now Nepal, is thought to have been brought to China around the tenth century of the Age of Aries (first century BC), though some traditions claim it actually arrived much earlier.

Confucianism is based on the teachings of Confucius (K'ung Fu Tzu, or Kong Fuzi), who lived from 649–721 Aquarius (551–479 BC). However, Confucius himself held that his teachings were based on traditional ideas that had fallen somewhat into disuse, and that he himself was reviving and expounding on these rather than creating them.

Confucius was born into a noble but impoverished family. Confucius's father died when the boy was three years old, leaving the widowed mother in strained circumstances. Nonetheless, she worked hard to provide Confucius with a good upbringing and education, which allowed him to set himself up as a teacher.

Considering himself an aristocrat, Confucius longed for a political career, which was mostly denied to him. He consoled himself by teaching his political and moral ideas to his students. Confucius's teachings focus strongly on ideas of personal virtue and duty, and the role of proper relationships and reciprocity in building society.

Dissatisfied with the government of his native Lu and his own inability to secure a high position in it, Confucius began a series of travels around China in his late fifties. He was accompanied by many of his students, and much of his work has its origin in this period.

Eventually Confucius returned home to Lu, where he died at the age of seventy-two. Confucius and his wife, Qi Quan, had a number of children, and their descendants achieved much of the high social standing Confucius desired for himself. The family is still very much alive today and very much respected.

The principal work chronicling Confucius's teaching is the LUN YU, or Analects of Confucius, which gives anecdotes from his students' experiences of him. He is also said to have written the LI CHI, or Book of Rites, which as its name implies is a book of rituals and ceremonies.

Some have held that Confucius wrote or edited all of the so-called Five Classics, or WU CHING. The Five Classics include the I Ching (Book of Changes), the Shu Ching (Book of History), Shih Ching (Book of Poetry), the Ch'un Ch'iu (Spring and Autumn), and the Li Chi itself.

Still others hold that none of the works attributed to Confucius were actually written by him, and that his life is largely mythical.

Taoism is usually thought of as being based upon the teachings of the sage Lao-tzu (or Laozi), notably the TAO TE CHING. However, it is also widely viewed that the ideas which form the basis of Taoism were already ancient within Chinese Paganism, and that Lao-tzu merely gave them their first written form.

Lao-tzu is traditionally held to have lived during the seventh century of the age of Aries (sixth century BC) and to have been a contemporary of Confucius, albeit a generation older. Lao-tzu is a title; his actual name was Li Er Boyang. Lao-tzu is said to have been Curator of Archives at the royal court of ZHOU during the EASTERN ZHOU period. Unlike Confucius, Lao-tzu never established a formal school, disseminating his teachings as a personal rather than a professional passion. Nonetheless, Lao-tzu attracted a number of followers and a great reputation for wisdom during his lifetime.

At a great age, dismayed by the moral decay of the state, Lao-tzu is said to have decided to leave the capital with the intention of becoming a hermit. He mounted an ox and began his trip—a form in which he is often shown in artwork—but was stopped at the western gate by a guardsman who recognized the celebrated sage. The guardsman prevailed upon Lao-tzu to write down his teachings for the benefit of future generations before he left the city. Convinced that this would be a good idea, Lao-tzu wrote the Tao Te Ching, or Book of the Way, in which he set out his understanding of the Tao, which would become central to all future Taoism. He then mounted his ox again and departed for the west, leaving the book behind for posterity.

Unlike Confucianism, which places its emphasis on outward behavior, Taoism places its emphasis on inner understandings and attunement to the Tao, or "the Way of Things."

There is considerable diversity of opinion as to whether Lao-tzu was an actual person, a mythical figure, or a combination of several actual people. Certainly his life is overlaid with mythical elements—much more so than Confucius. However, many people have claimed descent from Lao-tzu, notably the T'ANG DYNASTY, which ruled China from 218–507 Pisces (AD 618–907).

Beliefs of Confucianism

Confucianism stresses the role of the individual in creating and maintaining personal and social harmony. The individual does this by living a virtuous life and fulfilling their personal and social duties to the best of their ability. Confucianism emphasizes the virtues of honesty, loyalty, piety (respectful behavior), and benevolence as cornerstones of proper behavior, and the importance of education and moderation.

Confucianism takes the JUNZI (gentleperson) as its cultural ideal. The Junzi is distinguished by moral reflection and cultivation, filial and social piety, and generosity of spirit.

Confucianism teaches that respect and consideration for others is the basis of a good life, a healthy family, and a sound society. In Confucianism, all relationships are important and the expectations inherent in one's relationships must be honored if harmony in those relationships is to be maintained. Confucianism teaches that all relationships are reciprocal, with each party having a duty to the other. Thus, to get respect you must give respect—but in giving respect you also have a right to expect to be respected in accordance with your role in the given relationship.

Confucianism teaches that the proper role of each person in a relationship is important and must be adhered to. Many relationships are inherently unequal, as for example the relationship of parents to children, or of employers to employees. Indeed, this is the case for most relationships. However, this inequality does not mean that the relationship is any less reciprocal than if it were on an equal footing. On the contrary, while the child may be viewed as owing respect and obedience to the parent, the parent in turn owes nurturing, sustenance, and protection to the child. If either party fails in its role, the relationship is damaged and in turn damages all around it.

Confucianists apply this same concept to the state, holding that while people owe allegiance and obedience to their government, the government in turn owes honest and effective governance to the people. Again, if either party neglects its side of the relationship, damage occurs.

The teachings of Confucius addressed the behavior of people in life; he did not much address issues of the soul or the spirit realms. Confucius did not reject these, he simply did not address them in detail. Later Confucian thinkers did expound on spiritual issues, with ideas that correspond to aspects of both Taoism and Buddhism. These later Confucians are commonly termed Neo-Confucians—though they certainly did not think of themselves as being a separate movement.

Beliefs of Taoism

The most famous symbol of Taoism also best exemplifies its belief system: this is the TAIJITU (Tai Chi Tu) or yin/yang. The Taijitu depicts the two polar opposites yin and yang in an eternal cycle of balance. Yin is feminine, dark, receptive, and inward-turning; Yang is masculine, light, active, and outward-turning. They are not so much opposites as complements, each being necessary to the existence of the other and a necessary consequence of the other. It is said that when an energy has gone to the furthest extreme of yin or yang, it must perforce turn back and begin heading toward the other. Moreover, both yin and yang contain a bit of the other within them. In Taoism, all things that exist are defined in terms of their relationship to yin and yang and the interplay of these two forces.

It is this interplay of yin and yang that defines the universe and propels it forward. This interplay is the TAO, the "Way of Things." The goal of Taoism is to attune to the Tao and move with it, rather than fighting against it. It is believed that if one can move in harmony with the Tao—the natural movement of the universe—all things in life will flow easily and properly, just as the Tao itself does. Disharmony in life comes from moving against the Tao, either intentionally or because one has fallen out of alignment with it. A great deal of Taoist thought and practice is dedicated to achieving and maintaining proper alignment with the Tao.

The principal means of achieving alignment with the Tao is described as WEI WU WEI, or "Action without Action." What this means is that instead of propelling oneself forward against all odds, if one is aligned with the Tao, it will itself propel one forward—not unlike the current of a river. Taoists employ many metaphysical disciplines such as FENG SHUI to better attune their natural energy, CHI, to the Tao in order to take maximum advantage of this effect. Like Wiccans, Taoists believe that all things reflect the whole, and as a result, divination is an important part of Taoism.

Taoism teaches that if one is sufficiently aligned to the Tao and one's chi is sufficiently developed, one can become an immortal (Hsien). Sometimes this immortality is portrayed as being an immortality of the physical body, other times as an immortality of the spirit, not unlike the idea of the BODHISATTVA or the ASCENDED MASTER. A popular symbol in Taoism is that of the EIGHT IMMORTALS (Pa-Hsien or Baxian), a group of eight such immortals traveling together.

This idea of immortality led to the creation of elevated spiritual techniques intended to purify the chi and transform the being, preparing it for a spiritual immortality, the study of which can be very useful to the modern metaphysical practitioner. The same idea of immortality also led to more degraded attempts to create an actual ELIXIR OF LIFE, which was hoped to induce physical immortality simply by drinking it. On several celebrated occasions, such Elixirs of Life have in fact proved fatal.

Popular obsession with magic and alchemy at the expense of the deeper philosophies of Taoism caused the religion to be looked down upon by some, especially Christian missionaries. In reality, it is only natural that ordinary people will be most interested in those aspects of their religion that affect their daily life, while only those with a deeper vocation will aspire to the deeper practices of the faith, and this is seen in all religions. Today, Taoist ideas are popular not only in Chinese culture but throughout the world.

Beliefs of Buddhism

Buddhism was founded by Prince Siddhartha Gautama, who was born in 637 Aries (563 BC) at Lumbini in the city-state of Kapilavastu, in what is now Nepal. Siddhartha's father was King Suddhodana of the Shakya people. His mother is said to have been Queen Mayadevi.

According to legend, King Suddhodana and Queen Mayadevi longed to have a child, but since they were still childless after twenty years of marriage, they had given up hope of this ever coming to pass. Then one night the queen had a dream in which a white elephant entered her womb—an extremely auspicious symbol. Shortly afterwards, she found that she was pregnant.

The child was duly born, and a magnificent future was prophesied for him. It was said that the infant prince would grow up to be either a great king or a great holy man. Suddhodana knew which he preferred his son to be, and it was not a holy man. Consequently, Suddhodana ordered that his son be raised in a manner that he felt would guarantee the kingly future.

The young prince was raised in a near—cloistered existence within the royal palaces. The prince was kept away from all religious instruction so that his mind would not be swayed from his political future. Moreover, Suddhodana made sure his son was shielded as much as possible from all aspects of human suffering, so that he would not turn to metaphysical speculation on his own. In best mythological form, this very strategy would prove to be the very undoing of Suddhodana's hopes for his son.

Queen Mayadevi had died either in childbirth or very soon after, and the upbringing of the young prince was entrusted to her younger sister, the Princess Prajapati Gotami. The princess had a decidedly spiritual bent and would later become the first Buddhist NUN. Although she honored the king's commands, one cannot help but think her influence may have helped the young prince to realize that material well-being was not all there was to life.

At the age of sixteen, Prince Siddhartha was married to the Princess Yasodhara, a first cousin of the same age as he. The young couple were happy together and would share a strong bond all their lives, despite the vicissitudes yet to come. But like Suddhodana and Mayadevi, Siddhartha and Yasodhara remained childless for many years.

According to legend, it was a series of chance encounters that led Siddhartha to begin his spiritual seeking. At the age of twenty-nine, Siddhartha, while traveling outside the royal palaces with his charioteer Channa, happened to encounter a man ravaged by sickness. Not long after, while on another similar trip, Siddhartha encountered an old man ravaged by the effects of advanced senility. On yet a third occasion, he happened across a funeral in progress.

Because the prince had been raised in such a sheltered manner and had never been exposed to these things before, he was not inured to them, as an ordinary person might be, and found them profoundly shocking. Having never set eyes upon illness, senility, or death, these commonplace things utterly shattered the prince's worldview and triggered a deep spiritual crisis.

Siddhartha's spiritual crisis may also have been intensified by the fact that Yasodhara was at last pregnant, and the birth of their first child was approaching—always a watershed in one's life.

In any event, Siddhartha felt he received an answer to his spiritual crisis when a fourth and final chance encounter brought him to see a SRAMANA, or ascetic holy man.

Sramanas were and are common in India. They are mendicant holy men who lead a wandering life and seek to perfect their soul through the practice of intense meditation, an austere lifestyle, and sometimes mortification of the flesh. By perfecting their soul, the sramana hopes to achieve release from the cycle of life and death. Such sramanas may travel alone or as part of a small group.

Siddhartha felt that the sramana provided the answer to his spiritual crisis and decided to devote himself to this lifestyle. Aided by Channa, Siddhartha stole out of the city by night and began his life as

a mystic. In Buddhism, this is known as "The Great Departure." That same night, Yasodhara gave birth to their son, Prince Rahula.

For the next six years, Siddhartha pursued the life of a sramana, practicing deep austerities. After a time, he became one of a group of five sramanas traveling the countryside. In his zeal to perfect himself, Siddhartha restricted his diet to the point of starvation. Images of Siddhartha in this state, as an emaciated sramana, are a staple of Buddhist art.

This intense regimen nearly led to his death—but not his enlightenment. Seeing that he was not making progress, Siddhartha reconsidered the desirability of the sramanic lifestyle and departed from his companions.

Siddhartha now discovered THE MIDDLE WAY, a key tenet of Buddhism: this is the idea that virtue is to be found in moderation, not extremity. Siddhartha charted a new course that lay between the extreme luxury of his youth and the extreme asceticism of the sramanas. He accepted nourishment and then sat down to meditate beneath a nearby fig tree—the famous BODHI TREE. He swore to himself that he would not leave the tree or cease to meditate until he had found the spiritual answers he sought.

For forty-nine days Siddhartha meditated. At this point, Siddhartha achieved

Bodhi, or "ENLIGHTENMENT," a spiritual opening and inner awakening that brought him a oneness with all things and opened the way for him to transcend the cycle of life and death. This state of being is called NIRVANA, or spiritual liberation. Siddhartha considered the possibility of leaving his earthly life and moving forward into PARINIRVANA as a fully realized immortal being, but decided that what he truly desired was to use his new enlightenment to help others—a pattern that many later BODDHISATTVAS followed. So he got up from under the bodhi tree. Thereafter, Siddhartha was known as BUDDHA, the Enlightened One.

After this, Buddha journeyed to the sacred city of BENARES, in what is now Uttar Pradesh. Here he met up again with the band of ascetics he had formerly traveled with. Buddha spoke to the five sramanas about his enlightenment and the DHARMA, or teachings, he had derived from it. The sramanas joined with Buddha, becoming the first *sangha*, or Buddhist religious community. This event was called the "Setting in Motion of the Wheel of Dharma" and was, in effect, the beginning of Buddhism as a movement.

The sangha grew rapidly, and the movement spread. In time, Buddha would carry his message back to Kapilavastu, and many of the royal house would become members of the sangha. Although Buddha did not initially wish to accept women into the sangha, his royal aunt Maha Prajapati in time convinced him to do so by her determination to follow him. The Princess Yasodhara also became a nun, and their son Rahula would become a monk.

After many years of successful teaching, the Buddha died peacefully at the age of eighty, entering into Parinirvana.

Teachings of Buddhism

Buddhism is a gigantic religion, having millions of adherents and hundreds of sects; consequently, in a forum such as this, the best we could possibly do is to give a very simplified overview of Buddhist ideas. All of these ideas exist in many versions, so anything we say about any of them is likely to be imperfect according to another understanding. However, we will attempt to convey the gist of it without dealing with sectarian divisions.

Buddhism is first and foremost a development of Hinduism and accepts many of the same suppositions that underlie Hinduism. However, Buddhism takes these suppositions in very different directions. The most notable of these underlying concepts is SAMSARA, or the cycle of rebirth. In both Hinduism and Buddhism, the goal of the spiritual person is liberation from the cycle of life and death, and from the karma that accompanies it. However, what that liberation means to the Buddhist is very different from what it means to the Hindu, as is the method of obtaining it.

Where the Hindu seeks to escape the cycle of life and death by fulfilling its requirements, the Buddhist seeks to escape the cycle of life and death by DISATTACH-ING from it—a "short cut," if you will. Buddha discovered the method of doing this in his meditation beneath the bodhi tree.

In Buddhism, Siddhartha Gautama is conceived of as being only one of the many Buddhas who have lived over time, though he is the only one commonly referred to as "The Buddha." Siddhartha Buddha is distinguished from the others because he is the one who taught the Dharma to the people. Many other Buddhas came before Siddhartha Buddha, and many have come after and will come. Generally, those who come after Siddhartha Buddha are called ARHATS or Arahats, because they had the benefit of Siddhartha's teaching to point the way, whereas earlier Buddhas did not.

As illustrated by Siddhartha's life, one becomes a Buddha by experiencing Bodhi, or Enlightenment, which leads one to Nirvana—a state of spiritual transcendence. Siddhartha Buddha's teachings for how to do this are set forth below. At death one may achieve Parinirvana—complete transcendence of the cycle of life and death in a state of immortal bliss. At that point, one becomes a full Arhat, or Buddha.

However, one can also delay the full buddhic state to become a boddhisattva, using one's enlightened state to help others on the path.

It is often said that Buddhism is not actually a religion but rather a philosophy. This is, however, really a semantic issue dependent upon one's definition of religion. The difference between religion and philosophy, and whether there is in fact any difference between them, depends very much upon who is speaking.

It is also said that Buddhism has no concept of God; this is also a semantic issue dependent upon how wide or narrow one's definition of the term "God" is. Buddhism does not separate the creator from the creation as certain religions do, but rather regards existence as creating itself. In religions that confuse ideas of "universal" and "personal" deity, this can be difficult to understand, as they are accustomed to thinking of God as a limited being separate from creation. Our Correllian understanding of Universal Deity, however, has no difficulty in understanding the unity of creator and created.

In the sense of what we Correllians generally term "Personal Deity," Buddhism has no dogma to speak of, though it does teach that "the gods" are also bound to the cycle of life and death and moving toward the transcendence of it. However, for many Buddhists, the Buddha himself and a variety of boddhisattvas and Arhats are themselves used as personal deities in the sense that we understand the term.

Buddhism teaches that all the things we normally perceive as "reality" are impermanent and illusory in nature, including our sense of self; attempting to create permanent attachments to these transient conditions is the root of suffering. Understanding and transcending the illusory nature of reality is an important aspect of Buddhism. Inherent in this teaching is the idea that those things which appear to irreparably bind one, including physical situations as well as spiritual situations like karma and the cycle of life and death, are really quite plastic and cannot actually bind one at all. That is why it is possible to transcend them through the practice of Buddhism.

Another important aspect of Buddhism is the rejection of the idea of that spiritual growth can be obtained by conference. Buddha taught that all true understanding must be acquired through experience and cannot be conferred through scripture or teaching—thus the extreme importance of personal meditation. An individual having attained Enlightenment can choose to teach others, but in this capacity is only an advisor and can only attempt to guide the student, who must make their own journey.

Thus belief in Buddha or his teachings does not in itself in any way confer Enlightenment, but rather Enlightenment must be worked for. However, this process can be assisted by using the teachings as a guide.

The Dharma Chakra, or Wheel of Doctrine, which Buddha set into motion at the Deer Park in Banares, contains these principle teachings:

The Four Noble Truths
1) Life is Suffering

2) Suffering is caused by ATTACHMENT

3) Suffering ends when one ceases to attach to things

4) One can cease to attach to things by following the Eightfold Path

The Eightfold Path
1) Right Understanding

2) Right Intent

3) Right Speech

4) Right Action

5) Right Livelihood

6) Right Effort

7) Right Mindfulness

8) Right Concentration

"Right," in the context of the Eightfold Path, means proceeding in each instance from a correct understanding of the Four Noble Truths. Each aspect of the Eightfold Path should help one to live by the Four Noble Truths and not to form transient attachments. The eight provisions of the Eightfold Path must also be understood to be not a sequence of steps to follow but rather a holistic program to be followed all together.

The Big and Little Boats

Like all religions, Buddhism has many branches. The two dominant branches are usually said to be the Big and Little Boats (as defined by the Big Boat).

Theravada Buddhism is the oldest surviving school of Buddhism. Theravada Buddhism arose around 950 Aries (250 BC) during the reign of the Mauryan Emperor ASOKA, himself a Buddhist. Theravada Buddhism relies upon the original Pali scriptures of Buddhist teaching, rejecting the later Mahayana scriptures. Theravada Buddhism is the kind of Buddhism practiced historically in most of southeast Asia. Theravada Buddhism is also sometimes termed Hinayana (Little Boat) Buddhism—though many consider the term *Hinayana* something of a slur, rather as Correllians regard the term *Neopagan*.

Mahayana (Big Boat) Buddhism arose in India around 1100 Aries (100 BC). Mahayana Buddhism places its emphasis on the idea of helping all people to attain Enlightenment (hence the name). Mahayana uses the term *Hinayana* to characterize other branches of Buddhism, which it regards as placing emphasis only on the individual pursuit of Enlightenment (hence "Little Boat"). Mahayana Buddhism has many branches of its own, which differ widely among themselves. It is generally regarded as the more "religious" form of Buddhism because of its more populist outlook and iconography. Mahayana Buddhism is the kind of Buddhism practiced historically in Tibet, China, Japan, and Korea.

Within Mahayana Buddhism there are many branches, of which only a few will be mentioned here.

Tibetan Buddhism: Tibetan Buddhism is the particular form of Mahayana Buddhism that developed in Tibet. It is distinguished by the belief in and widespread practice of conscious incarnation—that is, the intentional focus of one's reincarnations to continue the same goals through several lifetimes with conscious awareness of this fact. Such a person is called a TULKU, and although the Dalai Lama is the most famous example of a Tulku, Tibetan Buddhism in fact has hundreds of them. Tibetan Buddhism is also called LAMAISM.

Pure Land Buddhism: Pure Land Buddhism is a form of Buddhism that developed in China around the start of the age of Pisces (AD 400) or slightly earlier. Pure Land Buddhism places great emphasis on Amitabha Buddha, who is believed to preside over the "Pure Land" and to confer Enlightenment on his followers because of their pure devotion, as opposed to the personal effort required by other branches of Buddhism.

Zen Buddhism: Although best known by its Japanese name of Zen, this form of Buddhism first developed in China as Chan Buddhism. Zen Buddhism places its emphasis upon techniques of meditation in which the mind is made "blank" and thoughts are allowed to drift through it without attachment, sometimes for long periods. To assist in blanking the mind the practitioner may count, chant, order the rhythm of their breath, or focus upon the navel (that is, the solar plexus chakra). The idea behind this is that once the mind is no longer hindered by attachment, the inner buddhic nature will be realized and Enlightenment will result.

. . . .

Afro-diasporic Religion: Vodun and Santeria

Afro-diasporic religion is a term used to describe religions that owe their origin to Africa but that owe their further development to the New World. Afro-diasporic religions are based in traditional African practices that have been expanded or altered by exposure to other societies brought about by the African DIASPORA created by the SLAVE TRADE.

There are many different branches of Afro-diasporic religion, including but not limited to Condomble, Lucumi, Macumba, Santeria, and Vodun, as well as the magical tradition known as HOODOO. However, for ease of description, it is not uncommon to speak of Afro-diasaporic religions as being divided between Vodun and Santeria, using these as umbrella terms for those descending from French-speaking areas (Vodun) and those descending from Spanish-speaking areas (Santeria). Although it can be said that this is an oversimplification, it is an effective one for the purpose of giving a brief overview of these movements.

Vodun

Vodun, or Voodoo, is an Afro-diasporic religion found historically in Haiti and parts of the southern United States, notably New Orleans. These were French colonial territories and were freed from French control relatively early: Haiti by revolution, New Orleans as part of the Louisiana Purchase. Because of this, Vodun retains much of its older character, as opposed to Santeria, which is more assimilated.

Vodun is based upon the Vodu religion of the DAHOMEAN people, which is still very much practiced in Africa. The word *Vodu* means "spirit," and the religion is, in effect, the "Way of the Spirits." Historically, many Vodun leaders traveled to Africa for training under traditional teachers.

In Vodun, the creator is usually said to be DANBALLAH, the Serpent of the Universe. Danballah represents the motion of creation, flowing forth fluidly like a snake. Sometimes Danballah is called Bondye, the "Good God," but other times Bondye is thought of as a separate deity who is the origin of creation, while Danballah is the unfolding motion of creation. Danballah is also sometimes called Blanc Dani, or "White Dani."

In addition to Danballah, Vodun has many other deities, known as LOA. Danballah is thought of as being the origin of existence, but not as being involved in it in a personal manner. The loa are looked to for more personal interaction. Vodun has literally hundreds of loa, many of whom exist in several different variations. It might be said that there is a loa for every purpose—and not infrequently several for the same purpose.

It would be impossible to list all of the loa here, but many of them correspond to the Seven African Powers found in Santeria. Vodun loa are grouped together in houses, or families, which share similar characteristics. One of the most distinctive of these is the House of the GUEDES, or Gods of Death. The Guedes are distinct to Vodun and include the important BARON SAMEDI and MAMAN BRIGITTE.

Each loa is held to have a special heraldic sigil known as a VEVER, or veve. These usually quite elegant sigils are used in a variety of ways, but most notably are drawn out on the temple floor to invoke the deity.

Every person is held to have their own patron loa, who functions for them just as a patron deity would in any religion. Sometimes there are several of these. In addition, the spirits of the ancestors are of great importance in Vodun, and the ancestors are considered to remain actively involved in the lives of their descendants. Particularly important ancestors are sometimes classed among the loa, being regarded no longer as merely ancestors of a single house, but of the whole community.

Perhaps the most important of the loas is Legba, who is the gatekeeper of the loas and must be invoked anytime any loa is to be worked with. Legba is not invoked in working with the ancestors, however, because of the direct nature of the blood relationship between ancestor and descendant.

Ordinary worship takes place in the home, where a devout person may maintain several altars to loas and ancestors. Community worship takes place in the temple, in ceremonies organized by the priesthood. In Vodun, a priest is known as a *houngan*, while a priestess is known as a *mambo*. Exact practices vary from temple to temple and can be quite diverse.

The Vodun temple is usually oriented around a central pillar, known as the *porteau mitan*. The porteau mitan represents the axis of the universe; thus the temple represents the universe in microcosm. Ceremonies and offerings take place at the foot of the porteau mitan, and dances often circle around it. A central aspect of such Vodun ceremonies is the possession of the worshiper by his or her loa. This possession is generally induced through rhythmic drumming and ecstatic dance.

Another important aspect of Vodun is ANIMAL SACRIFICE. Animal sacrifice was once a feature of all of the world's religions—its practice is well attested in the so-called Old Testament, for example—but it has been gradually removed from most. Vodun is one of the few religions in the modern world whose followers still practice animal sacrifice, which has sometimes caused friction with other religions that have long since abandoned the practice.

And famously the Vodun religion also practices magic. Magic is very important in Vodun; however, most people not familiar with the religion have a distorted view of Vodun magic based largely upon sensational accounts that stress BLACK MAGIC practices—that is to say, magic meant to harm others. Although there are individuals who practice "black magic" in the Vodun religion, as in most religions they are regarded as doing something morally wrong. In Vodun, a black magic practitioner is known as a *bokor*.

Interestingly, it should be noted that in the days of slavery, a slave was not permitted to become a Vodun priest/ess. The reasoning behind this was that if the would-be priest/ess had a true vocation, they would also have enough magical ability to obtain their freedom. An exception to this rule was made for the New Orleans Voodoo Queen MARIE SALOPPE, because she had a romantic relationship with her master that would have been disrupted if she had been freed.

Vodun has two main divisions: Haitian Vodun and New Orleans Vodun. Over the centuries, these two forms have somewhat diverged in practice. A notable difference is the presence in New Orleans Vodun of the VOODOO QUEEN, powerful priestesses who exerted great control over the

New Orleans Vodun community. Many of the divergences between Haitian and New Orleans Vodun are the result of the policies of the Voodoo queens and their less-prominent male counterparts, commonly called VOODOO DOCTORS.

The term *Voodoo queen* refers to a certain level of preeminence, but there were usually several at any given time. The exception to this is during the long dominance of the MARIE LAVEAUS. Marie Laveau was an exceptionally powerful Vodun leader who came to totally dominate the New Orleans Vodun community in the early fifteenth century Pisces (nineteenth century AD). Under Marie Laveau's leadership, the Vodun community became very powerful in New Orleans and attracted a wide range of adherents from all ethnic and social backgrounds. Laveau is also said to have begun the process of identifying Vodun loas with Roman Catholic saints as a way of gaining greater social acceptance for her faith in an intolerant wider society.

Marie Laveau was succeeded by her daughter, who became MARIE LAVEAU II. The exchange of office took place in a memorable ceremony in which the elder Marie entered a room from which the younger Marie subsequently re-emerged, which gave rise to a legend that Marie Laveau had magically made herself young again. Marie Laveau II did not have her mother's political skill, however, and the cohesion of the New Orleans Vodun community began to falter. Marie Laveau II may have been succeeded by a Marie Laveau III, but by that time the family dynasty had lost most of its power and prominence, to the point that what actually became of them is unclear.

Although New Orleans continued to produce Voodoo queens after Marie Laveau II, these became increasingly minor figures and in time disappeared. The New Orleans Vodun community fell on hard times in the early sixteenth century Pisces (twentieth century AD) but began a resurgence after World War II and is very active today.

Santeria

As Vodun was practiced in French colonial areas, so Santeria was practiced in Spanish colonial areas. Santeria is to some extent an umbrella term, and it is certainly being used in that way here, covering a number of related movements with the same origin and similar characteristics.

Santeria originates among the YORUBA people of sub-Saharan West Africa, neighbors of the Dahomeans from whom Vodun descends, and there are many similarities in beliefs.

As in Vodun, Santeria places great importance upon the patron deity or deities, called the *encantado*, as well as upon the ancestors. Worshipers will usually maintain several altars in the home to the encantado and ancestors. Worshipers may be lay believers or become initiated clergy of the faith, and temple worship is an important feature of religious practice. Drumming, dance, and ecstatic possession are principal aspects of temple ritual, as is animal sacrifice. Magic is an important tradition and widely practiced.

In Santeria, the deities are known as *orishas*, or *orixas*, and are analogous to the Vodun loa. There are, however, far fewer orishas than loa, with seven major orishas taking the most prominent role. These are the Seven African Powers that will be discussed below. Ellegua, analogous to Legba, is the gatekeeper of the orishas and must be invoked in order to work with them.

Another distinctive aspect of Santeria is the extent to which the orishas are identified with Roman Catholic saints (hence the name Santeria). As in Vodun, this identification with the more dominant religion was originally undertaken as a prophylactic measure to ward off persecution. Today the identification of the orishas with the saints is often much less important than formerly, and it was never so complete that the original nature of the orisha was forgotten.

The Seven African Powers

Obatalah: The creator, Obatalah, is often thought of as both masculine and feminine.

Yemaya: The goddess of the ocean, an abundant and loving Mother Goddess.

Ogun: God of smithcraft, the forest, and war.

Orunmila: God of fate, wisdom, and divination.

Shango: God of thunder and fertility.

Oshun: Goddess of fresh water, love, beauty, and sexuality.

Ellegua: God of magic and mysteries, gatekeeper and messenger of the gods.

In addition to these major orishas there are also a variety of other orishas, often with more localized followings. These include all manner of Deity, but two shall be mentioned here as having particular relevance. These are:

Oya: Goddess of change and transformation, death and rebirth—analogous to Maman Brigitte in Vodun. Many people count Oya as one of the Seven African Powers in place of Orunmila, after the teaching of LOUISAH TEISH.

Pomba Gira: In Brazilian usage, Pomba Gira is a goddess of fate and is the consort of Eshu (Ellegua).

The Afro-diasporic religions are very important in the modern world and are found throughout North and South America. In discussing them, we have given only an overview of their beliefs and practices, but hopefully it is enough to give you an idea of what they are about.

. . . .

Hinduism and Jainism

The word *Pagan* was coined by the Judeo-Christian (or Abrahamic) religions to refer to everyone who was not a Jew, Christian, or Muslim. Consequently, the term *Pagan* takes in a lot of territory. It is the same with the word *Hindu*. *Hinduism* is a term used to distinguish the traditional religions of India from more narrowly defined movements like Buddhism and Sikhism, and from movements of foreign origin like Christianity and Islam. Basically, if you are following Indian traditional religion and you are not one of these non-Hindu groups, then, ipso facto, you are a Hindu. Because of this, exactly what constitutes Hinduism is difficult to define in other than broad terms. Even then, different views exist as to what should and should not come under the term *Hindu*.

For example, does the religion of the ancient INDUS VALLEY civilization come under this heading? Are movements like Jainism and Tantricism part of Hinduism, or are they separate movements? These are questions on which many points of view exist, and which we are certainly not going to try and resolve here. Rather, let us simply caution that the definition of Hinduism can be a bit tricky and open to multiple interpretations.

Hinduism and the Vedas

For many people, Hinduism is defined by the Vedas, an ancient collection of scriptures written in the classic SANSKRIT language. Indian religion may be said to be divided into two branches on this: the *Astika*, or orthodox, who recognize the Vedas as being divinely inspired (*Shruti*) and the *Nastika*, or non-Vedic, who do not recognize the Vedas as scripture. The Jains, Buddhists, and Sikhs fall into the Nastika category.

Written between 1100 Taurus and 1050 Aries (1700–150 BC), the Vedas are the oldest writings in Sanskrit. The term *Veda* means "wisdom." There are four main Vedas, which are called *Samhita* ("collections") and are regarded as the core of the canon. These are:

The Rig Veda: The oldest of the Vedas, the Rig Veda is a book of hymns to the gods.

The Yajur Veda: The Yajur Veda is a book of ritual form laying out various important ceremonies and how to perform them.

The Sama Veda: The Sama Veda is a book of chants drawn from the Rig

Veda and expounded upon in other ways.

The Atharva Veda: The Atharva Veda deals with magic and medicine, as well as with more philosophical understandings of the nature of being.

In addition to these, there are a number of commentaries on the Vedas that are often included under the name. These include:

The Brahmanas: The Brahmanas are books of ritual written as commentaries to the Samhitas.

The Aranyakas: The Aranyakas, or "Books of the Wilderness," are mystical works written for SADHUS, mendicant Hindu holy men.

The Upanishads: The Upanishads are deeply philosophical books presented in the form of dialogues, which expound upon the Samhitas and are considered to be the completion as well as the fulfillment of the Vedic literature (*Vedanta*). The Upanishads develop the spiritual ideas of the Vedas to a greater extent and are thus termed the "Higher Enquiry," or *Uttar Mimamsa*.

And beyond those are the Puranas (Books of Ancient Things) and the Itahasas (Epic Narratives), which catalog a wide range of philosophical, cosmological, and historical issues. These are post-Vedic in origin but are also included under the general term *Veda* by many.

All of these works serve to set forth the basic tenets that define the center of Hindu belief. Around this center swirls thousands of years of additional teaching and exposition that carries the core teachings in many different directions. Because there are so many different directions, it must be understood in going forward that everything we say about Hindu belief must surely be regarded as overgeneralization, and in every particular there will surely be some school of Hindu thought that disagrees with our interpretation. Having given fair warning on this, we will now do our best to explain the particulars of Hindu belief.

Beliefs of Hinduism

Perhaps most central to Hindu belief is the idea of SAMSARA, or the cycle of life and death. The soul, or *Atman*, lives many lives in many forms, constantly reincarnating to live and die and live again. This idea is found in Orthodox Astika Hinduism as well as in Jainism and Buddhism. In each of these, the cycle of life and death is not regarded as a good thing but as a cycle of suffering to be escaped.

The conditions we experience in the cycle of life and death are determined by karma. The Hindu idea of karma might best be described as the equal return of our actions: all that we do comes back to us, measure for measure. As regards reincarnation, karma means that if you do good things in this life, you will be reborn into a better situation. If you do bad things in this life, your next life will be less favorable. This is very important, because traditional Hindu society is dominated by CASTE, a social system which decreed that children must follow their parents' profession. Consequently, one's birth determined much of one's life.

Modern Wicca acquires the word *karma* directly from Hinduism, but as you have learned, our ideas about karma are similar to but not identical with the Hindu concept. Our attitude toward the cycle of life and death is markedly different (looking upon it in much more positive terms), as are our perceptions of the cause of karma (growth and learning) and its effect, which we see as potentially multiple rather than in exact measure.

In Hinduism, the Atman is regarded as identical with Ultimate Deity, or BRAHMA, the creator and sustainer of the universe. Thus Deity is within all things and is the ultimate nature of all things. It is ignorance (*Avidya*) of this inner divine nature that binds us to the cycle of life and death and creates suffering.

For the Hindu, escape from the cycle of life and death is accomplished through MOKSHA, or "liberation." Moksha brings release from and transcendence of the cycle of life and death, and brings union with Deity. This is accomplished by the realization of the true Divine Self, which is within each person. This aspect of the self has been obscured by the cycle of life and death, to which the Atman has bound itself through desire and ignorance and which must be overcome through self-mastery.

In many branches of Hinduism, this true Divine Self is considered to be the only reality, all else being an illusion created by the soul's ignorance. This illusion is called "Maya." Thus moksha brings one from illusion to a true understanding of reality.

There are within Hinduism many different ideas of how to achieve moksha; all involve overcoming the ego and putting an end to worldly desires. The methods of pursuing moksha are generally described as YOGA, meaning "to unite." There are many different kinds of yoga, all of which seek to transcend the illusory and achieve union with the divine through spiritual practices usually involving meditation and development of the energetic centers and systems of the body.

Hindu yoga has developed a deep understanding of the energetic centers of the body. The term *chakra* is Hindu in origin, and though as we have observed in various places within our Second Degree studies, while many peoples had a knowledge of the energy centers of the body, including the ancient Greeks, Celts, and Taoist Chinese, it is the Hindus who developed that knowledge the furthest.

The goal of many kinds of Hindu yoga is to awaken the kundalini energy, which dwells at the base of the spine, and use it to unite all seven major chakras in a way that will ultimately trigger moksha. In Correllian parlance, we would describe this as the full activation of the lunar energetic circuit.

Four Stages of Life

In Hinduism, it is regarded that an ideal life has four stages (*Ashrams*). Each of these stages is harder to fulfill than the one which came before it, and not everyone will fulfill all four—though ideally one should attempt to. Traditionally, each one is said to ideally require twenty-five years to complete.

The four Ashrams are as follows:

Brahmacharya: Life as a student. This is the stage of learning and study, to prepare one for life.

Grahasta: Life as a householder. This is the stage at which one marries and has a family, building a life together within a wider community.

Vanaprastha: Life as a retiree. This is the stage where, as one's children are grown, one retires from public life to devote oneself to meditation and spiritual pursuits.

Sanyasa: Life as an ascetic. This is the stage at the end of life when one focuses on one's spiritual development and the pursuit of moksha to the exclusion of all else.

One Hundred Million Gods

In addition to this very intellectualized understanding of the universe, Hinduism also possesses another much more personal side. Like Wicca, Hinduism recognizes an ultimate form of Deity that is expressed through many other forms. It is said that Hinduism has one hundred million gods —and this may be an understatement.

Hinduism recognizes countless deities, some of which are worshiped throughout the Hindu world, others only within very narrow localities. Though we have spoken of Brahma as the ultimate form of Deity in Hinduism, this being the dominant view, many other Hindu deities are looked at as the ultimate form of Deity by their own followers.

Hinduism is also, like most Pagan religions, extremely syncretic. Deities that have nothing to do with one another in origin can become closely linked over time or even seen as being the same Deity under different names. This is true for the three most universal deities in Hinduism:

Brahma the Creator, Vishnu the Preserver, and Shiva the Transformer. It is generally regarded that these three gods began completely separately, but over time came to be viewed as a Divine Trinity (TRIMURTI), each being complementary aspects of the same ultimate power.

Another important aspect of Hinduism is the role of the Goddess as SHAKTI. Each god is associated with a goddess who plays the role of Shakti, personifying the divine power of the god. For example, the Shakti goddesses associated with the Trimurti described above are Saraswati (Shakti of Brahma), Lakshmi (Shakti of Vishnu), and Parvati (Shakti of Shiva). In some branches of Hinduism, it is Shakti as Great Goddess (Mahadevi) who is the ultimate form of Deity.

The three principal branches of modern Hinduism are the Vaishnava, Shaiva, and Shaktam, movements which focus respectively on Vishnu, Shiva, or Shakti as Ultimate Deity.

Some of the more important Hindu deities include:

Brahma: Called "the Creator," Brahma brought the universe into being and regulates its existence. In iconography, Brahma is normally depicted as a man with four heads, symbolizing the four directions and thus omniscience and omnipotence. Although considered a major deity, Brahma is also thought of as remote and is not normally the recipient of worship in his own right.

Saraswati: Saraswati is the consort of Brahma. Saraswati is the goddess of learning, knowledge, and the arts. In iconography, Saraswati's color is white, and she is often shown playing a musical instrument.

Vishnu: Called "the Preserver," Vishnu might be described as the god of life. Vishnu is perceived as a kindly and loving, deeply personal deity. Vishnu is thought of as having had many earthly incarnations (avatars), during which he has been of service to humankind. These incarnations include, among others, the classical figures of VAMANA, RAMA, and KRISHNA, and according to some also include such figures as Gautama Buddha, Jesus Christ, and Mahatma Gandhi. In iconography, Vishnu and his avatars are normally colored blue. To the Vaisnava, Vishnu is the ultimate form of Deity.

Lakshmi: Lakshmi is the consort of Vishnu. Lakshmi is the goddess of abundance, prosperity, and good fortune. In iconography, Lakshmi's color is red, and she is normally depicted upon a LOTUS, a sacred flower in Hinduism, symbolizing creation as well as enlightenment.

Shiva: Called "the Transformer"—often rendered as "the Destroyer"—Shiva is a god who breaks down old forms to create new ones. Shiva is connected with mysticism and asceticism. In iconography, Shiva is usually colored white. Perhaps the most famous image of Shiva is the NATARAJ, or Lord of the Dance, depicting Shiva as maintaining existence in the form of a dance. Shiva also has an androgynous form, called Ardhanarishvara, which is half god and half goddess. Shiva is also commonly depicted in the form of a SHIVA LINGA, or stylized divine phallus. To the Shaiva, Shiva is the ultimate form of Deity. To the Shaktam, Shiva is the servant of the transcendent goddess Shakti.

Parvati: Parvati is the consort of Shiva and is regarded as the reincarnation of his earlier consort Sati. Parvati is a loving and protective Mother Goddess and is usually regarded as an aspect of the transcendent goddess Shakti, and through Shakti is assimilated with many other goddesses. Notably, Parvati has an association with fiercer goddess forms like Kali and Durga. In iconography, Parvati is usually shown mounted upon a lion or tiger.

Shakti: Also termed Devi, Shakti is the transcendent form of Goddess, who can be viewed as the inner nature of all things and portrayed through any number of other goddess forms. To the Shaktam, Shakti is the ultimate form of Deity.

Kali: Kali is a complex goddess who is often conceived of as the ultimate form of Deity by her worshipers. Kali is most familiar to the Western world as a goddess of death and transformation, but she is also often thought of as a Mother Goddess. Kali is associated with Shiva and is often thought of as a form of Parvati (or vice versa). In iconography, Kali is usually colored black (*Kali* means "black") and often depicted as a female ascetic.

Ganesa: Ganesha is called the "Remover of Obstacles" and is a god of good fortune, wealth, and happiness. He is also a god of knowledge and of the arts and sciences. Ganesha is lord of beginnings, and he is invoked at the beginning of ceremonies and the beginning of all new ventures. Ganesha is the son of the goddess Parvati, either alone or with her consort Shiva. In iconography, Ganesha is portrayed with the head of an elephant and a plump belly, representing abundance.

Durga: Durga is the fiercer form of Parvati. Durga is a warrior goddess fully armed and mounted upon a lion or tiger and doing battle with evil.

Krisna: Krisna is an important avatar of Vishnu, whose qualities he shares. Krisna is well-known in the Western world from the Krisna Consciousness movement, which sees him as the ultimate form of Deity.

Jainism

Jainism is one of the principal indigenous religions of India. Some consider Jainism a separate movement from Hinduism, while others regard it as a heterodox (*Nastika*) movement within Hinduism. Jainism is generally spoken of as having been founded by MAHAVIRA SWAMI—a contemporary of Confucius, Lao-tzu, Pythagoras, and Buddha—though Jains regard Mahavira as only the most recent of their many spiritual teachers, or *Tirthankaras*.

Tirthankaras

Like Hinduism and Buddhism, Jainism believes in samsara, or the cycle of life and death. The soul, or *jiva* (life force), experiences endless incarnations in many different forms, which are dictated by its karma. In Jainism, karma is created by attach-ments formed through both thought and action.

Also like Hinduism and Buddhism, Jainism believes that one can transcend the cycle of life and death by achieving moksha, or Enlightenment. One achieves moksha after many lifetimes of working toward it through the practice of ASCETI-CISM. This asceticism includes refraining from worldly interactions or possessions, and strict practices regarding diet and meditation. The path to achieving moksha has been pointed out to people by a series of great spiritual teachers known as Tirthankaras.

A Tirthankara is one who, after achieving moksha, teaches others how to pursue it. At death, the Tirthankara leaves behind the cycle of life and death, entering Nirvana as a *Jina*, or spiritual victor over samsara. The term *Jain* means a "Devotee of the Jina."

Having achieved moksha, the Tirthankara enters into a state of perfect knowledge and omniscience, according to Jain thought. All Tirthankaras have this same perfect knowledge. However, the successive Tirthankaras appear to reveal successive layers of knowledge and build upon their predecessors because they reveal only as much knowledge as the people of their day can understand. Thus each Tirthankara, although having all knowledge at hand, teaches a bit more of it than his predecessors.

Jains believe that time is infinite, having no beginning and no end, but operating on regular cycles. Such a cycle of time is called a *kalchakra*. A kalchakra, in turn, is divided into two hemicycles, called an *utsarpini* (ascending hemicycle) and an *avsarpini* (descending hemicycle). Jains believe that we are currently in the avsarpini hemicycle of the present kalchakra. Tirthankaras do not randomly happen but appear during these cycles of time according to a set cosmic pattern. Forty-eight Tirthankaras are born during each kalchakra, making for twenty-four Tirthankaras during each hemicycle. The most recent of these Tirthankaras was Mahavira Swami.

The Tirthankaras are highly honored in Jainism, and their statues appear in Jain temples; however, they are revered as honored guides who point the way toward moksha rather than as gods or cosmic forces.

Three Principles

The three principles of Jainism set forth by Mahavira are non-sidedness, maybeness, and karma.

Non-sidedness, or *Anekantavada*, is the opposite of one-sidedness and refers to the belief that all understanding is subjective in nature and that the perception is never separate from the perceiver. This means that one can never understand the totality of existence, only different aspects of it, which one must assume to be influenced by point of view. Because one can never assume one sees the whole, one must remember that many points of view are potentially of equal validity.

Maybeness, or *Syadvada*, is the means of examining a thing to try to determine its relative truth within the context of non-sidedness. Syadvada asks a series of seven statements that may be used to consider whether a thing is or is not true. The seven statements are:

- "Maybe it is true."
- "Maybe it isn't true."
- "Maybe it is true but at the same time it isn't true."
- "Maybe you can't tell if it's true."
- "Maybe it is true…but you still can't tell if it is."
- "Maybe it isn't true…but you still can't tell that it isn't."
- "Maybe it is true but at the same time isn't true…but you still can't tell either way."

And finally, karma—as discussed above—is the idea that one's thoughts and actions bind one into the cycle of life and death, bringing about good or bad conditions in life that reflect the karma one has previously earned. Karma is extremely important in Jainism, as is illustrated by the Nine Tattwas.

The Nine Tattwas

The Nine Tattwas are a further series of nine principles that encapsulate Jain thought and also set forth the path to moksha.

1) **Jiva:** Jiva means "life force" and refers to the soul of any living thing. Jainism regards all souls as being equal and as having the same nature and the same potential to achieve moksha. This equality of souls is the basis for much that is unique in the Jain moral system.

2) **Ajiva:** Ajiva refers to things that are not physically living. Unlike Correllianism, Jainism regards things that are not physically living as having no soul or higher nature, nor any karma.

3) **Asrava:** Asrava refers to the acquisition of karma. To the Jain, karma is created by both thoughts and actions, and has a kind of physicality thought of as "dust" that accrues to the soul. In this sense, the Jain regards karma to some extent as we might think of an energy blockage.

4) **Bhanda:** Bhanda means "binding" and refers to the bondage created by the acquisition of karma. This karma may be good or bad, as either is equally a bond that holds the soul in the cycle of life and death. Moksha is possible only through the elimination of Bhanda.

5) **Samvara:** Samvara refers to the point at which one ceases to acquire new karma.

6) **Nirjara:** Nirjara refers to lightening one's karma through the practice of spiritual disciplines that allow karma to be released or overcome.

7) **Moksha:** Moksha means "enlightenment," as in Hinduism, and refers to the transcendence of the cycle of life and death and the achievement of Nirvana.

8) **Punya:** Punya means "merit" and refers to the positive karma accrued through positive actions, which helps to move one toward eventual moksha and improves one's karmic lot in the meantime.

9) **Papa:** Papa means "demerit" and refers to the negative karma created by improper actions. Such negative karma brings about negative circumstances in one's life and must be overcome before moksha can be reached.

The Five Vows

To help people reach moksha, Mahavira set forth five vows that would help them if followed. In Jainism, only monks and nuns follow the Five Vows strenuously, but every person is expected to make an effort to follow them as much as they are able.

The Five Vows are:

Ahisma, or Nonviolence: Because Jains regard all life as being of equal value, nonviolence is of extreme importance to them. Nonviolence means refraining from doing either emotional or physical harm to any living thing, even at the cost of your own life. Jain monks and nuns traditionally carry a ceremonial broom, which they use to gently sweep insects from their path, and some wear a special mask over their nose and mouth to ensure that they never accidentally inhale an insect.

Satya, or Truthfulness: This means exactly what it would imply: careful adherence to strictest honesty, both with others and with oneself.

Asteya, or Not Taking What Is Not Yours: Asteya is often termed more simply as "non-stealing"; however, there is more in this concept than what that phrase implies. In Asteya, the Jain not only refrains from stealing as such, but also from taking things that, while not actually owned by another, are nevertheless not their own. Asteya can also refer to nonphysical concepts; for example, As-

teya would include not attributing to oneself qualities which one does not possess.

Brahmacharya, or Celibacy: Brahmacharya refers to abstinence from sexual stimulation of all sorts.

Aparigraha, or Nonattachment: Aparigraha means not attaching to physical things and is the basis of the Jain renunciation of physical possessions. However, it also means not attaching to emotions, people, events, or anything which might cause karma and bind one to the cycle of birth and death. Nonattachment is the vital element in achieving moksha.

Djigambara and Svetambara

Jainism has two main branches: the Djigambara and the Svetambara. These two schools of thought share much in common but are also separated by certain key beliefs.

Djigambara means "SKY CLAD" and is the older and more severe of the two branches, while *Svetambara* means "white clad."

The principal difference between the Djigambara and the Svetambara regards their attitude toward women. The Djigambara have only monks, while the Svetambara have both monks and nuns. This is because the Djigambara believe that women cannot achieve moksha until reincarnating in male form, while the Svetambara believe that both men and women can achieve moksha in the present life. In fact, the Svetambara believe that the nineteenth Tirthankara, MALLINATH, was female—a view rejected by the Djigambara.

Another notable difference is that while both the Djigambara and the Svetambara believe in the renunciation of physical possessions, the Djigambara take this to the greater extreme. Djigambara monks own only two things: the broom used to sweep away insects from the path, which must be made from naturally shed peacock feathers, and a drinking gourd. Otherwise, Djigambara monks own nothing—not clothing, for they go nude at all times, hence the term "sky clad" (a term Wiccans acquired from the Jains), and not even a bowl for eating, as they eat from their hands. The Svetambara monk or nun, on the other hand, is allowed wrapped garments of plain white cloth (hence the term "white clad")—one worn around the waist like a skirt and the other around the shoulders like a shawl— and they may have a bowl in which to receive donations of food.

Of course, the ordinary members of both branches do not live like this; this level of asceticism is for the monks and nuns only. However, everyone honors the teachings of the faith and integrates as much of these teachings into their life as they can.

Both Hinduism and Jainism are extremely ancient, extremely current movements around the world today. The teachings of these two great religions have not only informed their own peoples' practice but have also influenced many other movements. As we see in the section on Buddhism, both Hindu and Jain practice were fundamental to the origin of that faith. It will also be immediately evident to the student the degree to which both Hindu and Jain teaching have influenced contemporary Wicca and other Western metaphysical movements.

. . . .

Platonism, Hermeticism, and Alchemy

Platonism

One of the great religions of the ancient world, Platonism has exerted a powerful influence on people's ideas throughout western history.

Platonism is the movement founded by PLATO and named for him.

One of the foremost of Greek philosophers, Plato was a student of SOCRATES and the teacher of ARISTOTLE: a trio whose work is formative to modern ideas of philosophy.

Plato was born as Aristocles, son of Ariston, in 776 Aries (424 BC), in the Athenian colony of Aegina. Plato (Greek

431

Platon) was a nickname given to him in his youth by Ariston of Argos and means "broad." Plato's mother was the lady Perictione, a descendant of the great Athenian statesman SOLON. After the death of Plato's father, Ariston, Perictione married her own maternal uncle Pyrilampes, who was a powerful figure in the Athenian government and close friend of PERICLES. His family's prominence meant that young Plato received the best of educations. Perictione herself was a Pythagorean and made certain that her son was familiar with Pythagorean ideas.

As a youth, Plato was a student of Socrates, whose teachings so alarmed the Athenian authorities that they had him tried, condemned, and executed (via suicide) in 801 Aries (399 BC)—one of the more famous MARTYRDOMS of history.

The execution of Socrates, which Plato saw as profoundly unjust, had a deep effect on Plato, and Socrates' ideas are expounded upon in Plato's work, as is Socrates' method of teaching through dialog, intended to lead the student to finding the truth rather than merely presenting the truth as a *fait accompli.*

Not unlike Pythagoras, Plato traveled widely in his youth, returning permanently to Athens only at the age of forty. In 815 Aries (385 BC), Plato opened his own school of philosophy, called the ACADEMY. The Academy was located outside the walls of Athens in an area known generally as Akademia, after an ancient olive grove of that name which was sacred to the goddess Athena.

Here Plato taught his ideas to his students, the most famous of whom was Aristotle, who would later open a competing school known as the LYCEUM. Unlike many earlier philosophers, however, Plato did more than teach his ideas: he also wrote them down in numerous works.

Plato died peacefully at the age of eighty in 853 Aries (347 BC). At his death, Plato passed the Headship of the Academy to his nephew Speusippus. This is what caused Aristotle to open his Lyceum. The Academy remained a center of learning for many centuries, dying out during the Roman period, only to be revived by later Platonists. Plato's Academy was permanently closed by the Christian emperor Justinian I in 129 Pisces (AD 529), in an attempt to suppress Pagan ideas.

Teachings of Plato

Of course Plato was also important in the development of mathematics and science; however, as this is a course on religion, it is his religious ideas that we shall exclusively concern ourselves with here.

Plato taught that the physical world was not the reality it appears to be, but rather an imperfect reflection of the true spiritual reality that underlies it. For Plato, the physical world is a manifestation of a larger spiritual world whose perfect archetypal forms can be re-created in the physical but rarely approach their true higher nature.

This world of archetypal forms will readily be seen as comparable to our own concept of the Higher Self, which is a transcendent and more perfect version of the physical self.

For Plato, all physical things were attempts to approximate these spiritual archetypes: a perfect version of any given thing existed in spirit, but the limitations of the physical world warped its attempts to find physical form. Better understanding of the archetypal form allowed a better approximation in the physical, and in time, through diligent application, all things can be made to perfectly approximate their archetypes.

The ultimate archetype, of course, is God, the One. The One is universal, eternal, and without limit. For Plato, the One is inherently good, and all things in existence would be good if they perfectly approximated the nature of the One. Indeed, the One is also simply called the Good.

The physical world comes directly from the One by a series of unfolding steps. Each of these steps places greater limitations on divine energy and thus removes it further from its original state of perfection. From the One emanates the divine consciousness (*Nous*), which constitutes the first limitation. Divine consciousness is a limitation because it imposes an order, which by definition must involve limitation. For Plato, the divine consciousness is the DEMIURGE, or creator (literally "builder"). Like the One from which it originates, the Demiurge is good and desires only to do good, but as it has imposed limitation upon itself in the form of consciousness, it is already limited in its ability to manifest perfect form. For later Platonic philosophers, often called Neo-Platonists, this made the Demiurge the origin of imperfection and jaundiced their view of it, but that was not true of the earlier Platonists.

From the Nous came forth Psyche, the soul. Psyche includes all souls: individual souls as well the WORLD SOUL. The soul seeks to manifest itself perfectly, according to its archetypal nature as an emanation of Nous, but the soul is even more limited than Nous and cannot manifest its perfect nature without hard work.

Finally, from Psyche comes Physis—the physical world. The physical world, and thus any physical being, is an emanation of the soul, which in turn is an emanation of Nous, which emanates from the One that underlies all and is itself perfect. However, the physical world is most limited of all and does not even at first realize its own imperfect nature, and must struggle to bring through the perfect archetypes that underlie it.

In this we may see the nascence of our own doctrine of the Planes of Existence.

But however greatly the successive steps into physical manifestation have limited it, the physical being still has its perfect archetype at its core, and this archetype can be accessed and aligned with to make the physical manifestation more perfect. This struggle for perfection is the *reason d'être* of Platonism, which—at least in its earlier form—maintains the hope of achieving perfect manifestation of the perfect archetypal form into the physical.

Anamnessis

Because a perfect archetypal form is at the core of our being, perfection can be accessed from within. Anamnessis, or remembering, is an important aspect of this process.

Plato taught that knowledge was inborn, a part of the perfect archetype. We already have all knowledge within us, we just don't realize it. Thus for Plato knowledge was not acquired but remembered. It was the duty of the teacher not to impart knowledge so much as to help the student uncover the pre-existing inner knowledge. This is the idea behind the SOCRATIC METHOD, which leads the student to understanding through questioning and discussion rather than simply passing on knowledge by rote.

Because they believe it possible to access a more perfect knowledge from within oneself, Platonists place great emphasis on issues of contemplation and meditation. The contemplation of the true spiritual reality is key to improving its physical manifestation, as well as to the advancement of the spirit.

Platonists believe that after death the soul will reincarnate. However, for some souls that have become particularly imperfect, this reincarnation will be delayed by purgative punishments intended to cleanse it of the effects of bad actions. For other souls that have perfected their nature, this reincarnation will be unnecessary, and they will live among the blessed in an afterworld paradise.

Evil

Like the contemporary Correllian, the Platonist does not believe in "EVIL" as a cosmic force. What people think of as evil, when not merely a matter of egocentric point of view, is not the opposite of good but rather the lack of good. The Platonic analogy is to shadow. A shadow may appear to exist but has no actual existence, as it is merely the effect of the blockage of light from a given area. Bring light to the area that is in shadow, and the shadow will be shown to be ephemeral. The shadow will not fight against the light and certainly cannot affect, let alone overcome, the light, because the shadow is itself merely the absence of light and does not exist in light's presence.

The Later Platonists

The term "Neo-Platonist" is a modern academic distinction that would have been highly offensive to the so-called Neo-Platonists themselves. They regarded themselves as being orthodox Platonists who were merely expounding upon the established ideas of their movement in a natural effort to gain deeper understanding. Therefore, let us refer to them as the later Platonists.

The later Platonist philosophers are those who lived during the latter Roman empire. The later Platonists are distinguished from the early Platonists by several features; notably, the later Platonists took a more jaundiced view of the physical world and the idea of its imperfection. In consequence, they placed a great emphasis on the idea of achieving perfection, which to them was a reuniting with the One. Toward this aim, they made increasing use of THEURGY, or magical ritual intended to bring them into alignment with the divine through direct experience of it.

The leading exponents of this later Platonism were:

Plotinus: Plotinus (1405–1470 Aries / AD 205–270) is often called the "Father of Neo-Platonism" and is considered the defining philosopher of later Platonic thought. Plotinus emphasized the negative character of the physical world. Plotinus was of Egyptian lineage.

Porphyry: Porphyry (1433–1509 Aries / AD 233–309) was a student of Plotinus who edited his teacher's works into their form as the *Enneads*. Porphyry also wrote influential biographies of Plotinus, Plato, and Pythagoras, and commentaries on Aristotle. Porphyry wrote widely on a wide range of moral and metaphysical subjects. He was also a noted opponent of Christianity who taught that Jesus was a great philosopher but held that contemporary Christians did not reflect Jesus's teachings. Porphyry was of Tyrian lineage.

Iamblichus: Iamblichus (1445–1525 Aries / AD 245–325) was a student of Porphyry but differed from Porphyry on the subject of theurgy, the use of magic to attune oneself to the divine. Iamblichus wrote commentaries on the work of Pythagoras, Plato, and Aristotle. He also wrote a number of works, including *De Mysteriis Aegytiorum* (On Egyptian Mysteries), which dealt with the practice of theurgy. Iamblichus was of Syrian lineage, a descendant of the priest kings of Emessa and thus a distant relative of the Emperor ELAGABALUS.

Julian: Flavius Claudius Julianus (1531–1553 Aries / AD 331–353) was the last great exponent of Platonic religion, as well as the last Pagan emperor of Rome. Emperor Julian wrote a number of religious works expounding upon Platonic ideas. He stressed personal spiritual experience and faith, as well as the importance of charity. Emperor Julian's writings about the nature of priesthood have been very important in the attitudes of many later Pagans. The emperor also wrote the *Contra Galileos*, responding to Christian claims against Pagans. As Emperor, Julian guaranteed religious freedom throughout the Roman Empire. He is called "the Apostate" by Christians and "the Restorer" (Restitutor) by Pagans.

Hermeticism

Hermeticism is a metaphysical school of thought that was developed in Greco-Roman Egypt, based upon writings attributed to HERMES TRISMEGISTUS, or Hermes "Thrice Greatest." In the Hermetic writings, Hermes Trismegistus is presented as a venerable Egyptian sage who has pur-

sued the secrets of the universe and now shares them with the reader. It is generally held that Hermes Trismegistus is actually a Greek name for the great Egyptian god THOTH, whose titulary in fact included the EPITHET "Thrice Greatest," and that the Hermetic writings were created by many authors who attributed their work to the god in the belief that he had inspired them. It is also possible that Hermes Trismegistus was a specific teacher, perhaps actually named Hermes or Thoth, who was confounded with the god either accidentally or intentionally. In any event, Hermes Trismegistus was traditionally looked upon by Hermetics as having been a mortal teacher like Pythagoras or Plato, and he is often still spoken of as such.

Egypt in the HELLENISTIC and imperial Roman periods was a meeting ground for many different cultural traditions whose interaction produced a vibrant cosmopolitan society combining the best (and sometimes worst) elements of its disparate components. In addition to the obvious mixture of Greek and native Egyptian ideas brought about by ALEXANDER THE GREAT'S conquest of Egypt in 868 Aries (332 BC) and the subsequent PTOLEMAIC Dynasty, there were other important elements in this mix, including a sizeable Jewish community.

These different peoples lived side by side in the great cities of Egypt, especially ALEXANDRIA, and despite occasional conflicts they shared their customs and ideas in a way that led to great innovations and created something of a cultural renaissance. This was especially true in the field of metaphysics where Egyptian magic, Greek philosophy, and Jewish mysticism combined in new and different ways to create several schools of thought which have remained important ever since.

Ptolemaic culture encouraged this religious syncretism, which is exemplified by Greco-Egyptian deities like SERAPIS, ZEUS-AMMON, and HERMANUBIS, who combined both native Egyptian and Greek aspects as well as new Greek interpretations of ancient Egyptian gods like Isis, who now found a wide new following beyond the borders of Egypt. Against this milieu it is not difficult to see how the Egyptian Thoth could become Hermes Trismegistus.

The CORPUS HERMETICUM is said to have comprised forty-two books attributed to the god Thoth, though this number is likely symbolic. Most of these works were written in Greek (at least in their surviving form), but some have been discovered written in the COPTIC language, which is the latter form of Egyptian. Historically, however, the Hermetic works have most often been disseminated in Latin.

Of the forty-two books said to have composed the Corpus Hermeticum, only sixteen would survive the fall of the Roman Empire. Many of the works are written in the form of dialogues in which a point of theology is expounded by a deity or teacher to a student. Most often the teacher is Hermes Trismegistus, but in some of the works Hermes himself is the student, instructed by a god.

This literary form is a traditional Egyptian one and can be found in such Egyptian works as the INSTRUCTIONS OF DUAUF or the TESTAMENT OF AMENEMHAT.

Indeed, much of the material expounded upon in the Hermetic texts is also of traditional Egyptian extraction, recensed for a new audience and reinterpreted in light of new cultural forces.

The most famous Hermetic text, however, and the one which is considered formative to many metaphysical movements, is the Tabula Smaragdina, or EMERALD TABLET—a term that might just as easily and perhaps more readily be rendered the "Green Book." This work, consisting of just fourteen lines, is a straightforward monologue setting forward the essentials of Hermetic thought in clear terms as if spoken by Hermes Trismegistus—man or God—himself.

The Emerald Tablet is the source of the famous maxim "As above, so below," considered by many to encapsulate the highest ideas of metaphysical thought and repeatedly quoted throughout our Correllian writings.

Since it is, as stated, only fourteen lines, and is absolutely fundamental to many schools of metaphysical thought, I reproduce the Emerald Tablet here in my own translation from the Latin (after Chrysogonas Polydorus, Nuremburg, 1141 Pisces /AD 1541).

Tabula Smaragdina
(The Emerald Tablet)

1) *Verum, sine mendacio, certum et verissimum.*

It is true, without falsity, certain and very true.

2) *Quod est inferius est sicut quod est superius*

That which is below is like unto that which is above

Quod est superius est sicut quod est inferius

That which is above is like unto that which is below

Ad perpetranda miracula rei unis.

This perpetrates the miracle of One-ness.

3) *Es sicunt res omnes fuerunt ab uno, meditatione unius*

As all things come from the One, by mental focus of the One

Sic omnes res natae ab hac una re, adaptione.

So all things are born of the One, through adaptation.

4) *Pater eius est Sol. Mater eius est Luna.*

Its father is the Sun. Its mother is the Moon.

5) *Portavit illud vertus in ventre suo. Nutrix eius Terra est.*

The wind has carried it in its womb. The Earth is its nurse.

6) *Pater omnes telesmi totius mundi est hic.*

The father of all that is perfect in the whole world is here.

7) *Virtus eius integra est si versa fuerit in terram*

Its force is integrated when it comes into earth (manifestation)

Separabis terram ab igne, subtile ab spisso, suaviter, mango cum ingenio

Separate the earth from the fire, subtle from gross, suavely and with great skill

8) *Ascendit a terra in coelum, interumque descendit in terram*

It rises from earth to the heavens, and again descends to earth

Et recipit vim superiorum et inferiorum.

And receives the power above and below.

9) *Sic habebis Gloriam totius mundi,*

In this way you shall have the Glory of the whole world,

Ideo fugiet a te omnis obscuritas.

And drive from you all obscurance.

10) *Haec est totius fortitudinis fortitude fortis,*

For its strength is stronger than all
strength,

*Quia vincet omnem rem subtilem, omne-
mque solidam penatrabit.*

Will overcome all things subtle, and
penetrate all things solid.

11) *Sic mundus creatus est.*

Thus was the world created.

12) *Hinc erunt adaptations mirabilis, quarum
modus est hic.*

From this come miraculous adaptations
through these means.

13) *Itaque vocatus sum Hermes Trismegistus,*

Thus am I called Hermes Thrice Greatest,

*Habens tres partes philosophiae totius
mundi.*

Having the three parts of the philosophy of the whole world.

14) *Completum est quod dixi de operatione
Solis.*

Complete is my speaking on the Opera-
tion of the Sun.

Beliefs of Hermeticism

Hermeticism, as can be seen in the
Emerald Tablet, teaches the idea that all
things are ultimately One. All things
that exist derive from the One and must
ultimately return to it. Everything that
exists is considered to exist as a thought
within the divine mind of the One. These
thoughts of the divine mind are not random but exist as a complex pattern of
being, or divine plan, within which everything has an appointed role and there is no
such thing as chance or coincidence.

Because all things derive from the
One, the One is within them and reflected
through them. This idea is expressed in the
doctrine of "As above, so below"—because
it originates "above" in the One, all that
exists reflects that divine nature here,
"below." Thus Deity can be observed and
studied through any aspect of creation.
This is why divinatory arts like astrology
and numerology can be used to reveal otherwise hidden aspects of existence.

In addition to these familiar ideas, the
Hermetics share a number of other ideas
with modern Wicca, including a belief in
the four elements and the idea of vibration—that is, that all things have a vibration whose frequency reflects their relative
spiritual development and which can be
affected through meditative and energetic
techniques. The higher the vibration, the
more spiritual and less physical the being
becomes.

Hermetics also believed in reincarnation. As a rule, Hermetics looked upon
the cycle of life and death as a state to be
escaped in favor of reunion with the One.

In order to achieve union with the One,
it was necessary to purify the soul and correct any imperfections. To the Hermetic, it

is these imperfections of the soul that hold it in the cycle of physical incarnation. The purifying and correcting of the soul is the major pursuit of Hermetic thought.

The tools used by Hermetics to purify the soul include the three disciplines referred to in the Emerald Tablet as the origin of the term *Trismegistus*.

In the Emerald Tablet, Hermes Trismegistus is made to attribute his name to the possession on his part of the "three parts of philosophy of the whole world." These three elements are said be the *Operatione Solis* (Work of the Sun), the *Operatione Lunae* (Work of the Moon), and the *Operatione Stellae* (Work of the Stars). These three works are thus posited as the cornerstones of Hermetic practice. They are, respectively, alchemy, astrology, and magic.

Alchemy, the Work of the Sun: We will talk in greater depth about alchemy in the next section, for it is also a major discipline in its own right. Here, let us only emphasize that alchemy is a path of personal transformation, described in coded symbolism, which seeks to break down and rebuild the self in such a way as to eliminate its imperfections and bring about spiritual Enlightenment.

Astrology, the Work of the Moon: In this sense, astrology should be understood not only as a predictive system used to study divine nature and one's own place in it via the principle of "As above, so below," but also as a way of understanding the inner nature of all things through the extensive system of planetary correspondences, whereby all things have their "planetary ruler."

Magic, the Work of the Stars: Magic here is used to refer to the use of theurgic practices to align oneself with the divine through direct spiritual experience of it. In particular, this refers to what we would call channeling or oracular work, wherein the worshiper embodies the deity through the trance state. In Hermetic thought, these practices are considered to help the person move toward the divine state by directly experiencing it for short periods.

Through these techniques and their myriad variations, the Hermetic seeks to align with Deity and ultimately achieve union with the divine.

Some people consider Hermeticism a religion while others consider it a philosophy. Personally, I do not see these definitions as being in contradiction to each other, because I subscribe to a Pagan understanding of the term *religion*, which does not imply the exclusivity of the book religions. Hermeticism, like many of the other religions we are looking at in these pages, is not exclusive in nature. That is to say that being Hermetic does not mean you cannot also be a Platonist, a Wiccan, or even a Christian—or, indeed, all of these.

Like Correllianism, Hermeticism teaches that the inner core of all religions ultimately reflects the same divine truth, though this may be obscured by external details and differences. All religions ultimately reflect the divine because it is the nature of all things to reflect the divine, though each reflection has its own idiosyncrasies. Moreover, the more spiritually advanced teachings of all religions reflect the same divine truth because the more spiritually advanced people in all religions have more in common with each other by virtue of being more spiritually advanced than they have in common with the less spiritually advanced members of their own movements who tend to focus on the differing external details of the religion rather than the unifying internal details of spiritual experience. Consequently, we say "all paths lead to the center" because no matter what path you are on, the "center" is still within you.

Alchemy

The third movement we shall look at in this lesson is alchemy.

Like Hermeticism, alchemy arose in the cosmopolitan cities of hellenistic Egypt, where many cultures came together under the auspices of the Ptolemy Dynasty. Alchemical ideas owe their origin to the mixing of traditional Egyptian ideas with Greek and other elements that led to new and vital interpretations of ancient ideas.

As we have seen, alchemy had an important role within Hermeticism; however, alchemy also enjoys the status of a movement in its own right. Indeed, alchemy can be pursued as a stand-alone art or combined with any other religious system.

The term alchemy comes from the Arabic Al khem, which in turn is said to come from the ancient Egyptian word Kem, which means "black." Thus, alchemy is sometimes called the "black art," though with a very different meaning than that normally ascribed to the term by the uninformed.

The Egyptians called their country Kemet, the "black land," in reference to the rich black topsoil renewed each year by the annual NILE FLOOD. This extremely fertile soil was the secret to Egypt's rich harvests and great wealth. To the Egyptians, the color black was associated with the renewal of life and rebirth of the land. Thus, the term black art actually refers to ideas of spiritual renewal and rebirth.

Others, however, say that the word alchemy comes from the Greek word Cheme.

However, as hellenistic Egypt is defined by nothing so much as the mixing of Greek and Egyptian culture, it is not only possible for the term *alchemy* to come from either *Kem* or *Cheme*, but it could well be related to both.

Most people today think of alchemy in terms of the supposed quest to transform lead into gold. While it is certainly true that many alchemists did in fact work with a variety of substances in an attempt to create arcane elixirs and effects—including, in some cases, the attempt to transmute base metals—this was a small aspect of alchemy and is based on something of a misunderstanding of its ideas.

In reality, alchemy is an advanced spiritual system that couches many of its concepts in symbolic terms. Thus, for example, the idea of turning lead into gold may be viewed as a symbolic way of describing the process of transforming the "lead" of an ordinary and undeveloped consciousness into the "gold" of a fully perfected and enlightened soul.

So the true quest of alchemy is the same quest to perfect the soul that we see in other religious movements. Alchemical writers, however, used a complicated code to convey their ideas, with the specific intent of obscuring the deeper meaning from those they regarded as unworthy. The result of this, of course, is that the ideas were and are often misunderstood, and consequently are sometimes misapplied.

To convey their ideas, alchemists drew on a rich array of allegorical images, combining elemental, planetary, and mineral symbolism, as well as ancient mythology. One of the principal themes of this symbolism is the union of opposites, which is expressed in many ways throughout alchemical art.

Many figures familiar to us today, including the four elements, the twin dragons, and OUROBOUROS, the great serpent of the universe shown swallowing its own tail, were of great importance in alchemy. Of even greater importance in alchemy is the image of the universe as a male/female duality, similar in concept to our own Goddess and God. The masculine polarity was thought of as red and fixed in nature, likened to the sun and the element of sulfur; the female polarity was characterized as white and volatile, likened to the moon and the element of Mercury. The union of these two polar opposites produced the physical world.

The Great Work, or ALCHEMICAL MARRIAGE, was the quest to unite and transcend this duality, achieving spiritual perfection. It is this Great Work that is represented by the analogy of lead into gold, and which is often misunderstood as the pursuit of the TRANSMUTATION OF METALS.

442

The Great Work began with what is termed "MATERIA PRIMA." This is the ordinary state of being—the "lead" in the analogy. The Great Work ended in the creation of the so-called "PHILOSOPHER'S STONE," which confers immortality upon the alchemist. This is Enlightenment, or the "gold" in the analogy.

The materia prima was believed to have both a masculine and a feminine aspect, which were in a state of opposition within it until brought into alignment through the Great Work—hence the term *alchemical marriage*.

The Great Work has three main parts: the NIGREDO, the ALBEDO, and finally the RUBEDO. It will be noted that these correspond to the colors of the Wiccan Goddess: black, white, and red. These are also the colors associated with the degree system in Correllian Wicca, as typified in both our degree sigils and the state robes.

In addition to these three main stages, there is also a fourth stage in the process, which is known as the CAUDA PAVONIS, or "peacock's tail." The cauda pavonis marked the transition between the nigredo and the albedo.

The materia prima is described symbolically as being placed into the ATHANOR, or alchemical furnace. The athanor subjected the materia prima to intense heat and steady pressure, causing it to dissolve into its constituent parts. What was left was a sticky black residue called the nigredo.

What this really means is that before one can grow spiritually, one must first eliminate old ideas and limitations. The athanor represents the process of self-discipline and meditation that brings this about, allowing the seeker to transcend the ego and the ordinary perceptions of being. This destruction of preconceived forms is necessary for new growth to occur, for, as the Zen Buddhists say, "Only an empty bowl can be filled."

Alchemists described this principle through the maxim "No generation without corruption"—an idea similar to the Wiccan "To rise, you must fall." New growth cannot take place until the old has been cleared away.

The nigredo then fermented until, at length, the cauda pavonis occurred; this was portrayed symbolically as a spray of many-colored lights. This means that when we have purified ourselves of old ideas, we may then experience many new ideas—and indeed will at first run riot with them, learning all we can from as many sources as possible.

During the cauda pavonis, we may find ourselves bedazzled or even blinded by this newfound light, but through the application of self-discipline we can learn to discern what is actually helpful to our spiritual growth and eliminate what is merely entertaining.

This process of discernment is thought of as a purification, and it in turn leads to the albedo. The albedo is a pure and receptive spiritual state. This means that after the initial euphoria of it all, a more controlled and focused spiritual growth can unfold, elevating and expanding the consciousness.

Finally, after being subjected to pressure again, the albedo becomes activated as the rubedo. The rubedo is the fully realized spiritual state. What this means is that spiritual knowledge (albedo), to be valuable, must be put into practice in one's life (rubedo); unless they are acted upon and integrated into one's life, spiritual ideas are merely decorative.

Thus the Great Work of alchemy may be described in this manner: first, old ideas must be transcended, then controlled spiritual growth can lead to spiritual enlightenment, which must be put into practice to be of value.

Alchemy may be seen to be a much more exalted system than it is generally given credit for. It will also be seen that alchemical ideas are directly and deeply involved in modern Wiccan thought.

There is, of course, much more that could be said of alchemy, if space permitted, but as it is, we shall make an ending here.

. . . .
Shinto

Shinto is the ancient religion of Japan.

Shinto is, in its origin, an animistic and shamanic religion that recognizes the divinity in all things and seeks to commune with it through ecstatic experience. Because it recognizes the divinity of all things, Shinto places tremendous importance on nature and communion with nature. Like most Pagan religions, Shinto is not an exclusive religion and has had a symbiotic relationship with Buddhism for well over a millennium, with most Japanese practicing both faiths simultaneously and turning to each for specific and complementary purposes.

Shinto is a highly personal, intuitive religion. It is an emotional and spiritual religion that does not place much emphasis on intellectual understanding of the divine. The kind of analyzing and categorizing of theological ideas that features in many religions is almost wholly absent from Shinto.

Kami

The central feature of Shinto is veneration of the idea of *kami*. The word *kami* is often translated as "God," and in the Pagan sense of "God," this is quite accurate—however, this idea is more intelligible in contemporary English if the word "spirit" is used instead. Everything that exists is a kami: people, animals, natural features like mountains and lakes, natural phenomena like lightning or wind. Not only are there individual kami for people and animals, but there are also kami for groups, families, nations, species, etc. Even ideas can be regarded as kami.

There are said to be eight million kami (*Yao Yorozu No Kami*). The number eight million is, of course, symbolic, as the kami are beyond the possibility of number.

Not all of these kami are worshiped, of course. One worships those kami who touch upon one. Though people are kami, they are not normally worshiped as such during their lifetime (though there are exceptions), but rather when they have become ancestors. Ancestor worship is very important in Japan.

The most important of the kami is AMATERASU NO MIKAMI, the goddess of the sun and ancestress of the Imperial House. Amaterasu has her principal shrine at ISE but is worshiped throughout Japan.

The kamidana, an altar maintained in the home, is the center of family worship. The kamidana may be very simple or it may be quite elaborate, depending upon one's taste and means. Here the family's protective kami and ancestors are worshiped through simple rites on a daily basis. Often the kamidana will include special amulets from the clan shrine (*Uji No Jinja*), other local shrines, or the Imperial Shrine at Ise.

Daily worship normally includes cleansing ABLUTIONS, ritual clapping of the hands to summon the kami, followed by a period of contemplative silence.

Shrines

In the earliest times, Shinto rites were very simple and performed outdoors in direct communion with nature. The central feature of worship was the priestess, who acted as a spirit medium, invoking the kami into herself through ecstatic dance. In this way, the kami was physically present through the body of the holy priestess.

When Buddhism began to become popular in Japan, the Buddhist temples inspired the idea of building shrines (*Jinja*) for the kami. Some of these shrines are very simple, others are quite large. Today there are over one hundred thousand such shrines in Japan.

Each clan has its own shrine (*Uji No Jinja*) where the clan's tutelary kami (*Ujigami*) is worshiped. Sometimes the Ujigami is perceived as a divine ancestor of the clan, as Amaterasu is the divine ancestor of the Imperial House. Other times the Ujigami is an actual physical ancestor from whom the clan is descended.

These shrines are focal points of Japanese cultural life. Almost all festivals in Japan are hosted by the local shrine and are open to everyone, whether they consider themselves to be Shinto or not. Some of these festivals are quite magnificent, and all serve to strengthen the whole community's sense of itself.

Shrines are normally built so that they face to the south. Although a shrine may occasionally face to the east, they are never constructed to face west or north. Usually a shrine is entered through a Torii, a free-standing ceremonial gateway that marks the entrance. The Torii is considered to mark the barrier between ordinary and sacred space. Because passing through a Torii is considered to be good luck, there are sometimes several in succession. Originally, Torii were made of cypress wood, but later it became permissible to construct them out of any substance. Today they are most commonly painted red, an effect of Buddhist influence.

Along with the Torii, the shrine entrance may be marked by ceremonial guardian figures. These guardian figures are usually made of stone and represented as Chinese-style lions. Some kami have special guardian figures, however; for example, the shrines of the goddess INARI usually have guardians in the form of stone foxes.

Another feature of most shrines are the sacred Sakaki trees often grown on the grounds. Written prayers are often tied into the branches of the Sakaki, and Sakaki branches are also used in ceremonies of blessing.

There will also be a pool or spring at the shrine, where worshipers may make ablutions by washing their hands and rinsing their mouths.

The kami is not normally portrayed being looked upon as NUMINOUS and ineffable in character. However, the kami may be represented symbolically within the shrine; for example, the great goddess Amaterasu is normally represented by a symbolic mirror.

Ritual hand clapping is used to call the kami for worship and to salute them. Worshippers make offerings (*Shinsen*) to the kami of the shrine in a variety of ways: offerings may be in the form of food, drink, symbolic items, or simply cash.

Prayers (*Norito*) may be offered by the shrine priests and are traditionally composed especially for the occasion. During the time when Shinto was controlled by the state, specific prayers were imposed by the Ministry of Religion in an attempt to formalize Shinto observance. However, since Shinto ceased to be the state religion in 1545 Pisces (AD 1945) at the close of WWII, Shinto priests have had their choice of using set prayers or following the ancient practice of improvising for the occasion.

In addition to the shrine priests, shrines normally also have priestesses, or *miko*. The miko serve a variety of functions but notably enact the ancient ritual dances (*kagura*)

that have evolved out of the ecstatic sha-
manistic dances of the ancients. Miko
kagura is performed in the shrines and at
festivals and is characterized by graceful,
circular movements and an emphasis on
the four directions. Though the modern
miko priestess enacts the kagura more as a
meditation than a trance in the shamanic
sense (*Kamigakuri*), the kagura is still considered to invoke and embody the kami.

State Shinto

The Japanese Imperial Family are said to
be descended from the sun goddess Amaterasu, and the Japanese emperor has traditionally been regarded as divine in his
own right. This was a recognition of the
emperor's special role and perceived spiritual holiness, but this did not prevent the
emperor from being reduced early on to the
role of powerless figurehead and occasionally impoverished prisoner of his august
role. It did, however, invest the emperor
with a sanctity that was undiminished by
the realities of his actual position.

The sudden forced ending by the Western powers of Japan's self-imposed isola-
tion and the resulting destabilization of
the SHOGUNATE led to a movement to
"restore the emperor," in the hope that the
emperor's innate holiness would help to re-
unify the country. This is called the MEIJI
RESTORATION and took place in 1468
Pisces (AD 1868). The emperor was not
really restored to power, just to a more
visible central role as cultural figurehead.
However, the idea of the emperor became
central to the new regime. As part of the
restoration, Shinto became the STATE
RELIGION of Japan, and the government
made it its business to formalize and organize the ancient religion of the islands.

The government's Ministry of Religion
undertook to organize the Shinto shrines,
codify the theology and mythology of the
religion, and create formalized prayers
for use across the country. Worship of the
emperor and veneration of the imperial
family were greatly emphasized as central
features of Shinto practice, the emperor
becoming in effect the human embodiment of the sanctity of the state.

During this period, Japan's increasingly
aggressive militarist government began a
massive imperial expansion into neighbor-
ing countries that would eventually trigger
WWII. These policies would bring great
hardships upon the Japanese people as the
war drained the nation's resources and consumed its youth. Eventually the war would
be lost and Japan would be defeated and
occupied by a foreign power for the first
time in its history. This led to the end of
Shinto's brief period as a state religion and
the emperor's formal renunciation of his
divinity, an event which was deeply shocking to the Japanese psyche at the time.

However, while he is no longer officially considered divine by the state, the Japanese emperor has not lost his special sanctity within Shinto, but it must be understood within the context of the explanation of kami given above.

Shinto Mythology

The oldest accounts of Shinto mythology are given in the Kojiki and the Nihon Shoki, two ancient texts dating from the NARA PERIOD. Among many other things, these include the story of creation, the birth of Amaterasu No Mikami, and the descent of the Japanese Imperial House from her.

In Shinto belief, the world was created by the divine pair Izanagi ("He Who Invites") and Izanami ("She Who Invites"). This primeval pair have often been likened to yin and yang in their qualities. Izanagi plunged his spear into the primordial ocean, sticking it deep into the ocean floor so that it stood upright, but shattering the spearhead in the process. The pieces of Izanagi's shattered spearhead became the Japanese islands. Izanagi pursued Izanami around the shaft of the spear in a dance of courtship somewhat reminiscent of the maypole. Allowing Izanagi to catch her, Izanami became his consort. As the result of this union, Izanami gave birth to many new deities: cosmic powers of various sorts who would play a great role in the later world.

At length, Izanami gave birth to Kagu-Tsuchi, the god of fire. The birth of this god proved more problematic for the Divine Mother than those who had come before, for as Fire was born, he burned his mother badly—so badly that the Goddess died and entered the Afterworld (*Yomi*).

Izanagi was inconsolable in his grief at the death of his beloved consort; nothing could assuage his grief. And so Izanagi resolved to go into the Afterworld, find Izanami, and bring her back to the world of the living.

Izanami loved Izanagi greatly, and when he found her in the Afterworld, she received him gladly. However, Izanami would not allow Izanagi to see her, hiding herself in shadow or behind a screen or fan. No matter how he pleaded, Izanami would not yield to Izanagi's plea that she return with him to the world of the living. At length, Izanagi grew impatient and pulled his dead wife to him, and in so doing saw her clearly.

Izanagi was horrified, for death had changed his wife: Izanami had begun to decay, and it was for this reason that she had hidden herself from Izanagi's gaze and had refused to return with him. Seeing Izanagi's repugnance, Izanami became angry. Izanami summoned an army of ghosts and drove Izanagi out of the Afterworld and back to the world of the living.

Knowing that Izanami could never return from the Afterworld, Izanagi was deeply sorrowful. He also felt contaminated by death and needed to purify himself. And so Izanagi went to the lake and performed ablutions, and as he did so, Izanagi brought new gods into existence.

When he washed his left eye, Izanagi produced Amaterasu, the goddess of the sun. When he washed his right eye, Izanagi produced Tsukuyomi, the god of the moon. When he washed his nose, Izanagi produced Susanowo, god of the storm.

These are considered the last children of Izanagi and Izanami.

The beautiful Amaterasu became the greatest of the kami. This led to a great deal of friction with her brother Susanowo, who believed that he should be the pre-eminent kami. This led Amaterasu and Susanowo to quarrel. The great goddess became so angry with her brother that she decided to retreat from the world and went off to hide in a cave.

The withdrawal of the sun plunged the world into darkness. All of the kami became very upset and began looking for Amaterasu everywhere. At last they found her brooding in her cave. The kami begged Amaterasu to come out of the cave and restore light to the world, but she was deeply hurt after her quarrel with Susanowo and refused to budge.

The kami now too were despondent. What would they do without the sun? They did not know what to do. At last one of the kami, a goddess called Uzume, came up with an idea.

Uzume began to dance. According to some versions, her dance was comic; according to others, it was erotic; according to others, it was simply beautiful. In any event, Uzume's dance cheered the grieving kami. At first the dance of Uzume lifted her fellow kami's spirits. Then Uzume's dance moved the kami to joy.

In her cave, Amaterasu heard the kami rejoicing and wondered what could have moved them to merriment so soon after they professed their grief to her. But although her curiosity was piqued, Amaterasu refused to leave the cave to see what was happening. Yet the merriment continued and grew louder, making Amaterasu more and more curious.

At last Amaterasu could stand it no longer; she had to know what was going on. She decided to peek out of the cave and steal a quick look. When Amaterasu peeked out of the cave's entrance, the kami were ready for her: they thrust a mirror before her face.

Amaterasu was amazed! She had never seen anything so beautiful and demanded to know what she was looking at. The kami informed her that she was looking at her own reflection, and that this was the glory her seclusion deprived them of. Moved by this and amazed by her own magnificence, Amaterasu agreed to return.

This myth is clearly seasonal in its origin, with the storms of winter (Susanowo) driving the sun into its winter decline. It is also thought to reflect ancient ceremonies held at the winter solstice intended to bring the sun back "out of its cave." In this way, Uzume's dance will be seen to be a shamanic kagura dance intended to invoke the sun's return.

Amaterasu did return, and from her the Imperial House of Japan was held to descend.

Types of Shinto

The description above speaks to the central themes of Shinto. There are, however, countless variations.

For many centuries, the Japanese regarded all religions as being either Shinto or Buddhist in nature. Anything that was not Buddhist was, per se, Shinto. With the introduction of Christianity, religions came to be seen as either Shinto, Buddhist, or Christian. During the period when Shinto was the state religion, all religious movements in Japan were required to be registered and organized as one of these three. All this changed after WWII, but because of these attitudes, Shinto has developed many branches.

Basically, Shinto may be said to be of two kinds:

Jinja Shinto: Jinja Shinto is shrine Shinto, as described above. This is the traditional form of Shinto, focused upon the worship of the countless kami in shrines and in the home. There are said to be around 100,000 such shrines.

Shuha Shinto: Shuha Shinto is sectarian Shinto. Sectarian Shinto is focused around specific doctrines developed by various teachers rather than around specific shrines. Consequently, sectarian Shinto does not have the local aspect of shrine Shinto, as a given sect may have a wide geography dispersal. There are many such sects, a few of which are Konkokyo (Shining Mind), Tenrikyo (Celestial Wisdom), and Omoto. The Shinto sects tend to be highly syncretistic and are often universalist in their outlook.

Today, Shinto is an extremely vibrant and diverse religious movement. New interpretations of Shinto exist side by side with the oldest practices. The end of state Shinto, far from weakening the religion, freed it from an unnatural governmental restraint that was not traditional to it; this has left Shinto free to resume its ancient diversity in modern variations that add to rather than distract from its essential nature.

• • • •
Druidism,
Ancient and Modern

Druid is the name given to the priesthood of the ancient Celtic peoples.

Although a great deal has been written about the druids, very little is actually known about them. The druids did not believe in committing their ideas to writing, and so no information exists about ancient druidism from a druid's perspective. Archeology as well as the study of other INDO-EUROPEAN peoples allows inferences to be made about druidic ideas and practices, but these must be regarded as speculative. Similarly, both classical Greek and Roman as well as later medieval writings do comment upon druidry, but the accuracy and impartiality of their information is open to question.

The Celtic peoples are generally held to have developed out of still older Indo-European peoples sometime around 500 Aries (700 BC) in what is now Austria. The earliest phase of Celtic culture is called the Hallstatt period, after the site in Austria from which it was identified. The great Celtic expansion began with the La Tene period, beginning around 700 Aries (500 BC) when large numbers of Celtic people began to migrate out of their original homeland and expand throughout Europe.

The Celts swept westward into what are now France, Spain, and the British Isles; they moved eastward into southeastern Europe and down into what is now Turkey, where they became known as Galatians. They also migrated south into Italy, founding cities such as Milan. In 810 Aries (390 BC), a Celtic army sacked the city of Rome, an experience that the Romans would never forget.

Exactly what the ancient Celts called themselves is unknown, but it would seem to have been close to "Kell" in sound, as revealed by the names used for them: to the Greeks they were *Keltoi*, to the Romans *Gauls* (Roman pronunciation: "Gowl"), in Asia Minor *Galatians*, and later in Ireland and Scotland they called themselves *Gaels*.

The Celtic peoples intermarried with the people already living in these areas, and in some cases preserved aspects of older cultures. This is seen in the fact that the Celts of central Europe lived in square houses, while the Celts of far western Europe and the Isles adopted an older, round style of house. This is of importance to the discussion of druidry because there are seeming differences between continental and British druids that may reflect the customs of earlier civilizations. Notably, the druids of the British Isles seem to have had more central organization than continental druidry.

451

The Celts also had close relations with the Mediterranean world, trading extensively with the Greek city-states and often hiring themselves out as mercenaries. For example, Alexander the Great had Celtic mercenaries among his armies. It is reasonable to assume that a certain amount of cultural exchange took place.

One of the most notable examples of such cultural exchange is the possibility that the Celts may have influenced Pythagoreanism, as some say Pythagoras studied under druids in Gaul during his youth and obtained some of his ideas from them. Though the story may be apocryphal, it is certainly not beyond possibility, as friendly relations between the Greeks and the Celts were often obtained, despite the fact that the Greeks considered the Celts "barbarians."

However, after 1001 Aries (199 BC) when the Romans defeated Hannibal, relations between the Celts and their southern neighbors began to change. Over the next centuries, the Romans moved against the Celts, first in Italy, then throughout Europe, and finally in Britannia.

This is not to say that the Celtic people were displaced from these areas. The various invasions and counter-invasions of history rarely actually displace people; rather, they introduce new elements into the population that change the culture. In this case, the Romans conquered the Celts, set themselves up as a ruling elite, and seeded the population with colonists, blending Roman and Celtic culture, just as the Celts themselves had blended with the peoples they had dominated.

The result of this was Romano-Celtic culture: a vibrant syncretism that combined Celtic cultural values with Roman civil administration. Although far from a painless process, the Celtic peoples of the Roman Empire in time came to see themselves as very much part of the Roman world, and in many cases would prove to be dogged preservers of Roman culture after the fall of the empire.

Druid Beliefs

The druids were the priests of the Celtic peoples. As a class, the druids were much more powerful than the priesthoods of Greece or Rome, more closely resembling the powerful priests of Egypt or the Hindu BRAHMINS to whom they are regarded as being related. The druids appear to have been especially powerful in the British Isles and to have had powerful centers there. As a rule, the druids are said to have been more powerful than the Celtic kings, though each had his own sphere of authority. This power came, in part, from the fact that druids administered the courts of law and interpreted the laws.

It is often asserted that the Romans wiped out the druids in the lands they conquered; this does not appear to be true. They did move to suppress druidic power and the social forms that had maintained it, and in certain cases moved against specific groups of druids who refused to accept Roman rule and Roman law. The Romans also outlawed specific druidic practices, notably human sacrifice, which the Romans abhorred.

Druids persisted after the Roman conquest, but without their previous political power they became relatively insignificant and in some cases seem to have developed an ascetic practice. Even in Ireland, where the Romans never ruled, the power of the druids waned, with bards taking a higher position in society, which they would retain down till the REFORMATION era.

It cannot exactly be said that bards replaced druids, however, as bards were a kind of druid. Although the druids did not record their beliefs and practices, classical Greek and Roman authors did write about them, and these describe druidry as having three divisions. These are the bards, the ovates, and the druids themselves.

The bards were singers and poets who also functioned as genealogists and record keepers. The OVATES, or more properly vates, were diviners and practitioners of the spiritual arts and sciences, while the druids as such were the presiding priesthood. The would-be druid progressed through these three levels, though many remained at any

of the three levels, finding their vocation best served there. It was said to take a minimum of twenty years to achieve standing as a druid, involving as it did the memorization of vast amounts of information in the absence of written material.

The druids were said to believe in reincarnation and the transmigration of souls, although exactly what they believed about this (and even *if* they believed it, according to some) is not really known. They are said to have been keen astrologers, but the form of astrology they practiced would be unlikely to be the same as Mediterranean astrology, and nothing much can be said about it. Above all, they organized private and public ritual and administered the law.

Worship was focused on the NEMETON, or sacred grove. The Nemeton was sacred to one or more deities, most of whom were intensely local in form. The Celts did have a few deities whose worship was widespread, but most were specific local variations of archetypal forms or deities associated with specific local places such as sacred pools or wells, groves, mountains, etc. Because of this intensely local character, it is hard to say a lot about Celtic divinities without appealing to archetypal forms to which they can be likened. As it happens, this is just what the Romans did, associating local Celtic gods with Roman gods based upon shared qualities. In our case, we will use the system of archetypes we introduced you to in First Degree to allow for a very, very brief overview of Celtic deities.

Hero: The Hero is the young god, who is an important figure in Celtic culture, with connotations of purity and innocence. Gods like Aengus and Mabon or Maponos exemplify the Hero archetype in Celtic culture. In Arthurian myth, the figure of Percival, or alternately Galahad, reflects this tradition.

Lover: In Celtic culture, the Lover archetype is represented by gods like Bel and Lugh, deities with associations to fire, the sun, and the yearly cycle of the seasons. Bealteinne, the great druidic festival that marked the beginning of summer, takes its name from Bel, who is also known as Beli and Belenos. The druidic harvest festival of Lughnassadh, meaning "Marriage of Lugh," takes its name from Lugh. Lugh was also known as Lugus and Lleu.

King: The King archetype in Celtic culture is said to have been exemplified by Nodens (or Nuada), Math, and similar figures.

Sorcerer: The Sorcerer archetype is the god of death, magic, and transformation, and also of forests and the hunt.

The Sorcerer also has an aspect as King of Fools. In Celtic culture, the Sorcerer is exemplified by Cernunnos, the Horned God familiar from the GUNDESTROP CAULDRON and a number of monuments. The Cerne Abbas Giant and Herne the Hunter are said to be Cernunnos, as is the later Herlichinus and Harlequin. Secculos the Good Striker is another form of this archetype, as is the Irish Dagda. In Arthurian myth, the Sorcerer archetype is, of course, Merlin.

Maiden: The Maiden archetype in Celtic culture is exemplified by the great goddess Brighid, or Bride, who was Brigantia and Brigantina in Britain. The Maiden was a goddess of arts and sciences as well as a warrior goddess.

Mother: The Mother archetype in Celtic culture is often associated with specific local topography, such as the PAPS OF ANU in Wales. This goddess is variously known as Danu, Dana, or Anu, but also takes the form of local river goddesses such as Boana, goddess of the Boyne, or Sequanna, goddess of the Seine. Other examples include Epona, Rhiannon, and Macha, for each of whom the horse was the *theophany*, or animal form.

Crone: Goddess of death, the Crone is associated with the ancestors and the idea of sovereignty in Celtic culture, often appearing in mythology to mark future kings for kingship. The preeminent form of the Crone in Celtic culture is Morgan, or Morrighan, the queen of phantoms. Other examples are Scathoch, Babd Catha, and Bocathia.

Druidism and Christianity

Encounters with druids continue to be mentioned long after the coming of Christianity, and so they presumably survived in some form. Perhaps at this stage the druid had become a solitary mystic as opposed to the highly organized priesthood they had once been.

In Ireland, where they retained their original status longer, they seem to have embraced CELTIC CHRISTIANITY and largely merged into the new priesthood. Celtic Christianity is distinguished by carrying forward a traditional Celtic emphasis on nature and personal mystical experience of Deity. Celtic Christians called Jesus the "Archdruid" and made an attempt to preserve ancient Celtic stories—our only source of anything resembling contemporary Pagan Celtic mythology, and that was often in a decadent form.

In Celtic lands, the bards generally remained a powerful body after the coming of Christianity, despite their druidic associations, and many have suggested that they kept druidic traditions alive. They certainly did a lot to keep Celtic nationalism alive.

When modern druidry began to emerge, it usually claimed a descent from ancient druidry via survivals such as these. Hereditary druidism is about as controversial as hereditary Witchcraft, and it is not my purpose to examine the subject here. What I will say is that modern druidry as exemplified by the groups described below is distinctly different from ancient druidry, especially in its more universal manifestations; however, this is not out of keeping with the idea of a living movement, where one would expect to see changes as a consequence of (and in direct proportion to) the passage of time, the introduction of new influences, and changed social circumstances.

Modern Druidry

The Ancient Druid Order (not to be confused with the ANCIENT ORDER OF DRUIDS) was founded on 22 September, 1317 Pisces (AD 1717), at a meeting supposedly attended by druidic delegates from throughout the British Isles. This meeting was called by JOHN TOLAND, who became the first Chosen Chief of the Ancient

Druid Order. The original name of the Ancient Druid Order was *An Druidh Uileach Braithreachas*, or the Druid Circle of the Universal Bond.

Although it claimed a druidic origin, the Ancient Druid Order was and is universalist and eclectic in practice. The founders may well have been completely sincere in their belief that they were legitimately druidic, but they represented what might be termed a folk druidism that drew from all sources to flesh out its ideas. They were druids because of their ancestry, not necessarily their specific practices, and felt that all knowledge was of equal value; thus they regarded no knowledge as being beyond their proper imperium.

Consequently, the Ancient Druid Order did not feel in any way obliged to re-create past practices but felt that their mission was to bring druidism as they understood it into the modern world, expanding its ideas from any sources that seemed worthy to them. This eclectic tendency only increased with time.

The Ancient Order of Druids was very successful and included some very prominent people, notably the Dowager Princess Augusta, mother of King George III, who was a member and patron of the order, holding the rank of Arch Druidess. The famous poet and metaphysician WILLIAM BLAKE was also a member of the order, serving as its fifth Chosen Chief.

At its inception, the Ancient Order of Druids was structured as a (theoretically) secret society. Today they are very public. Nonetheless, most functions of the Ancient Druid Order remain accessible to members only. The organization does hold three major public festivals a year, however, whose high profile makes them among the most visible of modern druidic events. These are:

The Spring Equinox Ceremony: The Spring Equinox Ceremony is held at Tower Hill, London.

The Summer Solstice Ceremony: The Summer Solstice Ceremony is held at Stonehenge.

The Fall Equinox Ceremony: The Fall Equinox Ceremony is held at Primrose Hill, London.

In 1564 Pisces (AD 1964), the Ancient Druid Order experienced a split brought on by the election of Dr. Robert Maughan as Chosen Chief of the Order. Dr. Maughan was not acceptable to some of the order's leadership, and they seceded from the organization.

Led by ROSS NICHOLS, the dissident druids founded a new order of their own, which they called the Order of Bards, Ovates, and Druids. A historian, Nichols felt that modern druidry should be more like ancient druidry. Considering the eclectic nature of the Ancient Druid Order, it is not surprising that Nichols' ideas did not find favor there, but in the new Order of Bards, Ovates, and Druids, these same ideas attracted a wide following.

The Order of Bards, Ovates, and Druids differed from the Ancient Druid Order in placing a much greater emphasis on Celtic mythology and introducing a greater alignment with ancient druidic structures. To this end, Nichols introduced a three-degree system in which the initiate moved from Bard to Ovate to Druid. Nichols also introduced the eight-festival Wheel of the Year; the Ancient Order of Druids had celebrated only the two equinoxes and the summer solstice.

Perhaps most notably, however, Nichols introduced a powerful new teaching system to disseminate his ideas. The Order of Bards, Ovates, and Druids introduced a distance study program that could be followed through correspondence by students anywhere in the world. A network of tutors was developed to guide the student through their studies. Real-time events were organized, at which the largely SOLITARY members of the order could meet and interact. An easy system for forming real-time groups was created, which allowed for two classes of group: the Seedgroup and the Grove. Members of any grade could found a Seedgroup, while only those of druid status could found a Grove. Moreover, the groups were allowed to be mostly self-governing, selecting the leadership styles and policies best fitted to their members.

Because of these enlightened policies, which made their teachings accessible on a wide scale, the Order of Bards, Ovates, and Druids spread quickly and far. Today, it is a global organization with branches in many countries around the world.

In 1588 Pisces (AD 1988), PHILLIP CARR-GOMM became Head of the Order of Bards, Ovates, and Druids.

American Druidism

A number of important druidic organizations have arisen in North America whose origins are very different from the British druidic groups described above.

The Reformed Druids of North America was started by students at Carleton College in Northfield, Minnesota, essentially as a joke. Carleton College had a requirement that all students must regularly attend religious services. In 1563 Pisces (AD 1963), a group of students who resented this requirement and felt that they did not wish to attend services with any of the local religious organizations available to them founded the Reformed Druids of North America and began to hold services

457

in order to fulfill the school's requirement while simultaneously protesting it. To their own surprise, the Reformed Druids quickly became a serious organization.

In 1566 Pisces (AD 1966), a Reformed Druid priest by the name of Robert Larson moved to Berkeley, California, where he met one ISAAC BONEWITS, a young visionary who would prove to be extremely important to the future of American druidism.

In 1583 Pisces (AD 1983), Isaac Bonewits founded the druid fellowship AR NDRAIOCHT FEIN. *Ar nDraiocht Fein* is Gaelic and means "our own druidry." The Ar nDraiocht Fein would quickly become a dominant force in American druidry.

Although the druids are a specifically Celtic form, they have strong parallels throughout Indo-European culture. The Ar nDraiocht Fein chose to focus not just on Celtic practice but on common patterns within Indo-European religions as a whole. In doing this, they were harkening back to the universalist focus of the Ancient Order of Druids.

The Ar nDraiocht Fein also strongly emphasizes its role as a public movement. It is organized into Groves and proto-Groves, which are required to hold public ritual as part of their *raison d'être*. Ideas of secrecy are frowned upon.

A third important North American druid group is the HENGE OF KELTRIA.

The Henge of Keltria is more specifically Celtic in focus than many of the forms of druidism we have discussed, which tend to have universalist aspects. The Henge of Keltria focuses on the veneration of nature, interpretation of Deity through Celtic mythology, the ancestors, and ideas of personal growth.

These are just a few of the many druidic orders active in the world today, but they do serve to provide something of an overview of modern druidry. Modern druidry is an extremely important movement within modern Western Paganism and one you are almost certain to run into quickly if you interact with the wider Pagan community.

. . . .

In writing this short discourse on comparative Paganism, it has not been my objective to tell you everything there is to know about each of the religions discussed; such a feat would be impossible, and even to attempt it would require many volumes. Rather, I have attempted to familiarize you with some of the major forms of Paganism that you are likely to encounter in literature and in the wider community, and from which you may seek to further your own spirituality.

There are many aspects of these religions as well as variations on these religions that I have not so much as touched upon here. Moreover, given the ever-changing nature of religion, new variations occur constantly. This is not an aberration or a contamination of "correct" forms, it is the nature of life and growth. As our understandings grow, naturally our religions must grow with them. When this does not occur, religion becomes a brittle and outmoded form that prevents rather than aids our deeper spiritual understanding.

One of the great errors of contemporary society is the attempt to analyze and categorize religious ideas in a manner that makes them appear to be wholly separate and unchanging concepts rather than the free-flowing river that religion actually is. For those who hold such a view, the druidic peas must never touch the Taoist corn, let alone the Vodun potatoes, so to speak.

This is partly the effect of the academic desire to give things a set definition, and partly also the fault of those religions whose priesthoods seek to ordain an unchanging understanding. Such a way of understanding religion is comparable to studying the photograph of a butterfly. Yes, you can get a good idea of the butterfly as it existed at the moment the photo was taken, but that aspect of the butterfly that is defined by its flight is wholly missed out on.

In religion, the butterfly flight is change and growth. It is the nature of faith that eternal spiritual truths are revealed again and again in new understandings and updated forms, which hopefully expand a little of our understanding each time. Thus we must not allow ourselves to be hidebound in our own understandings or forget that we can learn from others. Religion is not and must never be regarded as perfect, but rather it is a successive undertaking to gain a continually better understanding of and deeper relationship with God, by whatever name you know God.

As you have seen, most of the systems we have been discussing are nonexclusive and very flexible in nature, as is Correllianism itself. Thus the Correllian is free to study from all sources of knowledge in the understanding that all sources of knowledge can potentially expand our own understanding of spirituality. It is my hope that you will use this brief discussion of comparative Pagan religion as a launching board for your own wider study of higher Pagan thought from around the world and throughout time, and that you will, as I do, rejoice in the kaleidoscopic reflections of the great diamond that is Deity.

• • • •

Because this class is being offered as an appendix to the main book, we have not included the original glossary section. However, the glossary words are still indicated by SMALL CAPS within the text, and their definitions may be accessed online—along with all of the glossary words from all of our Witch School classes—through our searchable glossary at www.paganwords.com.

The Witch School Series

The Correllian Nativist Tradition is one of the largest and fastest-growing Wiccan traditions in the world! This 3-volume teaching series will prepare you for initiation into all three degrees of Correllian Wicca, and the fourth volume will help you master the art of ritual.

• • •

· ·

Witch School First Degree

Lessons in the Correllian Tradition

Rev. Donald Lewis-Highcorrell

In twelve lessons, you'll learn about magic, cosmology, personal power, the altar, the airts, the circle of art, invocation, garb, symbols, omens, and divination; basic energy work; herbs, oils, and incense; and stones and crystals. Appendices of a self-Wiccaning ritual and the Charge of the Goddess are also included. Every lesson features study questions, a glossary, and exercises to develop your psychic and magical skills.

978-0-7387-1301-4, 7½ x 9⅛, 288 PP. $19.95

Witch School Third Degree

Lessons in the Correllian Tradition

Rev. Donald Lewis-Highcorrell

Witch School Third Degree is for those who are called to Wicca as a vocation. This text explores Wiccan mysteries and spiritual concepts in depth and explains the responsibilities of the High Priesthood.

978-0-7387-1303-8, 7½ x 9⅛, 456 PP. $29.95

Witch School Ritual, Theory & Practice

Lessons in the Correllian Tradition

Rev. Donald Lewis-Highcorrell

From the Dance of Death for Samhain to fire jumping for Ostara, ritual is at the heart of religious devotion. Rev. Donald Lewis-Highcorrell, author of the Witch School series, is back with an in-depth exploration of ritual from the Correllian perspective. The Wheel of the Year is an ideal backdrop for mastering the art of ritual. Revolving through the Sabbats, Lewis-Highcorrell examines every step of formal ritual—casting the Circle, invoking the quarters, acts of power, and so on—along with traditional Correllian practices. Encouraging improvisation and innovation, Lewis-Highcorrell also offers tips for keeping ceremonies fresh. There are suggestions for decorating, costumes, colors, props, and more. Sample ceremonies and dialogue are also offered as templates for creating your own ritual.

978-0-7387-1339-7, 7½ x 9⅛, 240 pp. $19.95